STUDIES IN WELSH HISTORY

Editors

RALPH A. GRIFFITHS CHRIS WILLIAMS
ERYN M. WHITE

35

WALES AND SOCIALISM

'Senedd y Pentra – Dadl Sosialaeth yng Ngweithdy'r Crydd' (The Village Parliament – A debate on socialism in the Cobbler's Workshop), Yr Herald Cymraeg, 24 March 1908. Bangor University Archive.

WALES AND SOCIALISM
POLITICAL CULTURE AND NATIONAL IDENTITY BEFORE THE GREAT WAR

by

MARTIN WRIGHT

*Published on behalf of the
University of Wales*

CARDIFF
UNIVERSITY OF WALES PRESS
2016

© Martin Wright, 2016

All rights reserved. No part of this book may be reproduced in any material form (including photocopying or storing it in any medium by electronic means and whether or not transiently or incidentally to some other use of this publication) without the written permission of the copyright owner. Applications for the copyright owner's written permission to reproduce any part of this publication should be addressed to the University of Wales Press, 10 Columbus Walk, Brigantine Place, Cardiff CF10 4UP.

www.uwp.co.uk

British Library CIP Data
A catalogue record for this book is available from the British Library

ISBN 978-1-78316-916-0
eISBN 978-1-78316-917-7

The right of Martin Wright to be identified as author of this work has been asserted in accordance with sections 77 and 79 of the Copyright, Designs and Patents Act 1988.

Typeset by Mark Heslington Ltd, Scarborough, North Yorkshire
Printed by CPI Antony Rowe, Melksham

SERIES EDITORS' FOREWORD

Since the foundation of the series in 1977, the study of Wales's history has attracted growing attention among historians internationally and continues to enjoy a vigorous popularity. Not only are approaches, both traditional and new, to the study of history in general being successfully applied in a Welsh context, but Wales's historical experience is increasingly appreciated by writers on British, European and world history. These advances have been especially marked in the university institutions in Wales itself.

In order to make more widely available the conclusions of original research, much of it of limited accessibility in postgraduate dissertations and theses, in 1977 the History and Law Committee of the Board of Celtic Studies inaugurated this series of monographs, *Studies in Welsh History*. It was anticipated that many of the volumes would originate in research conducted in the University of Wales or under the auspices of the Board of Celtic Studies, and so it proved. Although the Board of Celtic Studies no longer exists, the University of Wales continues to sponsor the series. It seeks to publish significant contributions made by researchers in Wales and elsewhere. Its primary aim is to serve historical scholarship and to encourage the study of Welsh history.

CONTENTS

SERIES EDITORS' FOREWORD	v
ACKNOWLEDGEMENTS	ix
Introduction	1
1 Pioneers, 1790s – 1880s	5
2 Putting down roots, 1889–1899	34
(i) Cardiff and Fabianism	35
(ii) The Social Democratic Federation in south Wales	58
3 South Wales and the ILP ascendancy, 1891–1906	82
(i) The ILP and socialism in south Wales before 1898	83
(ii) The 1898 coal strike	105
(iii) The culture of socialism in south Wales	122
4 Beyond the heads of the valleys, c.1880s–1906	143
(i) British socialism and Welsh Wales	144
(ii) Socialists, quarrymen and Lord Penrhyn	161
(iii) Towards an indigenous Welsh socialism?	174
(iv) Robert Jones Derfel, 'Socialist Cymreig'	184
5 Progress and pluralism, 1906–1912	202
(i) The socialist movement in Wales after 1906	203
(ii) The struggle for a Welsh socialist consciousness	222
Conclusion	239
SELECT BIBLIOGRAPHY	243
INDEX	265

ACKNOWLEDGEMENTS

This book has been a long time in the making. In a sense, its roots might be traced back to both Lampeter and Daventry in the 1980s. It has grown out of the confluence of two major themes in my own life. On the one hand, it is informed by an interest in (and commitment to) socialist ideas that I have held since my teenage years, and which I was fortunate enough to study at Masters level as a student at Lampeter in the late 1980s. On the other hand, the desire to write about socialism in Wales, rather than in Britain generally, is a natural consequence of the fascination and love that I have felt since childhood for the land of Wales, its people and its language. The book could not have been written without the experience of being an Englishman making a life in Wales, where I have been lucky enough to live for the last thirty years. As with many of the individuals who feature in the following pages, I have lived at an interface between cultures. My life has been enriched as a result, and any insights that I might have brought to the study of socialist history have resulted directly from this experience.

During what has been an eventful and captivating journey I have accumulated many debts. It would be impossible to name all the individuals who have contributed to the making of this book (many of them unknowingly), but some general acknowledgements are due. Those involved in teaching me history at Lampeter (and indeed at Daventry), and those involved in teaching me the Welsh language at Aberystwyth, have all been responsible for placing foundation stones for this study. The students with whom I've been lucky to share and discuss ideas at Lampeter, across mid-Wales and at Cardiff have all played a role in helping me build upon those foundations. Likewise my colleagues at Aberystwyth University's Continuing Education Department in the 1990s and early 2000s, and my comrades in *Llafur: The Welsh People's*

History Society, have all played an essential part in my education. More critical still are the personal friends – musicians, mine-explorers, climbers, ramblers, and other general nonconformists – who have accompanied me through the years. Without them I wouldn't have got here.

Some individuals have played a crucial role in my academic development at critical moments. Professor Paul Ward of Huddersfield University deserves thanks for pulling me back into academic research at a time when it looked like I might have left it for good. Without the opportunity to work with him on the Huw T. Edwards project I wouldn't have been able to conceptualise the current book. I owe a greater debt still to Professor Bill Jones of Cardiff University, who supervised the PhD upon which this book is based. His professional support and personal friendship have been invaluable.

Institutions too have played their part. The research upon which this study is based would not have been undertaken without the award of a PhD studentship from the Coleg Cymraeg Cenedlaethol. Numerous archives and libraries have been used during the research for this book, and I have received help and support from a great number of their staff. In particular I wish to record my thanks to the staff of the following institutions: The National Library of Wales at Aberystwyth, Bangor University Library and Archive, The South Wales Miners' Library at Swansea, Swansea University Library and Archive, Cardiff University Library, The Hugh Owen Library at Aberystwyth University, Aberdare Public Library, The British Library of Political and Economic Science in London, Glamorgan Archives in Cardiff and Cardiff Central Library. Another institution that was essential to the completion of this book was the National Health Service. Thanks in particular are due to the staff of the Royal Gwent Hospital at Newport, the University Hospital Wales at Cardiff and the Church Surgery at Aberystwyth. Without them there would be no me, and hence no book. Their work is but one of the fruits of the socialism that the individuals featured in this book strove to create. Long may it endure! Various people have read the manuscript of this book at different stages, and their suggestions have without doubt improved it. Particular thanks are due to the Studies in Welsh

History series editors, and to Professor Sir Deian Hopkin and Professor Paul O'Leary. I must, however, take responsibility for any remaining errors.

Finally, and most importantly, I owe a debt of gratitude to my family. My wife, Ceri, and son, Aneurin, have had to put up with the preoccupation and interruptions to family life that seem inherent in book-writing projects of this type, and for this I thank them. I also owe a profound debt of thanks to my own parents. Anything I have achieved, I have done so by standing on their shoulders, so it is to them that this book is dedicated.

INTRODUCTION

The ideology of socialism was one of the formative influences upon twentieth-century Britain. Socialists, although only ever a minority within a much broader labour movement, were instrumental in the creation and rise of the Labour Party, and their collectivist values were central to the mid-century political settlement that resulted in the extensive nationalisation of British industries, the creation of the welfare state and the foundation of the National Health Service. The twentieth-century British socialist achievement, which has shaped the life of everyone born in Britain since the 1930s, was fundamentally unionist in character. The 'nation' in nationalisation and the NHS, and the 'state' in welfare, unmistakably refer to the British nation and the British state. Wales played an important role in the creation of these institutions. The south Wales coalfield in particular formed an integral part of the bedrock of Labour's support, and among its most creative socialist advocates were two of the chief architects of Britain's socialist infrastructure: Aneurin Bevan and James Griffiths.

In recent decades the central pillars of the mid-twentieth-century political settlement have been undermined. Its collectivism has been eroded by a wave of individualism that has, since the late 1970s, seen nationalised industry become a thing of the past. In the early twenty-first century even some of the most resilient features of the post-war settlement, such as the NHS, no longer seem inviolable. Likewise the unionist, pan-British base of the collectivist consensus appears to be less stable than was once assumed. The growing strength of political nationalism in Scotland and Wales, culminating in the spectacular success of the Scottish National Party, campaigning on a socialist platform, in the 2015 General Election, has opened up the possibility of a very different political future for the left in Britain. At the very least, the prospect of a more devolved form of British socialism seems not just likely, but necessary.

The aim of this book is to contribute some historical perspective to the present predicament of British socialism. Its focus is the immediate pre-history of the twentieth-century socialist project: the period from the 1880s, when modern socialist ideas were first popularised in Britain, to the years immediately before the Great War, which, by giving the Labour Party its first taste of power at home and hastening the ascendancy of Bolshevism abroad, marked a watershed in the history of the left. This period was one of intense fluidity for the socialist movement: its political structures and strategies, even the very content of its ideology, were subjects of almost permanent debate. Were socialists going to form a separate political party or were they going to permeate existing parties? Were they going to seek influence through an alliance with the trade unions or were they going to plough a more purist socialist furrow? Were they going to advocate Marxist class war or follow a more inclusive 'ethical socialism'? Historians have given considerable attention to these questions, but less attention has been given to another aspect of the fluidity of the socialist movement in this period: the way in which socialists related to the national consciousnesses of the British Isles.

This is an issue both specific and universal in nature. Although socialist ideology is fundamentally universalist, socialists everywhere and in every period have been obliged to contend with particularisms, whether local, regional or national. The attempt to implement socialism might be seen as part of a set of parallel dialogues between the universal and the local, the general and the particular, the theoretical and the practical. This book, therefore, aims simultaneously to illuminate some of the themes of modern Welsh history, modern British history, and, more generally, the history of ideas and their application to reality. Its focus is not on electoral politics, nor the evolution of political structures, both of which have received adequate attention from historians. Rather it is concerned with the everyday activities, experiences and ideas of political activists that collectively comprise what we understand as political culture. Rather than focusing upon a specific locality, it offers an analysis at a national (Welsh) level, and seeks to examine the ways in which the dynamic of socialist development was built upon interplay between Wales and the wider world, and also between the different regions of Wales. It is written in the spirit of 'four nations history', but also in the knowledge that it can offer but one step towards the greater understanding of our past that is necessary if the British left is to come to terms with the fact that it is the product of a national and cultural pluralism through which it should be enriched rather than hindered.

In pursuing this agenda, the book combines chronological and thematic approaches. Chapter 1 makes some observations about the historiography of Welsh socialism, before examining the activities of the first socialists in Wales in the 1880s. The majority of these were missionaries, coming into Wales from over the English border. Their activities are placed within both their long-term and immediate contexts, and examined in the light of what they tell us about the role of socialists as mediators in an ongoing dialogue between Wales and the wider world. Chapter 2 examines the development of the first socialist organisations to put down roots in Wales in the late 1880s and 1890s: the Fabian Society in Cardiff and the Social Democratic Federation in Swansea and Barry. Through a consideration of some of these organisations' leading members, the political culture of urban-cosmopolitan socialism in 1890s Wales is reconstructed. This allows, in addition to the exploration of general questions about the growth of socialism in south Wales, an assessment of its relationship with Welsh national consciousness.

The 1890s also witnessed a growth in socialist activities within the communities of the south Wales coalfield, which is the focus of chapter 3. The main agent of this was the Independent Labour Party, founded in 1893, the efforts of which were supported and enhanced by the propagandists of Robert Blatchford's *Clarion* movement. The chapter begins with a consideration of socialist activities before the momentous 1898 coal strike, then examines the influence of the strike upon the development of socialism, before broadening out to a more general consideration of the political culture of socialism in south Wales in the 1890s and early 1900s. In addition to socialist attitudes to questions of national consciousness, the chapter examines the developing regional dynamic of socialist growth within Wales, suggesting that socialism was a more active and prominent influence within the coalfield in the 1890s than historians have previously suggested.

Chapter 4 shifts focus away from the coalfield to examine the growth of socialism across Wales more generally. It considers the way that socialist ideas were received in Welsh communities from the 1880s onwards, before examining the role of socialists in the Penrhyn Quarry lockout of 1900–3 – an event which provided a northern parallel to the 1898 coal dispute, but with some important differences. Building upon this analysis, the chapter culminates in an examination of the development of indigenous Welsh radicalism towards socialism, by examining the ideas of a number of activists that effectively straddled the two political traditions. This discussion is developed in chapter 5, which combines a general discussion of the development of socialism in Wales after 1906 with a more specific examination of the increasingly self-conscious efforts of some Welsh socialists to develop what they considered to be an indigenous form of socialism in Wales.

The efforts of Welsh socialists in this period to resolve the tensions between nationalism and socialism, universalism and particularism, and, in more general terms, vision and reality, although often intense, were only partially successful. For much of the twentieth century it might have appeared, in most of Britain at any rate, that such questions were becoming irrelevant. This is clearly no longer the case. British socialism is again in a state of fluidity, and the relationship between the plural national structures and consciousnesses of the British Isles promises to play a formative role in its re-casting. In recovering a neglected dimension of the early years of modern British socialism, it is hoped that this book will make not just a contribution to historical scholarship, but will also provide at least part of a historical context that will inform the debates of the present.

1
PIONEERS, 1790s–1880s

Cyril Parry, the pioneering historian of socialism in Gwynedd, asserted over 40 years ago that 'there was no indigenous Welsh socialism',[1] and his stark statement still awaits full interrogation. In structural terms it is certainly true that modern socialism developed relatively late in Wales. Although provincial centres in England and Scotland witnessed the establishment of socialist societies in the early 1880s, it was not until the 1890s that similar societies were established in Wales on anything like a sustainable basis. It is also true that some of the most prominent socialists in Wales in this period were incomers. In terms of independent labour representation – the form of politics that was most often forced and pioneered by socialists – Wales was also a relatively late developer. While independent labour parliamentary candidates were returned in other parts of Britain as early as 1892, it was not until 1900 that a similar breakthrough was made in Wales. Indeed, Welsh historiography supports the view that in its early years socialism 'seemed an alien growth' in Wales.[2] Existing studies of the impact of socialism upon late-nineteenth-century Wales focus upon its structural growth, tending to see it in the context of the later emergence of the Labour Party, as, in other words, 'Labour's roots in Wales'.[3] Viewed in this way the weakness of early Welsh socialism is striking. In the words of Deian Hopkin, Wales was '[f]rankly, nowhere' in the events of the Socialist Revival of the 1880s, and remained a 'socialist

[1] Cyril Parry, 'Socialism in Gwynedd 1900–1920' (unpublished PhD thesis, University of Wales, Bangor, 1967), p. 183.
[2] K.O. Morgan, *Wales in British Politics, 1868–1922* (Cardiff, 1963), p. 212.
[3] Deian Hopkin, 'Labour's Roots in Wales, 1880–1900', in Duncan Tanner, Chris Williams and Deian Hopkin (eds), *The Labour Party in Wales 1900–2000* (Cardiff, 2000), pp. 40–60; Deian Hopkin, 'The Rise of Labour in Wales, 1890–1914', *Llafur*, 6/3 (1994), 120–41; Jon Parry, 'Trade Unionists and Early Socialism in South Wales, 1890–1908', *Llafur*, 4/3 (1986), 43–54.

desert' into the late 1890s.[4] Regional studies add weight to these conclusions. Chris Williams argues in his study of the Rhondda that socialism was 'marginal' in the politics of the two valleys up to 1898.[5] In Llanelli, as doubtless elsewhere in Wales, participation in socialist politics in the 1890s was 'an act of high individualism, at once risky and outré'.[6] In the anthracite district of the south Wales coalfield socialist and labour activity before 1900 was 'minimal',[7] and the workers of Swansea were 'singularly untouched'.[8] At the other end of the country in Gwynedd 'the concept of socialism as a distinct political faith remained ill defined ... few appreciated its meaning and fewer still were aware of its implications' until well into the 1900s.[9] In the large geographical space between, early socialism is generally agreed to be so much of a non-event that it is not even mentioned. According to the established historiography, socialism in Wales did not begin to make inroads into the social and political bedrock of nonconformist Liberalism until some time in the second half of the first decade of the twentieth century. As Ryland Wallace states, '[i]n general, geographical remoteness and linguistic and cultural differences ... kept the Principality almost immune from the doctrines of the Socialist societies of England'.[10]

While the substance of these statements is doubtless correct, it must be conceded that the tardiness of Wales in the socialist growth of the 1880s and 1890s does present a historical problem. When socialism and independent labour

[4] Hopkin, 'The Rise of Labour in Wales', p. 123; Hopkin, 'Labour's Roots in Wales', p. 55.
[5] Chris Williams, *Democratic Rhondda: Politics and Society, 1885–1951* (Cardiff, 1996), p. 59.
[6] Deian Hopkin, 'The Rise of Labour: Llanelli, 1890–1922', in Geraint H. Jenkins and J. Beverley Smith (eds), *Politics and Society in Wales, 1840–1922: Essays in Honour of Ieuan Gwynedd Jones* (Cardiff, 1988), pp. 161–82 (p. 163).
[7] Ioan Matthews, 'The World of the Anthracite Miner' (unpublished PhD thesis, University of Wales, Cardiff, 1995), p. 208.
[8] Thomas John McCarry, 'Labour and Society in Swansea, 1887–1918' (unpublished PhD thesis, University of Wales, Swansea, 1986), p. 87.
[9] Cyril Parry, 'The Independent Labour Party and Gwynedd Politics, 1900–1920', *Welsh History Review*, 4/1 (1968), 47–66 (49).
[10] Ryland Wallace, *Organise! Organise! Organise! A Study of Reform Agitations in Wales, 1840–1886* (Cardiff, 1991), p. 221.

representation did develop in Wales it did so with remarkable rapidity. More than this, within a short space of time the Welsh socialist and labour movement became an integral and deeply influential part of the wider British movement. By 1903 Keir Hardie could state that 'For some reason or other, Wales had become the cockpit in which the great questions affecting labour were being fought out'.[11] He wasn't wrong. The previous five years had witnessed a series of events of major significance in the history of British labour and socialism, all taking place in south Wales within barely a dozen square miles of each other. These included the formation of the South Wales Miners' Federation, Hardie's own return to Parliament at Merthyr Boroughs and the portentous Taff Vale rail dispute. In the course of the next decade not only was there a dramatic proliferation of Independent Labour Party (ILP) branches in Wales, but the name of south Wales in particular was to become synonymous with left-wing militancy, epitomised by the Cambrian Combine dispute and the publication of the *Miners' Next Step*. During the decade after that, moreover, the region was to become one of the engine houses of the British socialist and labour movement. This apparent dichotomy between the early absence of socialist activity in Wales and the country's subsequent centrality to British labour history invites questions about the apparent failure of Wales to take part in the early growth of British socialism. At the very least the sudden animation of socialism in Wales in the early 1900s might suggest that something more was going on beneath the surface of Welsh society in the final decades of the nineteenth century than the existing historiography admits.

This book does not contest the structural weakness of late-Victorian Welsh socialism. Rather it seeks to re-examine the period from another perspective. Instead of viewing the development of socialism as part of that collection of events which is often assumed to amount to 'the origins of the Labour Party', in which the creation of formal organisational structures is an all-important measure of progress, it aims to examine the spread of socialism in Wales in terms of

---

[11] National Library of Wales, D.A. Thomas Papers, C2, unidentified newspaper cutting. Hardie was speaking at the Rocking Stone on Pontypridd Common.

an interplay between Wales and the wider world. In this light, structural growth is less important than the spread of ideas. Such ideational development is, of course, more difficult to assess. It takes place, for the most part, beneath the level of the historical record, much of it in the private rather than the public sphere, and it is unquantifiable. It is also extremely complex. In the case of socialism new ideas were undoubtedly introduced to Wales by propagandists who arrived from beyond its borders, but the flow of these ideas was not unidirectional. Frequently, it was diverted and complicated by contact with Welsh culture and society. Sometimes it borrowed from and fused with existing traditions of Welsh radicalism, and sometimes it eddied and fed ideas and influences back into the mainstream of British socialism. It flowed unevenly across Wales as a whole, influencing different regions in different ways and at different speeds. Undeniably, though, the permeation of socialist ideas into Wales in the 1880s marked the beginning of a process that was to have a major long term impact upon both Wales and Britain.

Beginnings and ends of historical processes and movements must, of course, be approached with circumspection. Indeed, the tendency to see what used to be called the Socialist Revival of the 1880s as a historical watershed has long been under question,[12] and the elements of it that comprised the interplay under discussion here might be seen as part of a greater metanarrative concerning the place of Wales in the world. Certainly, radicals had been exchanging ideas and influences across the Welsh border for hundreds of years. The French Revolution initiated what might be considered the modern phase of this dialogue, and in its wake radical influences began to permeate Welsh society.[13] Sometimes these came in the form of individual activists from England,

---

[12] E.F. Biagini and A. Reid (eds), *Currents of Radicalism: Popular Radicalism, Organized Labour and Party Politics, 1850–1914* (Cambridge, 1991); Jon Lawrence, 'Popular Radicalism and the Socialist Revival in Britain', *Journal of British Studies*, 31/2 (1992), 163–86; Mark Bevir, 'The British Social Democratic Federation, 1880–1885: From O'Brienism to Marxism', *International Review of Social History*, 37/2 (1992), 207–29.

[13] David Davies, *The Influence of the French Revolution on Welsh Life and Literature* (Carmarthen, 1926). The work of the Centre for Advanced Welsh and Celtic Studies at Aberystwyth has recently added immeasurably to our knowledge of this period.

among whom was John Thelwall, one of the heroes of E.P. Thompson's great narrative, *The Making of the English Working Class*.[14] Escaping the intensity of London in the late 1790s, he tried to find his way back to the land – thus engaging in another of the great radical traditions of the British Isles, and one that has direct bearing upon the arguments in this book – at a smallholding near Llyswen in Breconshire. During what turned out to be a brief and near-disastrous stay there he made contact with Welsh radicals, including Iolo Morganwg, before ultimately abandoning his new life, his rural dream having warped in the rain.[15] A failure at farming though he was, Thelwall might be seen as a forebear of the socialists who came at the end of the next century to spread their beliefs under the same Welsh rain.

His experience was linked to theirs not just by the continuity of the weather, but by an ongoing interplay across the intervening generations. A prominent example of human and ideological traffic in the other direction, from the generation following Thelwall, is, of course, Robert Owen of Newtown. Often considered the 'Father of British Socialism', Owen was seen by some, in the words of another Welsh export, Tom Ellis, to be taking the message of Wales to the world. If this was the case, the Owenite communitarians who came from England to settle in Meirionnydd and Carmarthenshire in the 1840s and 1850s were bringing it back again.[16] Their ideological cousins in the Chartist movement were also furthering the same radical cross-border dialogue. It was, after all, the prosecution of a Londoner, Henry Vincent, in south Wales that acted as the catalyst for the Newport Rising in 1839.[17] Another Chartist, Thomas Powell, provides

See in particular Mary-Ann Constantine and Dafydd Johnston (eds), *'Footsteps of Liberty & Revolt': Essays on Wales and the French Revolution* (Cardiff, 2013).

[14] E.P. Thompson. *The Making of the English Working Class* (London, 1963), esp. pp. 172–6.

[15] E.P. Thompson, 'Hunting the Jacobin Fox', *Past and Present*, 142 (1994), 94–140; Penelope J. Corfield, 'Rhetoric, Radical Politics and Rainfall: John Thelwall in Breconshire, 1797–1800', *Brycheiniog*, 40 (2008), 17–39.

[16] For a discussion of Owen and Owenism in relation to Wales, see below pp. 175–8.

[17] David Williams, 'Chartism in Wales', in Asa Briggs (ed.), *Chartist Studies* (London, 1959), pp. 220–48.

a better example of the geographical complexity of this radical interplay. He moved from Newtown to Shrewsbury and then to London, before returning in the 1830s to Montgomeryshire, where he was prosecuted for his role in the Llanidloes disturbances of 1839. Throughout his life's journey he doubtless imparted and absorbed ideas and influences in various forms and at varying levels of intensity along the way.[18]

One final example from the next generation will suffice to make the link with the socialists of the 1880s. John Ruskin was a formative influence upon most of them, and although his work might be considered quintessentially English, he was no stranger to Wales. Indeed, Wales provided a perfect setting for the implementation of the pastoral ideal set out in works such as *Fors Clavigera*. In 1871, as part of this agenda, he established the Guild of St George, the ultimate aim of which was variously described as 'the salvation of England' or 'the health, wealth and long life of the British nation', and to this end the Guild received the gift of a row of cottages in Barmouth, to be run as a type of social housing. When, in 1876, Ruskin went to Barmouth to visit the cottages, he found that one of the established tenants was a Frenchman by the name of Monsieur Guyard, a 'reformer, experimenter and philanthropist' who had left France during the Franco-Prussian War. The two men got on well, and shared a belief in 'the practical conviction that in flying from cities and luxurious lives, and in leading laborious days combined with the education of heart and mind, the perfect way was to be found'. Their liaison on the steep hillsides of old Barmouth provides a fine illustration of the diverse and cosmopolitan nature of the interplay that embraced even some of the most apparently rural and isolated parts of Wales in the nineteenth century.[19]

This process of interplay was by no means limited to secular radicalism. Indeed, its main theatres were the closely related activities of religion and education. Wales was subject

[18] For Powell, see Malcolm Chase, *Chartism: A New History* (Manchester and New York, 2007), pp. 87–94. After his involvement at Llanidloes, Powell returned to London and then emigrated to the West Indies, thus continuing the process.

[19] Blanche Atkinson, *Ruskin's Social Experiment at Barmouth* (London, 1900).

to waves of heterogeneous religious and educational influences during the nineteenth century, which were mediated and shaped by a class of more or less cosmopolitan Welsh opinion formers, epitomised by individuals such as Kilsby Jones, William Williams, Hugh Owen and Henry Richard.[20] Of Henry Richard, for instance, it was written on his death in 1888 that 'he fulfilled for Wales a double political function: he not only stood in the breach between Wales and England to explain as a Welshman the mind and wishes of the Principality to the English people, he was also the political spokesman from England to Wales'.[21] By the late nineteenth century these influences had been fused to create a distinct and powerful sense of Welsh identity. The ability of Wales to absorb such apparently foreign influences and make them its own was, moreover, not lost on some Welsh socialists, who saw their own creed as another religion and sought to mould it to the same ends. 'Just as Christianity came here from Palestine', one of them observed, 'and Protestantism from Germany, and Nonconformity from England, and Calvinism from Geneva, and were welcomed here, each in its turn – so also will it be with Socialism.'[22] Welsh patriots, on the other hand, were also aware of the ambiguities beneath their own identity, and towards the end of the nineteenth century they were increasingly making a case on behalf of Welsh particularism: that 'the sentiment that cherishes and strives to maintain all the particular institutions that belong to Wales as a nation apart from England' should be developed.[23] 'The most unlovely feature of modern civilization is the tendency to destroy distinction. Originality is dying out, and we are in danger of settling down on a dead level of universal mediocrity',[24] argued one such patriot (from beyond the

---

[20] J. Vyrnwy Morgan, *Kilsby Jones* (Wrexham, n.d.); Daniel Evans, *The Life and Work of William Williams* (Llandysul, n.d.); Gwyn Griffiths, *Henry Richard: Apostle of Peace and Welsh Patriot* (London, 2012).

[21] *Cymru Fydd*, 1/9 (September 1888), 505.

[22] National Library of Wales, David Thomas Papers, Box 3, undated unpublished manuscript, 'Wales and the Politics of the Future'.

[23] Robert Owen, 'A Plea for Welsh Particularism II: Anglicising Dangers', *Young Wales*, 5/51 (1899), 52–4, p. 53.

[24] Harry Jones, 'Another Plea for Welsh Particularism', *Young Wales*, 5/52 (1899), 88–90, p. 88.

Welsh border), and socialism might have been counted among the influences he had in mind. These debates were barely underway when the first socialists began their propaganda in Wales,[25] but they remained unresolved throughout the period under discussion in this book.[26] Considered as a whole, they form an essential context in which to understand the activities of early socialists in Wales who, when they began to propagate their ideas in the 1880s, were initiating yet another phase in a long historical process of ideological interplay between Wales and the wider world.

If the national context for the arrival of socialism was fluid, the socialists' own ideology was likewise suffused with what R.H. Tawney later called 'radiant ambiguities'.[27] Already by the early 1880s there were several different varieties of thought that were broadly grouped under the term socialism. These included the 'utopian' ideas of Proudhon, Saint-Simon and Robert Owen, the Christian socialism of Kingsley and Maurice, and the more recent 'scientific socialism' of Marx and Engels. The diversity of socialist belief was to become even more marked as socialism grew in popularity in the 1890s, but even in the 1880s the problematic nature of defining socialism was not lost on Welsh observers. One of them summarised his views in 1889: 'The difficulty one always has to encounter with modern Socialists is to attempt to get an approximate definition of their theory.' Their ideology, he continued, was imbued with 'vague teachings and fearful uncertainties', and

> if there is one thing certain at all about modern democratic Socialists it is this, that when they assemble together, the divergent views which

---

[25] For early contributions dealing specifically with aspects of the interplay under discussion here, see William Jones, 'Y Deffroad Cenedlaethol', *Cymru Fydd*, 1/12 (1888), 405–12; S.T. Jones, 'Cymry Cymreig', *Cymru Fydd*, 2/4 (1889); Soffos Ap, 'Arwyddion Deffroad', *Cymru Fydd*, 3/2 (1890), 107–10.

[26] Essentially the same debate that was conducted in *Cymru Fydd* and *Young Wales* in the 1880s and 1890s was rehearsed in *The Welsh Outlook* in the period after the Great War. Contributors complained that Welsh 'ideas are all heavily stamped "Made in England" or some other foreign country, and it is full time that we should attempt to develop the intellectual industry at home' (A Welsh Nationalist, 'Dangers of the Political Situation', *The Welsh Outlook*, 5 (1918), 244–6 [246]), or that Wales was, in intellectual terms, a 'nation of copyists' (Revd. Gwilym Davies, 'A Welsh Social Diary', *The Welsh Outlook*, 7 (1920), 44–5).

[27] R.H. Tawney, *The Attack and Other Papers* (London, 1953), p. 60.

they entertain, both as to the methods and meaning of their propaganda, are so extraordinary, that it places any material progress out of the question.[28]

Such statements were to some extent justified by the schismatic tendencies of the British socialist leadership of the 1880s, which by the middle of the decade had already resulted in the establishment of three main socialist societies. The Social Democratic Federation (SDF) was originally founded in 1881 as the Democratic Federation, and had adopted a Marxian socialist programme by 1883 which was reflected by the addition of the prefix 'Social' to the organisation's title in 1884. The Socialist League, another Marxist group, broke away from the SDF at the end of 1884, after a series of strategic disagreements and personal wranglings, to embark upon a short career in more purist and uncompromising socialist politics. The Fabian Society, on the other hand, which was also founded in 1884, espoused a more gradualist and flexible political agenda and a more heterodox, less strictly Marxist, socio-economic analysis. All three of these organisations attempted to influence Wales to some degree during the 1880s and 1890s, but it was the Marxists of the SDF and the Socialist League that were in the vanguard.

The views of the Marxian socialists regarding nationalism, small nations and (so far as they existed at all) Wales were, however, rather unhelpful as far as conducting a specifically Welsh propaganda campaign was concerned. One of their key foundation texts, after all, famously asserted that 'the working men have no country',[29] and it is likely that many of the leading socialists of the 1880s would have agreed with Engels that the Welsh, like the Highland Gaels, were mere 'remnants of peoples long gone' upon whose behalf any claim to a separate political existence would have been 'absurd'.[30] The SDF leader, H.M. Hyndman, in his

[28] Ivor Bowen, 'Welsh Radicalism and German Socialism', *Cymru Fydd*, 2/2 (1889), 57–63 (57, 58).
[29] Karl Marx and Friedrich Engels, *The Communist Manifesto* (ed. A.J.P. Taylor, London, 1968), p. 102. An English translation of *The Communist Manifesto* was published in *Justice*, 7 January 1887.
[30] Robert Griffiths, *Marx and Engels on Wales and the Welsh* (Cardiff, 2006), pp. 31–2.

tellingly named *England for All*, favoured decentralisation in general terms, but explicitly dismissed legislative devolution to Wales on the grounds that there was no demand for it.[31] There were socialist leaders who may have provided an exception to this generally dismissive view of Welsh nationality. William Morris, of Welsh descent himself, presented a vision of a multilingual society, in which Welsh was spoken and sung alongside other languages, in his socialist utopia of 1891, *News From Nowhere*.[32] He was, however, exceptional in this. More representative of early British Marxist views of Wales was an article published in the SDF's *Justice* in 1886, which derided the childish and 'petty race prejudice which makes Welshmen hate Englishmen simply because they are Englishmen, and speak Welsh simply because it is Welsh', and lamented the growth of nationalist feeling in Wales, opining that 'at the time when the economical situation absolutely requires that the social problem should be regarded from an international standpoint, this recrudescence of national antipathies should puzzle all observers'.[33] In the SDF world view Wales was a 'spurious nationality' which, along with Scotland and Ireland, would ultimately 'receive honourable interment'. 'To endeavour to resuscitate them', commented *Justice*, 'is only to play into the hands of the exploiting classes whose game it is to spread dissension between the workers of one country and another.'[34] When considered alongside the putative propensity of the SDF for free thought and atheism, such attitudes did not augur well for successful propaganda in Wales.

It is, possible, however, to overstate the limitations of the early British Marxist organisations in this respect. Indeed, some of the older representations of the SDF, as an inflexible, dogmatic sect, 'a rather weedy growth in the political garden, with few attractive features',[35] have long been subject

[31] H.M. Hyndman, *England for All* (London, 1881), pp. 99, 126.
[32] William Morris, *News From Nowhere* (London, 1897) (first published 1891), pp. 32, 114–15.
[33] *Justice*, 2 January 1886.
[34] *Justice*, 17 September 1892.
[35] Henry Pelling, *Origins of the Labour Party* (London, 1954), p. 172; Eric Hobsbawm, 'Hyndman and the SDF', in *Labouring Men: Studies in the History of Labour* (London, 1964), pp. 231–8, states that the SDF 'showed a lack of political

to revision. The Federation is now viewed as a more pragmatic organisation, which grew out of, and adapted to, local circumstances in the regions where it was strong, notably the north-west of England, and within which there was a significant gap between the official ideology of the leadership and the everyday activities of local activists.[36] This interpretation has barely been tested as far as Wales is concerned, but several points might be noted that suggest the context for the introduction of socialist ideas into the country was not wholly negative. First, the issue of Irish Home Rule was one with which socialists of all persuasions were familiar and towards which many were, up to a point, sympathetic – official views about 'spurious nationalities' notwithstanding.[37] This sympathy was by no means automatically transferred to the Welsh situation, but the prominence of Ireland as a

realism unparalleled by any other contemporary group of socialists', and that the group was a 'sect rather than a serious political organization'. Similarly critical of the SDF for its lack of ideological flexibility and realism are Henry Collins, 'The Marxism of the Social Democratic Federation', in Asa Briggs and John Saville (eds), *Essays in Labour History* (London, 1967), pp. 47–69, and Chushichi Tsuzuki, *H.M. Hyndman and British Socialism* (Oxford, 1961).

[36] Mark Bevir, 'H.M. Hyndman: A Re-reading and a Re-assessment', *History of Political Thought*, 13/1 (1991), 125–45; Martin Crick, *The History of the Social Democratic Federation* (Ryburn, 1994); Jeffrey Hill, 'Social Democracy and the Labour Movement: The Social Democratic Federation in Lancashire', *Bulletin of the North West Labour History Society*, 8 (1982), 44–55; Kenneth Hilton, 'John Spargo, The Social Democratic Federation and the 1898 South Wales Coal Strike', *Welsh History Review*, 16/4 (1993), 542–50; Graham Johnson, 'Social Democracy and Labour Politics in Britain, 1892–1911', *History*, 85/277 (2002), 67–87; A.J. Kidd, 'The Social Democratic Federation and Popular Agitation amongst the Unemployed of Edwardian Manchester', *International Review of Social History*, 29/3 (1984), 336–58; James Owen, 'Dissident Missionaries?: Re-Narrating the Political Strategy of the Social Democratic Federation, 1884–1887', *Labour History Review*, 73/2 (2008), 187–207.

[37] *Justice*, 23 February 1884 commented that 'the Irish National Party is doing great service by hastening on the crisis of the social question' in Ireland. Also see Michael Davitt in *Justice*, 22 March 1884; J.L. Joynes summed up the SDF ambivalence regarding the Irish issue in *Justice*, 4 October 1884: 'It is deeply to be regretted that in Ireland the question [of the class struggle] is complicated by the idea of nationality, which the oppression and interference of the English constantly tends to aggravate and foment. Socialists are nothing if not international, but we must all recognise the entire right of the Irish to settle their own difficulties, and to work out the solution of their own economical problem in their own way. It is upon the free Irish nation of the future that we confidently count for assistance and fellowship in the development of the great idea of Socialism for which we all strive'; *Justice*, 27 March 1886, 17 April 1886 and 2 April 1887.

political issue in the 1880s did at least ensure that most early socialists had some awareness of the predicament of Britain's 'Celtic fringe' in more general terms.

A more significant area of ideological confluence between the Marxists and Welsh radicals was provided by an issue that was closely related to Irish Home Rule: the land. Already a highly inflammatory issue in Ireland, this was in the 1880s fast becoming a key theme in Welsh politics too – a development not entirely lost on the SDF, which occasionally included reports of the Welsh land agitation in *Justice*.[38] The ideas of the American land reformer Henry George, moreover, had been an influence upon many members of the early socialist groups, often providing them with a stepping stone towards full acceptance of socialist ideology.[39] By the mid-1880s George was also extending his influence to Wales. In 1884 he visited Cardiff, where he lectured to a 'large and enthusiastic' audience, mainly of working men, at the New Public Hall on 16 January,[40] and the following afternoon he held a 'conference' on the land question, attended by twenty gentlemen and two ladies, at Cardiff's Swiss Hall. During the course of the afternoon meeting George explained that the 'movement was not a local one. It was going on all over the world', and illustrated his point with reference to examples from New Zealand, Australia and America.[41] The intellectual digestion of George's internationally informed, trans-Atlantic influence in south Wales is confirmed by the flurry of letters and comments in the *Western Mail* during the following weeks, some of which were negative, but others, in

---

[38] *Justice*, 11 September 1886 and 18 February 1888.
[39] For example, Tom Mann, who recalled in the 1920s the impact of reading Henry George's *Progress and Poverty* in 1881: 'it impressed me as by far the most valuable book I had so far read ... and never since I gave it careful attention have I had one hour of doubt but that the destiny of the human race is assured, and that the workers will, in due time, come to occupy their rightful position', Tom Mann, *Memoirs* (London, 1923), pp. 27–8. Also see H.H. Champion, 'Henry George and the Land Question', *Justice*, 19 January 1884. Whereas George argued for a single land tax, socialists went further and advocated full land nationalisation: 'All Socialists, without exception, are in favour of Nationalisation of the Land. It is one of the most important points in our whole programme', *Justice*, 11 October 1884.
[40] *Justice*, 26 January 1884.
[41] *Western Mail*, 18 January 1884.

the words of one correspondent, bore 'the tooth mark of the Socialist'.[42]

More influential was Michael Davitt's tour of Wales in 1886.[43] This controversial series of meetings was instigated and organised by Welsh radicals Michael D. Jones and Evan Pan Jones,[44] and, significantly, it was also approved of from afar by the English socialists.[45] The tour included meetings at Flint, Llandudno, Blaenau Ffestiniog and Swansea,[46] and although it was sharply divisive it must be viewed as an important landmark in the development of Welsh opinion on the land issue, as Davitt's presence in Wales not only drew important emerging radical figures such as Lloyd George and T.E. Ellis into the land debate, but also linked the issue with labour representatives from the industrial south of the country, notably the miners' leader William Abraham (Mabon).[47] More than this, though, Davitt's tour provides another example of an agitator mapping international radical issues onto a specific set of Welsh circumstances, a sense of which is illustrated by his opening remarks at Blaenau Ffestiniog:

> a ddywedai ei fod wedi anerch cannoedd o gyfarfodydd yn yr Iwerddon, Lloegr, Ysgotland, a'r America, o fewn y saith mlynedd diweddaf, ond ni theimlodd erioed fwy bleser i sefyll o flaen cynnulleidfa nag a deimlai wrth sefyll o flaen y gynnulleidfa hon.

Davitt went on to congratulate the Welsh for preserving their language, suggesting that the Irish could learn something from their example.[48] He sensed an opportunity, moreover,

---

[42] *Western Mail*, 22 January 1884.

[43] J. Graham Jones, 'Michael Davitt, David Lloyd George and T.E. Ellis: the Welsh Experience, 1886', *Welsh History Review*, 18/3 (1997), 450–82.

[44] Evan Pan Jones, *Oes Gofion: Fraslun o Hanes fy Mywyd* (Bala, n.d.), pp. 176–7. The plans for the tour highlighted a fault line in Welsh radicalism; Thomas Gee stood aloof.

[45] *Justice*, 9 January 1886 and 13 February 1886.

[46] *Baner ac Amserau Cymru*, 13 February, 17 February, 20 February and 29 May 1886.

[47] *Baner ac Amserau Cymru*, 12 May 1886; J. Graham Jones, 'Michael Davitt, Lloyd George and T.E. Ellis', 477.

[48] *Baner ac Amserau Cymru*, 20 February 1886 ('he said that he had addressed hundreds of meetings in Ireland, England, Scotland and America during the last seven years, but he had never felt more pleasure to stand in front of an audience as he felt standing in front of that audience'). All translations from the original Welsh are by the author. The orthography, spelling, punctuation etc. of quotations

in the 'intense national feeling' that he witnessed at Blaenau Ffestiniog. Although the Welsh were 'only in the A.B.C. of the great social and political problems of the day', he asserted, 'I think they will become apt scholars'. The Welsh people were, in his view, natural republicans, 'as the teachings of Nonconformity essentially tend towards republican ideas'. The meeting at Blaenau was closed by the singing of *Hen Wlad Fy Nhadau* which was, for Davitt, a 'most agreeable incident', and he attributed what he saw as a superior intelligence on the part of the Welsh quarrymen to the cultivation of their musical culture.[49] The singing of the Welsh anthem to celebrate the visit of the Irish agitator was a fitting expression of the meeting of the culture that it represented with the ideas that Davitt brought to Wales in 1886. His visit, along with that of Henry George, may be seen as a further episode in the interplay between Wales and the wider world, drawing Irish and Atlantic influences into the mainstream of Welsh life through the vortex of land agitation. Quite literally George's and Davitt's campaigns might be seen as contributing to the grounding of late-nineteenth-century international radical and democratic feeling in Welsh soil. They also formed the immediate context for the entry of socialist ideas into Wales.

The first instances of this were sporadic and random in nature, the result of happenstance or individual initiative, rather than any strategic effort. Most of them probably went unrecorded, but one or two left traces that are worth examining for what they tell us about early socialist attitudes to Wales. Among the first socialist visitors to the country was SDF member and Eton schoolmaster James Leigh Joynes, who visited Llandudno as a holiday-maker in 1884. Joynes was no stranger to either Celtic Britain or the land agitation, as he had toured Ireland with Henry George in 1882 – an adventure that cost him his job at Eton.[50] He was not, however, impressed with the hybrid Welsh holiday settlement that Llandudno had become by the 1880s, and found his natural propagandist instincts frustrated there. He wrote to

in Welsh have been retained, except in the case of a small number where minor silent emendations clarify meaning.

[49] *Baner ac Amserau Cymru*, 21 April 1886.

[50] J.L. Joynes, *The Adventures of a Tourist in Ireland* (London, 1882).

a colleague from a Llandudno guest house in the summer of 1884 in acerbic terms:

> This place is not one for propaganda. The scum of the rich Liverpool shop-keepers and their unspeakable wives and daughters disport themselves on the esplanade. The honest part of the population is at present employed in catering for their various tastes in the way of dead animals and black-faced minstrelsy. Besides nobody except these depraved scoundrels can speak English, and I cannot convert a Taffy without knowing Welsh. There is one blind man whom I have hopes of, as he sees more than most, but it is no use giving him *Justice* unless you have it printed for the purpose in raised type that he can feel.[51]

Joynes was not alone among the SDF leadership in visiting Wales in the 1880s. Indeed, the next high-profile SDF-er to record a visit was none other than the organisation's leader Henry Hyndman. Hyndman had first visited the country in the 1850s, and returned in 1886 to investigate an industrial dispute at the Llanberis slate quarries.[52] His observations are revealing, particularly with regard to the issue that Joynes found so obstructive, the Welsh language. Hyndman was not entirely negative about the language, and in some senses saw it as a tool that might be used advantageously in pursuit of the class struggle by Welsh workers. He observed later that it gave them a 'special advantage in strike organisation', offering 'almost all the gains with none of the drawbacks of the secret society'.[53] Hyndman's approval of this aspect of the use of Welsh was, however, tempered by a more general ambivalence, as revealed in his immediate impressions of the situation at Llanberis:

> ... the Welshmen are soon able to talk English when they find that the Englishman who wishes them to do so is on their side. 'Dym Sassenach,' 'No English,' is the answer to those only whom they feel pretty sure are against them. The National feeling which is rising in Wales so rapidly is really far more social than political; but they use their language among themselves and are forming secret societies from which Englishmen are excluded, because they hope in this way to organise better ... It would certainly be well to have our short

---

[51] British Library of Political and Economic Science, London, COLL MISC 522/2/11, J.L. Joynes to [?] Fitzgerald, 10 August 1884.

[52] *Justice*, 23 January 1886.

[53] H.M. Hyndman, *Further Reminiscences* (London, 1912), p. 447.

literature translated into Welsh and distributed in the Principality. The people are much quicker to grasp revolutionary ideas than our own rural population, and seem to turn naturally towards Socialism, though their language may interfere somewhat with the spread of our doctrines.

This passage reveals much about early socialist attitudes to the Welsh language and culture. Hyndman does his best to identify and insinuate himself with the Welsh workmen. He also articulates a view that was to become common currency in socialist circles in Wales, that the Welsh 'turn naturally towards socialism'. He cannot, however, hide his suspicion of the Welsh language and Welsh nationalism. He sees the language as something used wilfully to exclude Englishmen, and as something which will 'interfere' with the natural spread of ideas. To Hyndman, socialist ideas would only spread in Wales 'in spite of the Nationalism of the people'.[54]

Despite such attitudes on the part of the organisation's leadership, Wales was not devoid of indigenous socialist activity in the 1880s. Indeed, the first formal socialist society to be formed within Wales was a branch of the SDF, which was established near Brynmawr, in Breconshire, in the industrial south-east of the country. In 1885 a 'small body of earnest workers' organised themselves there 'after careful study of the principles of Socialism', with the intent of 'carrying on an active propaganda among their ill-paid and over-tasked fellow-workers'.[55] The workers, in a region of high unemployment, largely dependent upon a declining iron industry, were, it was reported, 'always glad to receive any of the Federation literature'.[56] The branch was, however, short-lived, and dissolved after the death of its leading light, John Price of Waen Avon, in the summer of 1885. Despite this, the work was carried on in the region by David Williams, an 'active Propagandist' from Clydach, and it was reported at the SDF's annual conference that year that 'large quantities of literature' had been 'put about' in Breconshire and

---

[54] *Justice*, 23 January 1886.
[55] *Justice*, 10 January 1885.
[56] *Justice*, 7 March 1885.

Monmouthshire.[57] Unfortunately, the historical record is sparse, and we do not know exactly where the branch met, how big it was, or where its members came from. It is fairly safe to assume, though, that they were reading and distributing literature supplied from SDF headquarters in London, including the Federation's newspaper, *Justice*, and pamphlets by the likes of Hyndman, Morris and Joynes.

It was not until March 1887 that socialists began to organise meetings in Wales in any strategic way. In that month John Fielding of the SDF began 'breaking fresh ground' by lecturing in south Wales. On Wednesday, 16 March 1887 he delivered a lecture on socialism at the Albert Hall in Swansea which, according to *Justice*, left the local workmen 'discussing the principles of Social Democracy on the following days with much animation and interest'.[58] Significantly, the meeting was chaired by a local Liberal, C.H. Perkins, who, in his opening remarks, recorded a sense of intellectual and ideological interplay between the UK capital and its distant satellite by observing that 'Mr. Fielding had come from London to give them information they very much lacked in Swansea'.[59] Fielding followed his lecture in Swansea with an open air meeting near Landore steelworks, where he delivered a 'long speech which was listened to with the greatest attention throughout' by local workmen who, after the meeting, urged him to return again to speak in Swansea.[60] Further meetings at Cardiff were unfortunately disrupted by snowstorms and poorly attended, but a Comrade Parr of Cardiff – 'the only avowed Socialist in this town' – managed to collect 26 names for the purpose of forming a branch of the SDF there. *Justice* concluded that the success of Fielding's visit 'has proved conclusively that the people are beginning to see that their only hope is in Social Democracy. A vigorous propaganda', it surmised, 'would most certainly result in the formation of powerful branches of the SDF in all the principal towns of Wales.'[61] The optimism of *Justice*'s

[57] *Justice*, 8 August 1885.
[58] *Justice*, 26 March 1887.
[59] *Cambria Daily Leader*, 17 March 1887.
[60] *Cambria Daily Leader*, 21 March 1887.
[61] *Justice*, 26 March 1887.

coverage far exceeded the reality of the situation, and the establishment of branches did not follow in the wake of Fielding's visit. There is, nevertheless, evidence that socialist ideas were being discussed in south Wales in this period, and that Fielding's visit was not wholly without impact. The Swansea Literary and Debating Society considered socialism at a meeting held in the Unitarian Schoolroom, just days before Fielding's first lecture, at which there was a 'capital attendance'. Presided over by the Revd. J.E. Manning, the members debated a motion put forward by the same C.H. Perkins who chaired Fielding's lecture that 'Socialism, properly carried out, affords the best remedy for the poverty and depression that so widely prevail'. The motion was defeated, but not without gaining some support.[62] A week or so later, in the wake of Fielding's lecture, socialism was the topic of debate at Swansea Liberal Club. Some of the local Liberal councillors had been present to hear Fielding at the Albert Hall, and many of them were clearly sympathetic to socialist ideas. Perkins was again active in the advocacy of the socialists, arguing that radicals and socialists were in close alliance and should mould their principles into one programme. Many of his colleagues were also sympathetic and, as one of them put it, 'failed to see any difference between an advanced Radical and a cautious Socialist'. Another argued that while socialism was too theoretical 'it was for the Radicals to give it practical form', and after a debate of two hours a motion in favour of socialism was passed.[63]

These reports highlight a central theme in the fortunes of socialism in Wales: its relationship with the advanced radical wing of Liberalism. Clearly, there was to some extent an ideological continuum that embraced both socialists and radical Liberals, of which at least some of the Swansea Liberals were a part. Care is needed, however, in evaluating this relationship. Many socialists were hostile to radicals attempting to give their theories practical form for them, and tended to see such expressions of sympathy as threatening to neuter their revolutionary beliefs. Liberals, on the other hand,

---

[62] *Cambria Daily Leader*, 16 March 1887.
[63] *Cambria Daily Leader*, 23 March 1887.

were more favourably disposed towards socialism while it remained abstract and theoretical than they were when it was translated into independent political action. More critical to the fortunes of socialism, though, was the extent to which Fielding's ideas found a receptive audience beyond the advanced wing of Swansea radicalism, and if the remarks of 'Paethsyllydd', the Welsh-language columnist of the *Cambria Daily Leader,* are at all representative of local opinion, prospects for socialism in the area were not bright. The columnist had attended Fielding's lecture, and had interviewed him afterwards, but was unimpressed with his ideas. Accepting that more would be heard of socialism in the future, and, significantly, that it was necessary to find a Welsh name for the movement, his column nevertheless dismissed socialist ideas as wholly unrealistic, and socialist agitators as false prophets:

> *y mae Mr. Fielding a'i gyfeillion yn myned o amgylch y wlad, gan addaw gwaredigaeth, pan y bydd y bedd wedi cau arnynt hwy ac ar eu plant cyn y sylweddolir un o'u dychmygion. Gwyr Mr. Fielding hyn yn dda, ond y mae yn talu iddo ef i anog dynion yn mlaen at bethau anhygoel. Y mae munud o ystyriaeth yn ddigon i oleuo meddwl unrhyw un fod y chwyldroadau y mae y Socialists yn dweyd rhaid eu cael cyn bydd y byd yn ddedwydd, yn bethau mor fawr fel nad all neb ddisgwyl cyflawniad o honynt. Dyma un peth, yn ol Mr. Fielding ei hun, cyn y gall Socialism fod yn ddaioni digymysg, rhaid fod holl genedloedd y ddaear wedi mabwysiadau yr un gyfundrefn. Pwy ond yr ehud a ddisgwyliai weled, yn ei oes fer, y fath chwyldroad? Gobeithio nad oes neb mor ynfyd yn mhlith fy ngenedl.*

Such ideas were, moreover, all the more unwelcome when presented by an incomer from England:

> *Cefais cyfle i ddweyd wrth Mr. Fielding fod gweithwyr Cymru, er ys blynyddau, yn barod i ddiwygiadau mawrion tra yr oedd y Saeson yn atalfa ar ein ffordd i'w cael.*[64]

---

[64] *Cambria Daily Leader,* 30 March 1887 ('Mr Fielding and his friends go around the country promising salvation when the grave will be closed over them and their children before one of their fancies is realised. Mr Fielding knows this well, but it pays him to encourage men to strive for the unbelievable. A minute of consideration is enough to enlighten the thought of anyone that the revolutions that the socialists say they must have before the world becomes happy are so great that no-one can expect them to be completed. Here is one thing, according to Mr Fielding himself, before socialism can be an unmixed blessing, all of the nations of the earth must adopt the same system. Who but the simple minded can expect to see in their short

Hostility of this type, with its nationalist undertones, was to become a familiar obstacle to socialist activists in Wales during the following decades.

Five months later it was the turn of the rival Socialist League to try to bring 'the Cause' to Wales. On 13 August 1887 Sam Mainwaring and Frank Kitz, members of the League in London, joined the throngs returning from the National Eisteddfod, which had been held in London that year, and boarded a train to Cardiff. They took with them 'an enormous sack' and another smaller bag filled with literature, which together were 'terrible encumbrances' on their subsequent week-long journey. Overnighting at Cardiff, they proceeded the next day to Pontypridd, where they held a meeting at the Rocking Stone on Pontypridd Common. 'Our audience', they later claimed, 'poured towards us from all points. They listened attentively to our exposition of Socialism, and cheered us to the echo', ultimately giving a unanimous show of hands in favour of socialism. After another enthusiastic meeting at the Rocking Stone the next day Kitz and Mainwaring left Pontypridd and headed up the Rhondda to Tylorstown, where they held another meeting, and then walked to Aberdare, where they collected the names of local men interested in forming a branch of the Socialist League. From Aberdare, they went to Merthyr, where they held two enthusiastic meetings, at one of which 'a forest of hands' was held up in their favour. At Merthyr they also collected names for the formation of a branch of the League, and appointed agents for the sale of the League's journal, *The Commonweal*. Having secured Merthyr for socialism, they returned to Aberdare and 'held a great meeting' in the town, at Boot Square. Here they arranged more agents for *Commonweal* and distributed 'a vast amount of literature'. Satisfied that their work would be 'crowned with lasting success', they then returned to Pontypridd, where they held two further meetings at the Rocking Stone – one of which was an 'immense gathering' – and formed a branch of the Socialist League, before departing for home.[65]

lives this kind of revolution? Hopefully there is no-one so insane among my compatriots ... I had a chance to tell Mr. Fielding that the workers of Wales, for years, have been ready for great reforms, while the English have been standing in their way').

[65] *Commonweal*, 27 August 1887. The sack of literature contained, among other

Kitz's and Mainwaring's hyperbolic account of their 'Socialist Campaign in South Wales' must be treated with caution. Unsurprisingly, the *Western Mail* gave a different account of their visit. According to that paper, the attendance at the first meeting in Pontypridd was 'scanty', and 'those who did attend were composed of the social dregs of the place, who listened but very inattentively to the feeble attempt at addresses made'.[66] More tellingly, perhaps, nothing more is recorded of either the branch that the two propagandists were hoping would be formed at Aberdare, or the one they claimed to have formed at Pontypridd. In May of the following year, moreover, it was lamented at the Socialist League's annual conference in London that the trip to south Wales had not increased membership of the League or *Commonweal* sales at all.[67] Nevertheless, the visit is of interest for several reasons. Kitz's and Mainwaring's account of it is one of the fullest descriptions we have of an early socialist propaganda visit to Wales. Carefully studied, it yields important clues about the nature of socialist interaction with Welsh culture in this period, and a consideration of the two individuals involved also sheds significant light upon the process of ideological interplay central to the present discussion.

Frank Kitz would seem to provide a fairly straightforward example of a foreign socialist bringing his doctrine to Wales from outside. Born in the East End of London in the late 1840s, Kitz was the son of a German exile, and spoke fluent German.[68] He had become involved in leftist-radical politics

socialist publications, 5,000 specially printed leaflets for south Wales. See Joseph Lane's 'Report of the Strike Committee of the Socialist League', *Report of the Fourth Annual Conference of the Socialist League, May 20 1888* (London, 1888), pp. 8–9.

[66] *Western Mail*, 15 August 1887. Kitz and Mainwaring make reference to, and quote from, another report of their meetings, which appeared in the *Pontypridd Herald*, and which treats their campaign far more sympathetically. Unfortunately, there seem to be no extant copies of this.

[67] *Report of the Fourth Annual Conference of the Socialist League*, p. 9.

[68] E.P. Thompson, *William Morris: Romantic to Revolutionary* (New York, 1976 (first published, 1955)), pp. 281–3. Florence Boos, *William Morris's Socialist Diary* (London and New York, 1982), p. 65, asserts that Kitz was the name assumed by Francis Platt, the illegitimate son of Mary Platt and John Lewis, a watchmaker, although she does not give a source for this. For an account of the context in which Kitz was politically active in London, see Hermia Olivier, *The International Anarchist Movement in Late Victorian London* (London, 1983). Kitz's own 'Recollections and Reflections' were published in *Freedom*, January–July 1912.

in London in the 1870s, and his views, which were influenced by the refugees Johan Most and Victor Dave, might be more accurately described as anarchist rather than strictly socialist. Kitz's foreign origins were, moreover, apparent to the Welsh audiences he addressed during the visit. At the first meeting in Pontypridd Kitz was assailed by a local schoolmaster, who told him that 'he had no business in Wales because of his German origin'.[69] The same could not be said of Mainwaring. The son of a Welsh collier, born in Neath in 1841, Mainwaring was a native Welsh speaker.[70] He was, according to a reminiscence written years after his death, 'a Celt, with all the fire and enthusiasm of his race' and maintained that Welsh was 'the finest speaking language in the world'.[71] He addressed meetings in Welsh on the tour of 1887.[72] He also had first-hand knowledge of the region that he was attempting to propagandise, having worked in Aberdare as a fitter in the 1860s, before spending some time in America in the 1870s. By the 1880s Mainwaring was resident and working as an engineer in London. He had adopted Marxist views and become an active socialist, initially in the SDF and then the Socialist League. On the anti-parliamentary side of the League, Mainwaring's views, like Kitz's, tended towards anarchism – or what would later be called anarcho-syndicalism.[73] Mainwaring's son later reflected that 'It is a strange commentary on the progress of ideas that South Wales, now a stronghold of Marxism, should have had the first lessons in revolutionary Socialism from two such staunch Anarchist Communists as Kitz and Mainwaring.'[74]

Where exactly Mainwaring's views were formed is a matter for speculation. Certainly, his association with William Morris and other leading London socialists would have been

[69] *Commonweal*, 3 September 1887.
[70] Ken John, 'Sam Mainwaring and the Autonomist Tradition', *Llafur*, 4/3 (1986), 55–66.
[71] Mat Kavanagh, in *Freedom*, 1934, quoted in Ken John, 'Sam Mainwaring', 55.
[72] Frank Kitz, 'Recollections and Reflections', *Freedom*, June 1912.
[73] Mainwaring is credited with coining the term. Ken John, 'Anti-Parliamentary Passage: South Wales and the Internationalism of Sam Mainwaring, 1841–1907' (unpublished PhD thesis, University of Greenwich, London, 2001), p. 109.
[74] W.M. [William Mainwaring], 'A Fighter of Forlorn Hopes', *Freedom*, January 1927.

a considerable influence, but so too would his experiences of industrial capitalism in south Wales and America in the 1860s and 1870s. Ken John has argued that his anarchistic socialism was derived from a reading of Auguste Comte, Karl Marx and the American socialist Ira Steward, but also that elements of a Welsh unitarian religious inheritance were present in Mainwaring's ideological make-up. Among the most significant contributors to this inheritance was 'Publicola', the 'Welsh Communist', who published articles in David Rees's *Y Diwygiwr* in the 1830s. John argues that Mainwaring had read these by the 1870s, when he had 'arrived at an understanding of both a processal view of history and of exploitation at the point of production'.[75] Neither was Mainwaring's 1887 visit to Wales a one-off event. He returned to live in south Wales in the 1890s, where he continued to be involved in socialist activities, before again returning to London, where he died in 1907 – in full flow on a socialist platform.[76] A consideration of Mainwaring thus makes the stereotype of early socialists in Wales as outsiders bringing a foreign doctrine to the country seem a little less tenable than first impressions would suggest. Rather it throws light upon what is clearly a complex process of ideological development involving the interplay of influences and ideas from a range of sources, including those indigenous to Wales.

Further observations on Kitz's and Mainwaring's propagandist mission of 1887 also raise questions about the assumptions that the tour was a mission into virgin territory. The socialists certainly had contacts in the area prior to their visit. Their report in *Commonweal* makes reference to a prearranged meeting with 'friends' at Cardiff, who gave them a 'hearty Welsh welcome'.[77] These may have been members of Mainwaring's family, contacts made by him when he worked at Aberdare in the 1860s, or contacts made the previous

[75] John, *Anti-Parliamentary Passage*, p. 134.
[76] Mann, *Memoirs*, p. 47. Mainwaring was Mann's foreman at one point, and Mann credits him with being 'one of the very first to understand the significance of the revolutionary movement'. It might be possible, in the light of this, to see Mainwaring's Welsh inheritance as one of the influences that propelled Mann himself towards socialism. See below pp. 64–7 for Mainwaring's subsequent socialist activities in Wales.
[77] *Commonweal*, 27 August 1887.

year when he acted as a Socialist League delegate to miners in south Wales, as part of his activities with the League's Strike Committee.[78] Either way, this suggests that there was an informal network of socialist sympathisers in south Wales prior to 1887, in addition to those already mentioned at Clydach. Their activities and ideological beliefs are absent from the historical record, and we do not know whether they were indigenous Welsh or otherwise. Their implied existence, though, adds weight to the contention that socialist ideas were already spreading in south Wales – albeit below the level of mainstream political discourse.

Kitz and Mainwaring were certainly of the opinion that the Welsh were predisposed towards radical and socialist thought, and saw no necessary conflict between Welsh national feeling and socialism. 'The vitality of the Welsh language and the depth of national feeling is strikingly evident throughout these valleys', they wrote, the 'recrudescence of national feeling' manifesting itself in two forms: 'the commercial and the Celtic'. The commercial, as expressed by figures such as Henry Richard, was a form of 'bastard nationalism' and was friendly to capitalism. On the other hand,

> the Celtic feeling ... is that which causes 'grave disquiet' to the friends of 'law and order,' and which antagonises at every step the progress of Anglo-Saxon commercialism. In Wales it is opposition to tithes and mining royalties, and I am glad to be able to add now, landlordism. In Ireland and Skye it is the land war. It has a trinity of tribunes in Davitt, Pan Jones and Macdonald. It harks back to the historical times when the Celtic tribes were free from the curse of landlordism; and whilst, of course, it would not revive the cruelties of those olden days, it yet clings to the old tongue that has no equivalents wherewith to give expression to the modern profit-grinding which has blighted the land of their fathers.[79]

These comments are significant because they mark an early attempt by a native Welsh socialist (the writing is almost certainly Mainwaring's) to graft socialist feeling and ideology onto Welsh national identity. This would become

---

[78] For the Strike Committee, see *Commonweal*, 20 November 1886; *Report of the Third Conference of the Socialist League, May 29ᵗʰ 1887* (London, 1887), p. 8.

[79] *Commonweal*, 3 September 1887.

an important theme for successive generations of socialists in and from Wales.

The extent to which Mainwaring was successful in this task is questionable. Certainly, the Socialist League was not in a position to follow up its initial efforts in south Wales. In September 1887 *Commonweal* urged that, if the work done by Kitz and Mainwaring was to be of 'permanent benefit', speakers must be sent at once, but lamented that funds for such work had run out.[80] During the next year the League began to tear itself apart through internal differences, and made no further officially sponsored forays into Wales. The extent to which Kitz's and Mainwaring's efforts helped to spread socialist ideas is, of course, extremely difficult to estimate. It is not unreasonable to assume, though, that at least some of their 5,000 leaflets and other literature found receptive homes. Evidence for this is sparse, but one hint survives in the papers of the Welsh Mancunian socialist R.J. Derfel. J. Gwalia Lewis, a tailor and draper of Ynysybwl, wrote to Derfel in late 1888, having seen some of Derfel's writing on socialism in *Cymru Fydd*:

> Yr wyf yn dyheu am wastadhau llawer iawn ar ddosbarthiadau cymdeithasol ac 'o fewn ychydyg i fod' yn Socialist ... Yr wyf dros feddiannu yr oll weithfeydd cyhoeddus – Rheilffyrdd porthladdoedd, Dwfrweithiau, nwyweithiau ac yn benaf oll Tir. Gwelais bamphletyn gan W. Morris a B. Bax ... Yr wyf wedi gweled rhai rhifynau o 'Commonweal' a 'To day'.[81]

Lewis ('ap Gwalia') seems to have been connected to both the Rhondda Miners' Association and the Aberdare Liberal Association.[82] He also attended lectures organised by the Aberdare Nationalist Society, and shared with Derfel an interest in rationalism. This letter provides tantalising evidence that socialist ideas were being discussed in such

---

[80] *Commonweal*, 10 and 17 September 1887.

[81] National Library of Wales, NLW MS 23440D, Letters to R.J. Derfel ('I long for a much greater levelling of the social classes and I am close to being a socialist ... I am in favour of the public ownership of all the works – railways, ports, waterworks, gasworks, and above all else, the land. I saw a pamphlet by W. Morris and B. Bax. ... I have seen some issues of *Commonweal* and *To-day*').

[82] The letter quoted was written from Trecynon, Aberdare, and is undated, but is on the reverse side of notepaper of the two organisations. One of the sheets is a notice from the Aberdare Liberal Association dated 31 November 1888.

circles in the wake of the League's campaign, and it is not unreasonable to speculate that the copies of *Commonweal* and *Today* and the pamphlet by Morris and Bax may have come from the enormous sack that had encumbered Kitz and Mainwaring on their journey up the Rhondda.

There were, however, strict limits to the influence of Kitz's and Mainwaring's propaganda that are revealed in letters sent from south Wales to the Socialist League's head office in London during the summer and autumn of 1887. At the end of August John Rees of Dowlais, who had been present at the meeting in Merthyr, wrote in generally sanguine terms. The message of 'the holidaymakers of your League' had, in his view, 'taken deep root in some of the listeners' hearts'. 'All the workers', he continued, 'endorse the opinion that we the toiling masses by all common sense and justice ought to be on a higher level than we now are.' There was, however, a reason why workers would not become actively involved in the socialist cause:

> The fact of the matter to speak plain [is] men are afraid one of the other. I refer to tale-bearing and its consequences. I heartily wish better principles and better feelings could be instilled in them so that we could confide one in the other. I was sorry to find so many walking away without signing their names that night in Merthyr ... as a matter of course, if I signed I thought I might be a marked man.[83]

More problems were reported in September by another correspondent, R. Gregory from Treforest, who had tried, without success, to arrange a meeting place for League activity. Significantly, he reported a local lack of the necessary oratorical talent for such a venture – or at least a lack of self-confidence on the part of local would-be activists: 'there are nobody here', as he put it, 'that think themselves capable of speaking on the subject' [of socialism]. Worse still, it was even proving difficult to sell *Commonweal*, again due to fear of the personal consequences of being identified as a socialist sympathiser:

---

[83] International Institute of Social History, Amsterdam, Socialist League Papers item 2531, John Rees, 3 Alma Street Dowlais, to Socialist League office, 28 August 1887, quoted in John, 'Anti-Parliamentary Passage', p. 204.

I understand that Mr. Hughes Bookseller was going to sell them but I have been to him about it and he positively declines to have anything to do with them as he says that they would do harm to his business.[84]

Any account of the spread of socialist ideas in Wales in this period must, then, be strictly tempered by recognition of the obvious limits of socialist influence. It is nevertheless safe to argue that socialism was by no means unheard of in south Wales in the 1880s, and that the flow of socialist ideas was already reflecting and creating a cultural and ideological interplay between Wales and the wider world that worked on various levels. Some of the themes of this interplay are well illustrated by the experience of the final Marxist visitor of the 1880s to be discussed in this chapter.

The early Marxist groups focused their interest largely upon the industrial south of the country. Nevertheless, it was a member of the Socialist League, Haydn Sanders, who was responsible for the first significant recorded socialist propagandist effort in north Wales when he took it upon himself to turn a holiday at Barmouth into a socialist mission in late September 1887.[85] The son of a lock maker, Sanders was a native of Bloxwich in Staffordshire, and himself worked as a lock maker in Walsall. In 1887 he was in his mid-twenties, and probably a fairly recent convert to socialism.[86] He was rambling in the Barmouth area when, after visiting some local quarries, he 'decided to hold a meeting that very evening in Barmouth, and lay before such as chanced to listen the views of a Socialist. So at half-past six [he] took up a stand on the quay at Barmouth and began the first address on Socialism ever delivered there.' Like Mainwaring in the south, Sanders perceived a natural affinity among the locals

---

[84] International Institute of Social History, Amsterdam, Socialist League Papers item 1592, R. Gregory, Graig yr Alma, Treforest, to Socialist League office, 26 September 1887, quoted in John, 'Anti-Parliamentary Passage', p. 205. John speculates that Gregory was Mainwairing's brother-in-law. He also quotes another letter in the Socialist League correspondence from Mainwaring's son Robert (23 October 1887) reporting similar difficulties in selling *Commonweal.*
[85] *Commonweal,* 22 October 1887.
[86] He is recorded on the 1881 Census as being born in 1861. By the 1891 Census Sanders had married and moved to Rotherham in Yorkshire with his young family and was recorded as a trade union or guild secretary. It is not clear whether he came to Barmouth from Walsall or Rotherham.

for socialist ideas. 'It was soon evident', he reported, 'that however new the ideas of Socialism were to those present, there was much that was in accord with their natural feelings as regards the duty of one man to another; that they as much disapproved of the present system of society as I did.' The upshot of Sanders's impromptu performance on Barmouth quay was a request from some of those present to hold an indoor lecture on the subject of 'Christian Socialism'. He gladly agreed, and the minister and deacons of the local Congregational church offered the use of their schoolroom for the lecture at no cost.

Before giving his lecture Sanders delivered another piece of impromptu open-air oratory which, despite taking place in the rain, was 'one of the most fervent meetings that ever I addressed or witnessed'. He also managed to convert a local shopkeeper and his brother to the ideals of socialism. The indoor lecture, moreover, was 'thoroughly successful': '[t]hat a complete revolution of the present system of society is absolutely necessary for the removal of existing evils was admitted by every one present'. Sanders also reported comments made by one of the audience:

> 'Yes,' said one, 'if we would only be as enthusiastic and self-sacrificing for the establishment of Socialism as we are for our ordinary politics and religion, it could soon be brought about; and when brought about it would be practical application of all the best teachings believed in to-day.' The same speaker also pointed out to me that there is a great amount of Socialism carried out in the different religious bodies, and instanced the manner in which they clung together for the good of all, and the equality insisted upon.

Finally, Sanders observed that there was one great difficulty of propagandising in north Wales: while most of the inhabitants could understand spoken English, very few could understand the language in its written form.[87]

Sanders's visit to Barmouth was an isolated act of happenstance. Indeed, incursions by English socialist societies into north Wales before the turn of the century were extremely rare. His account must also be treated with customary caution. As usual, his optimism that 'North Wales could

---

[87] *Commonweal*, 22 October 1887.

soon be successfully organised' proved to be unfounded. Nevertheless, it would be wrong to disregard what is the only detailed account of early socialist activity in the region. Apart from its rarity value, Sanders's report is of interest for the insights it provides into the relationship between socialists and Welsh culture. Indeed, there are a number of portentous elements in it that re-emerge as themes in the later history of socialism in Wales. The socialist belief that the Welsh were sympathetic by nature to their ideas has already been noted, and Sanders provides specific instances to support such a belief. The request to lecture on 'Christian Socialism' is also significant, and presages a long campaign to relate socialist and Christian ideas that was undertaken with a particular intensity in Wales. The fact that it was the local Congregationalist minister who 'cordially approved' of the idea of holding such a lecture in the local schoolroom is also possibly significant. Congregationalists were arguably more sympathetic to socialist ideas than members of some of the other religious denominations, and the sect produced, in T.E. Nicholas, one of the most influential and outstanding Welsh socialists of the early twentieth century. The un-named minister who was amenable to the needs of an alien socialist was, perhaps, one of the first of his denomination to exhibit this trait with regard to modern Marxian socialism. The audience member who saw the activities of the chapels as inherently socialistic was also pre-empting arguments that would later be mobilised by Welsh socialists seeking to graft socialism onto their native culture. Finally, of course, Sanders recognised the difficulties posed by the Welsh language for socialist propagandists. In so doing he was among the first of the modern socialists to identify what would become a matter of deep significance to Welsh socialists of the next generation. Indeed, Haydn Sanders's spontaneous one-man socialist campaign in Barmouth in September 1887 raised most of the issues that would, within the next quarter of a century, become central to the attempt to reconcile socialism and Welsh culture.

2
PUTTING DOWN ROOTS, 1889–1899

Nid bywyd Cymru dawel, ac nid bywyd tawel, naturiol, gwlad, - na thref gymedrol faint, – a gynhyrchodd Sosialiaeth, ond yn hytrach bywyd y dinasoedd mawrion. Megir ef, fel y megir pethau afiach eraill, lle y mae aneirif nifer o fodau dynol yn byw bywyd annaturiol; lle mae tlodi, fel cyfoeth, yn ymdrybaeddu mewn pethau anhygar; lle nad oes nwyfre ond caddug afiach.[1]

Such was the verdict of Edward Foulkes, a contributor from Llanberis to the nationalist *Geninen* in 1908. Part of the argument of this book is that the reality of the development of socialism in Wales was more complex than this statement suggests. There is nevertheless a sense in which Foulkes was correct. When socialist organisations began to put down roots in Wales, during the early 1890s, they did so not in the slate quarries of Caernarfonshire, where H.M. Hyndman claimed to have detected secret societies ready to use the Welsh language in their pursuit of the class struggle, nor even initially in the burgeoning coal mining settlements of Glamorgan, through which Kitz and Mainwaring had hauled their sack of socialist literature, but in the coastal towns and ports of south Wales. In 1892 Joseph Burgess's *Workman's Times* issued a call for the names of individuals who were interested in establishing an independent labour party, which may to some extent be taken as an index of interest in socialism across Britain.[2] By the end of the year only twenty-five names had been sent from Wales – from a British total of over 2,500.[3] Of these, fifteen were from Cardiff, five from Cadoxton and Barry Dock, four from Newport and one

---

[1] Edward Foulkes, 'Sosialiaeth', *Y Geninen* (1908), 21–5, 21 ('It is not the life of quiet Wales, and not the quiet natural life of the country nor the moderate-sized town that generated socialism, but instead the life of the great cities. It is nurtured, as other unhealthy things are nurtured, where countless numbers of human beings live an un-natural life; where poverty, like wealth, wallows in things unlikeable; where there is no sky but an unhealthy gloom').
[2] *Workman's Times*, 30 April 1892.
[3] *Workman's Times*, 14 May 1892–31 December 1892.

from Llantrisant. More than anything, this suggests that the demand for independent labour representation in Wales was weak. It does, however, point to the urban coast of south Wales as a starting point for an investigation of the country's early socialist movement. The growth of socialism there during the 1890s represents a distinct phase in the history of socialism in Wales. During this period socialism ceased to be an ideology that was simply imported by external proselytes, and became a belief that was sustained by domestic organisation. Two main groups were initially involved in this process: the Fabian Society and the SDF. This chapter will therefore examine the main theatres of influence of these two organisations. It will begin with a study of Fabian activity in Cardiff, and then discuss the role of the SDF across south Wales.

(I) Cardiff and Fabianism

Cardiff was the most important of the Welsh communities in which socialists attempted to organise in the early years of their movement. It was also a town with an ambiguous identity. The product of spectacularly rapid growth from obscure origins during the nineteenth century, by 1871 Cardiff had become the largest town in Wales and was without dispute the commercial centre of the Welsh industrial revolution – a supremacy reflected in the last decades of the nineteenth century by the adoption of its multiple soubriquets, the 'Welsh Metropolis', the 'Coal Metropolis', or the 'Chicago of Wales'. Cardiff's commercial success was built upon its unique geographical position, and resulted from its development, in stages throughout the nineteenth century, as a communications hub connecting industrial Wales with both England and the wider world. With London and its range of socialist societies only three hours away, and Bristol, where a vigorous socialist society had been established in 1885,[4] even closer, Cardiff was a gateway through which socialist ideology could enter Wales. Kitz and Mainwaring may have been among the first socialists to use it, when they battled

---

[4] Samson Bryher, *An Account of the Labour and Socialist Movement in Bristol* (2 vols, Bristol, 1929).

through the returning *eisteddfodwyr* to manhandle their sack of literature across the platforms of Central Station in 1887, but they were not the last.

By the 1890s many more individuals with socialist proclivities had disembarked at Cardiff Central, some to live in the town, and others to take part in increasingly frequent propaganda tours of south Wales. The town in which they arrived, moreover, hosted the greatest critical mass of concentrated cultural and intellectual activity in Wales, particularly among its growing middle class.[5] In character – and directly as a result of Cardiff's nodal position, transitory nature and diverse immigrant population – this culture was highly cosmopolitan. Cardiff may have been geographically situated in Wales, but it was ambivalent about its Welshness, which had been linguistically and culturally diluted by an anglicising tide of urban growth. That is not to say that Welshness, however defined, was absent from the town's cultural fabric. Far from it: if Cardiff was a product of in-migration this included in-migration from within Wales. In 1891 12,492 of Cardiff borough's 116,207 inhabitants (10.7 per cent) were Welsh speakers. There were at least a dozen strong Welsh chapels, and a range of Welsh cultural institutions. This included the Cardiff Cymrodorion Society, founded in 1885 in a coffee tavern owned by the notable Edward Thomas (Cochfarf). A native of Betws, Maesteg, a monoglot Welsh speaker until he was 13, carpenter, coffee house owner and businessman, *eisteddfodwr*, antiquarian, Pan-Celticist, temperance advocate, Baptist and Liberal politician, Cochfarf exemplified the virtues and diversity of urban Welsh middle-class culture. Elected a town councillor in 1890, and ultimately mayor of Cardiff (in 1902), he also represented its political accommodation.[6] Indeed, Welshness – thanks partly to the conscious

---

[5] Neil Evans, 'The Welsh Victorian City: The Middle Class and Civic and National Consciousness in Cardiff, 1850–1914', *Welsh History Review*, 12/3 (1985), 350–87; Neil Evans, 'Urbanisation, Elite Attitudes and Philanthropy: Cardiff, 1850–1914', *International Review of Social History*, 27/3 (1982), 290–323.

[6] J. Gwynfor Jones, 'Y Ddelwedd Gymreig Ddinesig yng Nghaerdydd, c.1885–1939', in Hywel Teifi Edwards (ed.), *Merthyr a Thaf* (Llandysul, 2001), pp. 325–63; Owen John Thomas, 'The Welsh Language in Cardiff, c.1800–1914', in Geraint H. Jenkins (ed.), *Language and Community in the Nineteenth Century* (Cardiff, 1998), pp. 181–201; Gwynedd Pierce, 'The Welsh Connection', in Gwyn Jones and Michael

efforts of individuals like Cochfarf – was a part of Cardiff's cosmopolitanism, and this balance was to be reflected in the nature of the town's socialism, some of the representatives of which were on good terms with the man himself.

Cardiff socialism was also the product of the town's occupational and social structure. The economic dominance of commerce and transport had tended towards the creation of a fragmented working class.[7] As a result, and despite the creation of the Cardiff Trades Council in 1883, the labour movement in the town was weak, and failed to develop any real momentum towards independent political action for the best part of another two decades.[8] Consequently, Cardiff socialism tended to be dominated by the town's middle class. Care must, however, be taken in advancing this argument too far, as by the end of the 1880s there were signs of activity among Cardiff's working class that would at least create a context for the emergence of socialism in the town. One of these was the election, with Liberal support, of John Jenkins, president of both the Shipwright's Society and the Trades Council, to the Grangetown ward of the town council in 1890, as 'the advocate of the claims of the labouring classes to secure themselves adequate representation, and to support their efforts at combination'.[9] More challenging to existing social relations, however, was the upsurge of trade unionism among previously unorganised workers at the turn of the decade.[10] Far from indicating a level of social quiescence,

Quinn (eds), *Fountains of Praise: University College, Cardiff, 1883–1983* (Cardiff, 1983), pp. 25–40; J. Gwynfor Jones, 'Edward Thomas (Cochfarf): Dinesydd, Dyngarwr a Gwladgarwr', *Trafodion Cymdeithas Hanes Bedyddwyr Cymru* (1987), 26–45.

[7] Martin Daunton, *Coal Metropolis: Cardiff, 1870–1914* (Leicester, 1977), p. 181.

[8] Daunton, *Coal Metropolis*, pp. 178–214; M.J. Daunton, 'Aspects of the Social and Economic Structure of Cardiff, 1870–1914' (unpublished PhD thesis, Canterbury, 1974), pp. 391–477, includes more detail; Neil Evans, 'Cardiff's Labour Tradition', *Llafur*, 4/2 (1985), 77–90, offers a slightly more sanguine view and takes the history of Cardiff trade unionism beyond the Great War; McCarry, 'Labour and Society in Swansea, 1887–1918', p. 379, contrasts the situation in Swansea with 'the feeble image of the movement in Cardiff' in the early 1900s.

[9] *South Wales Daily News*, 4 March 1890.

[10] L.J. Williams, 'The New Unionism in Wales, 1889–92', *Welsh History Review*, 1/4 (1963), 413–29; Philip J. Leng, *The Welsh Dockers* (Ormskirk, 1981), pp. 13–32; Martin Daunton, 'The Cardiff Coal Trimmers Union, 1888–1914', *Llafur* 2/3 (1978), 10–23; Martin Daunton, 'Inter-Union Rivalries on the Waterfront: Cardiff, 1888–1914', *International Review of Social History*, 22/3 (1977), 350–78.

this marked the emergence of Cardiff, in the words of the Webbs, as 'a regular cockpit for the trades union struggles of all South Wales'.[11]

This outbreak of 'new unionism' had several important implications. Firstly, as represented by national (UK) figures such as Tom Mann, John Burns and Ben Tillett – all of whom visited Wales frequently in this period – it was in itself an influence which both created and confirmed links between Wales and the other great commercial and industrial centres of Britain. As L.J. Williams noted, the most important feature of new unions was their national (UK) affiliation, which made them 'a potent source of Anglicisation'.[12] Indeed, the supposed externality of the unions' leaders was used as an argument against them by their opponents in Cardiff, who contrasted the 'rabid nonsense these Londoners are talking with the calm, deliberate, measured utterances' of the Welsh trade unionists, 'Welshmen born and bred', such as Mabon and the miners' agent David Morgan (Dai o'r Nant).[13] The view that Cardiff workers were being manipulated by London was an oversimplification, and a significant part of the initiative towards general unionism came from within south Wales itself.[14] Nevertheless, the 'new' or 'general' unionism of the late 1880s, which tended to recruit workers wherever and of whatever type it could find, held a more tenuous relationship to place than the older craft-based unions, which tended to be more deeply rooted in more static communities.[15] This was a tendency of long-term significance for south Wales. It meant that the region's trade unionists were being drawn into an organisational and psychological relationship with a greater whole that stretched both along the rail lines to London and across the Bristol Channel, and which

---

[11] Quoted by Martin Daunton, 'Coal to Capital: Cardiff Since 1839', in Prys Morgan (ed.), *Glamorgan County History*, vol. 6: *Glamorgan Society, 1780–1980* (1988), pp. 203–24 (p. 221).

[12] Williams, 'The New Unionism in Wales', 428.

[13] *Western Mail*, 12 March 1891.

[14] Deian Hopkin and John Williams, 'New Light on the New Unionism in Wales, 1889–1912', *Llafur*, 4/3 (1986), 67–79.

[15] Joe England, 'Notes on a Neglected Topic: General Unionism in Wales', *Llafur*, 9/1 (2004), 45–58 (46–7).

spoke – both metaphorically and literally – the international language of trade unionism.

If the relationship of the new unionism to the local was abstruse, so too was its relationship to the universal, as represented by socialism. Alarmed observers may have feared the 'communistic tendency' of the unions,[16] but union leaders, although almost all were socialists, were aware that socialism was a secondary matter to the growth of their unions. Just as the London dockers had welcomed the involvement of socialist leaders 'not because of their Socialism, but in spite of it',[17] so too were the 3,000 unionised Cardiff dockers of the early 1890s motivated not by socialism, but by the desire to improve their living standards. This did not mean that socialism was absent from Cardiff trade unionism; rather it was sublimated. Ben Tillett, in particular, succeeded in weaving a socialist message into his speeches while avoiding explicit mention of socialism. In July 1891, for example, he addressed a mass meeting of striking dockers and railwaymen at Park Hall, to which he was escorted at the head of a procession with a brass band. The meeting opened with the singing of Harry Salt's explicitly socialist 'Hark the Battle Cry is Ringing' to the tune of 'Men of Harlech', and Tillett went on to 'tell the respectables – the capitalists – that they would have to look to labour organised for their security in the future', and that if they did not comply with the workers' demands 'the volcano would burst, and the wrath pent up for centuries would find a terrible outlet, and teach those who had scorned and spurned the working men ... a bitter lesson that would last for centuries'.[18] Tillett may not have mentioned the word socialism, but the revolutionary implications of his words were clear, and it was in this way that the new unionism provided a medium for the spread of socialist ideas in Cardiff.

A different context was offered by the cultural and intellectual activities organised by the town's middle class, sections

[16] *Cardiff Argus*, 7 December 1889.
[17] H.H. Champion, 'The Great Dock Strike', *Universal Review*, 5/18 (1890), 157–78 (163).
[18] *Western Mail*, 1 August 1891. See also *Cardiff Times and South Wales Weekly News*, 28 February 1891.

of which began to engage with socialist thought in the late 1880s. When the SDF's John Fielding passed through the town in March 1887, there was only one 'avowed socialist' there, 'Comrade Parr'.[19] Just over a year later Parr had lost his uniqueness, and been joined by a 'Comrade Meade', who had also begun to present papers on socialism to select audiences.[20] Neither was the discussion of socialism an entirely fringe activity; under certain circumstances it could be pursued with intellectual rigour and respectability. The new University College of South Wales offered one forum for this. In January 1888 Professor Sorley, the newly appointed professor of Logic and Philosophy, addressed its literary and debating society on socialism, with Professor Viriamu Jones in the chair.[21] The town's religious and political organisations offered further scope, which extended the debate on socialism to the more affluent and aspirational elements of the working class. In April 1889 the Cardiff Free Methodist Improvement Class heard a paper on 'The Higher Socialism' read by the Reverend William Bailey of Penarth, and considered it interesting enough to publish in pamphlet form.[22] Later in the same year Reverend W. Tuckwell, the 'Radical Parson' of Stockwell, county Durham, addressed a meeting in Park Hall, organised by the Cardiff Liberal Workmen's Institute, on 'Christian Socialism'. His extensive programme included an expansion of local government, land nationalisation, industrial and economic cooperation and a readjustment of taxation, and was greeted by a unanimous motion expressing 'cordial acceptance of his teaching'.[23] Socialist texts were also being discussed in the town's literary circles. In 1890 a paper on Edward Bellamy's *Looking Backward* was read by a Mr. Turner to a well-attended meeting of the Literary Society at the Presbyterian Schoolroom in Windsor Place. In this instance, however, the lecturer was less positive about the collectivist values it espoused: 'He shewed

[19] *Justice*, 26 March 1887.
[20] *Justice*, 23 June 1888.
[21] *Western Mail*, 20 February 1888.
[22] Revd. William Bailey, *The Higher Socialism: A Paper Read at the Cardiff Free Methodist Improvement Class, April 1889* (Cardiff, 1889).
[23] *Western Mail*, 24 October 1889.

that the scheme of Mr. Bellamy was pure communism; but in the past failure had been the result of such plans, and from experience, and from logic, it could not succeed.'[24] Despite such views, it is clear that by the turn of the decade, against the background of the new unionism, socialist ideology was becoming part of Cardiff's intellectual life.

The leading figure in this effort to propagate socialism was the 'Comrade Parr' referred to by John Fielding in 1887, otherwise known as Dr Arthur Charles Edward Parr, of 189 Richmond Road. Parr was a medical doctor, born in Wimborne, Dorset, in 1863 of Irish parentage, who had lived in London in the early 1880s,[25] and obtained his medical degree from King's College in 1885.[26] He probably came to Cardiff soon afterwards, and quickly became involved in the political and intellectual life of the town. Apart from his unsuccessful efforts to form a SDF branch in 1887,[27] Parr led an intellectually energetic existence. In December 1888 he read a paper on socialism at the Roath Church Institute.[28] In July 1888 he lectured the Cardiff Junior Liberal Association, of which he was a member, on 'Social Problems and How to Meet Them', advocating 'the control by the workers of the land and capital of the country, in short, the establishment of Social Democracy'. Not surprisingly, 'an animated discussion followed'.[29] In March of the following year he was again active in the Junior Liberals, presiding over a meeting at which Henry George made his second appearance in Cardiff. Parr's beliefs clearly went further than George's, and he stated from the chair that 'the Cardiff Junior Liberal Association was one of aggressive reform. That being so, they demanded the land for the people', and taxation of land values, he argued, was 'the first step towards that end'.[30] In calling for the 'land for the people' Parr was tapping into a core element of Welsh radicalism, which, along

[24] *Cardiff Argus*, 13 December 1890.
[25] The 1881 Census records him as a 'student of medicine', living in Lambeth.
[26] *British Medical Journal*, 14 March 1885.
[27] *Justice*, 26 March 1887.
[28] *Justice*, 15 December 1888.
[29] *Justice*, 21 July 1888.
[30] *Western Mail*, 27 March 1889.

with his position on the advanced wing of radical Liberalism, goes some way to locating the origins of socialism in Wales.[31]

So too does another sphere of Parr's activities in the 1880s: his involvement in the Cardiff Society for the Impartial Discussion of Political and Other Questions.[32] In November 1889, as vice president, he addressed the society on 'Is It Advantageous in Business to be a Rogue?', into which he doubtless worked a socialist message.[33] This potentially awkward topic didn't seem to damage his popularity, as by 1890 he had become president of the society.[34] The 'Cardiff Impartial' hosted a number of left-wing speakers in the 1880s and 1890s, including the exiled Russian revolutionary Sergius Stepniak,[35] and the debating society culture that it represented was an important nurturing ground for socialist ideas. Parr's contributions to it, and his frequent interventions in other areas of the town's intellectual life, were politically in advance of most of his contemporaries, and he was doubtless seen as a rather eccentric young man by many in the town. He must nevertheless be considered as the pioneer of socialism in Cardiff. Middle-class and cosmopolitan, he acted as a yeast in the social and intellectual life of Cardiff, often to be seen standing in the Hayes, addressing meetings in 'a delicious Dublin brogue, wearing a top hat, with a stethoscope sticking out of his breast-pocket, and flourishing an immaculate umbrella', and calling upon those who would listen 'to emulate our Paris comrades and storm the barricades'.[36]

When Parr and other Cardiff socialists combined to create their own discrete organisation they did not, however, storm any barricades. Instead they turned to Fabianism. Founded in London in 1884, the Fabian Society provided an

---

[31] Parr continued to offer support to both advanced Liberalism and George's land reform ideas into the 1890s. In 1892 he was present at a meeting in support of the Liberal municipal candidate Morgan Morgan, at which he argued for the Georgeite policy of taxation of land values, *Western Mail*, 26 March 1892.
[32] The 'Cardiff Impartial' was founded in 1886 and met at various venues in Cardiff, including the Cymmrodorion Hall. A brief history is recorded in a leaflet printed on its closure in 1906. Cardiff Central Library, Cochfarf Papers, Box 2. Unfortunately, its minute books appear to have been lost.
[33] *Western Mail*, 19 November 1889.
[34] *Western Mail*, 10 December 1890.
[35] *Western Mail*, 17 November 1891.
[36] Sam Hobson, *Pilgrim to the Left* (London, 1938), p. 29.

alternative to the socialism of the SDF and Socialist League. During the 1880s Fabian doctrine embraced many shades of opinion, ranging from anarchism to Marxism, but by the end of the decade it was becoming more clearly defined – a process marked by the publication in 1889 of the influential *Fabian Essays in Socialism*. In essence, this offered an indigenous approach to socialism. Although not free of Marxian influence, it drew upon the work of British social and economic thinkers, such as Stanley Jevons, John Stuart Mill and David Ricardo, and envisaged a transition to socialism through reasoned reform, logic and evolution rather than class struggle.[37] The roots of Fabianism were firmly planted in Hampstead, and in many respects the society was a direct product of London cosmopolitanism. It did nevertheless attempt to establish provincial branches,[38] and, despite its quintessential Englishness, exhibited an interest in Wales, which even extended to the translation of some of its influential *Tracts* into Welsh.[39] On 10 December 1890, moreover, one of the Fabians' most prominent speakers and essayists, Hubert Bland, arrived at the Cymrodorion Hall, Cardiff, to address the first public meeting of the town's newly formed Fabian Socialist Society.

The meeting, at which Bland addressed a 'very good and attentive audience' on 'What Socialism Is', was presided over by Dr Parr.[40] Bland's message was explicitly gradualist, he rejected the class war, and his intellectual touchstones were drawn from the canon of English political economy, side-stepping Marx, but including references to John Stuart Mill and Ricardo. Indeed, one commentator who attended his lecture

[37] Norman and Jeanne Mackenzie, *The First Fabians* (London, 1977); A.M. McBriar, *Fabian Socialism and English Politics* (Cambridge, 1962); Edward Pease, *History of the Fabian Society* (New York, 1916); Willard Wolfe, *From Radicalism to Socialism: Men and Ideas in the Formation of Fabian Socialist Doctrines, 1881–1889* (New Haven and London, 1975); Mark Bevir, 'The Marxism of George Bernard Shaw, 1883–1889', *History of Political Thought*, 13/2 (1992), 299–318; Mark Bevir, 'Fabianism and the Theory of Rent', *History of Political Thought*, 10/2 (1989), 313–27; Stanley Pierson, *Marxism and the Origins of British Socialism* (Ithaca and London, 1973), pp. 106–39.

[38] Edward Pease, *History of the Fabian Society*, pp. 95–8.

[39] The first of these, *Why Are The Many Poor?*, originally published in 1884, was translated and published in 1892 as *Paham Mae y Lluaws yn Dlawd*.

[40] The account of the meeting is based upon *Western Mail*, 11 December 1890. Also see the interview with Hubert Bland, *Western Mail*, 12 December 1890.

saw Bland less as a socialist than as an advanced radical.[41] The most explicitly socialist ideas in his lecture were, in fact, international in their origins and derived not from British sources, but from the Dutch-born American, Laurence Gronlund, author of *The Co-operative Commonwealth*.[42] This mix of influences illustrates well the diverse nature of socialist ideas entering Wales at the beginning of the 1890s, and the circuitous routes through which they came. Significantly, Bland's ideas were communicated from within specifically English frames of reference. Making no concession to the fact that he was in Wales, his speech was wholly geared to an English audience; his arguments were supported exclusively by English statistics, and his Gronlundian demonstration of the division of 'the national cake' referred explicitly to the English nation. Socialists, he told his audience, 'wanted to point out the monopolies to the English working men, and get them to return members to the House of Commons pledged to attack them in every direction'. That this statement was received with applause, moreover, suggests that Bland's audience was not unduly uncomfortable being considered part of 'the English working men'.

Indeed, the activities of the Cardiff Fabian Socialist Society in the early 1890s might suggest that it was to some extent a clone of other urban British socialist societies. The experience of its members was directly related to that of socialists elsewhere by their necessary involvement in a range of activities and issues that were universal to the late-nineteenth-century socialist movement. These included a campaign for free speech,[43] engagement with contemporary socialist strategic

[41] 'Cheviot', *Cardiff Argus*, 20 December and 27 December 1890. Bland's lecture prompted Cheviot to write a series of articles examining socialism, *Cardiff Argus*, 20 December 1890–2 February 1891.

[42] Laurence Gronlund, *The Co-operative Commonwealth in its Outlines: An Exposition of Modern Socialism* (Boston, 1884), along with Gronlund's journalism, was an important influence upon British socialists. For a good example of Gronlund's journalism, which summarises his rather eclectic mix of evolutionary and revolutionary views, see 'The Work Before Us', *Commonweal*, July 1885. The diffusion of Gronlund's views, of which the meeting at Cardiff was a part, might be seen as part of a process through which European ideas were exported to America and then found their way back to Britain. Gronlund explicitly stated that his object was 'to lead socialism into the main current of English thought' (*The Co-operative Commonwealth*, p. x).

[43] *Western Mail*, 27 February and 2 March 1892.

debates,[44] and efforts to achieve electoral representation at a municipal level through a Progressive Labour League that was largely modelled on the success of the Progressives on London County Council.[45] Primarily, however, the Cardiff Fabians' efforts were educational, and focused upon the organisation of public lectures. During 1892 visiting speakers included Keir Hardie, Ramsay MacDonald, Hugh Holmes Gore, W.S. De Mattos, Katharine Conway and Sidney Webb – all based in either London or Bristol.[46] In this way, the Cardiff activists initiated the importation of the latest arguments and debates of a generic British socialism into the intellectual life of their town. Their activities were communicated in turn to the wider British movement through the pages of the *Workman's Times*, which reported enthusiastically in 1893 that

> A more energetic body could not exist than the Cardiff Fabian Socialist Society. They are everywhere. On the Trades Council, on the Board of Guardians, and, so I'm told, even on the Cardiff County Council. If ever energy and enthusiasm, coupled with hard work, deserved to be rewarded with success, then our Cardiff Fabians ought to get it.[47]

The temporal activities of the Fabian Socialist Society were supplemented on a spiritual level by the Cardiff Labour Church, which must also be viewed within the context of a wider movement. Founded in Manchester in 1891, the Labour Church movement was a response to the failure of existing religious organisations to accommodate labourist and socialist aspirations.[48] As one of its Cardiff members explained, 'The principle upon which the Labour Church works, is, that the two great forming agencies, religion and economics, are inextricably mingled, each reacts upon the

---

[44] *South Wales Daily News*, 12 March 1892 and 5 May 1892.

[45] *South Wales Daily News*, 6 October 1892; *Western Mail*, 3 November 1892; Daunton, 'Aspects ...', p. 413.

[46] *South Wales Daily News*, 5 May 1892; British Library of Political and Economic Science, London, Fabian Society Archive, COLL MISC 375, Reports and Cuttings of Local Fabian Societies, Volume 1 contains a selection of posters for the meetings.

[47] *Workman's Times*, 21 May 1892.

[48] Kenneth Inglis, 'The Labour Church Movement', *International Review of Social History*, 3/3 (1958), 445–60; Stanley Pierson, 'John Trevor and the Labour Church Movement in England, 1891–1900', *Church History*, 29 (1960), 463–78; Mark Bevir, 'The Labour Church Movement, 1891–1902', *Journal of British Studies*, 38/2, (1999), 217–45.

other, and no permanent advance will ever be made without the simultaneous progression of these two forces.'[49] The movement's centre of gravity was the north of England, and it grew rapidly in the early 1890s, reaching a high point of 50 churches in 1895.[50] The establishment of Cardiff Labour Church was, therefore, an expression of a national (UK) movement in its ascendancy. As with Cardiff's other socialist activities, this involved a dialogue between local socialists and representatives of the wider movement, a process initiated by the presence of the prominent London socialist H. Halliday Sparling at the Church's launch in January 1893.[51] The Cardiff Labour Church met regularly in 1893–4, and although its meetings did feature some local speakers, including Dr. Parr, the miners' leader William Brace and Abertillery's John Powell,[52] it largely drew its speakers from outside Wales. These included Enid Stacy from Bristol,[53] Ben Tillett,[54] the Manchester-based Fred Brocklehurst[55] and Keir Hardie.[56] Reliance upon outside speakers was partly due to the limited supply of speakers in Cardiff itself. 'We shall have to get speakers from strange places to do any permanent good, as folk get used to faces, and often fancy they hear the same humdrum story', commented E.T. Robinson, the Church secretary, in the summer of 1893.[57] Whatever the

[49] *South Wales Labour Times*, 4 March 1893.
[50] Bevir, 'The Labour Church Movement', 234.
[51] *Western Mail*, 30 January 1893.
[52] *Labour Prophet*, December 1893 and August 1894; *Western Mail*, 26 February 1894.
[53] Other speakers from Bristol at Cardiff Labour Church included Enid's younger brother Paul Stacy, and Comrades Knight, Creese and Weaver, all of whom visited on more than one occasion. *Labour Prophet*, May, October, November and December 1893 and April 1894.
[54] Tillett was born in Bristol and maintained links to the city despite being based in London from the early 1890s onwards, Jonathan Schneer, *Ben Tillett: Portrait of a Labour Leader* (London and Canberra, 1982). On 13 August 1893 Tillett lectured 'to a very large meeting' at Cardiff Labour Church, *Labour Prophet*, October 1893. He returned again in early 1894 to speak in the Colonial Hall, *Labour Prophet*, January 1894. He also visited in February 1895, when it was rumoured that he would be seeking to stand as parliamentary candidate for Cardiff, *Western Mail*, 11 February 1895.
[55] Brocklehurst was organising secretary of the Labour Church and ILP candidate for Bolton. *Labour Prophet*, August 1894; *Western Mail*, 4 June 1894.
[56] *Western Mail*, 5 March 1894.
[57] *Labour Prophet*, June 1893.

reason, though, the influx of outside speakers ensured that the Labour Church was another agent in the integration of Cardiff's activists into a wider British socialist movement.

Indeed, evidence of the interests and connections of both the Socialist Fabian Society and the Labour Church in early-1890s Cardiff would, on the face of things, suggest that as organisations they were aligned not with the culture of Cardiff, nor of Wales, but with a culturally cosmopolitan socialist movement. At the Fabian Socialist Society's first Socialist Watch Night meeting, held at the Hotel Metropole on New Year's Eve 1891/2, the proceedings were not accompanied by the singing of *Hen Wlad Fy Nhadau*, but were opened with the *Marseillaise* and closed with a recitation of Shelley's *Men of England, Heirs of Glory*. Between the two songs was a resolution, which made the society's universalist affiliations clear:

> That we, the Fabian Socialists of Cardiff, on the eve of the New Year, cordially send our fraternal greetings to our friends in the cause the world over. Renewing our pledge to the Socialist faith, we call upon all comrades to unite in working for the solidarity of the Human Race.[58]

Such a declaration would seem to counter any suggestion of Welsh particularism on the part of the Cardiff Fabians. There is a difference, however, between the formal outlook of a society and the personal affiliations of its members. Consequently, before accepting this interpretation of the relationship of the Cardiff Fabians to the national and local cultures of which they were part, it is necessary to look within the society and examine some of the individuals who were present at that Watch Night in 1891/2.[59]

Among them, for instance, was none other than Cochfarf himself. Although not formally a Fabian, he was identified, by the *Western Mail* at least, as one of 'the prominent leaders

---

[58] British Library of Political and Economic Science, London, Fabian Society Archive, COLL MISC 375 – Volume 1, Programme of the Socialist Watch Night Meeting. Other songs included Salt's 'Hark The Battle Cry is Ringing' and 'Auld Lang Syne', *Fabian News*, February 1892.

[59] *Western Mail*, 1 January 1892, reports the event and provides a list of the principal attendees.

of the Labour Party in Cardiff',[60] and was clearly on good terms with members of the Fabian Socialist Society. Although in reality one of Cardiff's 'ardent Liberals',[61] he made efforts to draw the socialists into the political life of the town. In December 1892, for example, he invited them to a dinner at the Hotel Metropole, along with representatives from other political and labour organisations, at which the miners' leader, William Abraham (Mabon), spoke.[62] He also fostered links with national (UK) labour leaders, including a warm friendship with the Fabian and Labour MP Will Crooks,[63] which testify to a degree of confluence between Cochfarf's nationalistic Liberalism and the ideology of the wider labour movement. Neither was Cochfarf, and his brand of nationalism, without admirers on the socialistic left of Cardiff politics. The *South Wales Labour Times*, the organ of the Trades Council and Progressive Labour League, published a short story in 1893 entitled 'Looking Backwards, 1936'. Inspired by Edward Bellamy's influential text, it envisaged an independent Wales, with its own parliament in which all property was 'invested in the State. All for each and each for all'. In this utopia, Cochfarf held the position of chancellor of the Exchequer.[64]

The extent to which such proto-nationalist views were current among Cardiff socialists is difficult to estimate. A study of several of those present at the Watch Night, however, gives some clues as to the extent of national consciousness within the nascent Welsh socialism of this period, and also illustrates the complex relationship between that socialism and its locality. Dr. Parr, who read the resolution quoted above, has already been discussed, and might be categorised as a classic cosmopolitan. The same might also be argued for the individual who presided over the proceedings that evening, and who, by the early 1890s, had arguably overtaken Parr as the dominant character within Cardiff socialism, Sam Hobson.

---

[60] *Western Mail*, 24 March 1893.

[61] Cardiff Central Library, Cochfarf Papers, Box 1, Fred Maddison to Edward Thomas, 21 April 1904.

[62] *Western Mail*, 21 December 1892.

[63] Cardiff Central Library, Cochfarf Papers, Box 6, contains extensive correspondence from Will Crooks.

[64] *South Wales Labour Times*, 8 April 1893.

The son of a Quaker minister, Hobson was born in Bessbrook, County Down, in 1870, although his family moved to England when he was a child, and he was educated at Quaker schools in Saffron Walden and Sidcot. Having failed to win a university scholarship, he arrived in Cardiff in the late 1880s.[65] The Quaker foundations of Hobson's intellect had been developed in the direction of socialism, under the influence of a teacher at Sidcot, before he arrived in Wales. He also visited London in 1889, where he was influenced by the Great Dock Strike: 'I came back with a vivid sense of the potential power of an industrial democracy', he later recalled. It was in Cardiff in early 1890, however, when he discovered the *Fabian Essays in Socialism*, that he became a committed socialist, and within a short time he became a key figure in the town's socialist movement.[66] A founder member of the Fabian Socialist Society, he was also a leading light in the Cardiff Labour Church, and went on to become the most prominent representative of the ILP in Wales in the period prior to 1895.

Hobson's socialism was drawn from a range of sources. The *Fabian Essays* provided one element, but this was balanced with a strong ethical and religious drive, which came to the fore in his speeches to the Labour Church. In essence, his beliefs comprised 'articles of faith in relation to labour' which had been 'grafted' upon his pre-existing religious beliefs.[67] This process had been influenced by experience, but perhaps more by his wide reading. This encompassed most of the staples of late-Victorian British intellectual culture, including Ruskin, Carlyle, Frederic Harrison, Matthew Arnold and Charles Bradlaugh. His ideology also had a strong international dimension, and drew upon both European and American sources, including Mazzini, Emerson and Walt Whitman.[68] The result was a heady, idealistic cocktail, with arguably limited practical content. Keir Hardie later referred

---

[65] Marc Stears, 'Hobson, Samuel George (1870–1940)', *Oxford Dictionary of National Biography* (Oxford University Press, 2004) *http://www.oxforddnb.com/view/article/45909* (accessed 18 July 2009).

[66] Hobson, *Pilgrim to the Left*, pp. 23–5.

[67] S.G. Hobson, *Possibilities of the Labour Church: An Address to the Cardiff Labour Church on February the 19th 1893* (Cardiff, 1893), p. 1.

[68] *Possibilities of the Labour Church*; S.G. Hobson, 'Looking Forward', *South Wales Labour Times*, 4 March 1893.

to him as 'a good fellow, but an inveterate builder of sand castles'.[69] The extent to which Hobson related these ideological enthusiasms directly to his immediate local and national context is questionable. Despite his prominence within Cardiff socialism, and the fact that he almost fought a parliamentary seat there in 1895,[70] his relationship with the town was ambivalent. He worked as a travelling salesman, so was frequently absent, often for extensive periods.[71] He also sometimes gave the impression that he did not really like Cardiff. He opined to Thomas Jones, who was considering establishing a university settlement there in 1896, that the town was 'intellectually dead. I know of no town in the kingdom', he continued, 'so utterly destitute of real vitality and idealism.'[72]

Indeed, to Hobson Cardiff could have been any town in the UK, and his presence there was both accidental and incidental to his life's trajectory.

This did not mean that he was necessarily antipathetic to either nationalism or Welsh culture. He was on good terms with Cochfarf, whose election to the council in 1890 pleased him on two counts: firstly because Cochfarf was a 'working carpenter' and shared Hobson's socialistic enthusiasm for 'one or two pet schemes equally dear to both of us' (by which he meant measures of municipalisation). More than this, though, Hobson stated that he would 'have great pleasure in informing my friends [in Ireland] of the success of a nationalist'.[73] He also exhibited respect – awe even – for Welsh culture. He attended the funerals of the victims of the Albion Colliery disaster at Cilfynydd in 1894, and his journalistic account of the event is revealing. His reference to 'the vast choirs, with their subtle sense of harmonious melody,

---

[69] Francis Johnson Correspondence, 1897/53, Keir Hardie to John Penny, 13 August 1897.
[70] *South Wales Daily News*, 10 and 13 April, and 9 July 1895.
[71] *Pilgrim to the Left*, p. 31. The 1891 Census records him as a commercial traveller, staying at the Beauchamp Hotel in Malvern.
[72] National Library of Wales, Aberystwyth, Thomas Jones C.H. Collection, X (Family and Personal) 2, Sam Hobson to Thomas Jones, 25 February 1896.
[73] Cardiff Central Library, Cochfarf Papers, Box 2, Sam Hobson to Edward Thomas, 3 and 4 November 1890. Hobson was sympathetic to Irish Home Rule, see S.G. Hobson, *Irish Home Rule* (London, 1912).

singing their Welsh hymns so sweetly and truly that the music sinks into the soul even if we do not know the meaning of the words',[74] combines reverence with a sense of inevitable exclusion created by his ignorance of the Welsh language. Indeed, Hobson's position as observer at the funerals might be taken as a more general metaphor for his situation in Wales in the early 1890s. Despite playing an important role in the development of socialism, Hobson remained an outsider. His identity was essentially pan-British, as expressed in a tongue-in-cheek skit published in 1894, almost certainly written by Hobson himself, which asserted that 'Being thus an Irishman and a Welshman, Mr. Hobson has qualified as an Englishman'.[75]

The prominence of individuals like Sam Hobson and A.C.E. Parr in the early-1890s Cardiff socialist movement would support the contention that socialism was a heterogeneous influence within Wales. A study of some other individuals present at the Socialist Watch Night, however, rather confuses this notion. Indeed, Hobson and Parr only represent one element of Cardiff socialism, and it should be noted that Hobson's socialist education was only completed after his arrival in Cardiff. His main personal inspiration in this – someone who was also present at the Hotel Metropole that New Year's Eve – was a Welsh-speaking Welshman, R.E. Thomas.[76] Originally from Gelligaer, Thomas was the son of a Baptist minister, and grew up in Merthyr.[77] Sometime in the 1880s he moved to Cardiff, where he was employed as a postal clerk,[78] and by 1890, in his early 20s, he had become, according to Hobson, the 'virtual leader' of the small group which was busily studying the *Fabian Essays*.[79] A young, single, educated white-collar worker, with (according to Hobson) a small private income, Thomas was, perhaps, typical Fabian material. More than this, though, his personality was the

[74] *Labour Leader*, 7 July 1894.
[75] *Labour Prophet*, November 1894.
[76] Hobson, *Pilgrim to the Left*, p. 25.
[77] He appears on the 1881 Census as a 14-year-old scholar, living with his parents and two sisters at 89, Thomas Street, Merthyr.
[78] The 1891 Census records him living at 6, Beauchamp Street, just doors away from Sam Hobson.
[79] Hobson, *Pilgrim to the Left*, p. 25. Hobson describes Thomas as 'the most gifted mind I have ever known'.

product of the fusion of socialist ideas with native Welsh sensibilities. Hobson later wrote a character sketch of him:

> The last of an old and distinguished Welsh family, he carried his breeding lightly but palpably in speech and bearing. ... He would turn from his beloved Beethoven to Welsh mediaeval war-songs, of which he had collected a great number, setting some to his own music. He reconstructed the ancient architecture of St David's and Caerphilly. I think his revolt was at bottom directed against a system that had degraded his people from brave and chivalrous warriors into coal-miners and tinplate workers. The Welsh valleys, through which he sometimes tramped, beckoned to him to lead his people out and to smash the strange gods which they ignorantly worshipped. But he was by no means a mediaevalist. He had mastered Ricardo, Stanley Jevons and Marx.[80]

Thomas acted as a point of cultural interchange between late-nineteenth-century Wales and the British socialist movement. While playing an important role introducing the *Fabian Essays* to the Cardiff intellectual scene of the 1890s, he also contributed to the socialist press. Keir Hardie's *Labour Leader* published a short story written by him in 1895 which provides, as well as a striking insight into Thomas's own views on Welsh society, an extremely rare example of the mainstream socialist press dealing with rural Welsh life. Set on a Breconshire farm, and worthy of Caradoc Evans, it contains a scathing attack on the values of contemporary Welsh nonconformity, which had become 'the willing tool of the lower middle class of monied men, [which] [a]s is well known ... is the body of men the most unimaginative and reactionary in the community'. It also, however, contains a defence of the genuine religious devotion exhibited by earlier generations (including, perhaps, Thomas's own father), and, indeed, of the fundamental values of Welsh rural life.[81] Its author was both a pivotal figure in the intellectual life of the fledgling Welsh socialist movement of cosmopolitan Cardiff and a harbinger of what was to become a major change of consciousness on the part of the following generation.

---

[80] Anthony Farley [Sam Hobson], *Letters to My Nephew* (London, 1917), p. 229.
[81] 'Yesterday and To-day: An Incident of Welsh Life', *Labour Leader*, 16 and 23 February 1895.

The most interesting and important of the indigenous Welsh socialists in 1890s Cardiff, however, was the individual who seconded Dr Parr's resolution at the Hotel Metropole, another medical doctor: David Rhys Jones. Jones was born in Llangunllo, Cardiganshire, in 1845, the son of a tenant farmer, and was educated at Newcastle Emlyn Grammar School and Carmarthen College.[82] Before settling in Cardiff he travelled widely. In 1866, for health reasons, he went to Australia, where he lived for several years,[83] although by the 1870s he had returned to Britain and entered the medical profession.[84] During the early 1880s he held the position of deputy superintendent at the Joint Counties Lunatic Asylum, Carmarthen, and was an acknowledged expert in lunacy cases.[85] He spent some of the 1880s in London,[86] and moved to Cardiff in 1889 to set up in general practice.[87] It is possible that Jones came into contact with socialist ideas while in London, although the decisive phase in his development as a socialist occurred around 1890 in Cardiff, under the influence of Dr Parr. 'Thanks to Dr. Parr, I saw a "great light", and now all other science has second place', he wrote in 1893.[88] Enthused by his conversion, Jones became one of the most active Cardiff socialists, frequently driving his metaphorical 'Fabian Bus' through the correspondence columns of the *Western Mail*.[89] Apart from being a founder member of the Cardiff Fabian Socialist Society, he also attended the Cardiff Labour Church,[90] and was an early advocate of independent labour representation.[91] In 1894 he was elected to Cardiff's Board of Guardians.[92] What is of particular interest

[82] Obituary, *British Medical Journal*, January 1926.
[83] National Library of Wales, Aberystwyth, NLW MS3601E, Letters of Evidence to the Welsh Land Commission, 1894.
[84] *Medical Register*, 1887.
[85] *Western Mail*, 17 August 1893.
[86] He married there in 1885. His wife, Matilda, was born in Middlesex. The 1901 Census records two sons born in London, aged 13 and 14.
[87] *British Medical Journal*, January 1926.
[88] *Western Mail*, 6 January 1893.
[89] *Western Mail*, 28 December 1893, 6 and 19 January, 7 March, 7 and 8 May and 21 December 1894.
[90] *Celt*, 10 February 1893.
[91] *Workman's Times*, 14 May 1892.
[92] *Western Mail*, 18 and 31 December 1894, 28 January 1895.

about Jones, however, is that he was the most prominent of the Cardiff socialists to advocate socialism within a specifically Welsh context and through the medium of the Welsh language.

Although Jones's socialism may have been moulded into a finished product in Cardiff under the influence of Parr and Thomas, its roots were deeper. In 1894 he gave evidence to the Royal Commission on Land, and his written submission provides a valuable insight not just into the origins of his own socialist beliefs, but also into some of the influences that would soon shape the socialism of an increasing number of young Welsh professionals. Recounting the history of his family farm, Ffynnon-wen in Cardiganshire, he explained how, despite considerable kindness and paternalism on the part of the family's landlords (the Lloyds of Bronwydd), injustice was an inherent part of their landlord–tenant relationship. He recounted how 'very nearly all the surplus after a coarse living for farmer family and servants went in rent year by year which was gathered with immense toil and anxiety and spent in one night's feasting at the palace close by'. He explained how prohibitively high rent had made it almost impossible to run the farm and pay fair wages to its labourers, and that the implication of this was that 'Not from choice is the country deserted for unhealthy towns by its lads and lasses. Rent drives them.' As a solution he advocated land nationalisation.[93]

Jones's testimony yields important clues towards an understanding of his socialism. Significantly, it was not based upon bitterness. There are no episodes of harassment or evictions in his account of the history of Ffynnon-wen. His political convictions were essentially moderate, and gravitated naturally towards Fabianism. They were, nevertheless, based upon a stark analysis – derived from personal experience – of the iniquitous economics of private land ownership. Importantly, Jones's perception of the economics of his native country was sharpened by his time away from it. In Australia, he testified, 'I ... saw the vast advantage to its people of a country

---

[93] National Library of Wales, Aberystwyth, NLW MS 3601E; Herbert M. Vaughan, *The South Wales Squires: A Welsh Picture of Social Life* (London, 1926), pp. 175–7.

not devoured by rent'. The juxtaposition of cultures and economic systems he experienced had a striking impact upon his thought, opening his mind to new possibilities that led in the direction of socialism. Jones was not alone in coming to socialism as a result of contact with multiple cultures; the same pattern has already been observed in the case of Sam Mainwaring. If, however, part of the dynamic of a developing Welsh socialism was tension between experience of the local and knowledge of the wider world, it was sharpened by the reading of socialist literature. In David Rhys Jones's case, this probably included the publications of the Land Nationalisation Society.[94] It definitely included Sidney Webb's Fabian Tract on land nationalisation, which Jones translated into Welsh.[95] The most direct source of Jones's ideas on land reform, though, was not the English-based Land Nationalisation Society, nor even the Fabian Society, but the Welsh *Cymdeithas y Ddaear i'r Bobl*, founded in 1883 by Evan Pan Jones. The two Joneses, Rhys and Pan, originated from the same part of Cardiganshire, had what amounted to family ties and remained in contact through Rhys Jones's life in Cardiff.[96] They also shared the same mix of religious belief and concern for social justice which made their social teaching essentially a salvationist mission.[97] Rhys Jones's

[94] Alfred Russel Wallace, *Land Nationalisation: Its Necessity and Its Aims* (London, 1882); Alfred Russel Wallace, *The 'Why' and the 'How' of Land Nationalisation* (London, 1883); A.J. Ogilvy, *Land Nationalisation* (Manchester, 1890); Helen Taylor, *Nationalisation of the Land* (London, 1888). The Society's president, Alfred Russel Wallace (1823–1913), himself provides a fascinating study of the interplay between Wales and the wider world. Born near Usk in Monmouthshire of Scottish and English ancestry, he was brought up in Hertford and London, before returning to Wales, ultimately settling in Neath, although he seems to have considered himself an Englishman. Harry Clements, *Alfred Russel Wallace: Biologist and Social Reformer* (London, 1983).

[95] Sidney Webb, *Practicable Land Nationalization (Fabian Tract No. 12)* (London, 1890). Jones's translation, 'Y Ddaear i'r Bobl – Beth Allwn Wneud', appeared in *Tarian y Gweithiwr*, 1 October 1891.

[96] Evan Pan Jones was born at Waunlluest, near Llandysul, which was only a matter of miles from Ffynon-wen, and Rhys Jones later helped Pan Jones in the writing of his autobiography, Evan Pan Jones, *Oes Gofion: Fraslun o Hanes fy Mywyd* (Bala, 1911), pp. 4–5; David Rhys Jones worked with the brother of Pan Jones, also called David, in the establishment of a Fabian Society at Llandysul, *Fabian News*, April 1892.

[97] It is not clear to which denomination Rhys Jones belonged, but, as with almost all of his contemporaries, his socialism had a strong religious element: 'It seems to me very strange to hear of Socialism as pitched against Christianity ... Why, Jesus

links with Pan Jones, and the confluence of the former's Fabian socialism with the latter's agrarian radicalism, clearly demonstrate the way in which Welsh influences contributed to the making of socialism in Wales.

If, however, Jones's socialism was a product of the convergence of native Welsh influences and late-nineteenth-century 'scientific' socialism,[98] an important function of his career as a socialist was the way in which he attempted to interpret his ideology to the Welsh, making a determined effort to promote socialism beyond the confines of cosmopolitan Cardiff. Jones was certainly conscious and proud of his own Welshness. Sam Hobson once referred to him as a 'Welshman of mighty fervour which is sometimes embarrassing'.[99] He maintained his Welsh connections while in London by attending meetings of the London Cymmrodorion,[100] and once in Cardiff he continued to advocate particularist Welsh causes, such as the official recognition of the Welsh language in university education.[101] He was, however, aware of the limitations of Welsh culture in the modernised, urban, cosmopolitan world in which he lived, and he often equated the use of the English language with civilisation.[102] His arguments for Welsh particularism might be seen as an attempt to defend Welshness and the Welsh language in a rapidly anglicising environment. His attempts to propagate socialism through the medium of his native language might equally be seen as an effort to modernise and enrich his own native culture. During the 1890s this manifested itself in several ways. First,

---

Christ was, and, therefore, is the very comrade whom any downtrodden, bedraggled, aye, condemned man, woman, or child, on roadside or in cell, may find by his or her side'. *Western Mail*, 16 September 1893.

[98] With regard to the scientific element of his socialism, Jones stated 'Socialism is to me like the law of gravity', *Western Mail*, 28 December 1895.

[99] National Library of Wales, Aberystwyth, Thomas Jones C.H. Collection, X (Family and Personal) 2, Sam Hobson to Thomas Jones, 25 February 1896. The statement says as much about Hobson as it does Jones. Jones's obituary in the *British Medical Journal* also noted that he 'took a warm interest in everything appertaining to Wales'.

[100] *Baner ac Amserau Cymru*, 17 June 1885.

[101] *Western Mail*, 10 August 1893; *Genedl Gymreig*, 7 March 1893.

[102] For example, 'Whatever the Romans may have felt of the evil effects of the unrestricted development of hereditary greed and self-satisfying, it becomes more obvious year by year that these effects cannot be much longer tolerated among English-speaking people', *Western Mail*, 28 December 1893.

Jones translated socialist literature into Welsh.[103] He often stood up at the end of meetings in Cardiff, drawing attention to the availability of such material.[104] Secondly, he frequently travelled from Cardiff into the south Wales valleys to address socialist meetings in Welsh alongside English speakers.[105] In this respect, he provided a valuable extra dimension to the early socialist forays into industrial Wales.

It was not just in the south Wales valleys, though, that Jones attempted to promote socialism. He also used his personal connections and knowledge of Welsh cultural life to attempt to reach out into rural Wales. He was instrumental in setting up a branch of the Fabian Society at Llandysul.[106] He also made a prolific contribution to the Welsh-language press, including regular, detailed reports under the name *Fabius* in Evan Pan Jones's *Celt* and a series of letters signed '*Un o'r Ffabianiaid*' in the north Wales Liberal newspaper *Genedl Gymreig*.[107] Thanks to David Rhys Jones, the Welsh reading public could read accounts of Cardiff's series of Fabian lectures,[108] or follow a detailed explanation of the theory of rent,[109] in their own language.

David Rhys Jones represented a different face of Cardiff socialism to that of his younger comrades, Charles Parr and Sam Hobson. He lived between two cultural worlds with a foot firmly placed in each. As a correspondent to the *Workman's Times* put it in 1892, he was 'a typical Welshman yet withal a thorough cosmopolitan'.[110] His socialism was a hybrid creation – a product of the meeting of Welsh radical culture with scientific Fabianism – within which religion and science were interwoven in equal measure. He provided an important point of contact between cosmopolitan socialism

[103] Apart from Webb's pamphlet on land nationalisation, he also translated Fabian Tract no. 1, *Tarian y Gweithiwr*, 17 September 1891.
[104] *South Wales Daily News*, 3 and 5 May 1892.
[105] *Labour Leader*, 16 June 1894 and 14 September 1895.
[106] See below, chapter 4.
[107] *Celt*, November 1891–April 1893; *Genedl Gymreig*, 20 April 1892–7 September 1892.
[108] *Celt*, 20 November 1891 (W.S. De Mattos), 1 January 1892 (Sidney Webb), 18 March 1892 (Katherine Conway), 8 April 1892 (W.S. De Mattos), 21 October 1892 (Keir Hardie), 3 February 1893 (H. Halliday Sparling).
[109] *Genedl Gymreig*, 31 August 1892.
[110] *Workman's Times*, 21 May 1892.

and traditional Welsh culture, the urban and the rural, the universal and the local. It is possible that this was a limiting factor in his long-term impact upon the socialist movement. Whereas the footloose Hobson left Cardiff in the mid-1890s and went on to make a name for himself in various socialistic spheres in different parts of Britain, Jones seems to have retreated from the socialist movement towards the end of the 1890s, remaining in Grangetown and serving its inhabitants as a doctor until his death in 1926. As the socialist movement developed and expressed itself as a national movement, with aspirations and affiliations at a UK level, it may have left Jones, with his attachment to place and native culture, behind. This may be advancing the argument beyond the facts; Jones, after all, did not leave us a statement of his reasons for withdrawal from the socialist movement. It is, nevertheless, safe to conclude that Jones, and his fellow Fabian Socialists, represented a particular and self-contained phase of Welsh socialism. By the mid-1890s the type of socialism they represented was waning. As a regional phenomenon Fabianism was being displaced by the ILP. Nevertheless, the activities of the Fabian Socialists cannot be dismissed. They provided an important site of cultural and ideological interpenetration, a melting pot for ideas coming from different directions and arising from a variety of influences. Indeed, Cardiff provided a seedbed for socialism in Wales, from which it would spread and take root elsewhere.

(II) THE SOCIAL DEMOCRATIC FEDERATION IN SOUTH WALES

Fabianism was not the only form of socialism to take root in south Wales in the early 1890s. It may have been dominant in Cardiff, but elsewhere along the south Wales coast the SDF was in the vanguard. Llanelli, Swansea and, on Cardiff's doorstep, Barry all experienced some level of SDF activity in the 1890s. The industrialised south-west, which was the initial object of SDF interest, comprised the 'Tinopolis' of Llanelli, the 'Copperopolis' of Swansea and the industrial settlements strewn up the Loughor and Swansea Valleys and around the Gower Peninsula, and was one of the most important metal producing centres in the world. In addition to the region's miners, most of the country's 25,000 tinplate workers were concentrated in this area. They had traditions of trade unionism going back to the early 1870s, and had in 1887 established a new Tinplate Workers' Union.[111] Socialist interest was further encouraged by the strong degree of independent political consciousness that had been demonstrated by the workers of the Gower constituency in 1888, when they had combined to force the return to parliament of their own representative, David Randell, in a by-election.[112] The new unionism too had made rapid advances in the Swansea region by the early 1890s. A precursor to this was witnessed by delegates to the Trades Union Congress, held at Swansea in September 1887. Although the event is chiefly remembered for Keir Hardie's attack on Henry Broadhurst, an event of local significance was the speech given by W. Bevan, one of the representatives of Swansea Trades Council, in which he attacked 'the present system of society, which gives the riches of toil to those who do not produce', and argued for independent labour representation, declaring that 'socialism has lost its terror for us'.[113] After the successful Swansea dock strike of May 1890, moreover, trade unionism was extended significantly across the region. By 1891, it was estimated that there were 10,000 trade unionists in Swansea alone. As was the case in Cardiff, prominent socialists such as Ben Tillett and Tom Mann were frequent visitors to the south-west, where they attempted to radicalise the working class in the same way.[114]

This did not necessarily mean that workers in the west were, as a group, any better disposed towards socialism than those elsewhere. Quite the contrary: anti-socialist statements, such as that in the *Welsh Industrial Times,* organ of the Tinplate Workers' Union, which declared in 1889 that 'with

---

[111] Idris C. Bell, 'The Tinplate Workers' Union', in Goronwy Alun Hughes (ed.), *Men of No Property: Historical Studies of Welsh Trade Unions* (Caerwys, 1971), pp. 25–32.

[112] David Cleaver, 'Labour and Liberals in the Gower Constituency, 1885–1910', *Welsh History Review,* 12/3 (1985), 388–410 (390–2). Randell was a sympathetic solicitor from Llanelli who had assisted in the establishment of the Tinplate Workers' Union.

[113] Quoted in McCarry, 'Labour and Society in Swansea, 1887–1918', pp. 60–1.

[114] Leng, *The Welsh Dockers,* pp. 16–18; McCarry, 'Labour and Society in Swansea', pp. 114–38.

Socialism of the red flag we have no sympathy',[115] were more representative of working-class opinion in the region than Bevan's speech at the 1887 TUC. Indeed, the main forces in the politics of the south-west were Liberalism, religious nonconformity and localism, and this remained the case well into the early twentieth century.[116] This, however, did not dampen the interest of socialists from across the English border. William Morris had read reports of Bevan's speech at the 1887 TUC, and reflected that 'it affords gratifying evidence of the growth of Socialism in the ranks of organised Labour'.[117] H.H. Champion, formerly of the SDF and by the 1880s attempting to stimulate independent labour representation through the columns of his *Labour Elector*, had come to Swansea to support Randell in 1888.[118] The SDF's *Justice* also occasionally covered events in south Wales.[119] Although never more than a tiny fraction of the journal's content, these articles ensured that socialists in other parts of Britain were aware of at least some events in Wales. This sometimes sparked the interest of the Federation's members in England. John Paterson of the Colne branch wrote to *Justice* in November 1892, having read of the distress in the tinplate industry in south Wales, suggesting that a fund should be raised for 'an active propaganda of the principles of Social Democracy amongst the Welshmen'.[120] Despite his promise to raise the issue at his local branch, however, little seems to have come of the suggestion. Although seeing industrial south Wales as 'a splendid field for socialist propaganda', *Justice* complained that 'the cursed impecuniosity of the SDF prevents, as usual, the Socialist agitation being vigorously carried into a district which is now ripe for revolutionary teaching'.[121]

Despite this, the Federation did launch several propaganda campaigns in south Wales in the early 1890s. In July 1892, H. Alexander, a young member from London, held

[115] Quoted in McCarry, 'Labour and Society in Swansea', p. 87.
[116] Cleaver, 'Labour and Liberals in the Gower Constituency', p. 392.
[117] *Commonweal*, 17 September 1887.
[118] *Western Mail*, 27 March 1888.
[119] *Justice*, 11 February 1888, 14 February 1891, 8 and 22 October 1892.
[120] *Justice*, 12 November 1892.
[121] *Justice*, 29 October 1892.

a public meeting in the People's Park at Llanelli, with the aim of forming a branch of the organisation there,[122] and in December another London SDF-er, Harry Hobart, visited the area on a week-long tour. Hobart's visit was organised by a local sympathiser, E.A. Cleeves, and included meetings in Llanelli, Gorseinon, Kidwelly, Ammanford, Felinfoel and Penclawdd. The Federation also went to the trouble and expense of having three of its tracts translated into Welsh.[123] Despite this, Hobart's mission enjoyed only mixed success, and *Justice*'s coverage of it sheds light upon the SDF's problematic relationship to Wales. Indeed, it conveys the impression that as far as Hobart was concerned he might almost have been a missionary in Africa, rather than a propagandist in Wales. It was reported that 'he has received sufficient evidence of a desire amongst the natives to learn something of Social-Democracy to encourage him to believe that we shall eventually reap a plentiful and valuable harvest amongst the Welsh people'. The problem was that 'on the admission of Welshmen themselves, they are very slow and cautious in adopting new ideas',[124] and '[t]aking all their characteristics into consideration, it is not surprising that there was a show of timidity when a London Social-Democrat was known to have invaded their domains'. It came as a matter of surprise that on some issues – church disestablishment, tithes, land nationalisation and Sunday closing – 'they are apparently more advanced than the Englishman'.[125]

During his visit Hobart faced a number of problems that were, by the early 1890s, becoming recurrent issues facing English socialists in Wales. The first was the influence of the chapels. When Cleeves and Hobart tried to organise a meeting at Gorseinon, the attendance was poor, due to 'the interference of certain influential personages, who advised those who had resolved to come to stay away, because

[122] *Justice*, 13 August 1892; *South Wales Press*, 28 July 1892.
[123] *Justice*, 19 November and 3 December 1892. The SDF financed the leaflets from a Provincial Propaganda Fund. The tracts translated were *What Use is a Vote?*, *The Gospel of Discontent* and *What Social Democrats Want*. It has not been possible to trace extant copies.
[124] *Justice* 10 December 1892.
[125] *Justice*, 17 December 1892.

Socialism meant Atheism and everything else that was bad'. A meeting they organised at Felinfoel clashed with a chapel meeting and was consequently poorly attended. The local trade unions too stood aloof. Tom Phillips, the tinplate workers' secretary, withdrew his promise to chair one meeting at short notice without explanation, and 'the meeting was not nearly so large as it should have been'. At Pontarddulais Hobart experienced another disappointing meeting, which he attributed to the fact that the workers in the region had previously been subjected to 'a sort of bastard Socialism', which stressed the role of trade unionism and political pragmatism over 'a thorough collective principle of ownership. The men themselves therefore seem more disposed to be satisfied with a little improvement of their present condition than to strive for an entirely new system.'[126] This problem was common to socialists in all parts of Britain. In Welsh-speaking south-west Wales, though, it was compounded by the complication of the Welsh language, which, despite coming armed with the specially printed Welsh tracts, Hobart found a significant challenge. At some meetings local sympathisers helped him to overcome the language barrier. Lecturing at Seion Baptist Chapel in Gorseinon, he was introduced to a 'very attentive and enthusiastic audience' by a friend of Cleeves, a Welsh speaker by the name of Ludwig: Ludwig 'took the chair, and addressed them in their native tongue, and told them that Hobart would speak to them in English. Several of those present afterwards said they understood every word.'[127] Other meetings, though, were more difficult. At Felinfoel, when the chapel had finally emptied and a 'fairly good gathering' had been assembled, 'The great difficulty was the language. Most of the men understanding very little English; but by a careful and slow delivery *we made them* understand us.'[128] Hobart's words speak for themselves. The image they present of the Englishman abroad amongst the natives borders on the comic.

---

[126] *Justice*, 17 December 1892.
[127] *Justice*, 10 December 1892.
[128] *Justice*, 17 December 1892. Italics added.

Hobart's campaign was not, however, entirely without success. The fact that he succeeded in securing a number of chapels as venues for meetings suggests that local nonconformists were at least curious about his teachings. More significantly, his visit attracted the interest and patronage of David Randell, the local MP. Randell chaired one of Hobart's meetings, at the Athenaeum Hall in Llanelli, where he made a statement explicitly aligning himself with the SDF. He also echoed socialist assertions concerning the inherent socialism of the Welsh people:

> The Chairman, in opening the meeting, said that as one identified with movements, both social and political, he had pleasure in taking the chair that evening. To remove the doubt that might exist in the minds of the audience, he might say at once that as far as he was concerned, his own opinions and beliefs were tending more and more in the direction of Socialism ... The work of the Socialists of this country was chiefly propagandist, and amongst other associations the Social Democratic Federation was in the very front rank of the new movement. The Welsh workers were as instinctively Socialistic as any body of workers in this country.[129]

At the end of the meeting, moreover, 'Several names were taken to render assistance in the formation of a branch in Llanelly, and foremost amongst those who promised every assistance possible was Mr. Randell'.[130] Randell's interest in the SDF is remarkable. It might be ascribed to a maverick and politically eccentric personality. This would, though, underestimate its significance. Randell was a member of *Cymru Fydd* and an ally of Mabon, whose election campaign in the Rhondda he had supported in 1885. Only four months previously he had been adopted as the official Liberal candidate for Gower, a position he retained in 1895 despite there being no evidence that he had renounced his socialist affiliations. To the contrary, he seems to have held socialist views well beyond his retirement (due to ill health) as an MP in 1900.[131] Indeed, Randell's SDF sympathies provide further

---

[129] *South Wales Press*, 8 December 1892.
[130] *Justice*, 17 December 1892.
[131] He appeared on an ILP platform at Brynaman in 1908, stating '*fod ei fywyd a'i ddyheadau yn gyfryw nes cydweddu yn hollol ac egwyddorion syflaenol Cymdeithasiaeth yn eu gwahanol gyfeiriadau*' ('that his life and his aspirations were such that they fully

evidence of a relatively benign attitude among some sections of advanced Welsh Liberalism towards socialism. His comment that the work of socialists was 'chiefly propagandist' is significant in this respect. The confluence of social democratic and advanced Liberal thought was only tenable while socialist agitation remained 'chiefly propagandist'. Once it began to challenge Liberalism politically the accommodating attitude of individuals like Randell would become less common.

This was still some years away in 1892, and in the wake of Hobart's propaganda tour Social Democratic activity became a more constant feature of the political culture of south-west Wales. By the summer of 1893 an SDF branch was active in Llanelli, holding weekly meetings at the Temperance Hotel in Stepney Street.[132] By the autumn Swansea too was host to regular meetings. Sam Mainwaring, who by now was back in the SDF and living in Swansea, provided a series of regular reports for *Justice*. '"Gallant little Wales" is falling into line', he reported in September. Seven meetings had been held in Swansea and two in Llanelli in the previous week alone. Mainwaring was working alongside Cleeves, and the two had been joined for a fortnight by A.G. Wolfe, a visiting propagandist from Lancashire.[133] Landore, Morriston and Neath also came under their influence. Their first attempt at a meeting in Neath fell foul of the competition provided by the 'Great Neath Fair'. Nevertheless, despite there being no branch in the town, an SDF member was secretary of the Neath Trades Council, and another Neath sympathiser, Comrade Rees,[134] regularly travelled down to Swansea to attend SDF meetings. At Landore and Morriston the names of supporters were collected after open air meetings, and as the result of two weeks' propaganda work in September 1893 Mainwaring

corresponded to the basic principles of Socialism in their different manifestations'), *Llais Llafur*, 4 April 1908.

[132] *Justice*, 16 September 1893.
[133] *Justice*, 16 September 1893.
[134] W.J. Rees, later to be secretary of the South Wales ILP Federation, see *Labour Leader*, 5 May and 13 October 1894. His gravitation towards the ILP illustrates the way in which the SDF created interest in socialism that was to be harvested later by the ILP. In Rees's case the harvest was short-lived; he died in November 1895, *Labour Leader*, 23 November 1895.

estimated that about 150 new recruits had been attracted.[135] 'Wales is awakening. It is Cambria *rediviva*', he rejoiced, socialism would soon spread like a wildfire over the mining and manufacturing districts, and the people were 'ripe for it – rotten ripe'.[136] By October some form of regular branch activity was taking place in Llanelli, Landore, Morriston and Swansea, and by the winter of 1893 the Swansea branch was stable enough to have set up a penny-a-month circulating library[137] and to have made its own banner.[138] By the end of November it was even contemplating building a meeting hall.[139] Signs appeared promising for the SDF in south-west Wales.

Behind *Justice*'s exuberant reports, however, the SDF's position was fragile. In reality its fortunes were overdependent upon the presence of experienced speakers from the SDF strongholds of London and Lancashire. It was only the visits of Alexander, Hobart and Wolfe that attracted significant attention. Once they had gone it was difficult to sustain either interest or organisation. 'Unfortunately the district is too large to be organised sufficiently rapidly by the few experienced comrades in the district', lamented Mainwaring on Wolfe's departure in late September 1893, 'and we think if Wolfe could return here for two months the results would be very satisfactory.'[140] The SDF did not have the resources to arrange such extended visits, neither was it in possession of sufficient human capital on a local level to sustain a satisfactory level of activity in the absence of external help. 'I think there is good ground for sowing Socialist seed in Wales, – all we need is speakers', opined J. Arnold of the Swansea branch in November 1893,[141] implying a deficit of local oratorical talent. The few committed local activists who did exist also faced problems beyond their control. One of these was opposition from both irate members of the public and the police,

[135] *Justice*, 23 September 1893.
[136] *Justice*, 30 September 1893.
[137] *Justice*, 30 September 1893.
[138] *Justice*, 4 November 1893.
[139] *Justice*, 25 November 1893.
[140] *Justice*, 30 September 1893.
[141] *Justice*, 25 November 1893.

who attempted to break up their meetings.[142] The chapels too continued to be a source of frustration. 'The pulpits are using their influence against the movement as they did in London twelve years ago, and the fact of our holding a meeting on Sunday morning is turned to our disadvantage', complained Mainwaring.[143] The work patterns practised in the industries of the region also militated against organisation, particularly the prevalence of night work, which prevented local workers from attending meetings.[144] The work of the small group of socialists in industrial south-west Wales in the early 1890s was indeed uphill.

About that group's membership we know little. Griff Jones, who in 1902 became secretary of the Swansea Socialist Society (the SDF's successor in the town), later lamented that the early history of socialism in Swansea, which was the primary centre of socialist activity in the south-west in this period, was 'shrouded in impenetrable darkness'.[145] It unfortunately remains so, although a precious few gleanings from contemporary sources and reminiscences do allow some tentative conclusions about the nature of the membership. Clearly, the leading individual in the region was Sam Mainwaring.[146] As already discussed, he had local origins and was a Welsh speaker. He had returned to live in south Wales in 1892, initially spending ten months in the Rhondda (where he organised informal economics classes in the room of an inn), and then settling with his family in Swansea.[147] He continued to use Welsh at meetings, which drew appreciation from his audiences.[148] He also, despite a pragmatic realignment with the SDF, retained a level of commitment to anarchist rather than strictly socialist ideology, thus ensuring a degree

---

[142] *Justice*, 16 September and 4 November 1893.
[143] *Justice*, 4 November 1893.
[144] *Justice*, 30 September 1893.
[145] Glamorgan County Record Office, Cardiff, D/D AW H14/4, Griff Jones, 'Script of Swansea Socialist Party and Labour Party' [1956].
[146] Stan Awbery, *Labour's Early Struggles in Swansea* (Swansea, 1949), pp. 49–50, discusses Mainwaring, 'whose pioneering work for Socialism was of the highest quality' and describes him as 'the man chiefly responsible' for the permeation of socialism into Swansea politics by the end of the 1890s. Awbery joined the labour movement in Swansea a decade after Mainwaring's involvement.
[147] *Freedom*, February 1927.
[148] *Justice*, 23 September 1893.

of ideological heterodoxy on the part of the local branch. Under his influence the group's meeting place was named 'Liberty Hall', and alongside *Justice*, the anarchist-communist newspaper *Liberty* was 'pushed most whole-heartedly in Swansea and south Wales generally'.[149] The influence of Mainwaring, an 'eloquent, deeply-read man, possessing a fascinating personality', was clearly seminal, and when he left Swansea in the mid-1890s Sir Hussey Vivian declared, with satisfaction, that there were no socialists left.[150] This was not, however, strictly accurate. Other socialists who worked alongside Mainwaring included some of the local trade unionists, such as George Hollett of the Dockers,[151] and William Morris of the Engineers. Morris is, perhaps, of particular interest. A native of Swansea, he was also a long-standing member of the Independent Order of Rechabites, a benefit society which promoted temperance. His primary intellectual influences were John Ruskin and his namesake William Morris, and he went on to serve as president of Swansea Trades Council and to represent St. John's ward on Swansea council.[152] He might thus be seen as both an early link between the native Swansea working class and socialist ideology, and an element of continuity between the origins and later development of the socialist and labour movement in Swansea.

The single other most important figure was E.A. Cleeves, who had been instrumental in arranging Hobart's visit in 1892, and whose background was the very opposite of a trade unionist. Another Swansea SDF-er reported of him that he 'belongs to the middle classes; which somewhat astonishes the people; but he boldly tells them they are fools to let him remain so'.[153] Edmund Cleeves, in his early 20s in the early 1890s, was a colliery owner and coal exporter, originally from Yorkshire who had, most likely, only been in Swansea a year

[149] *Freedom*, February 1927; *Liberty*, April–October 1894.
[150] John Littlejohns, 'The Rise of the Swansea Labour Party', in W.C. Jenkins (ed.), *Swansea Trade Union Congress Souvenir* (Swansea, 1901), pp. 101–9, p. 104.
[151] Awbery, *Labour's Early Struggles in Swansea*, p. 43. Hollett was originally from Plymouth, and is recorded on the 1891 Census as George Howlett at 5, Baptist Well Street (occupation, fuel shipper).
[152] Awbery, *Labour's Early Struggles in Swansea*, p. 40; *Swansea and District Workers' Journal*, September 1899; *Swansea Trade Union Congress Souvenir*, pp. 139–40.
[153] *Justice*, 25 November 1893.

or two in 1893.[154] An outsider from the start, his elevated social position put him beyond the reach of victimisation,[155] and also enabled him to give financial support to the Swansea branch.[156] His prominence, however, underlines the extent to which the Swansea SDF, notwithstanding the contributions of Mainwaring and Morris, was driven by individuals who, although they may have been domiciled in Swansea, were essentially outsiders.[157] By the summer of 1894, the relatively shallow roots of SDF-ism in the south-west were exposed, and the local branches collapsed. H.W. Lee, the Federation's secretary, expressed regret in August 1894 at 'the unsuccessful attempt to spread Socialism in Wales'.[158] The work of Mainwaring, Cleeves and the others, was nevertheless not without significance. It marked a distinct phase in the history of socialism in the region. As Stan Awbery later observed, its protagonists were 'teaching each other. They were feeling their way, and seeking in their discussions the direction in which they should advance.'[159]

Neither was the collapse of the south-western branches in 1894 the end of the SDF in Wales. In 1896 the Federation appeared in the newest of all the south Walian coastal

---

[154] Griff Jones, Glamorgan Archive D/D AW H14/4, refers to him as a colliery owner and coal exporter. He does not seem to appear on the 1891 Census at all, but is recorded on the 1901 Census, along with his wife from Neath, three young children, two Welsh domestic servants and a French governess at 'Chez Nous', Gower Road, Cockett. His occupation is given as Colliery Agent (Employer). The only members of the household recorded as Welsh speakers are the two domestic servants. If Cleeves's house name is anything to go on, his awareness of Welsh sensibilities was probably limited.

[155] It also enabled him to protect other socialists. A few years later, Paul Cocks, a member of the Swansea Socialist Society at the turn of the century and representative of the shop assistants on Swansea Trades Council, was employed by Cleeves. Griff Jones, Glamorgan Archive D/D AW H14/4, states, 'How he [Cocks] must have enjoyed "thumbing-his-nose" in the faces of the impotent shop-keepers, who were powerless to injure him. And no doubt his employer Mr E.A. Cleeves must have enjoyed the unique situation, just as keenly, for he was not without a sense of humour.'

[156] *Justice*, 4 July 1896.

[157] Even Mainwaring's attitude towards the locality may have been less than homely. William Mainwaring states that his return to Wales 'was nothing less ... than a species of self-inflicted exile' and that 'he himself regarded these years as a sort of banishment'. He returned to London in 1896, *Freedom*, February 1927.

[158] *Western Mail*, 6 August 1894.

[159] Awbery, *Labour's Early Struggles in Swansea*, p. 52.

towns, Barry.[160] The branch owed its initial existence to Sam McCorde, who had migrated to Wales from London twelve months previously.[161] He was joined by another new arrival in Wales, Cornishman John Spargo, who had moved to Barry in 1895, at the age of 19, after spending his teenage years working in the tin mines and quarries of his native county. On his arrival in Barry he found work as a stone cutter and threw himself into socialist activism, soon taking a place on the SDF's Executive Council.[162] Another key member was the branch secretary, Matthew Sheppard. Sheppard seems to be the only prominent member of the Barry SDF to have been born in Wales, at Undy, Monmouthshire, in 1868, although – following a pattern already observed in other Welsh activists – he had travelled abroad before returning to the country. Moving to Cardiff at the age of 11, he worked for a spell in a market garden, until moving to America and working as a printer in the mid-1880s. In 1887 he returned to Cardiff, and then moved to Barry, where he worked as a railwayman. *Justice* described him as 'an uncompromising Socialist of the Marxian School', and like Spargo he was active within the SDF at a national level.[163] The likes of McCorde, Spargo and Sheppard represented something of a socialist vanguard in Barry. 'Whatever may be said of Socialism or Socialistic organisation', commented the *Barry Herald* in May 1896, 'it would be difficult to find a more determined go-ahead set of fellows than those who comprise the local branch of the Social Democratic Federation'.[164]

The branch sustained a vigorous level of activity in Barry for several years. It held a weekly economics class at rooms in the Universal Restaurant, led by the local activists, among whom, it was reported, 'there is no dearth of speakers'.[165] The talents

[160] *Justice*, 25 January 1896 claims a branch of 30 members at Barry, and *Justice*, 6 June 1896 reports a 'financial membership' of 40.
[161] *Justice*, 6 June 1896. McCorde seems to have been involved in the socialist movement in London. He gave 'some interesting reminiscences of the early days of the movement in London' to the branch in October 1896, *Barry Herald*, 23 October 1896.
[162] Kenneth Hilton, 'John Spargo, the Social Democratic Federation and the 1898 South Wales Coal Strike', *Welsh History Review*, 16/4 (1993), 542–50.
[163] *Justice*, 4 July 1896; *Barry Herald*, 19 June 1896.
[164] *Barry Herald*, 29 May 1896.
[165] *Justice*, 25 January 1896.

of such aspirant orators were regularly exercised throughout 1896 and 1897 at open air meetings outside the Free Library at Barry Dock and outside Barry gasworks.[166] Local trade unionists were a particular target for propaganda, and the branch enjoyed close links with the unions. Sheppard served as both treasurer and secretary of the Barry branch of the Amalgamated Railway Servants, and both he and Spargo held the presidency of Barry Trades Council at various times in the 1890s.[167] It was amongst the navvies, however – thousands of whom were at work on dock building projects in Barry in the 1880s and 1890s – that most efforts were made to extend socialism to the local working class. McCord addressed meetings under the banner of the Navvies' Union at Barry Dock in January 1896,[168] and Sheppard lectured to its members on 'The Historical Basis of Socialism' the following month.[169]

The Barry SDF also acted as a contact point for representatives of the wider socialist movement. Foremost among these was the SDF's political secretary, Joseph Chatterton, who was a frequent visitor to south Wales in this period. Chatterton addressed meetings, along with another London activist, W.G. Pearson, on several occasions in 1896,[170] and returned alone for two weeks the following summer.[171] James MacDonald, secretary of the London Trades Council, also visited in 1896.[172] Visitors were not restricted to SDF representatives, and included ILP members such as Enid Stacy and Tom Taylor,[173] as well as Joseph Hyder of the Land Nationalisation League, who illustrated his lecture with the use of oxy-hydrogen limelight apparatus.[174] An even more exotic visitor was the refugee Russian revolutionist, R. Rosetti, who spoke three times in June 1897 to 'good audiences' at Barry and Cadoxton on 'Socialism: Past, Present, and Future'. Most spectacular, though, was his lecture 'How

[166] *Justice*, 10 July 1897.
[167] *Justice*, 4 July 1896.
[168] *Justice*, 25 January 1896.
[169] *Justice*, 29 February 1896.
[170] *Barry Herald*, 29 May and 28 August 1896; *Justice*, 14 November 1896.
[171] *Justice*, 7 August 1897.
[172] *Barry Herald*, 6 November 1896; *Justice*, 14 November 1896.
[173] *Barry Herald*, 11 September and 11 December 1896.
[174] *Barry Herald*, 1 January 1897.

I Escaped Death and Siberia', which attracted an audience of between 1,500 and 2,000 and yielded a 23 shilling collection.[175]

Rosetti's lecture was part of an ideological and informational interchange between Barry and the outer world; it was also an expression of a growing socialist culture, which was becoming a common and defining aspect of the 1890s socialist movement. John Spargo made efforts to enhance the possibilities for a culture of comradeship in the summer of 1897 by working to establish a 'club' at York House in Wyndham Street. 'For a long time we have felt the need of such an institution', he wrote, 'where members can meet each other more frequently than at present, and enjoy themselves in the fashion of comrades. We have secured fine premises in a central position, and intend having a reference library of books on social, political and general subjects; a reading room, branch room, lecture hall, &c..' This, he claimed, would be 'the first Socialist club in Wales'.[176] Spargo appealed through the columns of *Justice* for help in gathering resources for the club, and received donations from nearby Newport, and far-off Blackburn and Manchester.[177] Chatterton was impressed, and reported the hope that the club rooms would 'become a good centre for Socialist propaganda in the district'. He also enjoyed the branch's social and cultural activities, which included frequent parties and musical recitations. 'The members of Barry SDF possess a capacity for enjoyment in a marked degree', he remarked approvingly.[178]

It is through a consideration of these cultural activities that the branch's relationship with Welshness might be assessed. Evidence is sparse, but suggests that the branch had only tenuous links with Welsh culture. Its musical culture drew on the established canon of the British socialist movement. James MacDonald's Cardiff meeting in October 1896 was preceded, for example, by the singing of 'England Arise'.

---

[175] *Justice*, 10 July 1897.
[176] *Justice*, 3 July, 1897. The club had seating for 150 people, *Justice*, 28 August 1897. and the rent was £50 per annum, *Justice*, 7 August 1897.
[177] *Justice*, 28 August 1897. The donation from Manchester came from R.J. Derfel.
[178] *Justice*, 7 August 1897.

His meeting at Barry Dock (which opened with the singing of William Morris's 'No Master' and included a piano recital) saw his audience sing Harry Salt's 'Hark the Battle Cry is Ringing' to the tune of 'Men of Harlech' – a song, as already seen, favoured by the Cardiff Fabians.[179] While this should not be read as any sort of locally initiated concession to Welshness – it was the standard arrangement used by socialists for this anthem – it does present an example of cultural blending going on within the wider socialist movement. Otherwise the branch largely accepted the standard culture of British socialism. The work of William Morris was prominent in the tastes of its members. When Morris died in October 1896 a William Morris Memorial Night was held, which included performances of Morris's works set to piano accompaniment,[180] and the author of Morris's eulogy in the *Barry Herald* claimed to have been humming Morris's 'All For The Cause' when he heard the news of its composer's death.[181] When not drawing upon the culture supplied by the British socialist movement, Barry SDF-ers tended to borrow from existing British popular culture. Their New Year's meeting in 1896/7, for example, opened with Kelso Carter's 'The Hope of the Ages' and closed with 'Good Night', and there is no evidence of any specifically Welsh cultural content.[182]

The Barry SDF's lack of Welsh cultural credentials did not reflect the nature of its locality. Barry may have been a new and cosmopolitan town, but it was host to a vibrant Welsh culture in the 1890s. St David's Day was enthusiastically celebrated and, according to one English observer, was 'in all things ... distinctly Welsh'.[183] The town had an active branch of *Cymru Fydd*, which organised a wide range of social activities,[184] there were columns in Welsh in the local press and there was an ongoing debate about the promotion and

[179] *Justice*, 14 November 1896; *Barry Herald*, 6 November 1896.
[180] *Barry Herald*, 23 October 1896.
[181] *Barry Herald*, 9 October 1896.
[182] *Barry Herald*, 8 January 1897.
[183] *Barry Herald*, 6 March 1896. See also *Barry Herald*, 5 March 1897.
[184] *Barry Herald*, 20 March, 2 October and 20 November 1896.

teaching of Welsh in the town's schools.[185] Advocates of Welsh culture were, moreover, cognisant of Barry's cosmopolitan nature and made efforts to make their activities inclusive of all of Barry's inhabitants – a sentiment symbolised by the opening of the local *Cymru Fydd* St David's dinner to English guests in 1897.[186] The local SDF, though, seemed oblivious to this, and remained largely disconnected from Welsh culture. They had no equivalent of Cardiff's Dr Rhys Jones to provide a link. The closest the Barry SDF could offer was probably the Undy-born Matthew Sheppard. Sheppard did not speak Welsh,[187] but he did sing in Welsh. Chatterton – impressed and tongue-twisted in equal measure – reported one such performance at the SDF club: 'To hear comrade Sheppard sing "Wrhydmlynofdooyd" would have touched a tender spot in a "Patti's" heart, even as it did in Spargo's'.[188]

The relationship of the Barry SDF to Welsh culture may have been tangential rather than integral, but this did not prevent its members from reaching out beyond Barry into the industrial valleys. Indeed, with the encouragement and involvement of Chatterton, the branch made a concerted effort to export social democracy into the south Wales coalfield. The main object of their aspirations was Aberdare, where a small socialist society had been independently established in 1896. Chatterton and Pierson went there shortly after its formation,[189] and Chatterton returned with Matthew Sheppard on a three-day speaking tour in August 1897, which included meetings at Aberaman and Cwmbach. As a result, the Aberdare Socialist Society voted unanimously to affiliate to the SDF, and Chatterton and Sheppard cycled back to Barry satisfied with their success. This was not, however, before Chatterton had experienced the perennial language problem, which he attempted to solve in the usual manner. 'The majority of those present', he wrote of the meeting at Cwmbach, 'understood the Welsh language much better than English, and consequently I had to speak rather slowly

---

[185] *Barry Herald*, 28 February, 10 April and 18 December 1896.
[186] *Barry Herald*, 22 January 1897.
[187] The 1901 Census records his language as English.
[188] *Justice*, 7 August 1897.
[189] *Justice*, 14 November 1896.

and deliberately and adopt an explanatory tone in order to make myself understood.' Although he was satisfied with his success in this respect, Chatterton had begun to grasp the nature of some of the challenges of socialist work in Wales. Conscious of this, perhaps, he advised that 'it would be wise to build up and strengthen the movement a little in both Barry and Aberdare before extending propagandist efforts to districts further afield'.[190]

The Barry activists, however, did not follow his advice, and by the autumn of 1897 they had Pontypridd in their sights.[191] In late September Spargo and another branch member, Buzzo,[192] travelled from Barry to hold a series of meetings there, which resulted in the formation of a new branch.[193] Spargo returned in early October, when he was impressed by the calibre of the new branch, which was arranging to supply *Justice* to the local free library's reading room, and was taken by one of the local activists to address a meeting at Tonypandy.[194] Reports of Spargo's activity in the coalfield in 1897 reveal something of the nature of nascent social democracy in the south Wales coalfield. Some of the members of the branch at Pontypridd were of Welsh origin. The activist who accompanied Spargo to Tonypandy, for example, Comrade Gower, was bilingual and addressed an open air meeting there in English and Welsh, attracting an audience of 200 before Spargo got up to speak.[195] Possibly more representative, though, was the branch's president, Moses Severn. Born in Nottinghamshire in 1850, before moving to Wales in 1888, Severn had lived in Yorkshire, Derbyshire and Nottinghamshire where he had worked in the coal industry, ultimately as a colliery manager. His unexplained move to south Wales involved a return to the coalface, and also precipitated his involvement in socialist politics.[196] His chief contribution to that cause, before serving as president of the

---

[190] *Justice*, 14 August 1897.
[191] *Justice*, 11 September 1897.
[192] Buzzo had migrated to Barry from Southampton, where he had been a member of the ILP, *Justice*, 10 July 1897.
[193] *Justice*, 9 October 1897.
[194] *Justice*, 23 October 1897.
[195] *Justice*, 23 October 1897.
[196] I am grateful to Vicki McKenna and Clare Fuller for information on their

SDF branch, was the publication of an extended pamphlet, *The Miners' Evangel*,[197] in 1895 – a text which must be ascribed importance as one of the earliest pieces of socialist propaganda to be generated within the heart of the south Wales coalfield.

Severn's socialism, as expounded in the *Evangel*, was clearly informed by a Marxist reading of economics, which held that 'Capital always has been, and always will be derived from Labour' and that labour was 'the sole element of wealth'.[198] His Marxism, though, was part of a catholic ideology which drew not just upon Marx, but upon a range of other thinkers, including the Irish political economist Cliffe Leslie, Ferdinand Lassalle, Mazzini, Saint Simon and Ruskin. It was also based upon religious faith, encapsulated in the argument that 'true religion is on the side of Labour'.[199] The *Evangel* is, however, by no means an abstract ideological treatise. Rather, the bulk of the text is concerned not with ideology, but with the practical issues of economics and organisation within the coal industry, and in this respect it represents an effort to apply socialism to the reality of working life in the coalfield. Specifically, it contains an attack on the contemporary method of wage regulation in the south Wales coalfield, the 'mysterious winnowing machine' of the sliding scale.[200] It concludes with comments on the organisation of the miners, which are built upon a Marxist analysis of social change. 'What is called "Organisation of labour" is the problem of the whole future. Organisation of labour is the only key capable of unlocking the doors of the "Golden age" which lies before us,'[201] argued Severn, concluding that the way forward was for the south Wales miners to join the Miners Federation of Great Britain. In attacking the sliding scale and advocating membership of the MFGB, Severn was a few years in advance of the main body of the south Wales miners. Significantly,

great grandfather, Moses Severn. For biographical details, see Vicki McKenna, 'A Miner on a Mission', *Your Family Tree*, September 2010.
[197] Moses Severn, *The Miners' Evangel: A Text Book For All Manual Workers* (Pontypridd, 1895).
[198] Severn, *The Miners' Evangel*, pp. 5, 10.
[199] Severn, *The Miners' Evangel*, pp. 5–18 (p. 17).
[200] Severn, *The Miners' Evangel*, p. 52.
[201] Severn, *The Miners' Evangel*, p. 62.

in terms of union politics, he was also aligned on this issue with the English-speaking William Brace and the more anglicised Monmouthshire miners against Mabon – the personal embodiment of Welshness – and his Cambrian Miners Association.[202] In short, although its contemporary influence was doubtless limited, *The Miners' Evangel* was a harbinger of change within the coalfield. Published between the divisive and indecisive 1893 hauliers' strike and the most definitely more decisive 1898 lockout, its primary significance was in identifying the position of socialism on the anglicising wing of the miners' movement, aligned with the forces that wished to centralise trade unionism on a UK basis. Equally important, and a function of this process, it confirmed English as the primary medium for discussion of socialist ideas in print in the coalfield.

The SDF maintained a foothold in the coalfield up to and beyond the 1898 coal dispute. The branch at Pontypridd remained active through 1897 and into 1898,[203] and Spargo continued to invest his energy in the region. He was active in the 1898 coal strike, and took part in a major public debate in Pontypridd at the end of June on the theme 'Would Socialism Benefit the People?'.[204] The branch at Barry remained a

---

[202] For the dispute between Brace and Mabon over the sliding scale and federation, which resulted in considerable animosity and a lawsuit, see E.W. Evans, *Mabon (William Abraham 1842–1922): A Study in Trade Union Leadership* (Cardiff, 1959), pp. 47–63; E.W. Evans, *The Miners of South Wales* (Cardiff, 1961), chapters 10 and 11; E.W. Evans and John Saville, 'Abraham, William (Mabon)', in Joyce M. Bellamy and John Saville (eds), *Dictionary of Labour Biography* (London, 1972), vol. 1, pp. 1–4; R. Page Arnot, Joyce Bellamy and John Saville, 'Brace, William', *Dictionary of Labour Biography*, vol. 1, pp. 51–3; Robin Page Arnot, *South Wales Miners: A History of the South Wales Miners Federation, 1898–1914* (London, 1967), pp. 30–1. For a contemporary analysis of the division within miners' trade unionism perceived as a clash of Welsh and English influences, see the report by T. Daronwy Isaac on the meeting at Merthyr in *Tarian y Gweithiwr*, 3 August 1893.

[203] *Justice*, 4 and 18 December 1897, 1 January 1898.

[204] For further discussion of Spargo and the SDF attitude to the 1898 strike, see below pp. 107–11. For the debate at Pontypridd, see *Justice*, 23 and 30 July 1898. The title of the debate is of interest, as it took for its model debates between Hyndman and Charles Bradlaugh, and Ernest Belfort Bax and Bradlaugh in 1884 and 1887 respectively (*Will Socialism Benefit the English People: Verbatim Report of a Debate Between H.M. Hyndman and Charles Bradlaugh Held at St. James' Hall, April 17 1884* (London, 1884); *Will Socialism Benefit the English People: A Written Debate Between E. Belfort Bax and Charles Bradlaugh* (London, 1887)). In the case of the debate between Spargo and W.H. Davies, the word 'English' was quietly dropped, doubtless in deference to the

going concern,[205] and there seemed to be signs of SDF growth within the coalfield, branches being reported at Ynysybwl,[206] Porth,[207] Tonyrefail,[208] Abercynon[209] and Mountain Ash[210] up to and beyond the turn of the century. As far as the SDF went, though, this period represented a false dawn. Although the organisation did not thereafter vanish entirely from south Wales, neither did it prosper. The nature of the SDF's problems might be illustrated by going back to where this chapter began – cosmopolitan Cardiff, where it might be thought that prospects for the SDF were comparatively good. Certainly, the town was a target for the Barry activists. Since the dissipation of the Fabian Socialist Society around the middle of the 1890s some attempts had been made to establish an ILP branch in the town, although with only limited success.[211] From 1896 onwards the SDF attempted to muscle in and establish their own version of socialism in the town. Chatterton and Pierson spoke there on their visit in 1896, as did James MacDonald, during whose visit contact was made with SDF members in the town – a Glaswegian, James Colton, a German, Comrade Smith, and two unnamed Russians.[212] Four SDF sympathisers from Cardiff also attended one of Chatterton's meetings at Barry in July 1897, and urged him to help establish a branch in Cardiff. There were, however, difficulties. 'An attempt was made to form an SDF branch at Cardiff last summer', he explained in his report to *Justice*, 'but failed for want of support from the local Socialists ... if there really are any socialists in the town I shall be glad if they will come out of their shells and do some work.'[213]

A branch was eventually formed in Cardiff, in September 1897, and over the autumn meetings were addressed by

fact that the debate was being held in Wales. Interestingly, this marks a departure from the policy of earlier socialist lecturers in south Wales, and arguably reflects the shift in context from the anglicised towns of the coast to the coalfield.

[205] *Justice*, 25 August 1900.
[206] *Justice*, 11 June and 24 September 1898.
[207] *Justice*, 30 July 1898.
[208] *Justice*, 6 August 1898.
[209] *Justice*, 24 September 1898.
[210] *Justice*, 1 June and 20 July 1901.
[211] See below p. 86.
[212] *Justice*, 14 November 1896.
[213] *Justice*, 7 August 1897.

Spargo, Colton and others at St. Mary's Street on Sunday afternoons and The Hayes Market on Sunday evenings.[214] The branch even managed to establish its own bakery for a period in 1898.[215] The problem was, however, that it never succeeded in gaining a full ascendancy in the town. First there was the issue of competition with the ILP. James MacDonald's meeting in 1896 had raised the ire of local ILP-ers, who questioned him and 'seemed to dislike the idea of our forming a branch of the SDF in Cardiff',[216] and the issue was never truly resolved. Ultimately, the form of socialist organisation that represented Cardiff was a generic Cardiff Socialist Society, which refused to align exclusively with any of the established national organisations.[217] In May 1899 its members decided that the best way forward was to affiliate half their number with the SDF and half with the ILP.[218] As the Cardiff Socialist Party it went on to play a small, but lively part in the life of Cardiff into the twentieth century, distributing 'advanced literature' from its Labour Pioneer and Socialist Institute on the balcony of the Castle Arcade,[219] and publishing its own *Labour Pioneer* monthly newspaper. The same pattern was followed in Swansea, where a revival in socialist organisation in 1897 did not result in the establishment of an SDF branch but the non-aligned Swansea Socialist Society.[220] In Aberdare too, despite the enthusiasm for SDF affiliation reported to Spargo in 1896, the cluster of socialist societies in and around the town never seems to have used the SDF title, and indeed by 1902 they had affiliated, in several stages, to the ILP, under the title Aberdare Valley ILP.[221]

This failure of the SDF to survive and replicate on a local level in south Wales is puzzling, particularly when viewed in

---

[214] *Justice*, 25 September 1897.
[215] James Colton was a biscuit baker, but was sacked by his employer for his advocacy of socialism, so the branch established its own cooperative bakery as a response. *Justice*, 24 September and 29 October 1898.
[216] *Justice*, 14 November 1896.
[217] *South Wales Daily News*, 1 March 1899.
[218] ILP National Administrative Council minutes, 6 May 1899.
[219] *Labour Pioneer*, November 1901.
[220] McCarry, 'Labour and Society in Swansea', pp. 235–45.
[221] Glamorgan Record Office, Cardiff, Glamorgan Archive DXHJ2, Aberdare Valley ILP/Aberdare Socialist Society Papers.

the context of the later (but not much later) rise to prominence of Marxism in the south Wales coalfield. In one sense the problem might be seen as part of a wider discussion about the failure of social democracy in Britain, projected in terms of a debate about 'British exceptionalism' or the inherent conservatism of the British working class.[222] If so, the discussion needs relating specifically to the nature of the working class in south Wales. Certainly, some aspects of SDF-ism would have been particularly jarring in Liberal and nonconformist Wales. The inherent Toryism of the SDF leadership may have been one off-putting factor, although there does not seem to be any direct evidence for this.[223] In more general terms, though, the tone and nature of the SDF was clearly irritating to some within the radical wing of politics. One contributor to the *Barry Herald* in 1896 castigated the Barry socialists as 'that conglomeration of noise, cheek, discontent, and nothingness'.[224] There is also evidence that some of the more 'advanced' statements and beliefs of the Federation's members created opprobrium within south Walian society. After one meeting in Pontypridd, for example, the SDF was accused of being in favour of atheism and 'the hideous doctrine of free love', in support of which the accuser could legitimately quote SDF member Ernest Belfort Bax.[225] Despite replies by Chatterton and other socialist sympathisers from within the coalfield,[226] it is likely that the accusations stuck in the minds of many. Such arguments, though, were deployed indiscriminately against socialism in general, and although the SDF may have provided more ammunition than other socialist groups for its opponents in this respect, its failure cannot be explained on this basis alone. Indeed, an understanding of the failure of the SDF to put down firm roots in Welsh soil cannot be restricted to a study of the SDF alone. Ultimately SDF-ism failed to grow in Wales because it was

[222] Ross McKibbin, 'Why Was There No Marxism in Great Britain?', *The Ideologies of Class* (Oxford, 1990), pp. 1–41.
[223] The argument that independent political action would split the progressive vote and allow Tory victories was certainly used, but more against the ILP than the SDF. *Tarian y Gweithiwr*, 6 September 1894 and 19 November 1896.
[224] *Barry Herald*, 18 September 1896.
[225] *Glamorgan Free Press*, 7 and 21 May 1898.
[226] *Glamorgan Free Press*, 14 and 28 May 1898, 9 July 1898.

displaced by a quicker growing and better adapted plant in the form of the ILP, and this represented the advent of a new period in the history of socialism in Wales.

The periodisation of the growth of socialism in Wales is a hazardous business. It is potentially untidy, and must take account of the uneven development of socialist organisation in both territorial and ideological terms.[227] Between them, though, the activities of the Fabians and the SDF in urban south Wales in the 1890s represent a specific phase in the interaction between Wales and modern socialism. Through their activities the members of these societies initiated the development of socialism from an idea brought into Wales by missionaries from afar into a movement that was rooted in Wales itself. It is true, as Edward Foulkes suggested in the quotation that opened this chapter, that this was very largely an urban phenomenon, and that it was initiated to a large extent by incomers, rather than indigenous Welsh people. This is, however, only a partial truth. The growth of socialist societies in the urban centres of south Wales in the 1890s was a more complex process than the simple implantation of a foreign doctrine in Welsh soil. While they acted as a seedbed for the propagation of socialism in Welsh society beyond their urban horizons, the socialist societies of Cardiff, the Swansea and Loughor Valleys and the port of Barry also acted – admittedly in varying degrees – as meeting places between socialism and Welsh culture. The resulting cultural and ideological product was, in the long term, to change the course of Welsh history. In order for it to do this, however, it needed to move beyond the cosmopolitan world of Cardiff and the docks of Barry into the heart of Welsh society. It needed to develop the human capital that the early societies lacked. It needed to become embedded in Welsh communities and to reflect those communities in all of their aspects. This process demanded an even more intense interplay between ideology and practice, between the universal and the local and between Wales and the wider world. The primary medium for this was the

---

[227] Deian Hopkin, 'The Rise of Labour in Wales, 1890–1914', *Llafur*, 6/3 (1994), 120–41, makes a convincing attempt.

Independent Labour Party, which is the focus of the next chapter.

3

SOUTH WALES AND THE ILP ASCENDANCY, 1891–1906

Founded at Bradford in 1893, the Independent Labour Party was qualitatively different to its fellow socialist organisations. As its name implied, the ILP aspired to be a political party rather than a simple socialist society. In addition to 'making socialists', the party aimed to recast British politics to the benefit of the working class. '[W]orking with the grain of British politics',[1] its strategy was to create an alliance with the trade unions – most of whose members were not socialists – to achieve specific political aims. On a national level this resulted in the creation of the Labour Representation Committee in 1900, which in 1906 formally became the Labour Party.[2] Advocates of these organisations claimed that they represented an intrinsically British road to socialism.[3] Their critics argued that the political advance of labourism was inimical to socialism, and urged the creation of a united and explicitly socialist party.[4] This view may have had virtues from a socialist perspective, but the fact that the ILP quickly became the largest of all the British socialist organisations spoke for itself.[5] The party developed stronger and deeper

[1] David Howell, *British Workers and the Independent Labour Party* (Manchester, 1983), p. 5.
[2] Frank Bealey and Henry Pelling, *Labour and Politics, 1900–1906: A History of the Labour Representation Committee* (Oxford, 1958).
[3] J. Ramsay MacDonald, *Socialism and Society* (London, 1905), pp. 134–48; J. Ramsay MacDonald, 'Socialism and the Labour Party', *Socialist Review*, 1/1 (1908), 13–23.
[4] Keith Laybourn, 'The Failure of Socialist Unity in Britain, *c.*1893–1914', *Transactions of the Royal Historical Society*, 6/4 (1994) 153–75; Martin Crick, '"A Call to Arms": The Struggle for Socialist Unity in Britain, 1883–1914', in David James, Tony Jowitt and Keith Laybourn (eds), *The Centennial History of the Independent Labour Party* (Halifax, 1992), pp. 181–204.
[5] In 1901 the ILP claimed a membership of 13,000, as opposed to the SDF's 9,000 and the Fabian Society's 861, Pelling, *Origins of the Labour Party*, Appendix A, p. 229. See also Deian Hopkin, 'The Membership of the Independent Labour Party, 1904–1910: A Spatial and Occupational Analysis', *International Review of Social History*, 20/2 (1975), 175–97; P.A. Watmough, 'The Membership of the Social Democratic

roots in more communities than any of the other socialist groups, and consequently became the primary medium through which the universal ideals of socialism were related to local conditions. This was fundamentally a regional phenomenon: in Wales, up until 1906, the growth of the ILP was almost wholly confined to the south, and the party's subsequent dominance of Welsh socialist politics was built upon its southern ascendancy. This chapter will therefore examine the growth of the ILP in south Wales, focusing on the pre-1906 period. This structural and territorial development occurred alongside the continued ideational spread of socialism across the region, which was a closely related but separate process. The chapter will therefore combine a structural analysis of ILP growth with a more subjective assessment of the communication of socialist ideas. It will examine a crucial, yet neglected period in the implantation of socialism and its adaption to the local circumstances of a region that was to become one of the primary seedbeds of the British labour movement.

(i) The ILP and socialism in south Wales before 1898

The ILP's heartland was northern Britain. It was centred upon the woollen manufacturing districts of Yorkshire's West Riding, extended across the Pennines to Lancashire and included a significant outlying area in central Scotland.[6] By 1896 the party comprised 381 local groups: 222 were in the

Federation, 1885-1902', *Bulletin of the Society for the Study of Labour History*, 34 (1977), 35-40.

[6] Howell, *British Workers and the Independent Labour Party*, pp. 131-73, 174-229; Keith Laybourn and David James, *The Rising Sun of Socialism: The Independent Labour Party in the Textile District of the West Riding of Yorkshire between 1890 and 1914* (Wakefield, 1991); J.A. Jowitt and R.K.S. Taylor (eds), *Bradford, 1890-1914: The Cradle of the Independent Labour Party* (Leeds, 1980); Jack Reynolds and Keith Laybourn, 'The Emergence of the Independent Labour Party in Bradford', *International Review of Social History*, 20/3 (1975), 313-46; Alan McKinlay and R.J. Morris, *The ILP on Clydeside, 1893-1932: From Foundation to Disintegration* (Manchester, 1991); J. Hill, 'Manchester and Salford Politics and the Early Development of the Independent Labour Party', *International Review of Social History*, 26/2 (1981), 171-201; James Robert Moore, 'Progressive Pioneers: Manchester Liberalism, The Independent Labour Party and Local Politics in the 1890s', *Historical Journal*, 44/4 (2001), 989-1013.

north of England (including 118 in Yorkshire alone), and a further 41 in Scotland.[7] The party's geography was reflected in its leadership. Its National Administrative Council was dominated from the outset by northern English and Scottish delegates.[8] Of the four key figures who came to dominate the party in the late 1890s (Keir Hardie, Ramsay MacDonald, John Bruce Glasier and Philip Snowden), three were Scots and one a Yorkshireman.[9] The party's intellectual and cultural roots were nourished by the industrial culture of northern England. Of the 70 local ILP newspapers in Britain in the period before 1906, almost a third (22) were published in the West Riding of Yorkshire, and many of the others were based in Lancashire or Cheshire.[10] The work of their propagandists, such as Robert Blatchford, figurehead of the influential *Clarion* movement,[11] was often explicitly addressed to the inhabitants of the great northern conurbations. Blatchford's emblematic 'hard headed working man', 'John Smith', to whom his hugely influential *Merrie England* was addressed, was an Oldham cotton spinner,[12] and Blatchford referred to the socialist movement as 'the Northern Party of Progress'.[13] The movement's popular culture, which included an array of cycling, singing, nature study, rambling and philanthropic clubs, was a direct outgrowth of northern factory life – a product of the aspiration of those who lived it for a better, cleaner and freer existence.[14] The ILP was the

[7] *Report of the Fourth Annual Conference of the Independent Labour Party* (Glasgow, 1896), p. 10.
[8] Howell, *British Workers and the Independent Labour Party*, p. 296.
[9] Ward, *Red Flag and Union Jack*, pp. 45–51.
[10] Deian Hopkin, 'The Newspapers of the Independent Labour Party, 1893–1906' (unpublished PhD thesis, University of Wales, Aberystwyth, 1981), pp. 44–73.
[11] J. Fincher, 'The Clarion Movement: A Study of a Socialist Attempt to Implement the Co-operative Commonwealth in England, 1891–1914' (unpublished MA thesis, Manchester, 1971); Logie Barrow, 'The Socialism of Robert Blatchford and the Clarion Newspaper, 1889–1918' (unpublished, PhD thesis, London, 1975).
[12] Robert Blatchford, *Merrie England* (London, 1893), p. 3.
[13] Robert Blatchford, 'The New Party in the North', in Andrew Reid (ed.), *The New Party* (London, 1895), pp. 9–25 (p. 12).
[14] A.J. Ainsworth, 'Aspects of Socialism at Branch Level, 1890–1900: Some Notes Towards Analysis', *Bulletin of the North West Labour History Society*, 4 (1977), 6–35; Dennis Pye, 'Fellowship is Life: Bolton Clarion Cycling Club and the Clarion Movement, 1894–1914', *North West Labour History Society Bulletin*, 10 (1984), 20–30; D. Prynn, 'The Clarion Clubs, Rambling and the Holiday Associations in Britain

political expression of this culture, and was created, in the words of one of its members, by 'fusing local elements into one national whole'.[15]

Wales was initially marginal to these developments. Of the 115 delegates at the ILP's inaugural conference there was not one from Wales (Sam Hobson was meant to represent Cardiff, but missed his train),[16] and by 1896 only four of 381 local ILP groups were in Wales.[17] Until the south Wales coal strike of 1898, the main newspaper associated with the ILP, Keir Hardie's *Labour Leader*, gave considerably more column inches to events in distant New South Wales than it did to events in the Wales closer to home. This situation was, however, temporary, and the party's fortunes in Wales changed dramatically in the early twentieth century, as did the role of Wales within the wider British labour movement. This turnaround was the result of socialism outgrowing its roots in the coastal towns and becoming implanted in the communities of the coalfield, and the primary agent of this was the ILP. It is important not to overstress the ease, rapidity or completeness of this process in the period before the Great War. The Liberal Party remained a formidable barrier to the advance of labour and socialism in the region until at least the 1920s.[18] Nevertheless, the influence of the ILP in south Wales was profound. In the ten years prior to 1916 it was estimated that the party organised 20,000 meetings in the coalfield alone.[19] A powerful engine of political progress and education, it was a formative influence upon the key Welsh politicians of the interwar period. Its ascendancy was, however, not imposed upon Wales from outside; it was equally initiated from within. In order to understand how a political party formed in, and driven from, northern Britain

since the 1890s', *Journal of Contemporary History*, 11 (1976), 65–77; Chris Waters, *British Socialists and the Politics of Popular Culture, 1884–1914* (Manchester, 1990).

[15] Joseph Clayton, quoted in Ainsworth, 'Aspects of Socialism at Branch Level', p. 9.

[16] *Independent Labour Party, Report of the First General Conference* (Glasgow, 1893), p. 8; Hobson, *Pilgrim to the Left*, p. 35.

[17] *Independent Labour Party, Report of Fourth Annual Conference*, p. 10.

[18] K.O. Morgan, 'The New Liberalism and the Challenge of Labour: The Welsh Experience, 1885–1929', *Welsh History Review*, 6/3 (1973), 288–312.

[19] 'Observer', 'The Mind of the Miner', *Welsh Outlook*, 1916, p. 218.

could become central to the politics of Wales it is necessary to begin in the early 1890s.

The first stirrings of interest in socialist-inspired independent labour politics in Wales may be traced, not unexpectedly, to the coastal towns of the south. As early as July 1892, six months before the official launch of the national ILP, a group met in Cardiff with the aim of establishing a local branch, and 'decided to commence active propaganda ... of the principles of the party, by means of indoor and outdoor meetings'.[20] It took several more years, however, for the ILP to gain a real foothold in the town. A teetotal ILP club existed in Splott in 1894,[21] although it was not until the following year that a formal branch of the party developed out of the Fabian Socialist Society. Soon after its foundation, it invited Sam Hobson to stand as a parliamentary candidate,[22] and put up Rhys Jones for the local school board.[23] Its secretary, Ben Evans, reported to Thomas Jones in March 1896 that the branch had about 40 members,[24] but it hardly seems to have prospered. It was reported as 'still alive' near the end of 1897,[25] although by February 1898 it had amalgamated with the local SDF.[26] Newport similarly showed early signs of an ILP presence. A branch was established there in 1893,[27] and by October 1895 it had 28 members. Its club and lecture rooms were open every evening, and it organised regular Wednesday evening lectures.[28] By March 1896 its membership had reportedly grown to 40,[29] although its secretary had reported months previously that progress was 'very slow'.[30] In December 1897 the branch was reported

[20] *Western Mail*, 12 July 1892.
[21] *Labour Leader*, 5 May 1894.
[22] *South Wales Daily News*, 10 and 13 April 1895.
[23] *Labour Leader*, 7 December 1895.
[24] National Library of Wales, Thomas Jones C.H. Papers X2, Benjamin Evans to Thomas Jones, 1 March 1896.
[25] *Labour Leader*, 11 December 1897.
[26] *Labour Leader*, 26 February 1898.
[27] *Western Mail*, 13 January 1893.
[28] *Labour Leader*, 19 October 1895.
[29] National Library of Wales, Thomas Jones C.H. Papers X2, Benjamin Evans to Thomas Jones, 1 March 1896.
[30] *Labour Leader*, 18 January 1896.

to be reorganising,[31] and by February 1898 it was claiming to be the largest branch in the district.[32] If the testimony of the SDF's Joseph Chatterton is to be trusted, though, the situation was hardly promising. He reported in 1896 that 'At Newport and Cardiff there are supposed to exist branches of the ILP, but they are doing nothing'.[33]

Chatterton's words may have contained grains of truth, but they were not entirely fair. One thing that the Cardiff ILP-ers had been doing was proselytising in the coalfield, as one of them reported in August 1895:

> On Monday, Bank Holiday, some of our comrades went as missionaries up into the colliery district to try and convert the natives to Socialism, and show them the necessity for I.L. [independent labour] representation. They, the natives, were deeply impressed with the truths they heard, many impressions made will encourage our comrades to pay another visit, armed with a big supply of 'M.E.s' [*Merrie England*s].[34]

On some of these trips they took guest speakers with them. In June 1894 Rhys Jones, Sam Hobson and Ben Evans escorted Fred Brocklehurst on a journey up the Rhondda, during which Jones addressed meetings in Welsh.[35] These expeditions were a portent of what quickly became a flood of socialist speakers in the region. Some were locally based, like John H. Roberts of Preston Cottage, Newport, 'an experienced lecturer' who offered his services in return for third-class rail fare and hospitality,[36] or Edward Robinson, of the Cardiff ILP, who offered a lantern show and lecture, in the making of which he 'spared no expense to make the affair interesting and instructive'.[37] In addition to the local activists some of the big names of the movement visited the region – individuals like Tom Mann[38] and Keir Hardie.

---

[31] *Labour Leader*, 11 December 1897.
[32] *Labour Leader*, 5 February 1898.
[33] *Justice*, 6 June 1896.
[34] *Clarion*, 24 August 1895.
[35] *Labour Leader*, 16 June 1894. Brocklehurst also visited Swansea on this visit, where he worked alongside Sam Mainwaring, *Labour Leader*, 30 June 1894.
[36] *Labour Leader*, 24 August 1895.
[37] *Labour Leader*, 5 February 1898.
[38] Mann was a frequent visitor to south Wales. He spoke at Neath, Morriston and Cardiff in 1894, *Labour Leader*, 7 June 1894, and extended his activities into

Hardie, in particular, attracted attention, as he began to forge a relationship with south Wales that would be central to the rest of his political career. He visited Cardiff and Neath in 1892,[39] and returned to south Wales in 1894, speaking at Cardiff, Swansea and Llanelli.[40] In addition to this, Hardie dramatically drew attention to the plight of the families of the colliers killed in the 1894 Albion Colliery explosion at Cilfynydd by raising the issue in the House of Commons.[41] Hardie's interest in south Wales gave the socialist movement a boost. 'The meetings, through his presence, were larger than the labour meetings generally [had] been hitherto', it was reported in 1892,[42] and local activists were delighted and encouraged. 'When [Hardie] came amongst us there was no actual ILP organisation, although there was a few Labour societies based on ILP principles ... Before this year is much older there will be twenty more', one reported confidently in 1894.[43] In their efforts to stimulate this, national stars like Mann and Hardie were supported by a cast of less prominent personalities, up-and-coming professional socialist agitators such as J.S. Hamilton,[44] Enid Stacy[45] and Tom Taylor.[46] This incursion of speakers represented the most significant level of interaction between Wales and the wider socialist movement thus far.

The society – or, rather, mosaic of societies – into which they were taking their message offered promise and challenge in equal measure. In the 1890s the 'magnetic south'

the coalfield in 1896, speaking at Treharris, Merthyr, Aberdare and Maerdy. At Aberdare he urged south Walians not to 'stand aloof' from the British trade union movement, *Merthyr Express*, 4 and 11 July 1896.

[39] *Western Mail*, 14 and 29 October 1892.

[40] *Western Mail*, 5 and 7 March 1894; *Labour Leader*, 26 May and 23 June 1894.

[41] *Labour Leader*, 30 June 1894; Emrys Hughes (ed.), *Keir Hardie's Speeches and Writings* (Glasgow, 1915), pp. 32–6; William Stewart, *Keir Hardie* (London, 1921), pp. 88–90; Morgan, *Keir Hardie*, pp. 71–3; Benn, *Keir Hardie*, pp. 122–3.

[42] *Western Mail*, 28 October 1892.

[43] *Labour Leader*, 26 May 1894.

[44] Hamilton delivered a series of 'well attended' lectures at Cardiff, Newport, Treharris, Maerdy, Merthyr, Pontypool, Neath and Bury Port in 1896. *Labour Leader*, 5 December 1896.

[45] *Labour Leader*, 12 and 19 March and 7 May 1898.

[46] In 1896 Taylor lectured, among other venues, at Bedlinog, Nelson and Aberdare, supporting his talks with a lantern show entitled 'Darkest England'. His style was that of an evangelical preacher. *Labour Leader*, 9 January 1897.

was in the process of transition from a frontier of 'colonies in the desert'[47] to a vibrant industrial society, with its own regional consciousness and culture. This transformation was driven by astonishing rates of in-migration, which even before the 1890s were beginning to shift the ethnic, cultural and linguistic balance of the region away from its traditional Welsh roots towards the 'American Wales' that Alfred Zimmern was to discern in the 1920s.[48] This process took place at varying speeds and levels of intensity. Some parts of the coalfield – Merthyr, for example – had long-established communities with relatively long traditions of industrial and social organisation, while others – such as Senghenydd – were no more than tiny villages in 1890, but had become substantial industrial settlements by the end of the decade.[49] The regional process of cultural and linguistic change was therefore uneven, and Welsh remained the language of many of the communities – and communities within communities – of the coalfield.[50] What the old and the new, the Welsh and the anglicised, the religious and the secular aspects of this society had in common, and what made it attractive to socialist propagandists, was the huge discrepancy in wealth and power between its masters – coal owners like D.A. Thomas, later Viscount Rhondda and William Lewis, later Lord Merthyr of Senghennydd – and its workers. In short, south Wales hosted a society in which the process of capitalist exploitation was stark and transparent.

It was also a society in which labour was beginning to flex its political muscle, as the workers of the Rhondda demonstrated in 1885, when they elected the miners' leader William

[47] The phrase was used by one of the government's Commissioners of Education in 1847. Thomas Jones C.H., *Rhymney Memories* (Aberystwyth, 1990, first published 1938), pp. 1–29.

[48] Alfred Zimmern, *My Impressions of Wales* (London, 1921); Dai Smith, *Wales! Wales?* (London and Sydney, 1984); Philip N. Jones, 'Some Aspects of Immigration Into the Glamorgan Coalfield Between 1881 and 1911', *Transactions of the Honourable Society of Cymmrodorion*, 1 (1969), 82–98.

[49] Glanmor Williams (ed.), *Merthyr Politics: The Making of a Working Class Tradition* (Cardiff, 1966); Michael Lieven, *Senghennydd: The Universal Pit Village, 1890–1930* (Llandysul, 1994).

[50] Philip N. Jones, 'The Welsh Language in the Valleys of Glamorgan, c.1800–1914', in Geraint H. Jenkins (ed.), *Language and Community in the Nineteenth Century*, pp. 147–80.

Abraham (Mabon) as their MP.[51] Mabon was not sympathetic to the socialism of the 1890s, but some of his constituents were. One of them wrote to the *Western Mail* from Maerdy in January 1893 celebrating the advent of the ILP and predicting that 'Socialism ... in the future – maybe the near future – will sweep everything before it'.[52] The author of this letter was one of a small, but growing minority. By early 1894, stimulated by a visit from Keir Hardie, ILP branch activity was being reported in a range of centres beyond Cardiff and Newport. These included Morriston, Cwmavon, Swansea and Neath in the west, but also the coalfield communities of Abertillery and Pontypridd.[53] By the middle of the decade, though, the greatest concentration of ILP activity in the coalfield was at Treharris, which might legitimately be regarded as the party's birthplace in the south Wales valleys. The 40-strong[54] Treharris branch organised numerous speakers in the mid-1890s. These included James Sexton, leader of the Liverpool Dockers, and Jesse Butler of the Manchester ILP,[55] Hugh Holmes Gore of Bristol,[56] Tom McCarthy[57] and Fred Brocklehurst.[58] One sign of progress was a declaration in October 1895 from the local branch of the Railwaymens' Union in favour of independent labour representation,[59] and by February 1896 the Treharris ILP-ers were contemplating contesting local elections and sending a delegate to the ILP conference at Nottingham.[60]

The most significant feature of the branch's work, however, was the way in which its members methodically exported socialism to the surrounding area. In this way they took the initiative from the Cardiff activists and established a propagandist dynamic internal to the coalfield

---

[51] L.J. Williams, 'The First Welsh "Labour" M.P.: The Rhondda Election of 1885', *Morgannwg*, 6 (1962), 78–94; Williams, *Democratic Rhondda*, pp. 29–37.
[52] *Western Mail*, 19 January 1893.
[53] *Labour Leader*, 26 May 1894.
[54] National Library of Wales, Thomas Jones C.H. Papers X2, Benjamin Evans to Thomas Jones, 1 March 1896.
[55] *Labour Leader*, 14 September 1895.
[56] *Labour Leader*, 30 November 1895; *Merthyr Express*, 23 November 1895.
[57] *Labour Leader*, 7 December 1895; *Merthyr Express*, 7 December 1895.
[58] *Clarion*, 22 February 1896.
[59] *Labour Leader*, 5 October 1895.
[60] *Labour Leader*, 1 and 15 February 1896.

itself. In the summer of 1896, for example, they organised a lecture campaign that took in Cilfynydd, Nelson, Bedlinog, Llanbradach, Pontypridd, Merthyr, Merthyr Vale, Troedyrhiw, Maesycymmer, Mountain Ash and Aberdare, during which 10,000 assorted leaflets and socialist newspapers were distributed.[61] The Treharris ILP was also instrumental in establishing a branch at Merthyr,[62] which in turn organised joint meetings with sympathisers in Dowlais.[63] In this way a rudimentary ILP branch structure began to spread across the coalfield. Although most advanced around Treharris and Merthyr, a similar process was underway in other valleys. A branch was established at Maerdy in 1896,[64] and at Abertillery a rather grandly termed 'conference of Socialists' took place in the home of an ILP sympathiser in March 1898.[65] Thus, as south Wales drifted towards the great conflict of the 1898 coal strike, socialists there began to identify one another and coalesce. By the end of 1897, ILP branches were reported in nine locations: Abertillery, Cardiff, Dowlais, Ebbw Vale, Maerdy, Maesycymmer, Merthyr Tydfil, Newport and Treharris.[66] Some of them were of questionable strength. One activist later observed that 'Many of them were weak, none were really powerful as they are in the North [of England], and some of them had almost shuffled off the mortal coil, after doing what they could against great odds.'[67] They nevertheless represented the public expression of an underlying proliferation of socialist ideas, and promised to justify the statement of the Treharris branch secretary to his local newspaper in 1895 that 'we as Independent Labourites, and as a political party in this country have come to stay'.[68]

The socialists of south Wales also aspired to create an overarching structure for their activities, and an examination of their attempts at organisation reveals the nature of

[61] *Labour Leader*, 15 and 22 August 1896.
[62] *Labour Leader*, 7 December 1895.
[63] *Labour Leader*, 8 January 1898.
[64] *Labour Leader*, 5 December 1896 and 11 December 1897.
[65] *Labour Leader*, 12 March 1898.
[66] *ILP News*, August and December 1897.
[67] *ILP News*, September 1898.
[68] *Merthyr Express*, 14 September 1895.

their regional and national identity. At the end of March 1894 a conference of around twenty delegates assembled at Liberty Hall, the headquarters of the Swansea socialists, with Sam Hobson in the chair. Its aim was the adoption of a constitution and programme for a 'Welsh Independent Labour Party', and it established an Administrative Council, with Hobson as chairman, W.J. Rees of Neath as secretary and E.J. Clarke of Swansea as treasurer. All of the members of the Council, which included Sam Mainwaring, were from either Cardiff, Neath or Swansea, with the exception of Henry Davies, a young man from Cwmavon who was to play an important role in the rise of the ILP and Labour Party in south Wales over the next two decades. The first matter to be discussed was the issue of identity, and the first thing to be agreed was that the name of the organisation should be the 'ILP of South Wales and Monmouthshire', rather than the 'Welsh ILP'.[69] This limiting of territorial ambition was, even at this embryonic stage, of deep significance. It was the first sign that Welsh socialists would not be easily organised along national lines, and it suggested that regional consciousness would be a more important driving force within Welsh socialism than national consciousness. By May the new body had adopted the name of the 'South Wales ILP Federation', and was considering arranging for the production of a partially bilingual edition of the *Labour Leader*, with four pages devoted specifically to south Wales.[70] Ambitions of reaching beyond the heads of the valleys had been abandoned. Indeed, some were more inclined to reach across the Bristol Channel. The Newport branch passed a resolution in October 1896 inviting 'the other Socialist branches in Bristol and South Wales to consider the necessity of a district committee for the purpose of spreading the doctrine of Socialism amongst the workers'.[71] The resulting meeting, at which Bristol, Newport, Cardiff, Treharris and Merthyr ILP, as well as the Newport Fabian Society, were represented, took place on 6 November at Caerphilly. It was decided to form

[69] *Western Mail*, 2 April 1894; *Labour Leader*, 28 April 1894.
[70] *Labour Leader*, 5 May 1894.
[71] *Labour Leader*, 10 October 1896.

a 'federation of such socialist bodies as are in existence in S. Wales and the West of England', which was to be open to 'all bodies ... that advocate the socialisation of capital and industry'.[72] The new organisation, which met through the winter of 1896 at the Anchor Coffee Tavern in Cardiff,[73] was an expression of territorial ambiguity within the nascent Welsh socialist movement.

Its open membership policy also revealed a more general organisational fluidity, which expressed itself in the desire of many rank and file ILP members for a more inclusive organisation that would allow socialists of all persuasions to cooperate within one party. South Wales socialists tended to favour this agitation for 'socialist unity' in the 1890s, and their desire was expressed in their efforts at regional organisation. Early in 1896 the Newport branch unanimously passed a resolution 'favouring the union of the Socialist forces in one grand Socialist party',[74] and the Cardiff branch believed that 'the ILP might with advantage be merged in a National Socialistic Party'.[75] The Treharris ILP favoured the creation of a 'Socialist Political Party' in place of the existing socialist organisations,[76] and maintained a close relationship with the SDF. It received supplies of books from the Salford SDF,[77] and even went so far as to reconstitute itself briefly as an SDF branch in 1898.[78] The inclination for 'socialist unity' was confirmed on Jubilee day 1897, when, at the initiative of the Treharris ILP, 100 south Wales socialists of all persuasions held a rally, enlivened by the singing of 'revolutionary songs', outside Caerphilly Castle.[79] The gathering adopted the title of the 'West Glamorgan Socialist Society', and explicitly resolved to initiate the fusion of SDF and ILP branches in the region.[80] Such simultaneous expressions of socialist unity and regional solidarity were intermittent and confused in

[72] *Labour Leader*, 14 November 1896.
[73] *Labour Leader*, 5 December 1896.
[74] *Labour Leader*, 18 January 1896.
[75] *Clarion*, 25 January 1896.
[76] *Labour Leader*, 1 February 1896.
[77] *Labour Leader*, 15 February 1896.
[78] *Justice*, 10 December 1898.
[79] *Labour Leader*, 3 July 1897.
[80] *Merthyr Express*, 26 June 1897.

the 1890s. The SDF complained about the poor organisation of the Caerphilly meeting,[81] and other attempts at regional federation failed, as their most energetic protagonists either left the region (Hobson and Mainwaring), died (W.J. Rees) or gradually lessened their involvement in the movement (Rhys Jones). Such defections created a deficit of expertise, leading one observer to comment that 'The party suffers from inexperience and distrust of their own abilities'.[82] Despite this, the efforts of south Wales socialists to create a regional structure in the 1890s are significant. They represented a nascent popular movement finding its own form and, from the bottom up, reaching out to a wider movement. As such, they were an integral part of the dialogue between the local and the universal.

They also had the virtue of persistence. In March 1898 south Wales ILP-ers were attempting to reorganise into yet another federation.[83] By this time, though, the political context was changing. Towards the end of 1897 the number of socialist speakers showing an interest in south Wales began to increase significantly. Enid Stacy became a regular visitor.[84] Similarly, Harry Snell of the London Fabian Society, and ILP-er Joe Grady toured in the spring of 1898.[85] More significantly, ILP head office began to develop a more systematic interest in the region. This may partly have been a response to the outbreak of socialist unity evidenced at Caerphilly, or to the activity of the SDF, both of which threatened to undermine the ILP's influence. Whatever the case, the bottom-up socialist activity in the coalfield was being met by top-down interest, opening a new chapter in the dialogue between the local and the national. In early 1898 the NAC of the ILP voted a £5 grant for a tour in south Wales by two of its semi-professional propagandists, Pete Curran and Russell Smart.[86] Smart and Curran covered most of the eastern and central part of the coalfield during their tour, speaking at a range

[81] *Justice*, 10 July 1897.
[82] *ILP News*, March 1898.
[83] *Labour Leader*, 19 March 1898.
[84] *Merthyr Express*, 19 March 1898; *Labour Leader*, 22 January 1898, 12 and 19 March 1898.
[85] *Merthyr Express*, 7 and 21 May 1898; *Labour Leader*, 19 March 1898.
[86] ILP NAC Minute Books. Organising Committee, 8 January 1898.

of centres, including Newport, Cardiff, Dowlais, Treharris, Merthyr, Maerdy, Abertillery and Maesycymmer. Articulating the ILP message to the immediate and local concerns of their audiences, Curran addressed the issue of mining royalties, arguing to an audience at Treharris 'that the only way for the miner to get a living was through Socialism'.[87] On another evening he covered 'Trades Unionism and its Relationship to Socialism'.[88] Russell Smart, on the other hand, lectured specifically on 'The History of the ILP'.[89] Thus the ILP moved to cement its presence in the coalfield.

In early 1898 it was unclear which socialist party, if any, would ultimately gain ascendancy in south Wales. In any case, the establishment of formal groups was only one expression of the spread of socialism through the south Wales valleys. Equally important was the gradual infiltration of socialist ideas into the intellectual life of the region, which was stimulated by the reading and discussion of socialist publications – an activity that took place largely outside the public sphere. The most important element in the construction of this intellectual base was Robert Blatchford's *Clarion* newspaper, and his propaganda masterpiece *Merrie England*. On the face of things, the prospects for Blatchford's paper in Wales were not wholly favourable. Although Blatchford had visited Wales in the 1870s,[90] his staff's knowledge of the country was limited. Nor was the paper's celebrated frivolity calculated to appeal to Welsh nonconformist sensibilities. In 1893 a *Clarion* reporter visited south Wales to investigate the hauliers' dispute in the coal industry. He took with him a certain amount of prejudice. 'I have always been told ... that the Welsh are a suspicious people', he informed readers. Failing to find the 'coal war' that he had been promised, he went to the Gordon Coffee Tavern in Cardiff, where he interviewed Cochfarf, who informed him that the Welsh were, in fact, a 'quiet, industrious and religious people'.[91] One stereotype had been exchanged for another.

[87] *Labour Leader*, 5 February 1898.
[88] *Merthyr Express*, 5 February 1898.
[89] *Labour Leader*, 26 February 1898.
[90] Blatchford, *My Eighty Years*, pp. 154–60.
[91] *Clarion*, 26 August 1893.

Despite the *Clarion*'s apparent unfamiliarity with Wales, however, there were some senses in which its socialism was closer to Welsh nonconformist sensibilities than might be supposed. Until Blatchford's conversion to atheism in 1903, his emphasis on the classless, altruistic 'religion of socialism' did not directly challenge dominant nonconformist notions of morality or community. Rather, it subverted them. In any case, the extent to which south Wales exhibited a wholly monolithic nonconformist hegemony can be overplayed, and the fun-loving tone of the *Clarion* spoke very effectively to the new 'American Wales' of the south Wales valleys. Indeed, the popularity of the *Clarion* might even be seen as one of the elements in its creation. During the late 1890s and early 1900s the *Clarion* began to displace the more traditional radical Welsh newspapers, such as *Baner ac Amserau Cymru* and *Tarian Y Gweithiwr* in radical households across south Wales. This happened in the Tredegar home of David Bevan, father of Aneurin Bevan, sometime in the early 1900s.[92] Bevan's household may have become one of the most famous to take the paper, but it was representative of a radical and socialist culture that had begun to emerge in south Wales in the 1890s. Griff Jones of the Swansea Socialist Society became a *Clarion* reader late in the decade, and felt that 'a weekend without the *Clarion* was unthinkable'.[93] At Treherbert in 1898, a socialist agitator met William Morgan, '[a] *Clarion* reader for four years, and a fine intelligent chap'.[94] If there was one thing common to the experience of socialists who came into the movement from the 1890s until the Great War it was their *Clarion* readership.

What attracted many of them to Blatchford's paper in the first place was *Merrie England*. The most widely read book on socialism published in Britain in the 1890s, it presented socialism in a simple and convincing manner, as Ramsay MacDonald put it, 'like a man fully explaining a motor car

---

[92] Michael Foot, *Aneurin Bevan* (London, 1975), p. 15.

[93] Glamorgan Archive, D/D AW H14/4, Griff Jones, 'Script of Swansea Socialist Party and Labour Party'.

[94] ILP NAC Minutes, Willie Wright's Report from South Wales, 16 July–6 August 1898.

by describing a wheelbarrow'.[95] Its popularity acted as a unifying force across the British socialist movement: when south Wales socialists used it for self-education and propaganda they were sharing the same experience as socialists elsewhere in Britain. By 1895 it was available in mainstream shops in Cardiff.[96] It was not through shops, however, that *Merrie England* was chiefly distributed; it was through the direct efforts of socialists themselves, as reported by Ben Evans in 1894:

> *Merrie England* is being distributed over the whole of Glamorganshire by a member of our *Merrie England* class, who is getting rid of them at the rate of 40 a day throughout the colliery districts of South Wales. Last week he was asked by a detective whether he was the person that was selling 'Anarchist literature', to which he replied yes, and sold one to the detective.[97]

At Treharris, it was reported, '*Merrie England* is a byword',[98] and Oliver Jenkins, the branch secretary, claimed in 1897 that he had distributed over 1,000 copies single-handedly.[99] *Merrie England* classes allowed the book to be discussed, analysed and interrogated, and helped to turn those attending into more effective propagandists. The Cardiff branch ran them at the Victoria Coffee Tavern in Queen Street in 1894,[100] whereas the Treharris branch's Sunday class in 1896 rotated around members' houses.[101] The classes took the reading of the text from the private into the public sphere, and ensured it both a circulation and a social role. They also offered a challenge to the culture of the Sunday school and the chapel.

The *Merrie England* classes were not as directly challenging as the other main agent in the spread of socialism that hit the south Wales coalfield in 1897: the *Clarion* van. Launched in 1896, the *Clarion* van campaign involved a fleet

---

[95] Laurence Thompson, *Robert Blatchford, Portrait of an Englishman* (London, 1955), p. 96.
[96] *Clarion*, 2 March 1895.
[97] *Clarion*, 1 December 1894.
[98] *Labour Leader*, 9 November 1895.
[99] Francis Johnson Correspondence, 1897/55, Oliver Jenkins to Tom Mann, 18 August 1897.
[100] *Clarion*, 1 December 1894.
[101] *Labour Leader*, 1 and 15 February 1896.

of horse-drawn caravans, staffed by full-time volunteer propagandists and packed with socialist literature, touring Britain, taking the socialist message beyond the cities into the countryside and industrial villages.[102] The van that toured Wales in the summer of 1897 was the second of the *Clarion* vans to be built, the 'Caroline Martyn Memorial Van'. A description of it parked at Merthyr was published in the local press:

> The *Clarion* Van is a veritable home on wheels, and is neatly fitted up with sleeping bunks, side benches, with lockers underneath for literature and clothes, a marvellous sliding table which draws out and vanishes mysteriously when it is no longer required, while a cooking stove and patent wash stand, in addition to a food cupboard and clothes press, complete the indispensable furniture. When the Vanners are numerous or the ground permits, a tent is pitched for use as a sleeping place of the men, the van itself being appropriated for the ladies' use ... A feature of the van tour is the amount of free literature which is distributed in all places through which the van passes while actually en route.[103]

During August and early September 1897 the van toured the south Wales valleys, and either passed through, or dispatched propagandists on foot, to Newport, Pontypool, Abertillery, Llanhilleth, Aberbeeg, Blaina, Ebbw Vale, Aberdare, Rhymney, Pontlottyn, Merthyr, Dowlais, Pontmorlais, Troedyrhiw, Merthyr Vale, Treharris, Abercynon, Mountain Ash, Maerdy and Pontypridd.[104] This was the most extensive and sustained series of socialist meetings to take place in Wales before the coal strike of 1898, and the van's progress, as recorded in the pages of the *Clarion*, gives an invaluable insight into the trials and tribulations of socialist propaganda in the south Wales valleys in this period.

One of the most fundamental problems faced by the vanners was the physical geography of the region. A plan to take the van into Nant-y-Glo in early August was thwarted by a combination of steep, rough roads and heavy rain,[105] and later in the month, after a classic Welsh summer had set in, meetings were frequently broken up by rain and 'discussions

---

[102] Judith Fincher, 'The Clarion Movement', pp. 161–4.
[103] *Merthyr Express*, 28 August 1897.
[104] *Clarion*, 7 August–18 September 1897.
[105] *Clarion*, 28 August 1897.

carried on under umbrellas'.[106] Human agency also intervened to undermine progress. A plan to take the van by train to Abergavenny (because it was stranded in Merthyr and could not be taken out by road) collapsed because the rail company could not find a suitable carriage and then kept the van for three days. To make matters worse, the vanners, having made their own way to Abergavenny, were refused permission to hold meetings there.[107] The van also had to compete with other users of public space. At Bedlinog, a meeting could not be organised because temperance campaigners had already taken possession of the village's meeting place, and at Pontypridd the vanners had to compete with the Salvation Army for the town's square.[108] Despite these problems, the tour was considered a great success. Literature sales had been impressive. At Newport alone, where a handbarrow full of *Merrie England*s had been wheeled around the streets, over a thousand copies had been sold in four days.[109] Socialist literature was sold and delivered door-to-door throughout the valleys. Local socialists had been invigorated and inspired by the vanners, and ILP branch membership increased. In Newport the church organist planned to start a *Clarion* choir, and *Clarion* cycling clubs were planned for Newport and Treharris.[110]

It might be tempting to see the *Clarion* van campaign – and the general influx into the coalfield of other *Clarion* and ILP-related propaganda – as a foreign import, an anglicising influence working to draw the communities of the region into a homogeneous British socialist culture, in which the language and culture of Wales had little place. Evidence for such an interpretation is readily available. The composition of the *Clarion* van's staff was overwhelmingly pan-British in terms of nationality, with a bias towards the Anglo-Scottish tendency of the socialist movement. Members included Fenton and Mary Macpherson from Scotland, George Belt of Hull, a Mr Brabham of Bristol, the Irish-born Jim Connell

---

[106] *Clarion*, 4 September 1897.
[107] *Clarion*, 11 September 1897.
[108] *Clarion*, 11 and 18 September 1897.
[109] *Clarion*, 14 August 1897.
[110] *Clarion*, 4 and 11 September 1897.

(author of the socialist anthem, 'The Red Flag'), Bert Alpass from Gloucestershire and Amy Harrison and Isabel Tiplady from England. Their tour represented a territorial incursion to which many within the Welsh establishment were hostile. To the miners' leader, T. Daronwy Isaac, the socialists were 'like travelling gypsies, [who] travelled Wales in their vans [and] were the greatest frauds that ever ascended a platform'.[111] The reality is, however, more complex. In fact, the propaganda of the *Clarion*, and the 1897 van tour, represented the most thorough interaction that had yet occurred between socialism and Welsh culture. It was part of a wider dialogue across the linguistic divide which was taking place with a growing intensity by the late 1890s.

The *Clarion* van tour was, in fact, instigated by a Welshman, the Revd. Richard Roberts, who had drawn the attention of the van organisers to the fact that the National Eisteddfod was taking place in Newport in the first week of August, and insisted that the van should go there and capitalise on the opportunity to make contact with 'All Wales'.[112] There was, therefore, an element of sensitivity towards Welsh culture inherent in the arrangements. The London-based Roberts, who had attempted to initiate a debate on socialism within the *Cymru Fydd* movement in the late 1880s,[113] travelled with the van, and during the tour he addressed audiences of colliers in Welsh 'to their great satisfaction'. Two other Welshmen also joined the party, Thomas Jones of Rhymney and the Revd. Jenkyn Owen, secretary of the Aberystwyth University Fabian Society, who also addressed numerous meetings in Welsh.[114] If the van's members were pan-British in composition, then, Wales – with its language included - was represented as part of the mix. Neither was the presence of touring propaganda vans unfamiliar in Welsh towns and villages. In 1891, the first van 'crusade' of the Welsh land reformer Evan Pan Jones had involved very similar vans following almost exactly the same itinerary.[115] When the Rhymney correspondent for

---

[111] *Llais Llafur*, 19 August 1899.
[112] *Clarion*, 7 August 1897.
[113] Richard Roberts, 'Wales and Socialism', *Cymru Fydd*, January 1889, 35–9.
[114] *Clarion*, 28 August, 11 and 18 September 1897.
[115] Evan Pan Jones, *Oes Gofion*, pp. 189–90. Pan Jones's tour was more extensive,

Tarian y Gweithiwr saw the *Clarion* van pull up in 1897, he was so surprised not to see Pan Jones himself get out that he committed some lines to verse:

> *Dyma'r nef yn dod i Rymni*
> *Wrth cwt ceffyl yn y Van*
> *Dyma ddynion a menywod*
> *Ond pa le mae Dr Pan?*[116]

The *Clarion* was following in the wheel-tracks of Welsh radicalism.

Neither should the *Clarion* van be considered apart from the more general infiltration of socialist ideas that was beginning to take place across the language barrier in the coalfield. The most prolific Welsh-medium writer on socialism in this period was the Manchester-based R.J. Derfel, who had published an extensive series of letters in *Y Cymro* and *Cwrs y Byd* in the early 1890s.[117] It is difficult to ascertain how widely Derfel's letters were read in the coalfield, but *Cwrs y Byd*'s editor noted in June 1895 that the letters had received nothing but praise from readers.[118] That some of these readers were based in the coalfield, and that Derfel's letters were creating socialist converts, is suggested by a letter from 'Hen Lowr' (an old collier) in the following issue. Until reading Derfel's exposition, he reported, he had been opposed to socialism and even spoken against it at his local debating society, but having now considered the matter fully he realised that his previous opposition was based upon a misunderstanding of what socialism was, and he had become an enthusiastic advocate.[119] In 1896, moreover, a translation of Blatchford's *Merrie England* was published in the Aberdare-based *Tarian y Gweithiwr*, which had a circulation of 15,000 across the coalfield.[120] The translation was the

and his van went on to tour the anthracite region of the coalfield and then went north into rural Wales.

[116] *Tarian y Gweithiwr*, 26 August 1897 ('Here is heaven coming to Rhymney, On the tail of a horse in the van, Here are men and women, But where is Dr. Pan?').

[117] For discussion of Derfel see below pp. 189–201.

[118] *Cwrs y Byd*, June 1895.

[119] *Cwrs y Byd*, July 1895.

[120] *Tarian y Gweithiwr*, 9 January–3 December 1896; for circulation, see Aled Jones, *Press, Politics and Society: A History of Journalism in Wales* (Cardiff, 1993), p. 96.

work of a Congregational minister, D.D. Walters (Gwallter Ddu). The son of a colliery manager from Sketty, Walters had been pastor to two chapels near Pontardawe in the 1880s, although in 1890 – when in his late 20s and in the process of becoming 'a powerful Welsh preacher' – he moved to Cardiganshire.[121] At the time he translated *Merrie England*, Walters was just stepping into public life, as a popular speaker 'full of wit and humour',[122] and for the next three decades he devoted his talent to the promotion of socialism, both on the platform and in print. His work in translating and emulating Blatchford in the 1890s[123] was one of the first signs of the emergence of a new and distinct group of young Welsh ministers and professionals who were to make a determined and conscious attempt to integrate socialism into Welsh culture. Walters gave Blatchford's work a Welsh twist. Although largely faithful to Blatchford's original in terms of content and structure, Walters's *Cymry Ddedwydd* was not addressed to John Smith of Oldham, but to 'Annwyl Mr. Jones' – John Jones, not a hard-headed cotton spinner 'fond of facts', but a *'Cymro o waed coch cyfan'*.[124]

As with Derfel's letters, it is difficult to evaluate the reception of *Cymru Ddedwydd*. There was little discussion of it in the Welsh press, and a request for its publication as a pamphlet wasn't followed up.[125] On the other hand, there wasn't a negative response, and the idea that the coalfield's Welsh speakers were universally hostile to socialism is not viable. Certainly, there were ardent and prominent critics of socialism. 'Owain Glyndwr' of *Tarian y Gweithiwr* poured forth satirical scorn, painting socialism as an anti-Christian, anti-Welsh, anti-Liberal, wild, impractical tendency that would destroy personal freedom.[126] His outbursts, however, did not go uncontested. Two correspondents responded to his account of '*Y Socialiaid a'u Breuddwydion*' ('The Socialists

[121] *Cardigan and Tivyside Advertiser*, 14 January 1927.
[122] *Cardigan and Tivyside Advertiser*, 8 November 1895.
[123] Walters's article in *Tarian y Gweithiwr*, 21 May 1898, clearly shows Blatchford's influence.
[124] *Tarian y Gweithiwr*, 9 January 1896 ('A Welshman of pure red blood').
[125] *Tarian y Gweithiwr*, 10 December 1896.
[126] *Tarian y Gweithiwr*, 26 August, 16 September, 21 October, 4 November, 18 November and 2 December 1897.

and their Dreams'), and sustained a well-informed attack in the paper's letter column, which quoted scripture in equal measure with socialist theory, and forced Glyndwr's retreat – albeit temporarily – from the fray.[127] Indeed, the attitude of established Welsh radicalism, as represented by *Tarian y Gweithiwr*, towards socialism was complex and nuanced. It was bitterly hostile to both independent labour representation, which it considered divisive, and its principal spokesman, Keir Hardie, whom it considered insolent and lacking in authority.[128] Behind this defensive façade, however, there was another dimension to the paper's attitude. It had, after all, printed translations of socialist work by David Rhys Jones and D.D. Walters, and it was not universally hostile to all socialists. Tom Mann, for example, received favourable treatment in its columns.[129] While it stressed the mutual interests of capital and labour,[130] it also shared some common ground with the socialists in the belief that the 'labour question' – the relationship between labour, capital and the state – was *the* question of the future, and, like them, it foresaw a political realignment which would force oppressors and workers into mutually hostile political camps. What it differed on was the exact composition of those camps.[131] It would be fair to say that Welsh opinion within the coalfield was divided, or perhaps undecided, on socialism, but it would not be accurate to call it hostile.

The most convincing evidence for this is to be found in the launch, in early 1898, of a new bilingual newspaper which was explicitly supportive of both socialism and the ILP. *Llais Llafur – Labour Voice* was the inspired work of Ebenezer Rees of Ystalyfera. Born in 1848, Rees had been brought up in Cwm-twrch and had worked in the coal mines of Aberdare, Mountain Ash and Cwm-twrch. Victimised for trade union activism, Rees emigrated to the United States in 1869, but ultimately returned to south Wales and established himself as

[127] *Tarian y Gweithiwr*, 9 and 30 September, 28 October, 9 and 30 December 1897, 20 January and 16 February 1898.
[128] *Tarian y Gweithiwr*, 6 September 1894, 2 January and 19 November 1896.
[129] *Tarian y Gweithiwr*, 19 October 1893.
[130] *Tarian y Gweithiwr*, 2 September 1897.
[131] *Tarian y Gweithiwr*, 19 January 1893.

a printer.[132] *Llais Llafur* reflected Rees's own personality and interests, which are revealed in a fascinating notebook he kept in the 1870s. Written mainly in Welsh, it contains extensive notes on contemporary Ystalyfera and the local history of south Wales as well as a list of 'Rhai o'r helyntion cyhoeddedig yn y newyddion, 1878' ('Some affairs published in the news, 1878'). These include such diverse matters as famine in China, the selling of livings in the Church of England, the attempt on the life of the German emperor, the banning of women from Carmarthen reading rooms and people being fined in Llandovery for keeping dogs without a licence.[133] In other words, the book reveals a mind which was fascinated by the juxtaposition of the local and the universal, and it was this approach that made *Llais Llafur* so effective. Alongside local news, the results of eisteddfodau, profiles of local personalities and syndicated news from beyond Wales, the *Llais* published a constant flow of articles on socialism in Welsh and English.

In its first year these included a number of articles on the land issue by Evan Pan Jones, which linked the paper's socialism to Welsh radicalism.[134] Similarly, the Revd. D. Bassett (Twrchfab), also writing in Welsh, linked the cause of 'y werin' to the Welsh national awakening.[135] A selection of R.J. Derfel's Welsh letters on socialism was reprinted, along with other writings by Derfel in Welsh and English.[136] An exposition of more explicitly Marxist socialism was provided in Welsh, in the form of a catechism, by John Lewis,[137] whereas the leader writer, 'Carrusk' (Henry Davies of Cwmavon), expounded Marxist ideas on capital through the medium of English, advocating the nationalisation of the mines, and urging Welsh colliers to join the MFGB.[138] In addition to these practical matters, the *Llais* also published

[132] David Cleaver, 'Swansea and District's Labour Press, 1884–1914', *Llafur*, 4/1 (1984), 35–42, 37; Robert Smith, *'In the Direct and Homely Speech of the Workers': Llais Llafur, 1898–1915* (Aberystwyth, 2000), p. 1.
[133] Swansea University Archive, SWCC: MNA/PP/95/1, Ebenezer Rees Papers.
[134] *Llais Llafur*, 22 January, 26 February and 25 June 1898.
[135] *Llais Llafur*, 19 February and 5 March 1898
[136] *Llais Llafur*, 29 January–13 August 1898.
[137] *Llais Llafur*, 9 April and 7 May 1898.
[138] *Llais Llafur*, 14 May, 4 and 25 June 1898.

a translation of Edward Bellamy's *Looking Backwards*.[139] The paper consciously aligned itself with the socialist movement's national papers, sometimes reprinting pieces from the *Clarion*,[140] and stating that it was a *'cyw o'r un hatch'* ('a chicken from the same hatch') as the *Labour Leader*.[141] In fact, it was rather more. It represented the fusion of socialist journalism with local life to a depth that was rare among socialist newspapers, and its success as a business venture (which was exceptional for a socialist paper) reflected this. What was most remarkable about the emergence of *Llais Llafur*, however, was its immediate geographical context. It came from a part of the coalfield where significant ILP activism had not previously been recorded. James Griffiths later wrote of the origins of socialism in the western districts of the coalfield, commenting that it did not burst into life quickly: 'It was more like the fires of Anthracite – slow burning with sustained heat and long lasting as it spread through the valleys'.[142] The appearance – and positive reception – of *Llais Llafur* is compelling evidence that those fires were burning beneath the surface of coalfield society prior to 1898. *Llais Llafur* was the most impressive product of a wider dialogue that was taking place across south Wales in the 1890s. In two languages, in numerous communities and through diverse media, this dialogue was gradually linking the local and the national, the practical and the abstract, the specific and the universal. At the beginning of 1898, when the *Llais* was launched, the process of connection between socialism and south Wales society was incomplete – the dialogue was broken, indistinct and crowded by louder voices. It was, however, very much underway.

(II) THE 1898 COAL STRIKE

If Wales had been slower than some other parts of Britain in the uptake of socialism and the development of independent labour politics before 1898, that was not the case thereafter.

---

[139] *Llais Llafur*, 10 September–3 December 1898.
[140] *Llais Llafur*, 30 April and 14 May 1898.
[141] *Llais Llafur*, 25 June 1898.
[142] National Library of Wales, James Griffiths Papers, D 3/2, Notebooks 2 & 3.

In that year a series of events began to unfold that would both embed socialism into the political culture of south Wales and tie the region firmly to the British labour and socialist movement. The first of these was the coal strike of 1898, which has traditionally been seen as one of the great watersheds in the history of the south Wales coalfield.[143] The dispute – a strike or a lockout, depending upon how it is viewed – lasted from April to September of that year and resulted in crushing defeat for the miners. The colliers did not, however, fail to learn lessons from the experience,[144] and their response – the formation of the South Wales Miners' Federation – signalled 'the start of what would be a profound shift of emphasis' in the life of the region.[145] Part of this shift, as the classic histories of the south Wales miners and later revisionist works are agreed, 'was the introduction of socialist discourse into the coalfield on a scale hitherto unknown'.[146] It has also been observed that the dramatic improvement in socialist fortunes brought about by the strike was not sustained, and within months of the dispute ending socialist activity tailed off as dramatically as it had increased.[147] The socialist advances of 1898, it has been argued, were 'just a bubble',[148] and did not represent a genuine strengthening of socialist organisation in south Wales.

The sum of these conflicting interpretations suggests that the reality was more complex, and that the underlying continuities behind the narrative of socialist involvement in the dispute need to be considered. It has already been argued that the spread of socialism in south Wales during the 1890s had gone further than a mere tally of established socialist societies or ILP branches would suggest. It has also been shown that socialist activity was increasing on the eve of the

---

[143] John Williams, 'The Strike of 1898', in *Was Wales Industrialised?* (Llandysul, 1995), pp. 192–213.
[144] E.W. Evans, *The Miners of South Wales* (Cardiff, 1961), pp. 175–6.
[145] Hywel Francis and David Smith, *The Fed: A History of the South Wales Miners in the Twentieth Century* (London, 1980), p. 1.
[146] Williams, *Democratic Rhondda*, p. 60; also see Robin Page Arnot, *South Wales Miners: A History of the South Wales Miners' Federation, 1898–1914* (London, 1967), pp. 47–9.
[147] Hopkin, 'The Rise of Labour in Wales, 1890–1914', p. 127.
[148] Howell, *British Workers and the Independent Labour Party*, p. 245.

strike. That the strike was incidental to this trend, rather than causative, is suggested by the fact that most socialists were caught unawares by its outbreak. Strikes were not universally welcomed by socialists,[149] and in April 1898 the ambivalence of the ILP towards the coal strike was made clear at its annual conference. A motion (seconded by Pete Curran, who had not long returned from the region) congratulating the colliers on their stand and pledging ILP support was contested by Joseph Clayton (who also had experience of south Wales). Clayton argued that the miners had been misled into the strike, and 'questioned the desirability of congratulating a body of men who were not organised, and had no reasonable chance of success', and it was only after a rebuke from Keir Hardie that the motion was passed.[150] The SDF also expressed ambivalence about the strike, which it feared would divert energy and resources away from its own propaganda work. Joseph Chatterton appealed in *Justice* for financial support – not for the strikers, but for the SDF's work in south Wales. 'There is no hope of any help from the colliers', he complained, 'because ... they are all starving, and this includes a large portion of our own members',[151] and by June, John Spargo was predicting defeat for the miners. The strike, he argued, would be a 'lamentable and catastrophic failure', and he urged that the workers 'learn the lessons of the great failures of the old time methods against the ramifications of modern capitalism, and abandon the antiquated and inadequate weapon of the strike, in favour of the mightier and more easily wielded weapon of political action'.[152]

The socialists may have initially failed to grasp the implications of the dispute, but its long-term significance soon became clear, particularly its role in catalysing the integration of the south Wales miners into the wider British labour movement. In the words of Caroline Benn, 'the strike brought South Wales abruptly into the national labour

[149] John Bruce Glasier, *On Strikes* (Glasgow and Manchester, 1894).
[150] *ILP News*, April 1898.
[151] *Justice*, 7 May 1898.
[152] *Justice*, 11 June 1898.

family'.[153] The most obvious outcome of this was the decision of the new South Wales Miners' Federation to affiliate to the Miners' Federation of Great Britain after the strike. The process of integration, however, operated on different levels during the dispute, and socialists worked as its agents. Their press informed the wider socialist and labour movement of events. John Spargo provided regular, clear and intelligent reports in *Justice*,[154] but it was Keir Hardie's *Labour Leader* that was undoubtedly most effective. A series of impassioned articles by Hardie brought previously neglected Wales into the heart of ILP journalism.[155] The *Leader*'s coverage, which was highly critical of 'the stupidity, faithlessness, and inactivity' of the existing trade union leadership,[156] aimed simultaneously to draw the miners into the wider socialist movement while dividing them from their Lib-Lab trade union leaders. One element of this strategy was the launch in June of an ILP relief fund. Using the emotive issue of the miners' starving children, this successfully appealed to all parts of Britain,[157] and by mid-August almost £150 had been collected (representing meals for over 44,000 children).[158] This created an emotional bond between socialists in other parts of Britain and the coalfield. It also had a direct human dimension: miners' delegates travelled from the coalfield to England to enlist support. Two miners attended the Nottingham Labour Church in June, where they were allowed to make an address on the 'brave men of Wales'.[159] A similar deputation toured Yorkshire and the north of England in July, making emotive

[153] Benn, *Keir Hardie*, p. 142.
[154] Spargo's principal news reports appeared in *Justice*, 9 April 1898, 11 June 1898, 18 June 1898 and 3 September 1898. The dispute also made the front page of *Justice* on 16 April 1898, 30 April 1898 and 23 July 1898. In addition to Spargo's articles, Joseph Chatterton also provided coverage in *Justice*, 7 May and 21 May 1898, as did a miners' agent, 'W.S.', on 23 July 1898.
[155] The principal articles by Hardie were 'Peaceful Fighting Wales' (*Labour Leader*, 2 July 1898), 'Leaderless Wales' (*Labour Leader*, 9 July 1898), 'In Darkest Wales' (*Labour Leader*, 13 August 1898) and 'Maimed and Plundered Wales' (*Labour Leader*, 20 August 1898). Apart from Hardie's contributions, the *Leader* also published regular editorials and contributions from other socialists active in the region.
[156] *Labour Leader*, 28 May 1898.
[157] *Labour Leader*, 25 June 1898.
[158] *Labour Leader*, 13 August 1898.
[159] *Labour Leader*, 2 July 1898.

appeals for help,[160] and two miners visited Walden ILP in mid-August.[161] By August whole choirs were involved: the 31-strong Rhondda Valley Glee Singers performed twice daily for six days at Westminster Royal Aquarium in early August on a tour organised by the London Trades Council,[162] and they were followed later in the month by the Merthyr Male Voice Choir.[163] Such visits proved educational for both sides. The organiser of a visit to London in August commented that the two colliers involved 'had never seen the great town before, and were, of course, astonished at the traffic and display of wealth, and were equally surprised at the poverty of the slums'.[164] The strike was creating a Britain-wide labour consciousness.

The ILP role in this must be placed in perspective. The MFGB voted £1,000 in support early in the dispute, followed by a weekly grant of £500,[165] and substantial sums came in independently from the coalfields. The Nottinghamshire miners voted a grant of £500 in May,[166] and miners in Durham also contributed substantially,[167] as did various trades councils.[168] The ILP contribution was therefore a small part of a wider process. Importantly, however, it was by far the most significant effort made by any of the explicitly socialist organisations. It put the SDF, which failed to raise its own relief fund, to shame. This clearly irritated some members of the Federation. Tom Proctor, an SDF-er from Plymouth, chided the organisation for this, and contrasted its failure in the case of the miners with its willingness to support the engineers in the previous year's lockout. He raised six shillings at a SDF meeting in Plymouth, but in the absence of a relief fund was compelled to send it directly to John Spargo in south Wales

[160] *Labour Leader*, 16 July 1898.
[161] *Labour Leader*, 20 August 1898.
[162] *Lloyd's Weekly Newspaper*, 31 July 1898; *Morning Post*, 2 August 1898.
[163] *Labour Leader*, 20 August 1898.
[164] *Labour Leader*, 13 August 1898.
[165] *Pall Mall Gazette*, 28 April 1898; *Reynold's Newspaper*, 1 May 1898.
[166] *Nottinghamshire Guardian*, 7 May 1898, also see *Nottinghamshire Guardian*, 2 July 1898.
[167] *Morning Post*, 27 June 1898.
[168] The London Trades Council, apart from organising concerts, also collected £150 for the miners' relief in August. *Morning Post*, 17 August 1898.

'for distribution amongst the worst cases he comes across'.[169] A month later no action had been taken, and a member from Sevenoaks suggested, somewhat improbably, that pressure be brought through the Irish party in Parliament to vote £50,000 in relief for the local authorities in south Wales.[170] Still nothing was done at a national level by the SDF, and members had to be content with their contributions going to the ILP fund.[171]

The ILP also managed to marginalise the SDF during the strike through its more organised and far-sighted approach to literature distribution. The printed word was one of the most important tools that socialists used, in their own words, to 'drive home the lessons of the strike'.[172] Local activists repeatedly expressed an urgent need for supplies of socialist literature which was, in the early days of the strike, often frustrated. Hugh Lloyd, of the Maerdy ILP, complained in early June that 'the greatest drawback is the want of literature', and appealed through the *Labour Leader* for comrades in other parts of Britain to send him any spare pamphlets for distribution.[173] The ILP leadership acted decisively in response. By July the *Labour Leader* was supplied free to miners' committee rooms and to 'reliable parties' who would distribute it.[174] Hardie arranged with the *Leader*'s business manager in Glasgow, David Lowe, for copies of the paper to be sent to Dai Davies and Llewelyn Francis, ILP stalwarts in Merthyr and Penydarren, for distribution among members and sympathisers. He also arranged for a hundred copies of the paper to be distributed in each of the seven stoneyards in the Merthyr area, where locked-out miners were provided with work by the local authorities. This may have made propagandist sense, but it also represented a financial burden to a newspaper company that hovered on the point of bankruptcy, and Hardie felt the need to justify the policy to Lowe, arguing that a 'thousand papers don't cost much, and that

---

[169] *Justice*, 26 June 1898.
[170] *Justice*, 23 July 1898.
[171] *Justice*, 13 August 1898.
[172] *ILP News*, June 1898.
[173] *Labour Leader*, 4 June 1898.
[174] *Labour Leader*, 2 July 1898.

number will go a long way here'.[175] Hardie had his eye on the long-term possibilities of providing such a loss-leader, not just in educational but in business terms. He wrote to Llew Francis at the beginning of July with instructions: 'In distributing the *Leaders* that are being sent weekly, give a copy to each member of the Branch, that is to say, to each one who gives his name to join, and when the strike is over, try and get each of them to sign an order to have the paper weekly from their local news-agent.'[176] The SDF did not make a similar investment. Although its members reported distributing 'large numbers of leaflets' at meetings in Porth,[177] they more often reported disappointment at low levels of literature sales. Joseph Chatterton reported, after a series of meetings in May, that 'The sale of literature has only been moderate, but had the colliers been working we could have disposed of almost any amount of reading matter'.[178] The ILP had stolen a march on its Marxist rival.

It was, however, neither finance nor literature distribution that was the deciding factor in enabling the ILP to eclipse the SDF during the strike; it was the imbalance of human capital. The SDF's Spargo and Chatterton, who were energetic and committed propagandists,[179] were no match for the greater resources of the ILP. First and foremost among the numerous ILP speakers who travelled to the region during 1898 was Keir Hardie. Hardie played a critical role in the promotion of socialism, the ILP and himself during the strike. Unlike many in the ILP, he immediately realised its potential, reporting to the National Administrative Council after a visit to the region in April that 'a splendid field for ILP work was being opened up',[180] and during the dispute he combined powerful and sustained journalism with a strong

[175] Francis Johnson Correspondence, 1898/67, Keir Hardie to David Lowe (undated).
[176] Francis Johnson Correspondence, 1898/68, Keir Hardie to Llew Francis, 1 July 1898.
[177] *Justice*, 7 and 21 May 1898.
[178] *Justice*, 21 May 1898.
[179] Spargo's role is outlined in Kenneth Hilton, 'John Spargo, the Social Democratic Federation and the 1898 South Wales Coal Strike', *Welsh History Review*, 16/4 (1993), 542–50.
[180] ILP NAC Minutes, 12 April 1898.

personal presence on the ground. For two weeks in June he tramped an itinerary that included Abertillery, Rhymney, Pontypridd, the Rhondda, Mountain Ash, Treharris, Merthyr Vale, Troedyrhiw and Merthyr.[181] During this visit he addressed up to 15 meetings, which were exceptional in terms of their size and enthusiasm.[182] At Troedyrhiw, where he addressed a meeting of 5,000, the surrounding villages were decorated with bunting and streamers in anticipation of his visit, and five colliery bands led delegations from Plymouth colliery, Merthyr, Dowlais, Treharris and Merthyr Vale to hear him, despite pouring rain.[183] Neither was this an isolated event. Most of the meetings addressed by Hardie in June 1898 attracted audiences of at least 1,000, and even the correspondent from the unsympathetic *Tarian y Gweithiwr* was impressed by his oratory.[184] He returned to the coalfield several times before the strike was over. Early July saw him speaking to the newly formed Abertillery ILP,[185] but the majority of his meetings were in the Merthyr area. At the end of July he addressed a meeting of 6,000 at Dowlais, and his presence at a meeting in a packed Merthyr theatre swelled the membership of the newly reformed ILP branch there to 200.[186] During August he preached 'socialistic sermons' on the 'Cinder Hall' of Penydarren tips to audiences of up to 2,000.[187] Hardie was sowing seeds that would bear fruit for the rest of his political career, and after 1898 his name was increasingly 'mentioned with a respect approaching reverence' in the Merthyr district.[188]

Hardie was supported by a cast of talented deputies. Among them was his Welsh-speaking friend Robert Williams, originally from Llantrisant, who had grown up in Merthyr

[181] *Souvenir of Twentieth Annual Conference*, p. 10.
[182] Stewart, *Keir Hardie*, p. 138; *Labour Leader*, 2 July 1898.
[183] *Labour Leader*, 9 July 1898. *Merthyr Express*, 2 July 1898, supports the attendance figure of 5,000, although the less sympathetic *Tarian y Gweithiwr*, 30 June 1898, reports 4,000.
[184] *Merthyr Express*, 2 July 1898. *Tarian y Gweithiwr*, 30 June 1898, reports an audience of 2,000 at Aberdare.
[185] *Merthyr Express*, 9 July 1898.
[186] ILP NAC Minutes, Willie Wright's Report, 6–20 August 1898.
[187] ILP NAC Minutes, Willie Wright's Report, 25–31 July and 16 July–6 August 1898; *Merthyr Express*, 13 August 1898.
[188] W.J. Edwards, *From the Valley I Came* (London, 1956), p. 36.

SOUTH WALES AND THE ILP ASCENDANCY, 1891-1906   113

before moving to London to follow a career in architecture.[189] Williams acted as a key facilitator in the process of communication between the coalfield and the capital. He organised the tour of the Merthyr choir to London, arranged collections, spoke on behalf of the miners in England and campaigned on the ground in south Wales. He contributed articles to the *Labour Leader*, which appealed to the miners in explicitly Welsh terms, in their own language:

> Mae gweithwyr y cymry wedi llafurio er ys dwy fil o flynyddoedd yn yr ynys hon, mae'nt wedi hau a medi; maent wedi adeiladu fai, cestyll a themlau; mae'nt wedi gneid heolydd a fyrdd dwr; mae'nt wedi tori myrddiynau o dunelli o lo ac wedi troi y mwn yn haiarn yn ddicyfrif; eth, nid ydych chwi, eu hiliogaeth, yn llawer gwell na chaeth-weision.[190]

Yet he placed this nationalistic appeal within an internationalist, labourist framework, stressing the contribution that could be made by the Welsh to the wider labour struggle:

> Then arise, ye Welshmen; stand shoulder to shoulder, an unbroken phalanx! This is your Waterloo. Your Wellington is the God of Righteousness. Stand, then, as one man. Keep cool and determined, remembering always that you are not fighting your own battle only, but that of the world of Labour.[191]

Williams's contribution was extremely valuable to the ILP. As a Welsh-speaking Welshman, albeit an expatriate, he could legitimately make the case that socialism was not a foreign import. He aspired to represent a distinctive Welsh strain of socialism within the wider socialist ideal. There were inherent tensions in his ideological position, as suggested above by the use of what amounts to the language of sedition alongside the imagery of British militarism. His accommodation of a Welsh socialist identity within a British framework was essential, however, to the emerging socialist culture of south Wales.

[189] *Merthyr Express*, 17 September 1898.
[190] *Labour Leader*, 2 July 1898 ('The Welsh workers have laboured for two thousand years on this island, they have sown and reaped; they have built houses, castles and temples; they have made roads and water-ways; they have cut countless tons of coal, and turned an inestimable amount of ore to iron, yet, you, their offspring, are not much better than slaves').
[191] *Labour Leader*, 13 August 1898.

Arguably the most important of the socialist agitators in Wales during the strike made an appeal to the miners not on the basis of their nationality, but on the grounds of a shared occupational and class background. Willie Wright was a coal miner from Mexborough in Yorkshire, who had given up mining to become a full-time socialist agitator.[192] His presence in south Wales was in itself a sign of the growing professionalism of the ILP: he had been appointed by the party's NAC, on the initiative of the South Wales ILP Federation, as a full-time paid organiser just before the start of the strike.[193] Arriving in the region on 16 May, he reported that during the first month of the dispute the ILP had held 50 meetings, recruited 450 new members and established 10 new branches.[194] He immediately began to make his own contribution to the work, and during the following months he addressed up to 20 meetings a week. Initially focussing his efforts on the central part of the coalfield, where the ILP was already partially established, he visited Treharris, Dowlais, Merthyr Vale, Troedyrhiw, Merthyr and Mountain Ash, as well as Newport and Pontypridd in May. In June he expanded his activities, focusing upon the Rhondda, holding meetings in Pontypridd, Porth, Tonypandy, Gelli, Pentre, Maerdy and Ferndale, while continuing to work the Taff and Cynon Valleys.[195] In late June and early July he left Wales to work with the *Clarion* van in northern England,[196] but by 12 July he was back, and remained for most of the summer,

---

[192] It is probable that Wright originally came from Durham. A William Wright, coal miner, aged 29 and born in Durham, is recorded boarding at 20, Hall Gate, Mexborough, in the 1891 Census. By 1897 Wright was living one street away at Hirst Gate, and advertising his services as a socialist lecturer, *Labour Leader*, 24 April 1897.

[193] Wright was paid 25 shillings a week, and employed initially on a six-week contract, ILP NAC Minutes, April 1898. The idea of a nationally employed organiser had been raised as early as 1896, when the Treharris branch urged the appointment of J.W. Wood, *Labour Leader*, 15 and 22 August 1896. The idea was revived at the end of 1897, *Labour Leader*, 11 December 1897, and the decision to push ahead was made at the meeting of the South Wales ILP Federation in March 1898, at which the front runner for appointment seemed to be Joseph Clayton, *Labour Leader*, 19 March 1898. The appointment of Wright and the outbreak of the strike seem to have been entirely coincidental.

[194] *ILP News*, June 1898.

[195] *Labour Leader*, 28 May, 4 and 18 June 1898.

[196] ILP NAC Minutes, Willie Wright's Report, 8–25 June 1898; *Clarion*, 25 June 1898 and 9 July 1898.

propagandising under incessant rain.[197] He devoted most of his time to the central part of the coalfield, especially the Taff, Cynon and Rhondda Valleys, but occasionally visited Cardiff and Newport, and also ventured into the Rhymney Valley. At the end of August he opened a new agitation in the western part of the coalfield, holding a series of meetings in the Swansea Valley, before returning east again in September.[198] He remained in the coalfield for the rest of the year, until he was forced to leave for financial reasons.[199]

An effective organiser, Wright quickly attained a personal following. He was, according to local ILP-ers, 'the (W)right man in the (W)right place'.[200] His status as a former miner gave him credibility, while his oratorical skill created widespread enthusiasm. 'He is received everywhere with open arms', reported a local activist in July. 'The miners are eating every word as it leaves his lips. He has won his way into the hearts of my countrymen.'[201] Neither was his appeal limited to the English-speaking colliers. Ebenezer Rees recognised Wright's primacy among socialist speakers in south Wales:

> Diau y gwyr pawb o honoch am y person hwnw, o'r enw Willie Wright, - un o siaradwyr mwyaf derbyniol y dydd ar gwestiynau Llafur. Efe ydyw cynrychiolydd yr 'Independent Labour Party', yn Neheudir Cymru.[202]

The role played by Wright in the coalfield in 1898 would seem to fit that of the classic 'outside agitator', and confirm socialism as an imported doctrine. Even the sympathetic *Llais* seemed to concede this at times:

> Llawer o son sydd am y gwr enwog Willie Wright yn bresenol. Gwyr pawb ag sydd yn talu rhyw gymaint o sylw i lenyddiaeth y dydd am y cyffroad sydd wedi ei beri yn Nghymoedd Aberdâr a'r Rhondda, trwy ymweliadau y gwr dyeithr hwn, ag eraill, a hwynt.[203]

---

[197] He returned briefly to Mexborough to see his family in August, ILP NAC Minutes, 6–20 August 1898.
[198] ILP NAC Minutes, Willie Wright's Report, 29 August–17 September 1898.
[199] *Labour Leader*, 3 December 1898.
[200] *Labour Leader*, 4 June 1898.
[201] *Labour Leader*, 23 July 1898.
[202] *Llais Llafur*, 27 August 1898 ('Doubtless all of you know about this person, Willie Wright, – one of the most acceptable speakers of the day on labour questions. He is the representative of the "Independent Labour Party" in south Wales').
[203] *Llais Llafur*, 3 September 1898 ('There is a great deal of talk presently about the renowned Willie Wright. Everybody who pays any amount of attention to the

Wright himself, though, was clear that much of the credit for the growth of socialism in south Wales was due to the Welsh activists themselves: 'the success of Socialistic work in Wales is largely due to local men', he reported in July.[204] That Wright was a catalyst acting upon already existing socialist sympathies made itself repeatedly evident during his tour. At a meeting in Treherbert in July 'an old Socialist sprang up and had to go to the platform ... and is prepared to have a debate with any comer on Socialism'.[205] At Gwaencaegurwen, according to one local, there were 'a number of young men in our neighbourhood [who] have taken very keen interest in Socialism for some years past', as well as 'a large quantity of raw material ready to be made into socialists'.[206] Wright was a gifted propagandist, but his green fingers owed something to the fertile ground he was working.

He depended for everyday support upon the work of local activists. These included individuals like the Treharris photographer Dan Osborne, who, according to Keir Hardie, was 'well to the fore all the time' and came 'an easy first amongst the pioneers of Socialism in South Wales', or Hugh Lloyd of Maerdy, who 'trudged over hills and through dales, night and day almost, organising meetings and forming branches'.[207] At Penydarren, Wright was entertained by Llew Francis, the ILP branch secretary, whose barber's shop had become 'the local "floor of St. Stephen's", where Francis is chaplin [sic], speaker and barber combined'.[208] At Bedlinog, the 'ubiquitous' Joseph Sparkes provided the main inspiration for ILP organisation.[209] Such individuals acted as guides and interpreters. They made external agitators like Wright more acceptable to the Welsh community by providing a Welsh cultural dimension to socialist meetings. Seth Rees

literature of the day will know about the excitement that has been created in the Aberdare and Rhondda Valleys through the visit of this foreigner, and others, there').

[204] *Labour Leader*, 16 July 1898.
[205] ILP NAC Minutes, Report from Head Office, 25 June–16 July 1898, letter from Hugh Lloyd, Maerdy to ILP Head Office.
[206] *Llais Llafur*, 10 September 1898.
[207] *Labour Leader*, 9 July 1898.
[208] *Labour Leader*, 18 June 1898.
[209] *Labour Leader*, 3 September 1898.

of Merthyr spoke alongside Wright in Welsh at a meeting in Merthyr Vale on 20 July, while another local man 'gave "Land of my (step) Fathers" in fine style'.[210] Bert Alpass, who had cycled from Gloucestershire to address meetings in the Rhondda, was guided through the valleys by Tom Parker, an ILP-er from Porth, who 'proved a real boon companion, being guide ... and Director-in-Chief'.[211] In the anthracite region Ebenezer Rees and his son David facilitated the work of the visiting socialists in tandem with members of the Swansea Socialist Society.[212] This close working relationship resulted in a mutual affection between Wright and the local activists, and he developed a sensitivity towards the uniqueness and Welsh identity of the locality. The locals, he reported with delight to head office, 'said I was too good for an Englishman, and good enough for a Welshman! Henceforth I am to be known as Willie Wright Jones. (Talley Hooley!)'.[213] Thereafter he filed reports under his new name. The outside agitator had gone native.[214]

If the strike had a personal impact on agitators like Wright, it went some way towards reshaping the communities of the coalfield. It drew the Welsh miners into the politics of the UK, as the 'Great Strike' of 1889 had done the London dockers. Politically, its main beneficiaries were the socialists. The dispute weakened the miners' existing leadership, and raised the profile of the ILP dramatically. This was immediately evident in the number of ILP branches in the region. In addition to the nine that had existed at the start of the strike, Wright could list 12 new branches: Bedlinog, Fochriw, Rhymney, Penydarren, Merthyr Vale, Mountain Ash, Ferndale, Tylorstown, Ynyshir, Treherbert, Ystalyfera and

[210] ILP NAC Minutes, Willie Wright's Report, 16 July–6 August 1898.
[211] *Llais Llafur*, 3 September 1898; *Labour Leader*, 3 September 1898.
[212] ILP NAC Minutes, Willie Wright's Report, 29 August–17 September 1898.
[213] ILP NAC Minutes, Willie Wright's Report, Report from Head Office, 6–20 August 1898.
[214] After the strike he maintained close links with south Wales. In November 1898 he competed against Alfred Onions for the post of miners' agent at Tredegar, *Western Mail*, 10 November 1898. Despite failing to secure the post, he returned to south Wales frequently to attend ILP meetings, and took part in the next *Clarion* van tour in 1899, *Western Mail*, 15 and 18 November and 30 December 1898, 16 May 1899.

Gwauncaegurwen, and a prospective one at Pontypridd.[215] This marked a significant step forward. The core areas of ILP activity had been markedly strengthened, and many of the branches reported a substantial membership: Bedlinog claimed 120 members, Merthyr Vale and Penydarren both claimed 100 members, while Abercanaid, Abertillery, Maerdy and Treharris all reported 50 members or more. For the first time the size of the south Wales branches began to rival those of the northern English ILP heartland. In October 1898 Manchester reported only 20 more ILP members than Bedlinog![216] It is true that these figures cannot be taken at face value, and that many members quickly melted away, leaving some of the branches to fall into disrepair. If the strike did not result in a permanent structural gain for the ILP, however, it certainly stimulated a groundswell of sympathy and support. This was matched by a qualitative change in the nature of ILP activity, one manifestation of which was a growing level of regional consciousness and ambition. In early September 1898 delegates from all parts of the coalfield attended an ILP conference at Porth. The choice of location reflected a significant shift in the centre of gravity of socialism in south Wales, away from the coastal towns and into the coalfield. Various methods of strengthening the ILP were discussed and agreed upon, including a system of visitations of weak branches, a regional administrative council (funded by a levy on branches) and a tea and tobacco trading scheme (the profits of which would fund a regional organiser).[217] This meeting was followed by another at the Welcome Coffee Tavern in Merthyr the following week,[218] and although not all of the plans came immediately to fruition, their formulation represented a ratcheting up of ILP activity which was of long-term significance.

1898 also had a long-term psychological impact. W.J. Edwards recalled from his Merthyr childhood the memory of men marching during the strike and 'yearning ... for a

[215] *ILP News*, September 1898. *Labour Leader*, 10 September 1898, claimed that there were 31 branches in south Wales, some with a membership in excess of 200.
[216] *ILP News*, October 1898.
[217] *Llais Llafur*, 10 September 1898; *Labour Leader*, 10 September 1898.
[218] *Labour Leader*, 17 September 1898.

deeper richer life'.[219] The miners' crushing defeat meant that new avenues needed to be explored towards this end. One of their sympathisers, John Daniel of Aberdare, wrote to Keir Hardie in 1906, describing how 1898 had resulted in his own irreversible shift in consciousness:

> Very early in the year 1898, – 'A memorable year' in South Wales was 1898, something agitated me to write. The great Strike inspired me. So you see I am a convert of the ministration of loss. To be rid of a burden I wrote and ever since writing has been my safety valve.[220]

Under the name of Iwan Glyn, Daniel wrote, almost without a break, a weekly column in Welsh for *Llais Llafur* for the next fifteen years. It may be pushing the argument too far to say that Daniel's moment of epiphany represented that of a whole society, but he was certainly herald to a deep psychological shift in that society. In any case, there is a sense in which behind the dramatic-traumatic foreground of the 1898 strike, less dramatic but equally profound changes were taking place. The death of William Gladstone in May 1898, near the start of the strike, was followed by the death of two of the great radical voices of Welsh Liberalism near the end: Thomas Gee in September and Michael D. Jones in November. Henry Davies ('Carrusk'), the leader writer of *Llais Llafur*, observed that 'with Gladstone's death there comes also the irresistible reflection that the phase of Liberalism which he so ably represented also passes away'.[221] The same could have been argued with regard to Jones and Gee. A generational change was underway.

The most dramatic sign of this came two years after the end of the strike, in the general election of 1900, when Keir Hardie was returned as one of the MPs for the two-member constituency of Merthyr Boroughs. Hardie's return has received considerable attention from historians, who have generally agreed with John Bruce Glasier's assessment of it as 'one of those "providential occurrences" lying outside

---

[219] Edwards, *From the Valley I Came*, p. 37.
[220] Francis Johnson Correspondence, 1906/115, John Daniel to Keir Hardie, 25 February 1906.
[221] *Llais Llafur*, 28 May 1898.

the region of ordinary political probability'.[222] In securing it, Hardie had fortune working in his favour. Famously, he did most of his campaigning at Preston, only arriving at Merthyr at the last minute when his defeat at Preston was certain. Luckily, his Conservative opponent at Merthyr was so hopeless that he had difficulties even finding the constituency and didn't make it to the poll. Even more luckily, one of his sitting Liberal opponents, Pritchard Morgan, had spent much of the previous parliament abroad prospecting for gold, and was despised by the senior Liberal candidate, the industrialist D.A. Thomas, who gave Hardie his tacit support. Hardie's radical message and his opposition to the Boer War also chimed with the radical, pacifistic traditions of the constituency, which stretched back through Henry Richard to the days of Dic Penderyn.[223] Hardie's victory, though, was no mere conspiracy of circumstance. It was the consummation of a relationship that had been assiduously built up over the previous decade, and which had been intensified by the 1898 strike. Hardie made much of this in his election propaganda, 'WE ARE NO STRANGERS TO ONE ANOTHER', proclaimed his election address, drawing attention to his role in both the 1898 strike and his support for the hauliers in their dispute of 1893.[224] Although Hardie was only elected as junior member, the fact that he secured 867 'plumper' votes (that is voters who cast both their votes for him alone) is clear evidence that a core of voters in the Merthyr and Aberdare districts were embracing the new socialist creed that he represented.[225]

Unlike John Hodge, who had contested the Gower constituency in the same election on a labour ticket but lost to an opponent who 'banged the big Welsh drum' and claimed that 'my country's aims are mine',[226] and unlike Ben Tillett, who had been nominated to fight a seat at Swansea but had

---

[222] John Bruce Glasier, *Keir Hardie: The Man and his Message* (London, 1919), p. 9.
[223] K.O. Morgan, *Keir Hardie, Radical and Socialist*, pp. 112–19; Benn, *Keir Hardie*, pp. 162–5.
[224] National Library of Wales, D.A. Thomas Papers, C2, Keir Hardie Election Address, 1900.
[225] K.O. Fox, 'Labour and Merthyr's Khaki Election of 1900', *Welsh History Review*, 2/4 (1965), 351–66.
[226] John Hodge, *Workman's Cottage to Windsor Castle* (London, 1931), pp. 140–4;

been forced to withdraw before the poll,[227] Hardie – an outsider – succeeded in breaking into Welsh politics. This was of major significance. It seriously challenged Mabon, who had presented himself at the polls as 'the Labour Member for Wales',[228] and gave notice that the brand of Welsh Liberalism he represented was under attack. Mabon was quick to complain that Hardie's Merthyr seat was 'occupied by a stranger',[229] but his predictions that Hardie would fail to hold it at the next election were wrong. In 1906 Hardie managed to increase his vote substantially, despite a challenge from the Dowlais-born Cardiff shipowner Henry Radcliffe, in a contest that was described by one of Hardie's supporters as 'the dirtiest and meanest ever fought'.[230] If anything, the election of January 1910, at which Pritchard Morgan renewed his challenge – helped by the intervention of the Anti-Socialist Union – was even dirtier and meaner, yet Hardie still managed to improve his poll, and in December 1910 he won almost 40 per cent of the vote.[231]

The fact that one of the leading British socialist politicians represented a seat in south Wales had a major impact upon both Welsh and British politics. Not only did it act to raise the profile of socialism in south Wales, inspiring activists and capturing the attention of the public, it also raised the profile of south Wales within the British labour and socialist movement. 'A few years ago nobody outside of South Wales took any heed of the place; few, indeed, knew of its existence. Now it ranks in political importance with West Birmingham', John Bruce Glasier observed in 1904.[232] The importance of the region to socialist politics was implicitly recognised in the same year, when the ILP Annual Conference was held

Llais Llafur, 6 October 1900; K.O. Morgan, 'The "Khaki Election" in Gower', *Gower*, 13 (1960), pp. 20–5.

[227] McCarry, 'Labour and Society in Swansea', pp. 259–64.

[228] Roger Fagge, *Power, Culture and Conflict in the Coalfields: West Virginia and South Wales, 1900–1922* (Manchester and New York, 1996), p. 234.

[229] *Cardiff Times and South Wales Weekly News*, 20 October 1900.

[230] *Cardiff Times and South Wales Weekly News*, 27 January 1906; Radcliffe stressed on his election address his local origins, his Calvinistic Methodism and the fact that he was 'a handsome contributor' of funds to the local hospital, D.A. Thomas Papers, C2.

[231] Beti Jones, *Etholiadau'r Ganrif/Welsh Elections, 1885–1997* (Talybont, 1999).

[232] *Labour Leader*, 19 March 1904.

at Cardiff, a recognition that was confirmed in 1912, when (despite concerns about the remoteness of the location) it was held at Merthyr.[233] Hardie's tenure at Merthyr created a direct link between the movement in south Wales and the wider British labour movement, serving to draw industrial south Wales into that movement and to unify it at a British level. In the words of John Bruce Glasier, it 'fixed irrevocably the destiny of Labour policy in South Wales'.[234] A decade after Hardie's election, one of his supporters claimed *'Pan ddaeth Keir Hardie i Merthyr dechreuwyd cyfnod newydd yn hanes Cymru'*.[235] Hardie had been able to do this because of the catalytic effect of the 1898 strike, but also because of the efforts of his supporters, who created a political culture which sustained socialism in the region and, in so doing, played a crucial role in reshaping the politics of not just Wales, but of Britain as a whole.

(III) THE CULTURE OF SOCIALISM IN SOUTH WALES

Keir Hardie's supporters in Merthyr Tydfil were instrumental in securing his position. It was in response to their representations that he was persuaded to stand there in the first place, it was through their manipulation of the local labour electoral machinery that he was selected as a candidate, and it was through their ongoing work that he retained the seat. Hardie admitted that between 1900 and 1906 he 'was seldom in the constituency',[236] and although this caused 'nervousness and rage' among some of his supporters,[237] it did not prevent them working tirelessly for him and for the cause of socialism. Active socialists were a minority within their

---

[233] *Labour Leader*, 9 April 1904; *Report of the Twelfth Annual Conference of the Independent Labour Party, Cory Hall, Cardiff, April 4th & 5th 1904* (London, 1904); *Pioneer*, 24 June 1911; *Labour Leader*, 16 February and 31 May 1912; Andy Croll, *Civilizing The Urban: Popular Culture and Public Space in Merthyr, c. 1870–1914* (Cardiff, 2000), pp. 209–10.

[234] *South Wales Labour Annual* (1903), p. 74.

[235] *Pioneer*, 1 April 1911 ('When Keir Hardie came to Merthyr a new period began in the history of Wales').

[236] *Souvenir of 20th Annual Conference*, p. 12.

[237] Francis Johnson Correspondence, 1906/26, Frank Smith to Keir Hardie, 12 January 1906.

communities, but they were an important minority: their very existence changed the nature of political discourse at a local, and ultimately national (Welsh and British), level. They made their presence felt through the creation of a vibrant political culture, which, although particularly well developed in Hardie's Merthyr, existed across industrial south Wales during the 1890s and early 1900s. This chapter will close with a discussion of the nature of those activists and the political culture they created. What kind of people were they? To what extent did they represent their communities? How did their political culture reflect the way they related to socialism and to Wales?

First, and most obviously, they were overwhelmingly male. This did not mean that the south Wales socialist movement was not concerned with women's issues. Most of its members probably supported, at least in theory, agitation for sexual equality, and local socialist societies debated the suffrage and related issues intermittently. The Dowlais ILP resolved to support women's suffrage in 1902,[238] while the Cardiff ILP included the extension of electoral rights to women on its programme in the same year and opposed the 1902 Education Act on the grounds that it deprived women of the right to be directly elected.[239] Some individual male politicians proclaimed in favour of political sexual equality. In 1906 James Winstone emphasised that 'the ILP was in favour of Old Age Pensions for women as well as men',[240] and a year later Councillor T.E Davies of Trimsaran stated in an election leaflet that he was 'in favour of conferring full powers upon the common people', specifying that 'In this connection I include women as well as men'.[241] A consciousness that the movement needed to appeal to women also existed among the male rank and file. In 1898, after the launch of *Llais Llafur*, for example, the station master at Cwmllynfell contributed to its letters page urging the paper to include

---

[238] SWCC: MNA/PP/69/1, Dowlais ILP Minute Book.
[239] *Labour Pioneer*, May and September 1902.
[240] *Aberdare Leader*, 25 August 1906.
[241] Francis Johnson Correspondence, 1907/62, T.E. Davies, Trimsaran, Llanelly, to Johnson, 6 March 1907.

more for women.[242] There were, though, limits to male socialist support for female emancipation. The fact that the Aberdare ILP had to debate the question 'Should Women Sit in Parliament?' in 1906 indicates that socialist opinion was divided on the matter, and in 1908 Mr. J. Philips of the same ILP group could read a paper on women's suffrage, arguing against it on the grounds that 'the woman's proper sphere was the home, to educate and inspire the future generation'.[243]

The existence of such views did not prevent some female involvement in the movement. Like other aspects of socialist activity, this was stimulated by speakers from the movement in England. In 1897 Enid Stacy ('the accomplished lady socialist advocate') lectured to an audience in which 'several ladies were present' at Treharris.[244] She revisited a year later, expressing a hope that 'in future working men would bring their wives to these meetings as the idea was to educate both sexes'.[245] During the 1898 coal strike, Willie Wright organised some women's meetings, and reported the presence of women at other meetings: at Porth in June he recruited a Miss Thomas, who, he predicted, 'will spread her gentle influence over the party, and strengthen it, as only a woman can', and at Treherbert in July he reported meeting Mr. Morgan, a checkweigher from Treharris, who brought 'his wife and several other ladies' to a socialist meeting.[246] By the early 1900s there was some degree of confluence between the socialist movement and the women's suffrage movement. In 1906 Annie Kenney, the Manchester suffragette, lectured in Cardiff and the valleys, and twelve of her audience at Trecynon formed a branch of the Women's Social and Political Union and joined the ILP.[247] Mrs Pankhurst visited south Wales in 1906, arguing in her speeches that 'men as caretakers of women

---

[242] *Llais Llafur*, 26 March 1898.
[243] *Aberdare Leader*, 24 February 1906 and 7 March 1908.
[244] *Merthyr Express*, 3 April 1897.
[245] *Merthyr Express*, 19 March 1898.
[246] *Labour Leader*, 6 August 1898; ILP NAC Minutes: Report from Head Office, 25 June–16 July, 1898.
[247] *Cardiff Times and South Wales Weekly News*, 27 January 1906; Aberdare Socialist Party Minute Book, 1901–1906, Aberdare Public Library PY4/5, 27 January 1906.

are a failure'.[248] Mrs Cooper of Nelson, Lancashire, and the socialist-suffragette Charlotte Despard also spoke at ILP meetings in 1908, although the latter's meetings at Llanelli and Swansea were broken up by opponents.[249]

Some of the women attracted to such meetings found their way into the socialist movement as active members. In Swansea, around 1902, the Socialist Society counted thirty-four women out of a total membership of 463.[250] 'Lady members' from south Wales were involved in the preparations for the 1904 ILP conference at Cardiff,[251] and in some districts women's ILP branches were formed. The Aberdare Socialist Party had one by 1906 which had twenty members by 1908.[252] In February 1906, the main (that is male) branch discussed the appointment of 'an occasional member' to visit and 'give the women encouragement',[253] a comment which illuminates the nature of the political gender balance within the movement. Whether the male members did not have full confidence in the women's ability to organise themselves, or whether they were slightly uncomfortable with the existence of an autonomous women's group is a matter for speculation, but what is clear is that women were a small minority within the movement. They also played a supportive role within it, rather than occupying positions of authority. There is no record of a woman taking an official executive role in any of the south Wales socialist organisations in this period. Rather women were deployed in non-political cultural activities. In Cardiff Labour Church in the 1890s, for example, women were responsible for the musical programme.[254] Young, educated single women, such as Miss Trimnel, a student at Cardiff University College who lectured to the Cardiff Labour Church in 1894, were also allowed to contribute to

[248] *Aberdare Leader*, 8 September 1906.
[249] *Aberdare Leader*, 11 July 1908; Ursula Masson, *For Women for Wales and For Liberalism: Women in Liberal Politics in Wales, 1880–1914* (Cardiff, 2010), p. 156.
[250] Glamorgan Archive, D/D AW H14/4, Griff Jones, Script of Swansea Socialist Party and Labour Party.
[251] *Labour Leader*, 19 March 1904.
[252] Glamorgan Record Office, DXHJ2, Aberdare Socialist Society Papers.
[253] Aberdare Public Library, PY4/5, Aberdare Socialist Party Minute Book, 1901–1906.
[254] *Labour Prophet*, June, July and October 1893 and May 1894.

the intellectual life of the movement.[255] As the ILP developed in the early 1900s, however, women most commonly found themselves undertaking roles that reflected their social location within the domestic sphere. Thus, the recorded functions of groups such as the Aberdare ILP women's section included the supervision of the children's choir and the provision of teas at party functions.[256]

If these activities were politically limiting, they did give women a role in developing the political culture of socialism; they also offered scope for the subversion of existing gender norms. In November 1893 the Cardiff Labour Church 'made a departure from our usual service by giving the arrangements and conduct of the service into the hands of the women', the chair being taken by Mrs Rudland, the wife of the church secretary.[257] More controversially, the *Clarion* van offered the risqué spectacle of unmarried men and women travelling together and sleeping, if not under the same roof, in close proximity. It also offered the opportunity for the female vanners to assert their domestic superiority: 'it is a sight for gods and men to see the woman in charge, a B.A. in honours of London University – washing the dishes', commented the *Merthyr Express*, 'while prominent men in the Labour Movement, such as Tom Mann, or Bruce Glasier, sit round meekly "drying up" under her direction'.[258] A correspondent for *Tarian y Gweithiwr* saw the gender subversion of the vans as a portent that social order was about to collapse,[259] and a decade later Keir Hardie was also concerned when the Merthyr ILP similarly tampered with the gendered order by organising a social event for its women workers at which the men took their turn to provide the tea. Hardie, despite his support for women's suffrage, was not convinced that so radical a reversal of the separate spheres would result in a satisfactory tea.[260] So, despite the fact that the role of women

---

[255] *Labour Prophet*, July 1894; *Western Mail*, 21 August 1894.
[256] *Aberdare Leader*, 21 September 1907 and 4 January 1908.
[257] *Labour Prophet*, December 1893.
[258] *Merthyr Express*, 28 August 1897.
[259] *Tarian y Gweithiwr*, 26 August 1897.
[260] Francis Johnson Correspondence, 1910/76, Keir Hardie to Harry Morris, 26 February 1910.

within the socialist movement was restricted, their very presence threatened to confuse and undermine existing gendered assumptions, as betrayed by the comments of a contributor to the *Barry Herald* in 1908 who complained that 'Socialists talk much of the "uplift of woman", and yet some of them preach a doctrine of free love'.[261] It is important not to overstate the extent of this process in the early 1900s. Despite the efforts of activists such as Rose Davies and Elizabeth Andrews in the period before the Great War,[262] the women's pages of the socialist press continued to feature household tips and recipes,[263] and it was not until the postwar period that gender roles within the socialist movement really began to change. In this sense, the socialist movement in south Wales faithfully reflected both its host society and the wider British movement.[264]

This is less true with regard to the movement's male leadership. An impressionistic analysis of the most prominent ILP-ers would suggest that the party's leading activists did not wholly represent the structure of the society from which they came. Although heavy industrial workers were not unrepresented among their ranks, the majority, at least in the early years of the party's growth, were not industrial proletarians. S.D. Shallard, one of the group of supporters that was imported to canvass for Keir Hardie in 1900, observed that the ILP leadership in Merthyr comprised 'a little barber, a signalman, one or two insurance agents and Scotch drapers, and a handful of miners'.[265] In this respect the movement in south Wales exhibited similar characteristics to the wider British movement.[266] There were exceptions, and individuals who more closely reflected the region's heavy industrial

[261] *Barry Herald*, 31 July 1908.
[262] Keith Gildart and David Howell (eds), *Dictionary of Labour Biography*, vol. 11 (London, 2003), pp. 1–11, 39–47.
[263] See, for example 'Home Notes', by 'Elizabeth', *Rhondda Socialist*, 1 May 1912, which included a range of recipes supplied by wives of notable socialist leaders, under the motto 'Man makes houses, but woman makes homes'.
[264] June Hannam and Karen Hunt, *Socialist Women: Britain, 1880s–1920s* (London and New York, 2002); Krista Cowman, '"Giving Them Something To Do": How the Early ILP Appealed to Women', in Margaret Walsh (ed.), *Working Out Gender: Perspectives from Labour History* (Aldershot, 1999), pp. 119–34.
[265] *Labour Leader*, 20 October 1900.
[266] Deian Hopkin, 'The Membership of the Independent Labour Party,

economic base, such as Charles Stanton, James Winstone, Vernon Hartshorn and Edmund Stonelake,[267] did accede to the ILP leadership in the early 1900s. The men who were initially prominent in the making of socialist political culture in south Wales, though, tended to occupy positions which made them less vulnerable to blacklisting and victimisation. Llew Francis, secretary of the South Wales ILP Federation, treasurer of the Merthyr Trades Council and the linchpin of the movement in the Merthyr District – in Hardie's view 'the one man who had made it what it is'[268] – was the 'little barber' referred to by Shallard. Hugh Lloyd of Maerdy worked as an assurance agent, as did Henry Davies, of Cwmavon.[269] Matt Giles, the 'sun of the local Labour constellation' in Swansea',[270] who served as secretary of the Swansea Socialist Society, founded the Labour Press Association (publishers of the *Swansea & District Workers' Journal*) and ultimately became a full-time organiser for the Workers' Union in south Wales, worked for Fry's Chocolate of Bristol as their publicity agent in Swansea.[271]

For many prominent ILP-ers, their position outside the dominant occupational groups of the community was not a matter of choice. Ebenezer Rees, a former miner, ended up as a journalist due to victimisation because of his union activities. Joseph Sparkes of Bedlinog was forced out of mining because of his political activism during the 1890s, and resorted to selling meat to make a living, ultimately becoming a grocer.[272] Of the genuine industrial workers,

1904–1910: A Spatial and Occupational Analysis', *International Review of Social History*, 20/2 (1975), 175–97.

[267] Peter Stead, 'Vernon Hartshorn: Miners' Agent and Cabinet Minister', *Glamorgan Historian*, 6 (1969), 83–94; A. Mór O'Brien (ed.), *The Autobiography of Edmund Stonelake* (Mid Glamorgan, 1981); Ivor T. Rees, 'Charles Butt Stanton, 1873–1946, M.P. for Merthyr Tydfil, 1915–1918', *Merthyr Historian*, 25 (2013), pp. 161–79.

[268] Francis Johnson Correspondence, 1902/80, Keir Hardie to Llew Francis, 23 July 1902; *South Wales Labour Annual* (1902), p. 27.

[269] Hugh Lloyd in recorded in the 1891 Census as an assurance agent, and Henry Davies is recorded in the 1901 Census as an assurance agent and rate collector.

[270] *South Wales Labour Annual* (1903), p. 9.

[271] Jones, 'Script of Swansea Socialist Party and Labour Party'; Awbery, *Labour's Early Struggles in Swansea*, pp. 55–6; J. Graham Jones, 'John Littlejohns, Matt Giles and the ILP at Swansea: Some New Evidence', *Morgannwg*, 49 (2005), 79–99.

[272] South Wales Miners' Library, AUD/213, Edgar Evans (Broadhaven, Pembrokeshire), transcript of interview with D. Smith and H. Francis, 14 July 1973.

it was the railwaymen who were the most prominent, such as the signalmen Oliver Jenkins and George Richards of Merthyr and Aberaman respectively.[273] They were balanced, however, by members of the professions. John Littlejohns, for example – one of the leading lights of the Swansea Socialist Society – was an art teacher at the local grammar school, and exhibited his work in the Glynn Vivian Art Gallery.[274] Socially unrepresentative and internally disparate, the ILP's prominent members sought to become, in the words of John Davies of the Aberdare ILP, 'the intellectual and vital organs of the Labour body'.[275] By their very nature, local ILP leaders were exceptional. Once they had become involved in ILP activism they became even more so, and victimisation only served to accentuate this quality. They nevertheless articulated the aspirations of an important section of their society, and challenged to take over the representation of that society in the political process – a process that has received considerable attention from historians.[276]

The rank and file members that the local leadership represented, on the other hand, have received much less attention. Evidence relating to ordinary members who paid their dues, turned up to meetings, but otherwise did not play a prominent role in the movement is sparse, but what there is suggests that on this level the ILP was a relatively faithful mirror of its host community. Of the 302 male members recorded in the membership book of the Aberdare Socialist Party, which gives a snapshot of the group in 1907–8, 180 are identifiable in either the 1901 or the 1911 Census. Of these, well over half (117) were employed in the mining industry, most as workers underground. Over half (108) were born in the Aberdare district, with many of the remainder (thirty-two) coming from within south Wales. Only fourteen members

---

[273] Aberdare Public Library, PY4/5, Aberdare Socialist Party Minute Book, 1901–1906.
[274] Griff Jones, 'Script of Swansea Socialist Party and Labour Party'.
[275] *Labour Leader*, 23 January 1904.
[276] David Smith, *Aneurin Bevan and the World of South Wales* (Cardiff, 1993), pp. 67–89; S.E. Demont, 'Tredegar and Aneurin Bevan: A Society and its Political Articulation, 1890–1929' (unpublished PhD thesis, University of Wales, 1990); Jon Lawrence, *Speaking for the People: Party, Language and Popular Politics in England, 1867–1914*, pp. 229–40.

came from England, which belies assumptions about the socialist movement being a result of in-migration. The vast majority were Welsh speakers (145, including seven monoglots). The membership was also relatively young: a third of members were born after 1880 (so were in their mid-twenties in 1907), and almost half were born in the 1870s. Only nine were born before 1860.[277] Further research would be necessary to substantiate these conclusions, and it would need to be both ingenious and painstaking, as surviving membership lists like that of the Aberdare Socialist Party are extremely rare. If Aberdare is at all representative of the rest of south Wales, and if such a thing as an 'average socialist' existed in the early 1900s (both admittedly dangerous assumptions) it would seem that such a creature was a locally-born, Welsh-speaking male, probably a coal miner, in his twenties or thirties.

It was men like these, led by slightly less representative and less easily victimised proletarian-professionals (insurance salesmen, tradesmen, miners' checkweighmen), and supported (and sometimes subverted) by a small, but significant phalanx of women, who week by week and meeting by meeting, at a local and regional level, painstakingly created the political culture of south Walian socialism. Their efforts fluctuated between periods of energetic activity, which were perhaps stimulated by the visit of an outside speaker or a local electoral contest, and periods of dissipation, during which members fell away and branches fell into disrepair. Their main seedbed was the local branch meeting, which, along with its attendant activities of outdoor speaking, electioneering, fundraising and socialising, nourished a culture of mutual improvement and open debate. The Treharris branch was holding a weekly debating class by 1895,[278] and the Dowlais branch was running an economics class by 1897,[279]

---

[277] Glamorgan Record Office, DXHJ2, Aberdare Socialist Society Papers. In coming to these conclusions, I am grateful to Cardiff University student Anys Wood for undertaking analysis of Census returns relating to Aberdare Socialist Society membership, as part of a project made possible by Cardiff University CUROP funding.
[278] *Labour Leader*, 19 October 1895.
[279] *Labour Leader*, 11 December 1897.

by which time the Merthyr branch also boasted a 'literature department'.[280] At Penydarren, the local branch met in the Elim schoolroom and took turns, in the absence of visiting speakers, to read and debate papers on topics such as 'Does Socialism and the Bible Agree',[281] 'The Wages of Labour',[282] 'The Nationalisation of the Railways',[283] and 'Socialism and Drink',[284] to name just a few. The Merthyr branch met at the Welcome Coffee Tavern, and among its papers was an intriguing discussion on 'Socialism and Love, Are They Separate?'[285] Through such discussions local ILP-ers honed their public speaking skills, refined their arguments and orientated themselves intellectually.

The few surviving branch documents and minute books from this period reveal the ebbs and flows of ILP activity in some detail. At Dowlais, a branch met regularly throughout the early 1900s, with the exception of a year's break from September 1902 to September 1903, when it fell into disrepair and needed reviving. It hosted discussions on a wide range of issues, including 'Individualism and Collectivism', 'Labour Representation', 'Thrift'. 'Co-operation', 'Eight Hours By Law', 'Socialist Fusion' (which by this time they had agreed to oppose) and 'The Definition of Socialism'. It is recorded on occasions that 'members took part in a jocular and excellent way', or that the discussions were 'lively and edifying'. The branch also cooperated with the Penydarren branch – which was sometimes represented at its meetings by Llew Francis – to organise an open air speaking campaign. It organised systematic study of Blatchford's *Merrie England*, and his follow-up book, *Britain for the British*, and managed the distribution of the contents of a Fabian Society book box

---

[280] *Labour Leader*, 11 December 1897.

[281] *Merthyr Express*, 16 July 1898. Llew Francis presented this paper and after a debate, 'it was unanimously agreed that Socialism was in accordance with the Bible teaching'. Francis gave the same paper at Willis's rooms, Georgetown, later in the year, and it was followed by a discussion in which numerous members took part, *Merthyr Express*, 3 September 1898.

[282] *Merthyr Express*, 10 September 1898.

[283] *Merthyr Express*, 24 September 1898.

[284] *Merthyr Express*, 8 October 1898.

[285] *Merthyr Express*, 24 December 1898. ('The meeting came to the conclusion that they are one, because both were humanising in effect.')

among the members. It also engaged with the regional and national ILP structures, arranged visits by national speakers (including Philip Snowden, Katharine Bruce Glasier and John Penny) and dabbled in a tea trading scheme.[286] Elsewhere in Merthyr Boroughs, the Aberdare Valley ILP (formerly the Aberdare Socialist Society) had, by 1907, organised a market stall, an institute with its own caretaker and a socialist Sunday school. It also organised an annual children's concert, an annual branch tea and its own annual Christmas tree.[287] By 1908 its activities had extended to the organisation of an annual juvenile flower show, the aim of which was 'to foster a love of the beautiful in the hearts of the children'. Mr. W. Marsh, the representative of the local floral trade, who had been co-opted to help with arrangements, was gratified that 'the Socialists had taken the lead in Aberdare in juvenile horticulture'.[288]

This work was undertaken on a financial shoestring, as testified by the surviving account book of another ILP branch at Bedlinog, which shows that the bulk of branch income was derived from local contributions averaging less than a few shillings, and that income from the sale of pamphlets and photographs was cancelled out by the payment of fees for lecturers, the costs of purchasing propaganda, NAC fees and charges for conference attendance.[289] Despite these limitations, the south Wales ILP gradually built up a vibrant political culture which played a crucial role in developing the human capital of its membership – a process which was essential to its long-term existence as an influence in south Wales politics. Crucially, this culture incorporated most of the elements that were to be found in the more developed socialist movement across the English border, and in this sense it was a factor in the integration of the Welsh movement into the greater British whole. The influence of the *Clarion* continued to be important in this respect. The *Clarion* van,

---

[286] Swansea University Archive, SWCC: MNA/PP/69/1, Dowlais ILP Minute Book.
[287] Glamorgan Record Office, DXHJ2, Aberdare Valley ILP/Aberdare Socialist Society Papers.
[288] *Aberdare Leader*, 10 October 1908.
[289] Swansea University Archive, SWCC:MNA/POL/5/1, Independent Labour Party, Bedlinog Branch, Account Book and Press Cuttings, 1901–1921.

which returned in 1899 and 1907 and made extensive tours of the south Wales valleys, played its role in the further dissemination of socialist ideas across the region.[290] More diffuse was the influence of the printed word. Socialists placed a high premium on printed propaganda, and believed, as W.W. Price, secretary of the Aberdare ILP, put it, that 'once people begin to read about Socialism their ultimate conversion is certain'.[291] Pamphlets, books and newspapers therefore played a central role in socialist culture, and the influence of the *Clarion* was again dominant. Most notably, the publication of Blatchford's *Britain for the British* in 1902 recreated to some extent the excitement of *Merrie England*. The sales in the Swansea Socialist Society's shop 'went up with a bang' after its publication. David Richards, a signalman at Landore and a member of the society, hawked copies around the pubs of Swansea by the dozen and even sold them to passengers at Landore station.[292] The Society also ran a *Britain for the British* study class, as did the Aberdare ILP.[293]

Increasingly, after the turn of the century, the *Clarion*-related culture that went alongside ILP activism became something that was not simply imported, but which grew from the bottom up in south Wales itself. Initially this took place, like the early growth of socialism in the region, in the coastal towns. A *Clarion* club was launched at Newport in early 1900.[294] *Clarion* 'Cinderella Clubs', which organised meals for slum children, appeared at Newport as early as 1899,[295] and Swansea and Cardiff in 1900.[296] The Cardiff club claimed to have arranged meals for over 680 slum children during its first winter.[297] *Clarion* Fellowships were established at Swansea

---

[290] *Clarion*, 6 May–20 July 1899, 12 April–27 September 1907.
[291] Aberdare Public Library, W.W. Price to Aberdare Valley ILP, 7 November 1907, PY4/10.
[292] Jones, 'Script of Swansea Socialist Party and Labour Party'.
[293] *Labour Leader*, 31 January 1903; Glamorgan Record Office, DXHJ2, Aberdare Valley ILP / Aberdare Socialist Society Papers.
[294] *Clarion*, 27 January 1900.
[295] *Labour Leader*, 4 February 1899.
[296] *Labour Leader*, 22 December 1900; *Clarion*, 10 February 1900.
[297] *Labour Pioneer*, January, February and March 1901; *Clarion*, 10 March 1900, 11 May 1901.

in 1900,[298] Newport in 1902,[299] and Cardiff in 1904.[300] Cardiff even had a *Clarion* chess club.[301] Those who were more attracted to the open air – an integral part of British socialist culture – could join the squadrons of *Clarion* cyclists that departed from Cardiff on a weekly basis during the summer months from the early 1900s onwards to explore the Glamorgan coast, the valleys and rural Monmouthshire.[302] Another cycling group met regularly outside the Shaftesbury Hotel at Newport and included Raglan, Caerphilly and the western valleys of Monmouthshire in its itineraries.[303] Swansea too established a club in 1902, which explored the Mumbles on its opening run.[304] Gradually *Clarion* clubs spread from the coastal towns and became established in the valleys. By 1904 a *Clarion* cycling group was active in the Rhondda,[305] and by 1908 scout groups existed in Aberdare and the Swansea Valley. As the decade progressed, the cycle-mounted socialist scout became a familiar sight across south Wales.[306]

The ongoing dialogue between Wales and the wider British movement was also encouraged by the personal visits of socialist celebrities to south Wales. In 1904 the Cardiff cyclists were joined by A.J. Paton, otherwise known as the 'Flying Scotsman', editor of the regular *Clarion* 'Cyclorama' feature, for their annual picnic. Paton subsequently gave an account of his cycling adventures in south Wales in the *Clarion*, but unfortunately did not have many more opportunities to repeat the trip, as two years later he was found dead by the roadside near Nuneaton after a cycling accident. 'How the accident was sustained is not exactly known', reported

---

[298] *Swansea and District Workers' Journal*, December 1900.
[299] *Clarion*, 24 January and 18 July 1902, 13 March and 4 April 1903.
[300] *Clarion*, 11 November, 9 December 1904.
[301] *Labour Pioneer*, March 1902.
[302] *Labour Pioneer*, May 1901, refers to the group entering its third season. Also see *Labour Pioneer*, June 1901 and April and May 1902; *Clarion*, 25 August 1900 and 26 August 1904.
[303] *Clarion*, 19 May 1900, 23 and 30 June 1900.
[304] *Clarion*, 9 May 1902.
[305] *Clarion*, 14, 21 and 28 October 1904.
[306] *Labour Leader*, 16 October 1908; *Clarion*, 18 December 1908, 1 and 29 January 1909; *Llais Llafur*, 11 July 1908 and *Labour Leader*, 10 July 1908; *Aberdare Leader*, 19 September 1908.

the *Clarion*, 'but a book was found on the handle-bar of his bicycle. It is supposed that he was reading at the time.' The business of being a *Clarion* scout could be dangerous![307] Another visitor was G.A.H. Samuel, or 'Marxian', of the *Labour Leader*. Samuel was originally from Swansea, and although he had left the town at the age of six, he maintained a pride in his Welsh origins. He lectured frequently in the towns of south Wales and also contributed to the local socialist press, including writing a lengthy and detailed account of Swansea's history for the *Swansea and District Workers' Journal*.[308] Robert Blatchford also included south Wales on his after-dinner speaking circuit, visiting Cardiff, Swansea and Newport in February 1901.[309] At Newport, much to his delight, he met an old army friend, and the evening was a huge success.[310] At Swansea, though, he was reported to be 'uncommunicative and grave almost to grumpiness',[311] which might explain why he did not return there on his second trip to south Wales in November 1902 – although his unpredictable personality did not prevent *Clarionettes* travelling down from the valleys to hear him speak at Cardiff and Newport.[312] By getting involved in such activities and indulging in the culture of socialist fellowship, south Wales enthusiasts were consciously emulating their comrades across the English border. 'The fellowship in South Wales and Monmouth bids fair to equal that of the North and Midlands',[313] opined Cardiff's *Labour Pioneer* proudly in 1901.

Like their counterparts elsewhere in Britain, Welsh socialists generated a musical culture to accompany their activities. The Treharris ILP, which had a socialist string band as early as 1897, was a pioneer in this respect, but its efforts were not isolated.[314] The Newport branch was running monthly

[307] *Clarion*, 12, 19 and 26 August 1904, 20 July 1906.
[308] *Swansea and District Workers' Journal*, January, February and December 1900. 'Swansea's Lords' was serialised from August 1900 to June 1901.
[309] *Labour Pioneer*, March 1901; *Clarion*, 9 and 16 February 1901; *Swansea and District Workers' Journal*, March 1901.
[310] *Clarion*, 2 March 1901.
[311] *Swansea and District Workers' Journal*, March 1901.
[312] *Clarion*, 5 December 1902.
[313] *Labour Pioneer*, March 1901.
[314] *Merthyr Express*, 26 June 1897.

'smokers' (smoking concerts) by 1899,[315] and 'glees and solos [were] given in good style' at Blatchford's visit to Cardiff in February 1901.[316] By 1904 Cardiff had a *Clarion* choir,[317] and in 1908 it had a *Clarion* orchestra, which provided accompaniment to a Labour Day production of Shakespeare's *Midsummer Night's Dream*, for which members of the Cardiff labour movement provided the cast.[318] Up in the valleys, the Aberdare Valley ILP had its own branch pianist,[319] and in February 1906 it appointed Councillor John Davies to be conductor of singing at its meetings, the repertoires of which included Keir Hardie's election songs along with 'When Wilt Thou Save the People' and the *Marseillaise*. It seems, however, that not all Aberdare socialists were comfortable with the musical element of their activities. At a meeting on 18 February 1906 a motion that singing be curtailed at a forthcoming public lecture was debated, although it was ultimately rejected and singing was allowed.[320]

This debate over the presence of music at socialist meetings was, perhaps, an indication of an underlying tension. Socialist culture had two faces: behind its colourfully counter-cultural, fun-loving *Clarion* façade was a more austere set of core beliefs that revolved around the concepts of self and mutual improvement, and aspired to the pursuit of a strict moral code. This was partly the product of inherited notions concerning 'rational recreation', which socialists in south Wales shared with their contemporaries in other parts of Britain.[321] Welsh socialists both adopted and adapted this ideology, and in some respects it provided a link to other social movements in Wales. There was a degree

---

[315] *Labour Leader*, 4 February 1899.
[316] *Labour Pioneer*, March 1901.
[317] *Clarion*, 27 January 1904.
[318] Cardiff Central Library, Cochfarf Papers, Box 5, Labour and May Day Festival, Theatre Royal, Cardiff, 6 May 1908 (typescript).
[319] Aberdare Public Library, PY4/5, Aberdare Socialist Party Minute Book, 21 February 1901. It also proudly recorded in its papers the buying of a new piano for £30 in 1907, Glamorgan Record Office, DXHJ2, Aberdare Valley ILP/Aberdare Socialist Society Papers.
[320] Aberdare Socialist Party Minute Book, 18 February, 25 February and 5 March 1906.
[321] Chris Waters, *British Socialists and the Politics of Popular Culture* (Manchester, 1990).

of confluence, for example, between socialists and temperance advocates, as testified by John Littlejohns' pamphlet, *Black Glamorgan*, published by the Swansea Socialist Society in 1901, which appealed for the help of all political parties in south Wales to address the drink problem. It advocated a system of supervised municipal lodgings, where 'a desire for purer recreation and mental development' would supplant the desire for drink, so that 'this sin-ridden county may no longer deserve the name of "Black Glamorgan"'.[322] At the heart of this was an essentially revivalist message, and the role models that it encouraged were not that different to those of the religious revivalism with which it coexisted. In one of Keir Hardie's *Labour Leader* articles on the coal strike he recounted a meeting with a man who, much to the delight of his wife, had given up beer and tobacco since becoming a socialist. 'The man who can do that', he commented, 'that he may have more money for propaganda purposes is among the heroes of the movement.'[323]

Keir Hardie played a central role in promoting this aspect of the movement. Not only did his own life provide an object lesson in self-improvement, which was celebrated and communicated in contemporary publications,[324] but he also intervened personally in branch life to ensure that socialist societies in the region were run according to the appropriate codes of moral conduct. He gave some advice, for example, regarding the establishment of branch premises, to the members at Dowlais in June 1904:

> It is essential to the progress of the cause that each branch should have a home, where the members could gather to read papers, discuss important questions, and carry on the work of mutual improvement. Avoid a club make the headquarters a home. Keep out the drink and billiards. We want working thinking members and not a body of loungers.[325]

---

[322] John Littlejohns, *Black Glamorgan* (Swansea, 1901), pp. 11–12.
[323] *Labour Leader*, 9 July 1898.
[324] Anon, *From Coal Pit to Parliament: Complete Life of James Keir Hardie MP – Stories of Success No. 10* (London, 1907).
[325] SWCC: MNA/PP/69/1, Dowlais ILP Minute Book, 10 June 1904.

To what extent the rank and file membership of the movement lived up to Hardie's expectations is another matter, but what we know about the more prominent members suggests that they prided themselves on developing a rich intellectual culture. Henry Davies of Cwmavon (Carrusk of *Llais Llafur*) was, according to the *South Wales Labour Annual*, 'A marvel. Really well read in economics and many other sciences, general literature and theology.'[326] David Davies, of Briton Ferry, was a 'pioneer of the Free Library' there,[327] and in the Merthyr Valley in the early 1900s, the young W.J. Edwards used Robert Blatchford's *Clarion* book reviews to guide him through his local free library.[328]

If socialists were upstanding examples of self-improvement, they were also driven by a sense of social isolation, which was derived from widespread opposition to their beliefs. They quickly learnt to define themselves in opposition to their social environment. On the death in 1895 of W.J. Rees, the secretary of the first South Wales ILP Federation, one of his contemporaries commented that 'he and a few Socialist comrades lived an isolated life in the dreary desert of narrow Nonconformity and bigoted Liberalism'.[329] This naturally drove them to seek support from a wider movement. In some cases this went as far as direct material support for individuals. In 1895 W.J. Dunn of the ILP in Swansea was dying of consumption, like his friend and comrade Rees. He explained in a letter to Tom Mann how he hoped that Sam Hobson could send books of raffle tickets for a fund to help him to the branches in England 'where we are strong', because 'locally I don't expect support ... as we stink in the nostrils of this Hypocritical Community'.[330]

These attitudes may provide a key to an understanding of the south Wales socialist movement's relationship with Welshness, which was, at best, ambivalent. This is perhaps surprising, given what the Aberdare Socialist Party papers

[326] *South Wales Labour Annual* (1902), p. 27.
[327] *South Wales Labour Annual* (1903), p. 9.
[328] Edwards, *From the Valley I Came*, p. 96.
[329] *Labour Leader*, 23 November 1895.
[330] Francis Johnson Correspondence, 1895/138, W.J. Dunn to Tom Mann, 30 August 1895.

reveal about the origins and linguistic balance of its membership. Nevertheless, it is clear that from an early stage in the development of the south Walian socialist movement its leaders and spokesmen, incomers and Welsh alike, adopted a position of suspicion towards any form of Welsh particularism. Most fundamentally, this was reflected in the linguistic choices made by members. Welsh continued to be used at public meetings, at which Welsh culture was often implicitly celebrated. At the celebrations for Keir Hardie's re-election at Merthyr in 1906, for example, after the singing of 'Aberystwyth' and other customary musical proceedings, John Williams, the MP for Gower, spoke at length in Welsh, welcoming Hardie's re-election.[331] Hardie himself learnt some Welsh, had a Welsh election hymn written for him and had some of his propaganda materials translated into Welsh.[332] Quickly, though, Welsh became the second language of the movement, and English became the dominant language of branch life. All of the ILP's surviving minute books and branch records were kept in English, and branch discussions in Welsh seem to have been a rarity.[333] Even in the deeply Welsh-speaking anthracite region, by the turn of the century branches were sending their reports to the bilingual *Llais Llafur* in English only. This was an active choice. Activists known to be Welsh patriots tended to subjugate their Welsh patriotism to their socialism, and use the English language. Edgar Chappell, for example, originally from Ystalyfera, and an activist with the Swansea Socialist Society, was a Welsh speaker and a member of the patriotic *Cymdeithas y Ddraig Goch* (Red Dragon Society) in Ystalyfera. He chose, however, to contribute articles to *Llais Llafur* in English.[334]

---

[331] *Aberdare Leader*, 24 March 1906.

[332] Hardie's Welsh election hymn was printed by G.M. Evans at the office of *Y Darian*, Aberdare, and published by Frank Smith D.A. Thomas Papers, C2, National Library of Wales. John Daniel identifies himself as the author in Francis Johnson Correspondence, 1906/115. D.A. Thomas Papers C2 contains various Welsh medium election materials.

[333] For example, the Dowlais ILP Minute Book records only one discussion taking place in Welsh between January 1901 and October 1904.

[334] E. Margaret Humphries, 'Edgar Leyshon Chappell (1878–1949): A Biography', (unpublished Diploma in Higher Education dissertation, Cardiff, 1993); *Llais Llafur*, 4 April 1903.

The adoption of English as the socialists' primary medium of communication was partly a reflection of a wider shift in the language of Welsh politics, which saw the Welsh language relegated to a secondary position within the nation's political life.[335] It was, however, something more. As Ieuan Gwynedd Jones has observed, the adoption of English was a valuational and symbolic gesture of the rejection of old Liberal-nonconformist values on the one hand and the affirmation of new solidarities on the other.[336] It was also reflected in the wider cultural and political assumptions of the movement. Edgar Chappell, for example, did not simply write his *Llais Llafur* articles (such as his extensive series of 1903 on 'Social Movements of the Nineteenth Century') in English; he wrote them from a clearly British, rather than Welsh, historical perspective.[337] This pan-British socialist perspective was common across the south Walian movement. When Briton Ferry ILP published a book of *Socialist and Labour Hymns*, for example, it borrowed wholesale from a generically British socialist cultural canon. The first three songs in the book were William Morris's 'The Day is Coming', Jim Connell's 'The Red Flag' and Edward Carpenter's 'England Arise', and the remainder of the pamphlet did not contain a single Welsh tune or word of Welsh.[338]

Politically, Welsh national issues were occasionally raised by ILP-ers, but they were firmly subjugated to wider socialist concerns. John Littlejohns, for example, argued for 'Socialism as the end, Home Rule as the means'.[339] The consciousness of south Walian socialists was primarily regional, rather than national. This was exhibited by the launch in 1902 of a *South Wales Labour Annual*. This publication lasted two years, and combined news and

---

[335] Neil Evans and Kate Sullivan, '"Yn Llawn o Dân Cymreig" (Full of Welsh Fire): The Language of Politics in Wales, 1880–1914', in Geraint H. Jenkins (ed.), *The Welsh Language and its Social Domains, 1801–1911* (Cardiff, 2000), pp. 561–85.

[336] Ieuan Gwynedd Jones, 'Language and Community in Nineteenth Century Wales', in *Mid-Victorian Wales: The Observers and the Observed* (Cardiff, 1992), pp. 54–79, p. 78.

[337] *Llais Llafur*, 10 January 1903–11 April 1903.

[338] Independent Labour Party (Briton Ferry Branch), *Socialist and Labour Hymns* (Neath, n.d.).

[339] *Llais Llafur*, 14 and 21 February 1903.

information about the labour movement in south Wales with more general information about the national movement, as well as a curious section which contains a miscellany of articles on such topics as the British landscape and cooking. Any sign of a Welsh national consciousness was entirely absent. This was also reflected in the structural arrangements that were adopted by the ILP. A South Wales ILP Federation ultimately emerged after the 1898 coal strike, and any idea of creating a Welsh national structure was quietly abandoned.[340] Perhaps the best symbolic illustration of the attitude of the south Wales socialists towards Welshness was provided by the Aberdare Socialist Society, which held a complimentary dinner for Keir Hardie on St David's Day 1901. Despite the occasion, St David did not figure in the proceedings at all. The menu was printed in English, without even the presence of some token Welsh, and the toasts, apart from those to the guest and the branch, were to International Socialism and the Brotherhood of Man. *Hen Wlad Fy Nhadau* was conspicuous by its absence, and the banquet began and ended with the singing of the *Marseillaise*.[341]

It would be easy to see the culture of socialism in south Wales as part of a greater process of cultural homogenisation that was gripping south Wales in this period. 'Marxian' was aware of this process when he visited Cardiff in 1900: 'I paced the Metropolis of the country of my birth, and of the land of my fathers, only to discover afresh the weary characteristics of Liverpool and Hull and Birmingham', he mused, lamenting what he saw as 'the commercial repression of nationality and individuality'.[342] If, however, Welsh socialists were the recipients of an imported generic culture, they were also the agents of its adaptation for local use. When the Ystalyfera ILP Theatre Company put on its performance of 'The Poacher' in 1909, for instance, it informed the prospective audience that 'numerous local incidents connected

---

[340] *South Wales Labour Annual* (1902), p. 37; *South Wales Labour Annual* (1903), pp. 9–15.
[341] Swansea University Archive, SWCC: MNA/PP/131/3, Aberdare Socialist Society, Menu and Programme of Complimentary Banquet for Keir Hardie, 1 March 1901.
[342] *Labour Pioneer*, September 1900.

with industrial and political activities have been worked into the play'.[343] The outcome of this process of interplay was a singular socialist culture, rooted within the localities of south Wales and distinctive at a regional level. Undeniably Welsh, yet only ambiguously related to 'traditional' Welsh culture, it was tied to a pan-British identity. As the twentieth century progressed, and the culture of south Walian socialism developed and strengthened, the movement it represented and nourished became one of the primary engine rooms of the British labour movement. Through its political culture it played a crucial role in cementing south Wales into the great pan-British twentieth-century socialist project. The relationship of south Walian socialists to the rest of Britain was relatively straightforward. Their relationship with the rest of Wales was more complex.

[343] *Llais Llafur*, 6 January 1909.

4
BEYOND THE HEADS OF THE VALLEYS, c.1880s–1906

Wales is a singular noun but a plural experience.[1]

Welsh historiography has little to say about the fortunes of socialism outside south Wales in the period before 1906, but, if a full understanding of the relationship between Wales and socialism is to be achieved, there is a need to leave the coalfield, cross the heads of the valleys, and engage with the Wales beyond. This demands a geographical and cultural shift, but neither is straightforward because the geographical and cultural boundaries of Wales have never been coterminous. As Emrys Jones has recognised, 'had there not been a distinctive Welsh identity beyond Wales ... the cultural heritage of Wales would have been considerably diminished'.[2] Some major British cities had significant Welsh populations, which kept their native language and culture alive during this period,[3] and members of these expatriate communities played a role in the promotion of socialism. A full consideration of the interaction between Welshness and socialism cannot, therefore, be geographically restricted to Wales. If a geographical definition of Welshness is not possible, a cultural definition is similarly elusive. Wales was (and is) host to a variety of competing, evolving and sometimes

---

[1] Dai Smith, *Wales! Wales?* (London and Sydney, 1984), p. 1.
[2] Emrys Jones, 'The Welsh Language in England, c.1800–1914', in Geraint H. Jenkins (ed.), *Language and Community in the Nineteenth Century* (Cardiff, 1998), pp. 231–59, p. 231.
[3] Emrys Jones (ed.), *The Welsh in London, 1500–2000* (Cardiff, 2001); R. Merfyn Jones and D. Ben Rees, *Cymry Lerpwl a'u Crefydd: Dwy Ganrif o Fethodistiaeth Galfinaidd Gymreig/The Liverpool Welsh and their Religion: Two Centuries of Welsh Calvinistic Methodism* (Liverpool, 1984); D. Ben Rees, *The Welsh of Merseyside*, 2 vols (Liverpool, 1997 and 2001); William D. Jones, *Wales in America: Scranton and the Welsh, 1860–1920* (Cardiff, 1993); Ronald L. Lewis, *Welsh Americans: A History of Assimilation in the Coalfields* (Chapel Hill, NC, 2008); W. Ross Johnston, 'The Welsh Diaspora: Emigrating Around the World in the Late Nineteenth Century', *Llafur*, 6/2 (1993), 50–74.

overlapping cultures, ideologies and identities.[4] The concept of a 'national' or 'traditional' Welsh culture is potentially invidious; it is nevertheless unavoidable, and during the late nineteenth century such a culture was resurgent.[5] Neither was it geographically confined to any specific Welsh region. The geological barrier from the Black Mountain to the Black Mountains was culturally permeable. Consequently, Welsh national culture existed cheek by jowl with the new 'international' or 'American' culture of the south – often within individual personalities. Even Monmouthshire, which was legally English and apparently the most anglicised of all the Welsh counties, could appear, in terms of political tradition, 'more Welsh than Wales'.[6] In many respects, therefore, the boundary demarcating this chapter from the previous two is artificial, and a journey 'across the heads of the valleys' can demand a revisitation of Ystalyfera or Bedlinog, just as it can lead to Bethesda or Manchester. With these qualifications in mind, this chapter will examine the diffusion of socialism in the geographical entity of Wales beyond the heads of the valleys in the period prior to 1906; it will discuss the impact of the bitter Penrhyn lock-out of 1900–3, and it will examine some of the ways in which 'native' Welsh political culture related to socialism, both within Wales and, in one case, at the epicentre of industrial England.

(i) British socialism and Welsh Wales

Rural Wales provided less fertile ground for the growth of socialist organisations than the urban and industrial south. Penetration by socialist propagandists during the 1880s was extremely limited, while the development of formal socialist societies was restricted to the establishment of a Fabian group

---

[4] Merfyn Jones, 'Beyond Identity? The Reconstruction of the Welsh', *Journal of British Studies*, 31/4 (1992), 330–57; Neil Evans: 'Gogs, Cardis and Hwntws: Regions, Nation and State in Wales, 1840–1940', in Neil Evans (ed.), *National Identity in the British Isles* (Harlech, 1989), pp. 60–72; Emyr W. Williams: 'The Dynamic of Welsh Identity', in Neil Evans, *National Identity in the British Isles*, pp. 46–59.
[5] William Jones 'Y Deffroad Cenedlaethol', *Cymru Fydd*, November 1888, pp. 405–12.
[6] 'Gwent', 'The Revolution in Monmouthshire', *Cymru Fydd*, March 1889, pp. 131–4, p. 131.

at Aberystwyth University College in 1886.[7] This does not mean, however, that socialism was unheard of. Rather it was a familiar part of public discourse, both in the press and on the public platform, where its opponents took every opportunity to warn of its dangers. Opening a new chapel school in Wrexham in 1885, Benjamin Piercy JP, of nearby Marchwiel Hall, thought it appropriate to warn his audience of a range of contemporary evils, including 'Nihilism in Russia ... Socialism in Germany, Communism in France, and things in our own country and in Ireland [which] were all more or less traceable to the same cause'. Only a few days earlier he had told an audience at the Wrexham Music Festival of his hope that 'When music comes to reign supreme, such plants as the Nihilism of Russia, the Socialism of Germany, and the Communism of France will not thrive'.[8] Colonel Platt of Gorddinog, Llanfairfechan, shared the same concern with a Primrose League audience at Bangor's Masonic Hall in 1887: 'Socialism was making great progress in our midst, and unless it was combatted it could have but one ending – the ruination of the country.'[9] The leader writer of the *North Wales Chronicle* claimed to have met a socialist 'madcap' at Machynlleth in 1887, who was 'a pattern of many others in the Principality ... a man ... in advance of his time [who] for the sake of decency [should] have been born in the twentieth instead of the nineteenth century', and whose ideas threatened to endanger public morals.[10] Another press correspondent asserted that Montgomeryshire was a hotbed of socialism: 'Englishmen have long been blind to the fact that the fires of the spirit of lawlessness – call it Socialism or Communism, or what you will – have long been smouldering on the lonely hillsides of Wales'.[11] The bogey was so convincing that by the end of the decade a Conservative Registry had been established which aimed to vet tenants on behalf of landlords and

---

[7] Hopkin, 'Labour's Roots in Wales', p. 51.
[8] *Wrexham Advertiser and North Wales News*, 28 February 1885.
[9] *North Wales Chronicle*, 23 April 1887.
[10] *North Wales Chronicle*, 26 March 1887.
[11] *Wrexham Advertiser and North Wales News*, 3 December 1887.

'ascertain whether candidates for their farms are the friends of order and justice, or of anarchy and confiscation'.[12]

Not all coverage was so negative. By the mid-1880s Welsh journalists were increasingly agreeing that the questions raised by socialists in England were of fundamental importance, even if they were sceptical about socialist policies. *Baner ac Amserau Cymru* implicitly accepted the precepts of the socialists in 1886, when it stated in a series of articles on the labour question in Wales that '*Pwngc masnachol mawr y ganrif ddiweddaf oedd sut i gynnyrchu fwyaf o gyfoeth ... Ond pwngc mawr y dyddiau hyn ydyw sut i ranu cyfoeth*',[13] and within a year the paper was conceding the significance of the rise of socialism in Britain:

> Ni bu 'Sosialaeth' erioed yn dangos ei hun mor amlwg yn Mhrydain ag y gwna y flwyddyn hon. Un o 'arwyddion' amlycaf 'yr amseroedd,' yn ddiau, ydyw, cynnydd yr egwyddorion 'sosialaidd' yn mysg y werin Brydeinig.[14]

Y Faner was never reconciled to socialism, or independent labour representation. Rather it saw its own radicalism as an antidote to both socialism and anarchism,[15] and viewed socialist leaders like Keir Hardie as extremists.[16]

More sympathetic coverage was provided by *Cwrs y Byd*, published by Ebeneezer Rees of Ystalyfera and edited by Evan Pan Jones of Mostyn, Flintshire. The paper claimed to be independent Liberal in politics, identifying the land question, the drink trade and religious discrimination as the primary evils confronting society.[17] It nevertheless identified closely with working-class interests, seeing the miners and quarrymen of Wales as the most likely agents of the nation's social salvation.[18] It supported measures advocated by social-

---

[12] *Baner ac Amserau Cymru*, 30 October 1889.
[13] *Baner ac Amserau Cymru*, 25 August 1886 ('The great commercial question of the last century was how to produce the greatest amount of wealth ... but the great subject of the present is how to share wealth').
[14] *Baner ac Amserau Cymru*, 9 March 1887 ('Socialism has never manifested itself so prominently in Britain as it is doing this year. One of the most obvious "signs of the times" is surely the growth of "socialist" principles amongst the *gwerin* of Britain.')
[15] *Baner ac Amserau Cymru*, 20 January 1894.
[16] *Baner ac Amserau Cymru*, 4 July 1894.
[17] *Cwrs y Byd*, April 1891.
[18] *Cwrs y Byd*, May 1891.

ists, such as the eight-hour working day,[19] and increasingly during the 1890s published articles about socialism. These included the regular publication of the poetry and letters of the Mancunian socialist R.J. Derfel,[20] as well as articles with socialistic content by Ben Evans of Carmarthen,[21] and Ben Davies of Liverpool University.[22] In 1895 an editorial proclaimed approvingly '*I mi ac i filoedd yn Nghymru, y mae Sosialistiaeth yn fil pwysicach na Dadgysylltiad, ac os oes rhyw barti yn enill tir yn Nghymru, y Sosialistiaid yw hwnw.*'[23] The space *Cwrs y Byd* gave to socialist opinion in the 1890s was a sure sign that 'Welsh Wales' was contemplating the new doctrine, and not just from a hostile perspective. It represented, moreover, a substantial step towards the foundation of a more explicitly socialist Welsh-medium press, as represented by *Llais Llafur*, at the end of the 1890s.

Another arena for such discussion was provided by literary and debating societies, which acted as important centres of intellectual and cultural transmission across Wales. St Tudno's Literary Guild at Llandudno included a session on socialism in its programme in 1888,[24] and by the 1890s the topic was becoming a commonplace feature of debating society programmes. In Wrexham, the Wesleyan Mutual Improvement Society discussed a paper on socialism in April 1891,[25] and later in the same year a Mr Tickle of Liverpool visited the Christian Meeting House to deliver a paper especially aimed at the town's shop assistants, on 'the socialism of Christianity'.[26] The annual *Cylchwyl Lenyddol* at Salem chapel in Pwllheli offered a prize of one guinea at Easter 1893 for a winning essay on the subject of '*Cymdeithasiaeth Gristionogol*

[19] *Cwrs y Byd*, June 1891.
[20] For examples of Derfel's poetry, see *Cwrs y Byd*, July, August, October and December 1891, and January, May and June 1892. For political writings, see 'Aildrefniad Cymdeithas', *Cwrs y Byd* July–August 1892, and his letters on 'Cymdeithasiaeth', *Cwrs y Byd*, December 1892–June 1895.
[21] *Cwrs y Byd*, January 1891.
[22] 'Trefn o'r Tryblith', *Cwrs y Byd*, July–December 1891.
[23] *Cwrs y Byd*, September 1895 ('To me and to thousands in Wales, socialism is a thousand times more important than disestablishment, and if any party is winning ground in Wales, it is the socialists').
[24] *North Wales Chronicle*, 5 May 1888.
[25] *Wrexham Weekly Advertiser and North Wales News*, 11 April 1891.
[26] *Wrexham Weekly Advertiser and North Wales News*, 12 September 1891.

(Christian Socialism)'.[27] The subject of socialism was again on the agenda at Wrexham in 1893, when the Arena Society discussed a paper on the subject,[28] while at nearby Coedpoeth the *Cymdeithas Lenyddol yr Adwy* conducted a similar debate through the medium of Welsh in November 1894.[29] The subject was debated again at Llandudno in 1895, this time under the auspices of the Llandudno Literary and Scientific Society.[30] The *Cymdeithas Lenyddol* at Dinorwig joined the debate in 1896, under the presidency of the sympathetic Reverend Puleston Jones, but the majority voted against socialism.[31] The same was narrowly true at Porthmadog when its Presbyterian Church Literary Society held a debate on the socialism of *Merrie England* in 1897,[32] while members of the *Cymdeithas Lenyddol Ebenezer* at Pwllheli were content to hear a paper on '*Sosialaeth*', presented by the Reverend Owen Evans in 1898, without taking a vote.[33]

By the end of the decade there were signs that socialism was making progress. The Young Men's Literary Society at Ponkey debated 'Individualism and Socialism' in 1899, voting in favour of socialism.[34] Such events were signs that the cultural and intellectual leaders of some Welsh communities were finding socialism a topic of interest. In some cases this went beyond mere discussion. In 1899 the Reverend O.D. Williams, curate of Berse-Drelin Court, Wrexham, gained an MA from Durham University for a thesis on socialism.[35] Academic awareness of the subject was also shown by Professor Brough of Aberystwyth, who claimed in 1891 that land ownership among the early Welsh tribes was organised on a socialistic basis, thus adding an academic dimension to the debate about the inherent socialism of the Welsh.[36] Neither were such scholarly investigations restricted to the English language: the Anglesey schoolteacher and

[27] *Genedl Gymreig*, 14 December 1892.
[28] *Wrexham Weekly Advertiser and North Wales News*, 18 November 1893.
[29] *Baner ac Amserau Cymru*, 21 November 1894.
[30] *North Wales Chronicle*, 26 January 1895.
[31] *Genedl Gymreig*, 11 February 1896.
[32] *North Wales Chronicle*, 13 February 1897.
[33] *Genedl Gymreig*, 15 March 1898.
[34] *Wrexham Weekly Advertiser and North Wales News*, 28 October 1899.
[35] *North Wales Chronicle*, 24 June 1899.
[36] *North Wales Chronicle*, 27 June 1891.

antiquarian Owen Williamson produced a detailed survey in Welsh of the various schools of socialism, under the title '*Cymdeithasiad*'.[37]

What exactly was being debated under the name of socialism is another matter. The north Wales radical paper *Genedl Gymreig* discussed '*Sosialaeth – Hen a Diweddar*' in November 1898, but was forced to admit '*nid hawdd rhoddi i'r darllenydd ymofyngar ddeffiniad cyflawn o athrawiaeth Sosialaeth yn ei hagwedd bresenol. Y mae yr athrawon yn gwahaniaethu yn fawr.*'[38] Indeed, there was not even agreement on the correct Welsh term for socialism. The most popular term, *cymdeithasiaeth*, was coined in the late 1880s by the Mancunian socialist R.J. Derfel, although he complicated matters by also using the term *cymundebiaeth* for what might more commonly be called communism. Derfel's distinction between 'socialism' and 'communism' was not entirely straightforward. He used the two terms to differentiate what he called '*Cymdeithasiaeth rannol and Chymdeithasiaeth gyflawn*' (partial and complete socialism), a distinction which was less between socialism and communism and more in line with the distinction made between 'practical' and 'ideal' socialism by Robert Blatchford in *Merrie England* (the former referring to piecemeal social reform, and the latter referring to a complete socialist society).[39] During the 1890s and early 1900s, moreover, other writers began to complicate matters by introducing alternatives. These included *cymrodyddiaeth*,[40] *cyfranyddiaeth*,[41] *cydfeddianaeth*,[42] *cymrawdiaeth*,[43] and

[37] Bangor University Archive, Bangor MS 1781. It is not clear exactly when Williamson (1840–1910) wrote this document, although it is probable that it was produced sometime in the 1890s for a local *eisteddfod*.

[38] *Genedl Gymreig*, 8 November 1898 ('Socialism – Old and New'; 'It is not easy to give the inquiring reader a complete definition of socialist philosophy in its present form. The teachers differ greatly').

[39] R.J. Derfel, 'Cymundebiaeth', in D. Gwenallt Jones (ed.), *Detholiad o Ryddiaith Gymraeg R.J. Derfel* (Llandysul, 1945), vol. II, pp. 62–7; Blatchford, *Merrie England*, p. 44.

[40] Evan Davies, 'Cyfalaf a Llafur', *Geninen*, vol. 14 (1896), pp. 19–23.

[41] David Rhys Jones, *Celt*, 20 November 1891. He also refers to socialists as 'Cyfranyddion', *Genedl Gymreig*, 20 April 1892.

[42] Michael D. Jones, 'Cyfiawnder i'r Gweithiwr', *Geninen*, vol. 15 (1897), pp. 205–6; also *Tarian y Gweithiwr*, 7 March 1901.

[43] This was used by D.D. Walters, Natiomal Library of Wales, D.D. Walters Papers; *Llais Llafur*, 25 July 1908.

cymrodoliaeth.[44] The different terms conveyed an ideological spectrum, which in literal translation included 'societyism', 'communionism', 'co-contributionism', 'co-ownership' and 'comradeism' or 'fellowshipism'. It is significant, however, that all of these terms were ultimately superseded in common Welsh usage by terms directly imported from English. These included *socialyddiaeth*[45] and *socialistiaeth*,[46] both of which were supplanted by the almost universally used *sosialaeth* by the early 1900s. Tawney's 'radiant ambiguities' were just as obvious in Welsh as in English.[47] One approach to solving the ideological confusion was that taken by Owen Williamson, to whom *cymdeithasiaeth* was simply *'Yr enw cyffredinol am bob ymgais i wella cymdeithas'*.[48] Such inclusivity allowed individuals to define socialism for themselves, and in this respect they had much in common with their comrades across the English border.

One common popular conception of socialism was the vaguely defined 'Christian Socialism'. As Mr E.O.V. Lloyd put it when opening a new parish institute at Ruthin in 1889,

> They had heard a good deal those days about Socialism, a system which would put all men on the same level. That, of course, was impossible, but there was a kind of Christian Socialism, in which they could all be equal. In that Socialism he was a believer, and its doctrines he would recommend to them all.[49]

'Christian Socialism' was non-political, distinct from independent labour politics, and could be comfortably accommodated within Liberalism, as Mrs Tomkinson of Willington Hall, Cheshire, indicated when opening the Connah's Quay Liberal Club in 1891: *'Yr oeddynt wedi clywed pobl yn sôn yn fynych am Sosialaeth Gristionogol. Yr oedd Sosialaeth Gristionogol a Rhyddfrydiaeth yn dermau anghyfnewidiol ac anwahanol.'*[50] Despite their apparent imprecision, such beliefs

---

[44] Evan Pan Jones, 'Y Ddaear i'r Bobl', *Geninin* (1910), pp. 30–1.
[45] Evan Davies, 'Cyfalaf a Llafur'.
[46] *Cwrs y Byd*, February 1892.
[47] Tawney, *The Attack*, p. 60.
[48] Bangor University Archives, Bangor MS 1781, p. 8 ('The general name for every attempt to improve society').
[49] *North Wales Chronicle*, 26 June 1889.
[50] *Baner ac Amserau Cymru*, 17 October 1891 ('They had heard people speaking

could represent a powerful social doctrine, as revealed by W. Lewis Jones of Bangor, a journalist and aspiring newspaper editor, who outlined the issues which he thought Welsh Liberalism should address in 1889:

> How to redress the balance between class and class, how to solve the problem of the enormous inequalities which we see around us, how to readjust the relations between vast wealth and terrible poverty, between capital and labour, between the large-estated landlord and the toiling labourer – these are questions which we must face and which are common to all nations. I think we should learn to look a little beyond our own insular concerns, and take our stand shoulder to shoulder with the great party of freedom and justice throughout the world. In doing this, we would be striving to realise the great ideal of the Gospel in the brotherhood of all men ... In other words, what I believe in is nothing less than Socialism – but not the Socialism of anarchy and revolution; but what I believe can, without cant, be called Christian Socialism.[51]

In some abstract and selective forms, then, socialism was permeating Wales, and becoming part of its political consciousness, not just in the industrial south, but across the country.

The establishment of formal socialist societies was a slower process. The Fabians first established a branch at Aberystwyth in 1886, but did not organise on a sustained basis until the mid-1890s.[52] By then, however, the Aberystwyth society was deemed by the Fabian Executive as part of 'the most important branch of the Society's local organization'.[53] Its numerical strength wavered from 13 in 1898 to 32 in 1902, when it was the largest university Fabian society in Britain.[54] At the college election of 1897, the socialist candidate, W.H.

frequently about Christian Socialism. Christian Socialism and Liberalism were immutable and identical terms').

[51] Bangor University Archives, Bangor MS 479(iii), W. Lewis Jones, Bangor, to the Welsh Newspaper Company, 30 December 1889.
[52] *Thirteenth Annual Report of the Executive of the Fabian Society*, May 1896, p. 2.
[53] *Fourteenth Annual Report of the Executive of the Fabian Society*, May 1897, p. 7.
[54] *Sixteenth Annual Report of the Executive of the Fabian Society*, May 1899, p. 9; *Seventeenth Annual Report of the Executive of the Fabian Society*, May 1900, p. 22; *Eighteenth Annual Report of the Executive of the Fabian Society*, May 1901, p. 16; *Nineteenth Annual Report of the Executive of the Fabian Society*, May 1902, p. 11; A.M. MacBriar, *Fabian Socialism and English Politics*, pp. 168–9. The society collapsed in 1904, and was not revived until 1912.

Darby, polled a respectable 53 votes, well behind the Liberal candidate, but ahead of both the Welsh Nationalist and the Conservative candidates.[55] Admittedly, B. Scott Williams, the society's secretary, did less well the following year, and the socialists slipped into fourth place,[56] but the influence of socialism at Aberystwyth cannot be judged in quantitative terms alone. The vibrancy of the socialist contribution to academic debate must also be considered, as reported in the college magazine:

> For intensity of conviction and earnestness of tone the Socialist speakers, whether at College elections or debates, are always noticeable; and perhaps it would be safe to say that at elections the cogency of many of their arguments is keenly felt by many who, with the object of obtaining a more practical outlet for the political energy represented by a vote, give that vote to the Liberal cause.[57]

The Aberystwyth Fabians attracted important speakers to the town. In 1896 these included Hubert Bland and Enid Stacy,[58] and in 1897 Fred Brocklehurst lectured to an audience of 150.[59] In November 1898 Ramsay MacDonald battled his way through snow to lecture at the Buarth on 'Socialism and Current Politics',[60] and Bernard Shaw visited in 1899.[61] The group also hosted academic speakers from within Wales, including Professor Burrows of Cardiff, who lectured on 'Socialism – Ideal and Practical' in 1900.[62] Thus, the Aberystwyth Fabians introduced socialism to a significant and influential section of Welsh society. Among the students who were impressed by W.H. Darby's stand in 1897 was Mary Parry, who, as Mary Silyn Roberts, went on to make a major contribution to the adult education movement in north Wales.[63] An even more influential figure to come

---

[55] *University College of Wales Magazine*, vol. XX (1897–8), pp. 119–23.
[56] *University College of Wales Magazine*, vol. XXI (1898–9), pp. 47–50.
[57] *University College of Wales Magazine*, vol. XX (1897–8), p. 120.
[58] *Fabian News*, July 1896.
[59] *Fabian News*, January 1897.
[60] *University College of Wales Magazine*, vol. XXI (1898–9), p. 152.
[61] *Seventeenth Annual Report of the Executive of the Fabian Society*, May 1900, p. 22.
[62] *Goleuad*, 28 February 1900.
[63] National Library of Wales, Silyn Roberts Papers, Mary Parry to Robert Silyn Roberts, 24 October 1897.

in contact with socialism at Aberystwyth was Thomas Jones, later to serve as adviser to four prime ministers. Jones stood as a Labour candidate in the 1894 student elections, and by the time he left Aberystwyth for Glasgow had become a committed socialist.[64]

Aberystwyth was not the only university town to experience socialist influence. At Bangor too students were discussing socialism in the mid-1890s. William Eames, a future editor of *Genedl Gymreig*, recalled discussing Blatchford's *Merrie England* with members of the college football team around 1894,[65] after which socialism became 'one of those questions which seem to crop up in the [debating] Society with periodic regularity'.[66] The socialists were defeated in debate in 1894,[67] as was a motion in favour of trade unionism in 1895,[68] but this did not deter them from raising the matter again in 1896. Again they were defeated, but only after an intense debate with over 100 students present. Blatchford's *Merrie England*, 'the great *locus classicus* of the socialists', was a key influence, and the socialist speakers included John Jenkins ('Gwili'), who 'delighted his hearers by his poetical effusions on "dreams" in general and socialistic dreams in particular, and waxed eloquent over the question of equality'. Only after a speech by D. Miall Edwards that was considered 'the best heard for years' did opinion swing against the socialists.[69] Despite such setbacks, a formal Fabian Society was established at Bangor by the turn of the century, which aimed, in classic Fabian language, to 'assist in the formation of a healthy sentiment as to the duties which Society expects the educated to discharge'.[70] The group continued to advocate socialism at college debates,[71] although its formal allegiance

[64] E.L. Ellis, *T.J.: A Life of Dr. Thomas Jones CH* (Cardiff, 1992), pp. 28–53.
[65] William Eames, 'Brithgofion Newyddiadurwr', *Y Genhinen*, 11/2 (1961), 78–82, 79.
[66] *Magazine of the University College of North Wales*, vol V, no. 2 (March 1896), p. 34.
[67] *Magazine of the University College of North Wales*, vol. II, no. 2 (March 1894), p. 31.
[68] *Magazine of the University College of North Wales*, vol. IV, no. 2 (March 1895), p. 25.
[69] *Y Goleuad*, 29 January 1896; *Magazine of the University College of North Wales*, vol. V no. 2 (March 1896), pp. 34–5.
[70] *Magazine of the University College of North Wales*, vol. X, no. 1 (December 1900), p. 33.
[71] Other names appear amongst its membership that were to feature in the later history of socialism in the north – such as J.R. Jones, author of the only Fabian

to the Fabian Society was relatively short-lived. In 1902 it seceded from membership 'for the typically Fabian reason that its members think they can wield a wider influence if they are not officially associated with our name'.[72]

Although the university Fabian societies were important pioneers of socialism in rural Wales, they were preceded by an independent and surprisingly strong manifestation of Fabian socialism in rural Cardiganshire. In 1892 a Fabian Society was established near Llandysul,[73] under the influence of David Rhys Jones, the Cardiff doctor, who originated from southern Cardiganshire, but who had become a socialist in Cardiff a couple of years previously.[74] Jones launched the society, with an initial membership of fifteen, at Penrhiwllan on 11 March 1892.[75] At the end of April the society claimed 26 members, and started meeting monthly,[76] which it did for several years. Unlike the university societies, which consisted of a mobile, professional membership, and notwithstanding the role of the Cardiff-based Jones as an external catalyst in its formation, the *Cymdeithas Ffabianaid Dyffryn Orllwyn* was firmly rooted in its own local community. Its secretary, David Jones of Llyngwyn, Penrhiwllan, was a local minister,[77] and its membership included other locally prominent individuals, including at least one lay-preacher, John Jones of Blaentir.[78] David Jones was the brother of the land reformer Evan

---

Tract to be originally composed in Welsh (*Magazine of the University College of North Wales*, vol. 11, no. 1 (Dec. 1902), p. 46). The group met with only limited success in college debates. A Labour candidate came a bad third in the college elections of 1903 (*Magazine of the University College of North Wales*, vol. XIII, no. 3 (Dec. 1903), pp. 44–5), and socialism was considered impractical by a wide margin as late as 1907 (*Magazine of the University College of North Wales*, vol. XVI, no. 2 (March 1907), p. 41). However, the Literary and Debating Society did vote in favour of railway nationalisation in 1908 (*Magazine of the University College of North Wales*, vol. XVII, no. 2 (March 1908), p. 51).

[72] *Nineteenth Annual Report of the Executive of the Fabian Society*, May 1902, p. 7.
[73] *Fabian News*, April 1892.
[74] See above, pp. 53–8.
[75] *Baner ac Amserau Cymru*, 6 April 1892.
[76] Fabian Society Archive (British Library of Political and Economic Science), COLL MISC 375 – Volume 4 (newspaper cutting dated 28 April 1892).
[77] *Baner ac Amserau Cymru*, 6 April 1892.
[78] British Library of Political and Economic Science, Fabian Society Archive, COLL MISC 375 – Volume 4.

Pan Jones.[79] Significantly, the group transacted its business entirely through the medium of Welsh. This puzzled Edward Pease, the Fabian Society's secretary, who laboured under the mistaken belief that *Cymdeithas* was the name of the place where the society had been established.[80] It also, however, ensured that the Cardiganshire Fabians experienced virtually total autonomy. *Fabian News* noted that the society 'speaks Welsh, and consequently does not often communicate with headquarters'.[81] This was not merely incidental, and the group was clearly conscious of its role as a distinctly Welsh socialist society. It advertised itself in the press as '*y gymdeithas Gymreig gyntaf o Socialists*',[82] and advocated the formation of similar societies throughout Wales.[83]

This was not to be, however, and the Dyffryn Orllwyn Fabian Society must be seen as an exceptional flowering of Fabianism, due to a particular convergence of circumstances in a specific place. While Fabians may have played an important role in influencing key members of a coming generation, they did not create a political structure. The creation of such structures – in the form of ILP branches – was difficult enough in industrial south Wales. Beyond the southern ports and the coalfield it proved virtually impossible. A list of contributions to the ILP's election fund in 1899 included only two from beyond the industrial south, one from Builth Wells and one from Rhyl.[84] There were some signs of ILP influence over the border, such as in Oswestry, where a member was elected to the local school board in 1899.[85] There were also isolated individuals with ILP sympathies in rural Wales, such as W. Rees of Llechryd, who followed Keir Hardie's career with 'a kind of Hero-Worship' from the early 1890s onwards.[86] The obstacles to forming ILP branches

[79] *Fabian News*, April 1892. For Pan Jones, see below pp. 184–8.
[80] *Fabian News*, April 1892; National Library of Wales, T.J. Roberts Papers, NLW MS 23452 D, Edward Pease to T.J. Roberts, 3 March 1943.
[81] *Fabian News*, July 1894.
[82] *Celt*, 29 April 1892 ('the first Welsh society of Socialists').
[83] *Celt*, 16 September 1892.
[84] *Labour Leader* (Supplement), 6 May 1899.
[85] *ILP Annual Conference Report*, 1899.
[86] Francis Johnson Correspondence, 1914/468, undated letter (1914) from W. Rees to Keir Hardie.

were, however, overwhelming. Hugh D. Williams and his son, for example, were socialist sympathisers from Builth Wells. They distributed socialist literature in the town, with the help of a local newsagent who discretely recommended the material to likely customers. In frustration Williams even resorted to distributing the literature anonymously through the post, sending it to the *Clarion* office for forwarding. Overt activism was, however, not feasible, as he explained in a letter to ILP head office in 1899:

> I have given much thought to the subject of forming a branch of the ILP or other Socialist body in this town, and with a full knowledge of our supporters and their circumstances. I can confidently say that at present it is impracticable. The town contains only about 1,300 inhabitants. The people are consequently all known to each other, and are so intimately connected in their business and other relations, that it would be very easy to bring [pressure] to bear upon some of our people if they did anything publicly.[87]

One region which may have offered an exception, and where the ILP did show some signs of life in the 1890s, was the north-east, in the coalfield communities around Wrexham. The debating societies of the Wrexham area took a keen interest in socialism. Several prominent socialist speakers also visited the region during the 1890s, including Ben Tillett in 1892 and 1893 and Tom Mann in 1895.[88] There was also a *Clarion* inspired Cinderella Club in Wrexham in the mid-1890s, which organised feasts and magic lantern shows for children with the support of activists from Chester.[89] Attempts to establish ILP branches were, however, intermittent and of limited success. A 'Wrexham and District Independent Labour Party' organised a meeting at the Albion Hotel Assembly Room in the town in 1894, at which Robert Wheare of Liverpool spoke on 'Labour Politics'. The extent to which the branch was genuinely rooted in Wrexham is nevertheless

---

[87] Francis Johnson Correspondence, 1899/48, Hugh D. Williams to John Penny, 21 June 1899.
[88] *Wrexham Advertiser and North Wales News*, 2 April 1892, 28 October 1893 and 21 September 1895. Keir Hardie was also booked to attend a miners' demonstration at Pentre Broughton in 1893, but had to send apologies at the last minute, *Wrexham Advertiser and North Wales News*, 29 July 1893 and 5 August 1893.
[89] *Scout*, February 1896.

questionable, as attendance was small and the chair was taken by an ILP representative from Chester.[90] Several months later an ILP branch at Broughton hosted a lecture on 'The Evils of Capitalism'.[91] Although there is no evidence of sustained ILP activity at this stage, the north-eastern coalfield offered potential to the socialists commensurate with that of the southern coalfield.

A different context for the spread of socialist ideas was offered by the expanding holiday trade of the 1890s. By the end of the century *Clarion* readers were among the expanding number of visitors visiting the Welsh coastal resorts.[92] If they went to Llandudno, holidaymakers could visit the Masonic Hall and witness Mr Cheetham's Phrenological and Cinematographic Entertainment. In 1897 this included a series of 'Sunday talks for the people', one of which was on 'Christian Socialism' and was supported by limelight effects, songs and solos arranged by Mrs Cheetham.[93] Thus, socialist discourse found a place within the Welsh leisure industry. By the mid-1890s *Clarion* activists had begun to penetrate even more deeply into rural Wales. One of them subverted a Primrose League parade in Dolgellau in 1896 by joining the procession and sticking *Clarion* stickers to the marchers and their instruments.[94] Other Clarionettes used north Wales as a retreat for painting,[95] and by the end of the decade the Birmingham *Clarion* Cycle Club was organising an annual cycle tour of Wales. In 1900 this comprised a train ride to Llangollen, followed by a week-long bicycle ride, taking in Corwen, Cerrigydrudion, Beddgelert, Portmadoc, Llanberis, Caernarfon, Barmouth, Aberdyfi, Aberystwyth and Dolgellau.[96] During the early 1900s 'picturesque Wales' became an increasingly popular destination for *Clarion* cyclists from across the border. In 1901, the *Clarion*'s cycling correspondent took the north Wales steamer from Liverpool

[90] *Wrexham Advertiser and North Wales News*, 16 November 1894.
[91] *Wrexham Advertiser and North Wales News*, 23 March 1895.
[92] *Clarion*, 23 June 1900 (apartments are advertised in Rhyl and Llandudno); *Clarion* 21 July 1900 (apartments in Aberystwyth, Conwy, Llandudno and Rhyl).
[93] *North Wales Chronicle*, 14 August 1897.
[94] *Scout*, February 1896.
[95] *Clarion*, 7 November and 23 December 1896.
[96] *Clarion*, 18 August 1900.

to Llandudno and undertook a tour of north Wales which included Llangollen, Corwen, Llandrillo, Bala, Ffestiniog, Bettws y Coed, Llanrwst and Conwy.[97] The Wye Valley also became a popular destination in the early 1900s, particularly with *Clarion* cyclists from the English midlands.[98]

This increasingly leisure-orientated relationship between socialists from urban-industrial England and 'picturesque Wales' was problematic, however. The extent to which it involved serious propaganda work is difficult to measure, but there is little evidence in the published reports of such tours that propaganda was the chief priority, and it is quite likely that as the relationship developed propaganda work became a smaller and smaller part of it. Indeed, the more serious propagandists of the *Clarion* vans consciously avoided rural Wales. One reason for this was the problem presented by the Welsh language. When the van visited Wales for the second time, in 1899, it was intended, after a tour of the south Wales valleys, to travel from Neath 'through the wilds of Wales' to Aberystwyth. After discovering from Thomas Jones, however, that much of the route went through areas in which Welsh was the principal language, it was decided that the plan should be abandoned, and the van was taken by train directly to Shrewsbury. The revelation that the population of rural Wales was largely Welsh speaking came as a shock to John Bruce Glasier, who was the van's principal propagandist on the 1899 tour:

> it seemed as if the roof of the Van suddenly opened, and the truth flashed in upon my brain. The people of that remote part of the empire do not understand English! I had never thought of it before. I had imagined that the Welsh people like my kinsmen in the Highlands were everywhere nowadays familiar with the imperial tongue. Instead of which English is hardly better understood than Hindustanese in central Wales ... Did I not say that Wales was virtually an unknown land?[99]

This 'unknown land', with its mysterious language, picturesque landscape and abundance of ancient ruins, presented itself to most English socialists more as the subject of scientific

[97] *Clarion*, 27 July 1901.
[98] *Clarion*, 26 August 1904, 9 August 1907, 17 July 1908, 2 July 1909, 29 July 1910.
[99] *Clarion*, 27 May 1899.

inquiry than as a potential socialist seedbed. Even before the decision was made to abandon the van's tour, Bruce Glasier was envisaging a journey which had more in common with a scientific expedition than a socialist propaganda tour. 'By the time the Van winds up its tour at Aberystwyth', he wrote, 'its log-book, I venture to predict, will be replete with invaluable relics and variegated scientific lore pertaining to present day and primitive Cymric civilisation.'[100]

Bruce Glasier was not alone among British socialists in adopting a romantic, stereotypical view of rural Wales and its people. His idol, William Morris, toured mid-Wales in 1875. He was struck by the beauty of the landscape, and dreamt of settling in the Dyfi Valley: 'I thought that it would be so nice to have a little house & a cow there, & a Welsh poney [sic] or two', he wrote home to his family from Bala.[101] To Robert Blatchford, who recalled in his autobiography a walking tour he made of mid-Wales in the 1870s, a Welshman he met on the way 'clucked with his throat and rumbled in his chest, and made wild passes in the air with his arms, like Merlin working a spell',[102] and to John Burns, visiting north Wales in 1897, the Welsh were 'the kind of people one would associate with such beautiful scenery', and exhibited a melancholy, particularly in their language and song, which was 'natural to people living in mountaneuous [sic] countries'.[103] Keir Hardie too was prone to deal in stereotypes when discussing the Welsh. Most of Hardie's were rooted in the industrial south, where the people were 'simple, kindly, affectionate ... warm hearted and trusting ... [and] gregarious'.[104] His stereotypes of north-Walians were different: 'The Celtic fire which so brightly illumes the eye of the South Walian', he wrote after a visit to Caernarfonshire in 1901, 'seems to be smouldering in the dull sunken eye so common in the North.'[105] To Hardie, as to other socialists, the people of mid- and

---

[100] *Clarion*, 6 May 1899.
[101] William Morris to Jenny and May Morris, 5 April 1875, in Norman Kelvin (ed.), *The Collected Letters of William Morris, vol. 1, 1848–1880* (Princeton, 1984), p. 251.
[102] Robert Blatchford, *My Eighty Years* (London, 1931), p. 155.
[103] *North Wales Chronicle*, 15 May 1897.
[104] *Labour Leader*, 9 July 1898.
[105] *Labour Leader*, 17 August 1901.

north Wales were a breed apart, tied to their communities 'by the hallowed associations which inevitably grow up with the generations, and which appeal to the men and women of Wales in even a deeper way than to the average Briton'. Their sensibilities, he concluded, were 'attuned by the influences which emanate from the everlasting hills'.[106]

It was thus to a stereotype that British socialists related when confronting most of Wales in the 1890s and early 1900s. For most of them, the Wales beyond the heads of the valleys was a picturesque and romantic land of fairy tales and curiosities. In this sense it appealed to the anti-industrial, pastoral impulse that fed late-nineteenth and early-twentieth-century British socialism.[107] It also provided a perfect venue in which to enjoy the socialist culture of alternative recreation and fellowship. This was epitomised from 1907 to 1910 by the series of Fabian summer schools which took place at Pen yr Allt, near Llanbedr in Meirionnydd. The location was discovered by a Fabian, Dr Lawson Dodd, who was touring the region by bicycle in 1907, and was inspired by the surroundings to organise a series of summer schools that included not just socialist lectures, but also river and sea bathing, Swedish drill and walking excursions in 'scenery unsurpassed in wildness and grandeur'. This provided an inspiring experience for participants, whose eccentricities were looked upon askance by the locals.[108] Like the increasingly leisure-focused *Clarion* cycling programme, the Fabian summer schools were an expression of a one-way relationship between socialists and rural Wales. They were part of a process that saw rural, picturesque Wales appropriated to the rest of Britain as part of a hierarchy of recreational landscapes to be enjoyed under the banner of the twentieth-century amenity movement. Keir Hardie articulated this view of Britain in 1898, in some notes about the Co-operative Holidays Association, which was

---

[106] *Labour Leader*, 11 April 1903.
[107] Jan Marsh, *Back to the Land: The Pastoral Impulse in Victorian England from 1880 to 1914* (London, 1982).
[108] Katherine Watson, 'Some Letters Concerning the Fabian Summer Schools in Merioneth, 1907–10', *Journal of the Merioneth Historical and Record Society*, 13/4 (2001), 392–400.

planning, much to his approval, to open camps at Barmouth, Bangor and Conwy:

> Thanks to the influence of Jefferies, Thoreau, Ruskin, and comrades like Harry Lowerison we are getting a bit more reasonable in our ideas of holiday enjoyment. New love for meadows, woods, and mountains has bought into existence the fellowship called the Co-operative Holidays Association, in whose guesthouses so many Socialists have met during recent years. The illustrated programme conjures up visions of summer days spent in joyous comradeship amid the bewitching splendours of Snowdon and Scawfell, Borrowdale and Bettws-y-Coed. It tells of holidays in Wales, the Lake District, on the South Coast and at Whitby.[109]

Such was the context in which the relationship between Wales beyond the heads of the valleys and British socialism was defined. It may have provided socialists with opportunities for relaxation and fellowship in beautiful surroundings. Nevertheless, it encouraged a one-dimensional and partial view of Wales, which, beyond the industrial south, was seen as a retreat from the genuine theatres of socialist agitation in urban-industrial Britain. One *Clarion* cycling enthusiast wrote in 1901 that he had discovered a perfect holiday venue for Clarionettes. 'The roads are good for cycling', he reported. 'It is within easy reach of nearly every show place in North Wales; lodgings and food are good, and fairly cheap. There is good free (fly) fishing.'[110] He was referring to Bethesda, where almost 3,000 workers and their families were locked into an industrial dispute that made socialist views of picturesque Wales seem hollow in the extreme.

(II) SOCIALISTS, QUARRYMEN AND LORD PENRHYN

Aside from the coalfields, the most fertile ground for socialism in Wales was arguably in the quarrying regions of the north-west. In the valleys of Snowdonia, close-knit industrial communities with highly developed traditions of literacy and political debate had experienced decades of tense

---

[109] ILP Archive (Organisational and Regional Records, 1856–1955), Keir Hardie Manuscripts, 15 June 1898.
[110] *Clarion*, 11 May 1901.

industrial relations, which, by the 1880s, had created a strong sense of class solidarity among the quarrymen.[111] This was not lost on H.M. Hyndman, who reported that a 'formidable movement' existed among the district's workers when he visited Llanberis in 1886.[112] Neither was Hyndman alone in noticing a political awakening among the region's workers. The local press also discerned a growing political consciousness among them.[113] The Caernarfon-based *Genedl Gymreig* reported in 1891 that the quarrymen of Nantlle favoured state ownership of the quarries, which, it argued, effectively made them socialists. Dyffryn Nantlle, it conjectured, would be the perfect place to open a socialist college, due to the ready supply of willing students.[114] Notwithstanding its Liberalism, the *Genedl* was prepared to concede the relevance of socialist ideas. It approvingly viewed Gladstone's local government reforms as socialistic, and repeated William Harcourt's view that 'we are all socialists now'. '*Clywir llais y Sosialydd yn ein heolydd*', the paper noted in 1893, '*a gwr dawnus a dil-ildio [sic] ydyw efe. Dyrchafiad y lluaws ac nid yr ychydig ydyw baich ei genadwri ... Athrawiaeth ryfedd ydyw hon o eiddo y Sosialydd, ond y mae yn prysur lefeinio cymdeithas yn y dyddiau hyn ... Nid yw y gair Sosialaeth yn dychryn neb yn awr.*'[115]

The way had been prepared for socialism by the visit of Michael Davitt to Blaenau Ffestiniog, where he was given a rousing welcome in 1886,[116] and by the early 1890s it was reported that the quarrymen there were keen to entertain

---

[111] Cyril Parry, 'Socialism in Gwynedd', pp. 1–33; Cyril Parry, *The Radical Tradition in Welsh Politics: A Study of Liberal and Labour Politics in Gwynedd, 1900–1920* (Hull, 1970), pp. 1–21; R. Merfyn Jones, *The North Wales Quarrymen, 1874–1922* (Cardiff, 1982), pp. 1–174; Jean Lindsay, *The Great Strike: A History of the Penrhyn Quarry Dispute, 1900–1903* (London, 1987), pp. 7–60; Frank Price Jones, 'Gwleidyddiaeth Sir Gaernarfon yn y Bedwared Ganrif ar Bymtheg', in *Radicaliaeth a'r Werin Gymreig yn y Bedwaredd Ganrif ar Bymtheg* (Cardiff, 1977), pp. 148–80.

[112] *Justice*, 23 January 1886.

[113] *Genedl Gymreig*, 23 April and 21 May 1890.

[114] *Genedl Gymreig*, 29 April 1891.

[115] *Genedl Gymreig*, 14 February 1893 ('The voice of the socialist is heard in our streets, and he is a talented and unyielding individual. The elevation of the many and not the few is the onus of his message ... This philosophy of the socialist is surprising but it is busy leavening society these days ... The word socialism scares no-one now').

[116] Jones, *The North Wales Quarrymen*, p. 163.

a socialist speaker, such as John Burns or Ben Tillett.[117] Keir Hardie spoke at a quarrymen's demonstration at Blaenau Ffestiniog during the industrial dispute there in 1893,[118] but it was the first of the disputes at Bethesda's Penrhyn quarries in 1896–7 that really began to attract the attention of British socialists. Keir Hardie raised the quarrymen's plight at the ILP Annual Conference in London in April 1897, chiding Lord Penrhyn for his intransigent attitude and characterising him as 'the latest and most successful Socialist agitator'.[119] The SDF too poured scorn on the 'feudalist slave driver' Penrhyn, arguing that the dispute was 'sad for the quarrymen, but ... a lesson to the world'.[120] Socialist organisations in England were also involved in organising fund-raising concerts for the Bethesda Male Voice Choir.[121] Foreshadowing the events of three years later, the most detailed treatment of the dispute was given by the *Clarion*. Early in the lockout, the paper published a piece by the London Welshman Richard Roberts giving the background to what he called 'probably the most important event in the history of the North Wales slate industry',[122] and as events unfolded Blatchford himself contributed detailed articles drawing sharp socialist lessons from the dispute.[123]

The socialist response to the 1896–7 Penrhyn dispute was no more than a foretaste of what was to come in the more protracted and bitter dispute three years later. Nevertheless, it did mark the beginning of the gradual integration of the north Wales quarrying districts into the wider British labour movement. There is also evidence that socialist literature, most notably Blatchford's *Merrie England*, was circulating within the quarrying communities. In 1898 a popular young quarryman left the Oakley quarry at Blaenau Ffestiniog to work at a neighbouring quarry, and his workmates wanted to

[117] *Genedl Gymreig*, 28 October 1891.
[118] *Wrexham Advertiser and North Wales News*, 6 May 1893.
[119] *Labour Leader*, 24 April 1897.
[120] *Justice*, 13 February 1897.
[121] *Justice*, 27 February 1897; *Daily News*, 21 January 1897; *Leicester Chronicle and Leicestershire Mercury*, 14 and 17 April, 15 May, 24 and 31 July 1897.
[122] *Clarion*, 31 October 1896.
[123] *Clarion*, 9 January and 6 February 1897.

buy him a leaving gift. The press report of proceedings throws light upon the status of socialism among the quarrymen:

> Gwyddent ei fod yn llyfrbryf, ond ofnent ychwanegu at ei ystorfa o wybodaeth na blaenllymu ei eiriau, oblegyd cawsent brofi droion fin ei watwareg, yn eu barnu ac yn tynu i lawr seiliau cymdeithas fel y cerir hi yn mlaen yn bresenol. Am hyny, wedi dwys a maith ymgynghori, penderfynwyd rhoddi iddo offeryn y mae yn orhoff ohono i beri iddo freuddwydio am Merrie England a chymdeithasiaeth. Cyflwynwyd yr anrheg, sef cetyn hardd mewn case, iddo gan Mr. Evan Owen, Manod road.[124]

This story suggests not only that socialist literature was being read and discussed in the north Wales quarries of the 1890s, but that support for socialism did not necessarily lead to social ostracism. At worst, this socialist was seen as an eccentric, but he was clearly respected due to his wide reading. Keir Hardie claimed a few years later that eight out of ten members of an ambulance corps from Blaenau Ffestiniog attending the 1901 *Eisteddfod* at Merthyr were members of the ILP.[125] If this is true, it is unlikely that the crew was representative of its wider community, and it would be misleading to imply that socialism was a prominent topic in the proceedings of the quarrymen's *cabanau*.[126] Nevertheless, the *Merrie England* pipe dreamer represented an important toehold for socialism in north Walian society.

An opportunity for socialists to consolidate such toeholds was offered by the long and bitter lockout of 1900–3 at Bethesda. The most bitter and protracted dispute in the history of British industrial relations, the Penrhyn lockout had the potential to create a political watershed in north

---

[124] *Genedl Gymreig*, 20 September 1898 ('They knew he was a book-worm, but feared adding to his store of knowledge or further sharpening his vocabulary, because they had frequently experienced his cutting scorn, criticising them and pulling down the foundations of society as it is carried on at present. Consequently, after intense and protracted consultation it was decided to give him a tool that he was very fond of to induce him to dream about *Merrie England* and socialism. The gift, namely a beautiful pipe in a case was presented to him by Mr. Evan Owen, Manod Road').

[125] *Labour Leader*, 17 August 1901.

[126] Religious and denominational controversy dominated such discussions. Vivian P. Williams, 'Cipolwg ar Lyfr Cofnodion (1902–04) "Caban Sink y Mynydd", Chwarel Llechwedd, Blaenau Ffestiniog', *Journal of the Merioneth Historical and Record Society*, 14/3 (2004), 240–55.

Wales of the same nature as had the 1898 coal dispute in the south. The three years from the closure of the quarries in November 1900 to the end of the dispute in November 1903 saw a greater socialist presence in north Wales, and a greater coverage of north Wales in the socialist press, than ever before. Bethesda suddenly found itself on the circuit for socialist speakers. Keir Hardie made the ten-hour forty-five-minute train journey from Merthyr in August 1901, and urged an audience of between four and five thousand to continue the struggle. He assured them that the English trade unions would support them, and went on to raise the matter in the House of Commons.[127] Hardie was the most prominent of the socialists to visit Bethesda, but he was not alone. Robert Williams, who had been active in support of the south Wales miners in 1898, visited in the early months of the dispute and made contact with the quarrymen's supporters on behalf of Lambeth Trades Council,[128] and as the dispute unfolded other socialist speakers, including Pete Curran, Ben Tillett and Robert Blatchford, also visited.[129]

The socialist press took up the quarrymen's cause, particularly the *Clarion*, which published a series of articles by A.M. Thompson, the paper's co-founder, under the title 'Desolate Bethesda' in the spring of 1901.[130] Thompson visited Bethesda several times, with the help of an interpreter, and produced a detailed account of the history of industrial relations in the quarries and the background to the lockout, as well as an emotive account of the suffering of the quarrymen's families. In addition to Thompson's articles, the paper gave space to W.J. Parry, the quarrymen's most prominent local supporter, to give an account of some events in the dispute, although this backfired as Parry was sued by Penrhyn for libel and the *Clarion* had to appeal for funds for his defence.[131] The *Clarion* initiated the establishment of

---

[127] *Llais Llafur* 10 August 1901; *Labour Leader*, 17 August 1901; Jones, *The North Wales Quarrymen*, p. 253.
[128] *Llais Llafur*, 4 May 1901; *Justice*, 4 May 1901.
[129] Jones, *The North Wales Quarrymen*, p. 269.
[130] *Clarion*, 16, 23 and 30 March, 6 and 13 April 1901.
[131] J. Roose Williams, *Quarryman's Champion: The Life and Activities of William John Parry of Coetmor* (Denbigh, 1978), pp. 213–24.

a relief fund for the quarrymen's families, which raised over £1,800 by the time subscriptions were closed in December 1901,[132] and the fund-raising efforts of the various *Clarion* organisations were the most prominent among the socialist bodies in England. Local committees were established to coordinate the relief fund, and *Clarion* clubs arranged fund-raising concerts by the Penrhyn choir.[133] The *Clarion*'s leading role was tacitly acknowledged when Robert Blatchford took the chair at a crowded meeting in support of the quarrymen at the Memorial Hall in London on 22 May 1901, presiding over a cast of speakers that included socialists such as Keir Hardie, George Barnes and Pete Curran as well as Liberals like Lloyd George and the quarrymen's own leader D.R. Daniel.[134]

The *Clarion*'s efforts certainly raised the paper's profile in Bethesda. Mrs Myddleton-Worrall, better known as 'Julia Dawson', author of the paper's women's column, journeyed from her home at Wallasey to Bethesda in June 1901, and attended a meeting at which three cheers were given for the *Clarion*. Although she could not understand the details of the meeting, which was conducted in Welsh, she did report that

> The *Clarion* is a household word in Bethesda now! One old man at the meeting, who couldn't speak English, saw the badge in my husband's cap, and grasped his hand, with the word *Clarion* welling gratefully more from his heart than his lips. It was a golden moment.[135]

W.W. Lloyd, the secretary of the quarrymen's relief fund, also wrote to the *Clarion* in gratitude for its efforts,[136] and appreciation of the *Clarion*'s support was accompanied by a more general growth of interest in socialism. Quarrymen's leaders, such as W.W. Jones, began to articulate socialist ideas in the local press,[137] and in November 1901 the North Wales Quarrymen's Union bought and distributed 1,000 copies of Fabian Tract no. 87, the Welsh translation of Revd. J.

---

[132] *Clarion*, 27 December 1901.
[133] *Clarion*, 23 March and 11 May 1901.
[134] Lindsay, *The Great Strike*, p. 132.
[135] *Clarion*, 8 June 1901.
[136] *Clarion*, 13 July 1901.
[137] *Herald Cymraeg*, 18 February and 21 October 1902.

Clifford's *Socialism and Christ's Teaching*.[138] Such articulations of socialist sympathy confirmed the views of anti-socialists that the dispute was the result of socialist interference,[139] and the *Cambrian News* claimed that the whole affair was a socialist plot to take over Lord Penrhyn's quarries.[140]

Such fanciful claims notwithstanding, a number of important processes were underway during the dispute. As in the south in 1898, the lockout encouraged the development of stronger links with what Caroline Benn, in the 1898 context, called the 'national labour family'. At the outset the socialist press claimed that the quarrymen had 'not merely the sympathy and support of the neighbourhood where the quarries are, but practically of the nation', meaning, of course, the British nation.[141] The quarrymen also knew, in the words of W.W. Lloyd, that 'The success of the poor Penrhyn quarrymen depends upon the amount of support granted them by the British public, especially all friends of labour everywhere'.[142] It was agreed by all that the issues at stake were universal. The fight was against not just Lord Penrhyn himself, but against 'Penrhynism' – the extreme manifestation of individualistic landlordism and industrial exploitation.[143] 'For the honour of Trade Unionism, for the sake of all that is precious in our common humanity, this arch enemy of combination must be beaten', urged the *Labour Leader* as the dispute neared the end of its second year.[144]

Socialist arguments went beyond rhetoric to a more considered advocacy of solutions to the struggle being imposed within an all-Britain framework. One reader of the *Labour Leader* argued, under the pseudonym 'All Britain', in October 1902 that the dispute needed to be made '500 miles wider'. He suggested a compulsory court, constituted by Parliament,

---

[138] Jones, *The North Wales Quarrymen*, pp. 280–1.
[139] Jones, *The North Wales Quarrymen*, p. 273.
[140] *Labour Leader*, 20 July 1901.
[141] *Labour Leader*, 1 December 1900.
[142] *Clarion*, 20 April 1901.
[143] Lord Penrhyn too was aware that the struggle was part of a more universal campaign. See E.H. Douglas Pennant, 'Penrhynism: The Second Lord Penrhyn and Trade Unionism', *Transactions of the Caernarvonshire Historical Society*, 66 (2005), 126–36.
[144] *Labour Leader*, 11 October 1902.

which would 'represent all Britain, and give the verdict of all Britain': 'If the verdict of all Britain says "The men are found to be in the right" it shall then be all Britain's duty to bring about a settlement'.[145] Another correspondent argued that the struggle had 'become the common property of the workers of Great Britain', and that 22 November should be marked throughout the British Isles as 'Oppressors Day'.[146]

The efforts of the quarrymen and their community organisations to raise support across Britain had a directly personal dimension, as had been the case with the south Wales miners in 1898. Three choirs from Bethesda toured Britain between 1901 and 1903,[147] offering socialists in the industrial centres of England and Scotland a direct role in supporting the quarrymen. In April 1901 a group of six socialists organised two concerts in Sheffield, and a much wider group was involved in advertising the concerts, distributing tickets and providing accommodation for the singers.[148] During the spring and summer of 1901 the choir visited industrial towns in the midlands and north of England, and by 1902 it had extended the tour to include Scotland.[149] The opportunity for socialists to become involved in the arrangements continued, as did the contact between the singers and members of the labour and socialist movement. At Erith in London, in May 1901, socialists, co-operators, trade unionists and a local Baptist chapel came together to organise a concert.[150] In Bolton in September one of the choirs took part in a Labour Church service.[151] In 1903 the Stalybridge Trades and Labour Council entertained the Penrhyn Ladies' Choir, which was supported by the Mossley *Clarion* Quartette.[152] In all, the various choirs' tours raised over £31,000 for the distress fund.[153] The extent of the social and cultural interchange between their

[145] *Labour Leader*, 23 October 1902.
[146] *Labour Leader*, 5 November 1902.
[147] Jones, *The North Wales Quarrymen*, p. 275.
[148] *Clarion*, 27 April 1901.
[149] *Clarion*, 4 and 18 May 1901; *Labour Leader*, 3 August 1901, 18 and 23 October 1902.
[150] *Clarion*, 18 May 1901.
[151] *Labour Leader*, 21 September 1901.
[152] *Clarion*, 9 January 1903.
[153] *Clarion*, 15 January 1904.

members and the British labour and socialist movement was incalculable.

The Penrhyn dispute did not just promote a closer relationship with the labour movement across the English border. Possibly more significant was the relationship it fostered between the quarrying communities of the north and the coal mining communities of south Wales. Migration between these two regions – already a significant demographic feature before 1900 – was significantly accelerated by the dispute.[154] After the closure of the quarries, between 1,400 and 1,600 quarrymen left north Wales to find work in the south.[155] *Llais Llafur* urged the colliers of the south to show kindness to the newly arriving quarrymen, and to help them seek work in the mines, despite the potential difficulties this might raise for members of the Miners' Federation, who might have been uncomfortable acquiescing in the employment of non-Federation workers. '*BRAWD YW Y CHWARELWR*', urged the paper, '*a gobeithio yr ymddyga ei gydweithwyr a'i frodyr tuag ato yn yspryd y rheol euraidd*'.[156] The North Wales Quarrymen's Union, on the other hand, arranged for faithful union members to have their membership transferred to the South Wales Miners' Federation, to facilitate their move south.[157] As the dispute progressed, the relationship between the slate and the coal communities strengthened. In autumn 1901 the Penrhyn Ladies' Choir held a series of concerts in the Aberdare area,[158] and spring 1902 saw a more extensive tour, this time by the Penrhyn Male Voice Choir, through the anthracite region of the south, including concerts in Gorseinon, Ammanford, Glanamman, Brynamman, Swansea, Ystalyfera, Cwmtwrch, Cwmllynfell, Ystradgynlais and Clydach.[159] Quarrymen's emissaries also toured the south, speaking about the dispute and collecting for the relief fund. A 60-year-old quarryman, John Williams, lectured throughout the anthracite region during

---

[154] See Dafydd Roberts, *Y Chwarelwyr a'r Sowth* (Bethesda, 1982).
[155] Jones, *The North Wales Quarrymen*, p. 212.
[156] *Llais Llafur*, 1 December 1900 ('The quarryman is a brother, and hopefully his fellow workman and brothers will behave towards him in the spirit of the golden rule')
[157] Dafydd Roberts, *Y Chwarelwyr a'r Sowth*, p. 12.
[158] *Llais Llafur*, 26 October 1901.
[159] *Llais Llafur*, 24 and 31 May 1902.

late 1901 and 1902, for example, accompanied at times by a colleague, W.T. Jones, and both received a warm welcome and generous contributions.[160]

Such interactions worked upon the political consciousness of those involved. Ten months into the dispute, the general secretary of the North Wales Quarrymen's Union, D.R. Daniel, emphasised the importance of the relationship between the quarrying communities of the north and the coal mining communities of the south. The implications of the exodus to the south, he argued, went further than the provision of financial support:

> it kept the minds of the men healthy and independent ... He had no doubt that some day they would return to work once more at their old industry; but they would not be exactly the same men. (Hear, hear.) They would not be so easily enslaved as they had been in the past. (Cheers).[161]

Some of the uprooted quarrymen doubtless came in contact with ILP branches in south Wales, and brought socialist ideas back north on their frequent visits home.[162] The presence of a significant number of quarrymen in the south Wales coalfield, and the constant flow of news from the north, likewise had an impact upon southern opinion. It promoted knowledge of the north Wales labour movement, and worked to develop political opinion on specifically Welsh industrial affairs. This process may be observed in a debate that took place between two regular contributors to *Llais Llafur*, D. Jones of Chester and Henry Davies of Cwmavon, near the end of the dispute. Jones, writing in Welsh, argued that had the Liberals been in power the dispute would have been resolved earlier, and that the way to deal with Penrhynism was through the taxation of land values. Davies, replying in English, argued that the Liberals, even in power, would not have effected an end to the dispute and that the taxation of land values was merely an unnecessary half-way house on the

---

[160] *Llais Llafur*, 12 October and 9 November 1901, 26 July, 9 and 16 August 1902.
[161] *Llais Llafur*, 7 September 1901.
[162] Emyr Hywel Owen, 'Cyn y "Chwalfa" – ac Wedyn', *Lleufer*, 19/2 (1963), 55–60, 57.

road to full nationalisation, which would only be achieved by independent labour representation.[163]

It is tempting to see the debate between Jones and Davies as the (English) voice of the new combatting the (Welsh) voice of the old. In the final analysis, however, what is most striking about the socialist response to the Penrhyn dispute, when compared to the socialist role in the 1898 coal dispute, is the unresolved nature of this debate and the more modest nature of socialist influence in the quarry districts. In contrast to south Wales after 1898, there was no immediate flourishing of the ILP and no electoral breakthrough. There were several reasons for this, the primary one being the issue of the Welsh language. Far less influenced by inward migration than the coalfield, over three-fifths of Bethesda's inhabitants spoke and understood only Welsh in 1901.[164] This provided an instant barrier to the socialists which could have tragi-comic consequences. One socialist visitor to Bethesda mistook the hundreds of signs in cottage windows that read '*Nid Oes Bradwr yn y Tŷ Hwn*' to mean 'Apartments to Let'.[165] This was not a mistake that a representative of Welsh Liberalism could have made. As K.O. Morgan has recognised, the majority of Welsh Liberals were more attuned to the aspirations and trials of the Penrhyn quarrymen than they had been to the demands of the colliers in 1898, and their support 'revealed an instinctive and sympathetic appreciation of the small, chapel-going rural community fighting for its status'.[166] In the Welsh Liberal imagination the quarrymen were exemplary, heroic representatives of *y werin*.[167] The socialists, on the other hand, tended to portray the quarrymen less as heroes than as victims. While south Walian colliers were archetypal proletarians, the quarrymen of Bethesda were less integral to the socialist world view. 'Feudalism' was the word most often used in the socialist press in relation to the Penrhyn

[163] *Llais Llafur*, 31 May–20 June 1903.
[164] Roberts, *Y Chwarelwyr a'r Sowth*, Appendix A.
[165] *Clarion*, 29 June 1901. The signs actually meant 'There is not a traitor in this house'.
[166] Morgan, *Wales in British Politics, 1868–1922*, pp. 211–12.
[167] H. Paul Manning, 'The Streets of Bethesda: The Slate Quarrier and the Welsh Language in the Liberal Imagination', *Language in Society*, 33 (2004), 517–48.

dispute. Lord Penrhyn, admittedly with some justification, was portrayed as a 'feudal baron', while the quarrymen were seen as his serfs.[168] The 'too submissive and too "respectable" workers of Bethesda', complained A.M. Thompson, with a striking lack of cultural comprehension, 'have busied themselves more to build chapels and churches than to assert the rights of their manhood'.[169] Elsewhere, in a singularly misguided attempt to draw contemporary resonance, the quarrymen were referred to by socialists as 'outlanders'.[170]

The scale and length of the dispute also worked against the fostering of a sustainable relationship between socialists and quarrymen. 1898 was a much larger, yet much shorter, affair than 1900–3. Whereas it had made sense to keep a full-time organiser among 100,000 striking miners in south Wales in 1898, no such organiser could be justified for Bethesda in 1900–3. There is no record of the ILP's National Executive Committee even discussing the Penrhyn lockout during its three-year duration; neither did it feature in the official organ of the party, *ILP News*. As far as Wales was concerned, the attention of the ILP remained focused overwhelmingly upon the south. Beyond this, the *Labour Leader* betrayed something of the party's northern British centre of gravity by the far more extensive coverage it gave to the less significant quarry dispute at Ballachulish in Scotland in 1902–3.[171] Whereas the 18-month Ballachulish dispute was a long-drawn-out affair, the three-year Penrhyn dispute was a marathon, and this ultimately worked against the relationship between the quarrymen and their socialist supporters. As the dispute lengthened into its later phases the movement simply lost interest. Coverage declined markedly after the first year, and although socialists complained that the support offered by

---

[168] *Clarion*, 23 March, 29 June and 10 August 1901; *Justice*, 15 June 1901.
[169] *Clarion*, 16 March 1901.
[170] *Llais Llafur*, 5 October 1901; *Labour Leader*, 14 November 1903.
[171] *Labour Leader*, 23 and 30 August, 6, 13, 20 and 27 September, 4, 11 and 18 October and 6 December 1902, 17 and 31 January, 7 March 1903. For Ballachulish, see Neville Kirk, '"A State of War in the Valley of Glencoe": The Ballachulish Quarries Disputes, 1902–1905', *Scottish Labour History*, 38 (2003), 14–36; Neville Kirk, *Custom and Conflict in the Land of the Gael: Ballachulish, 1900–1910* (Monmouth, 2007).

the labour movement was inadequate,[172] their own organisations suffered a similar level of fatigue.

Aside from the ILP, the SDF lost interest relatively early. *Justice* reported what it saw as an inevitable victory for capital in June 1901,[173] and its reportage was thereafter either non-existent or reduced to near farce. In September it published a list of six carping questions about the dispute, on the grounds that if the SDF was to offer support it had a right to know the facts.[174] This amounted to a public admission of detachment. Only the *Clarion* maintained any significant interest in the later part of the struggle, and this began to drop off after the end of 1901. Even at the height of the dispute there was an underlying reticence on the part of some of the *Clarion* staff, which was revealed when Julia Dawson complained that efforts going into fundraising for the quarrymen were 'robbing the two *Clarion* vans'.[175] In November 1901 the paper ran a series of articles summarising the opinions of British trade union leaders on the dispute, and urged an 'organised and systematic effort' on behalf of the quarrymen.[176] This represented a last-ditch effort to generalise the struggle, and thereafter even the *Clarion*'s efforts were no more than a rearguard action in a defeated cause.

By the time the quarrymen finally conceded defeat in November 1903, the British socialist movement had long adopted a fatalistic approach, and to all intents and purposes had abandoned the quarrymen's cause. The lockout had brought the quarrying communities of north Wales into closer contact with the wider socialist and labour movement, both in England and in south Wales, but – in sharp contrast to the south Wales coal strike of 1898 – the spread of socialist influence seemed modest. The dispute did, however, have a long-term significance, which was powerfully articulated in *Llais Llafur*, alongside news of the quarrymen's vote to resume work:

---

[172] *Llais Llafur*, 29 June and 25 October 1901; *Clarion*, 8 June 1901.
[173] *Justice*, 15 June 1901.
[174] *Justice*, 7 September 1901.
[175] *Clarion*, 8 June 1901.
[176] *Clarion*, 2 to 23 November 1901.

174   BEYOND THE HEADS OF THE VALLEYS, c.1880s–1906

> *Enill am enyd ac enill arwynebol amheus, yn yr ystyr isaf yw enill brwnt Arglwydd Penrhyn, ond y mae yna enill arall yn y frwydr hon. O'r golwg y mae hyd yma, – o'r golwg yn y ddaear fel hedyn, ond wedi ei hau mewn dagrau a'i fwydo a gwaed a gweddiau. Fe ddaw i'r golwg maes o law, ac i'r golwg yn ffrwyth toreithiog iawn. Wedi hau mewn dagrau, mae medi mewn gorfoledd i ddilyn.*[177]

The words of the *Llais* were prophetic. Before the end of the decade a socialist movement would emerge in the north, and would exhibit a significantly different character from that based in the south Wales coalfield.

(III) TOWARDS AN INDIGENOUS WELSH SOCIALISM?

When Lord Penrhyn and his colleagues in the North Wales Property Defence Association complained of socialist influence, they did not generally have the ILP, the SDF or the *Clarion* in mind, but were more often referring to Welsh agitators like Michael D. Jones and Evan Pan Jones, who have not usually been considered by historians as part of the modern British socialist movement at all. Similarly, the lessons drawn from the Penrhyn struggle by many of the quarrymen's representatives, and even by the socialist *Llais Llafur* in the south, tended to revolve not around the socialist principles of class struggle or even production for use rather than profit, but instead focused on the more familiar Welsh radical totem of the land question. This raises some important questions. To what extent was Welsh radicalism moving towards socialism under its own volition? To what extent were the ideas of Welsh radicals influenced by the British socialist movement, and to what extent were they devising their own independent responses to the social question in Wales? Is it feasible to refer to an indigenous Welsh socialism in this period?

By the late nineteenth century, Wales already had a rich indigenous radical tradition, which reached back through

---

[177] *Llais Llafur*, 14 November 1903. ('Lord Penrhyn's dirty victory is truly a temporary, doubtful and superficial victory, but there is another victory in this struggle. So far, it is hidden from view, – hidden from view like a seed in the ground, but sown in tears and fed with blood and prayers. It will come to view in due course, and will come to view as a very plentiful fruit. Sown with tears, there is a joyous harvest to follow').

individuals such as David Rees ('Y Cynhyrfwr', 1801–1869), John Jones ('Jac Glan y Gors', 1766–1821), Morgan John Rhys (1760–1804), and Thomas Edwards ('Twm o'r Nant', 1739–1810) to the sixteenth-century protestant radicalism of John Penry (1559–1593). Most important from a socialist perspective, but also a figure with an ambiguous relationship to Wales, was Robert Owen of Newtown (1771–1858). Owen, best known for his utopian ideas and social experiments at New Lanark, has traditionally been seen as 'the father of British socialism', and historians have traditionally tended to concur with the view that 'Robert Owen, the Socialist, belongs rather to the World than to Wales',[178] agreeing that his 'influence on Wales has been part of the general impact of his work on the social history of Britain as a whole'.[179] Despite recent efforts to restore Owen to his Welsh context,[180] the limited evidence relating to his early years makes it difficult to come to any firm conclusion about his own sense of nationality. It is possible, though, to evaluate his legacy within Wales which during his own lifetime, and for several decades thereafter, was relatively slight.

Few Welshmen are known to have been involved in Owenite communities,[181] and although there were two such settlements in Wales in the 1840s and 1850s (in Meirionnydd and Carmarthenshire), they were both initiated and populated by incomers.[182] One of Owen's works was translated into Welsh (in Manchester),[183] but if the comments on the

---

[178] *The Welsh Outlook*, 5 (1918), p. 218.

[179] Brinley Thomas, 'Robert Owen of Newtown', *Transactions of the Honourable Society of Cymmrodorion* (1960), 18–35, 18.

[180] Ian Donnachie, 'Robert Owen's Welsh Childhood: kin, culture and environment, 1771–1781', *Montgomeryshire Collections*, 86 (1998), pp. 81–96; Geoffrey Powell, '"They shall no longer see as through a glass darkly": Robert Owen and the Welsh Enlightenment', *Montgomeryshire Collections*, 91 (2003), pp. 53–69; Jane Moore, '"Parallelograms and circles": Robert Owen and the satirists', in Damian Walford Davies and Lynda Pratt (eds), *Wales and the Romantic Imagination* (Cardiff, 2007), pp. 243–67; Chris Williams, 'Robert Owen and Wales', in Noel Thompson and Chris Williams (eds), *Robert Owen and His Legacy* (Cardiff, 2011), pp. 219–38.

[181] Thomas, 'Robert Owen of Newtown', p. 34.

[182] Williams, 'Robert Owen and Wales', pp. 225–8.; W.H.G. Armytage, 'Pant Glas: a communitarian experiment in Merionethshire', *Journal of the Merioneth Historical and Record Society*, 2 (1953–6: 1955), 232–4.

[183] Robert Owen, Yswain, *Talfyriad o'r Gyfundrefn Resymol, seiliedig ar ffeithiau diwrtheb-brawb yn amlygu cyfansoddiad a deddfau y natur ddynol, sef, yr unig foddion*

defaced copy in Cardiff University's Salisbury Collection, which brand it as '*un o'r llyfrau mwyaf cythreulig a gyfansoddwyd erioed*', are representative of Welsh opinion, it is safe to assume that Owen's written word had limited influence in Wales.[184] In particular, it was Owen's views on religion which inhibited the adoption of his ideas in Wales. When not referred to in the Welsh press as '*Robert Owen Y Socialist*', he was known as '*Robert Owen Yr Anffyddiwr*' ('the Atheist)'.[185] On account of his atheism, the local authority in Newtown refused to erect a monument to Owen after his death,[186] and his name was associated with atheism until the end of the century.[187]

Despite this, interest in Owen's work began to grow around the turn of the century. In 1893, Edward Edwards, the brother of O.M. Edwards, visited Owen's grave at Newtown and wrote an article on Owen for his brother's journal *Cymru*.[188] By 1902 the grave was restored with funds from the Co-operative Society.[189] In the same year, in another *Cymru* article, Richard Roberts of London (who had accompanied the *Clarion* van in 1897) detailed Owen's influence upon Wales and gave an account of the Owenite settlement at Pant Glas in Meirionnydd.[190] In 1900 Roberts won the National Eisteddfod essay prize with an essay on Owen, which, in an expanded form, was published in two volumes in 1907 and 1910.[191] Roberts used Owen's legacy to make a case for Welsh centrality in the development of the international working class movement:

> Nid lleiaf ymhlith clodydd Cymru yw mai hi, drwy Robert Owen, roddodd yr ysgogiad effeithiol cyntaf i ddiwygiad cymdeithasol yn yr ynysoedd hyn, a gobeithiwn mai blaenffrwyth yn unig yw o gnwd cyfoethog o Gymry a ymroddant i

effeithiol i symud y drygau sydd yn poeni ac yn dyrysu poblogaeth y byd (Bangor, n.d.) [1841].

[184] 'one of the most diabolical books ever composed'.
[185] *Baner ac Amserau Cymru*, 24 November 1858.
[186] *Baner ac Amserau Cymru*, 26 August 1868.
[187] *Goleuad*, 3 January 1900.
[188] Edward Edwards, 'Robert Owen o'r Drenewydd', *Cymru*, 4 (1893), 170–2, 309–11.
[189] *Robert Owen Co-operative Memorial at Newtown: The Unveiling Ceremony on July 12th, 1902* (Manchester, n.d. [1902]).
[190] Richard Roberts, 'Robert Owen a Chymru', *Cymru*, 13 (1902), 39–40.
[191] Richard Roberts, *Robert Owen* (2 vols, Caernarfon, 1907 and 1910).

gwblhau ei waith i sicrhau iawnderau gwerin, nid yr hen wlad yn unig, ond holl wledydd Prydain y tu yma a thu hwnt i'r môr.[192]

Nor was Roberts alone in his advocacy of Owen. Among those who assisted him in getting his book to press was Thomas Jones, by then in an academic post at Glasgow University.[193] There was also interest in Owen among the Welsh community in Manchester, where the Co-operative Society had its headquarters. Thomas Pugh published his *Nodiadau Hanesyddol a Beirniadol ar Fywyd a Gwaith Robert Owen o'r Drenewydd* in 1907, with the explicit aim of making Owen more familiar to his own countrymen.[194] His fellow Welsh Mancunian Robert Jones Derfel also promoted the work of Owen in the Welsh press, going so far as to suggest that Owen should replace St. David as the country's patron saint.[195]

Claims on Owen's legacy were also made from the upper echelons of Welsh Liberalism. In a speech at Bangor University in 1892 Tom Ellis urged the memorialisation of the heroes of the Welsh past, including Owen. His arguments went beyond nationalism, claiming that Britain and Europe were in the midst of a 'great movement for placing upon a stabler and a more satisfactory and permanent basis the social relations and duties of man to man' – a movement that he explicitly called socialism, and to which Wales was integral:

> Though Wales is, in modern times, largely individualist, we cannot but feel that it has been the land of *cyfraith, cyfar, cyfnawdd, cymorthau, and cymanfaoedd*, the land of social co-operation, of associative effort. It is significant that the initiator in Britain of the movement for collective and municipal activity in the common effort for the common good was Robert Owen, who embodied in these latter days the spirit of the old Welsh social economy.

---

[192] Richard Roberts, *Robert Owen*, vol. 1, pp. 5–6 ('Not least among the commendations of Wales is it that, through Robert Owen, she gave the first effective impulse to social reform in these islands, and it is to be hoped that this is the first fruit only of a rich crop of Welsh people that are devoted to completing his work in ensuring the rights of the common people, not just of the old country, but of all the countries of Britain and those beyond the sea').

[193] Roberts acknowledges Jones's help in vol. 1 of his work.

[194] Thomas Pugh, *Nodiadau Hanesyddol a Beirniadol ar Fywyd a Gwaith Robert Owen o'r Drenewydd* (Treffynnon, 1907).

[195] See R.J. Derfel, 'Dewi Sant: Saint Newydd yn Eisiau', in D. Gwenallt Jones (ed.), *Detholiad o Ryddiaeth Gymraeg R.J. Derfel*, vol. II, pp. 82–4.

Owen, he argued, apart from being the father of British Socialism was 'the bearer of *Neges Cymru* [the message of Wales] to the modern world'.[196] Ellis's claim upon Owen's legacy raises the wider question of the extent to which socialist ideas were being developed within the radical Liberalism that he represented. Some Welsh historians have emphasised the deep differences between the mentalities of socialists and Liberals in Wales in this period, arguing that the two traditions were 'worlds apart'.[197] Welsh Liberalism, it has been argued, subscribed to a broadly conceived 'Progressivism' that stressed the class harmony of the 'productive' classes and was wedded to the old themes of disestablishment, education, temperance, home rule and eternal memories of the 'Great Election' of 1868. Those advocating socialism or labour-orientated politics were prone to charges of sectionalism and perceived as hostile to the unity of the Welsh nation.[198] This view assumes a false dichotomy. It contrasts coalfield Marxists like Noah Ablett with traditional Liberal nationalists like O.M. Edwards, and ignores substantial areas of ideological confluence. We have already seen that this dichotomy could be bridged by some abstract expressions of socialism, particularly the concept of 'Christian socialism', and Ellis's claim on Owen's legacy is further evidence of the assumption of socialist ideas within Welsh Liberalism.

Tom Ellis provided a significant point of contact between radical Welsh Liberal nationalism and the socialist movement in other ways too. He rubbed shoulders with the London socialist leadership: his Westminster rooms at Palace Chambers, where *Cymru Fydd* was founded in 1886, shared the same building as the SDF's committee meetings. In 1885 Ellis and O.M. Edwards attended a meeting of the Socialist League in Oxford, at which William Morris and Edward Aveling spoke, staying afterwards to discuss socialism with the two speakers.[199] Ellis also followed events surrounding

---

[196] T.E. Ellis, 'The Memory of the Kymric Dead, Delivered at the University College Bangor, October 21 1892', in Annie J. Ellis (ed.), *Speeches and Addresses by the late Thomas E. Ellis M.P.* (Wrexham, 1912), pp. 3–26, pp. 22, 23–4.
[197] Morgan, *Wales, 1880–1980: Rebirth of A Nation*, p. 154.
[198] Morgan, 'The New Liberalism and the Challenge of Labour'.
[199] Dewi Rowland Hughes, 'Y Coch a'r Gwyrdd: Cymru Fydd a'r Mudiad Llafur

the socialist movement in London. In 1886 he witnessed the demonstrations instigated by the SDF in Trafalgar Square.[200] Two years later he drew parallels in the House of Commons between the use of the military against anti-tithe protesters in Denbighshire and the violence against socialists in London on 'Bloody Sunday' in November 1887.[201] Ellis's contact with socialism in the late 1880s, moreover, overlaid his experience earlier in the decade at Oxford, where he had developed a stake in the same intellectual hinterland as the socialists of the 1880s. Joint influences ranged from John Ruskin to Arnold Toynbee, and included the social thought of the Fabian Society.[202] At Oxford too he discovered the artistic ideas of Edward Burne-Jones and William Morris,[203] and the extent to which Morris's essentially pastoral vision of the ideal society harmonised with Ellis's belief in the virtue of agrarian life is striking. Ellis's agrarian radicalism, which extended at times to the advocacy of the nationalisation or municipalisation of land 'as an instrument for furthering social equality', overlapped with the views of socialists.[204] He tended to represent all of his enthusiasms as a means of restricting, in words that were his own, but which closely shadowed those of the first *Fabian Tract*, '*awdurdod a breintiau i'r ychydig, a blinder a llafur a chaethiwed i'r lluaws*'.[205] Indeed, Ellis considered, as he put it in a letter to the Liberal candidate for Flintshire, Herbert Lewis, in 1891, that 'Nationality and Labour are the two main principles'. He predicted that 'when disestablishment

Cymreig, 1886–96', *Llafur*, 6/4 (1995), 60–79, 60; Dewi Rowland Hughes, *Cymru Fydd* (Cardiff, 2006), p. 15.

[200] Hughes, *Cymru Fydd*, p. 16.

[201] Neville Masterman, *The Forerunner: The Dilemmas of Tom Ellis* (Llandybie, 1972), pp. 94–5.

[202] K.O. Morgan, 'Tom Ellis Versus Lloyd George: The Fractured Consciousness of Fin-de-Siècle Wales', in Geraint H. Jenkins and J. Beverley Smith (eds), *Politics and Society in Wales, 1840–1922: Essays in Honour of Ieuan Gwynedd Jones* (Cardiff, 1988), pp. 93–112, pp. 98–9.

[203] Masterman, *The Forerunner*, pp. 46–7.

[204] Masterman, *The Forerunner*, p. 83; Jones, 'Michael Davitt, Lloyd George and T.E. Ellis: The Welsh Experience, 1886', p. 475; Price Jones, 'Tom Ellis', in *Radicaliaeth a'r Werin Gymreig yn y Bedwaredd Ganrif ar Bymtheg*, pp. 181–95, p. 192.

[205] Quoted in T.I. Ellis, *Thomas Edwards Ellis, Cofiant, Cyfrol II (1886–1899)* (Liverpool, 1948), p. 161 ('the authority and privilege of the few, and the distress, labour and bondage of the many').

is settled Wales will throw herself heart and soul into the Labour movement'.[206]

Ellis was not alone among *Cymru Fyddwyr* in sharing the ideological heritage of the socialists or in using socialistic rhetoric. Like many socialists, Ellis's colleague Lloyd George counted the ideas of John Ruskin and Henry George, alongside the municipal radicalism of Joseph Chamberlain's 'Unauthorised Programme' and the agrarian socialism of Michael Davitt, among his early influences.[207] He also frequently advocated the redistribution of wealth, as at Bangor in 1891, when he told an audience that 'it is not in the creation of wealth that England lacks, but in its distribution'.[208] He occasionally used the word 'socialism' directly. His original vision for the newspaper *Yr Udgorn Rhyddid* was, as expressed to D.R. Daniel in 1887, for it to be 'thorough, nationalist and socialist – a regenerator in every respect'.[209] Some members of *Cymru Fydd* went even further. The Gower MP David Randell gave explicit support to socialist organisations.[210] Even Mabon, doyen of Welsh Lib-Labism and fervent critic of Keir Hardie, could accommodate socialism in his world view by making the distinction between 'Christian socialism' and 'material socialism'. The latter, he told an audience in the Rhondda in 1896, 'meant the levelling of all properties and of social positions', 'was intended to be obligatory and general' and was an erroneous doctrine. Nevertheless, 'he did not think it was ever intended that there should be such a vast difference in the distribution of wealth and the suffering of poverty, that the selfish and the glutton should be so extremely rich while the striving workman was half famished by poverty'. Consequently, he supported Christian socialism which 'meant nothing but what was voluntary and special' and 'was based upon sacrifice, and sympathy, and charity'.[211] This may have been

---

[206] Quoted in Masterman, *The Forerunner*, pp. 170–1.
[207] Emyr Price, *David Lloyd George* (Cardiff, 2006), pp. 8–25.
[208] Quoted in Chris Wrigley, *David Lloyd George and the British Labour Movement* (Brighton, 1976), p. 7.
[209] Quoted in Price, *David Lloyd George*, p. 46.
[210] See above pp. 63–4.
[211] *Cardiff Times and South Wales Weekly News*, 28 November 1896.

ideologically vague, but it left the door open for his eventual acceptance of wider socialist doctrines. By 1908, when it appeared that socialism was going to be a permanent part of Welsh life, Mabon was claiming: 'It is well known that I have been an evolutionary Socialist for many years, and mean to be till the end of my days. More than that, I have at the present moment very little faith in anything else as a real means of liberating and elevating the people.'[212]

All this would suggest that there was an ideological continuum between Liberalism and socialism. William Harcourt had, after all, stated in the House of Commons in 1887 that 'we are all socialists now'.[213] His statement was widely repeated during the following decades, and by 1910 Ellis W. Davies, a Liberal from north Wales, could argue that 'the socialist principle is now an essential part of our national life and the question that remains is not of principle but of degree'.[214] The coherence of this ideological linkage was, however, not always convincing. Keir Hardie's running partner at Merthyr, the industrialist D.A. Thomas, included socialistic elements, such as the eight-hour day, in his electoral appeals as a 'Liberal and Labour' candidate,[215] yet he was accurately described as a man 'born and cradled in the strongest form of individualism' who explicitly and implacably opposed socialism to the end of his life, as the striking workers at his Cambrian Combine discovered in 1910.[216] Neither is there a need to resort to examples like Thomas to demonstrate that radical Liberals were separated from socialists in some important ways. Tom Ellis may have been prepared to dabble with Robert Owen and adopt socialist rhetoric, but he had little time for most socialist leaders. He saw Hyndman as 'a thoroughly hollow fellow',[217] and viewed the revolutionary speeches of socialists at Trafalgar Square in

---

[212] *Labour Leader*, 17 April 1908.
[213] *Times*, 12 August 1887.
[214] Quoted in Tanner, *Political Change and the Labour Party*, p. 307.
[215] National Library of Wales, D.A. Thomas Papers, C2, 1900 and 1906 electoral material.
[216] Harold Begbie, 'His Philosophy', in *D.A. Thomas, Viscount Rhondda by His Daughter and Others* (London, 1921), pp. 278–90.
[217] Masterman, *The Forerunner*, p. 80.

the 1880s as 'a disturbing sign'.[218] As for Lloyd George, Chris Wrigley notes that beneath his fiercer rhetoric he differed markedly from the socialists on issues such as land, industry and profits.[219] The concept of full public ownership of the means of production, distribution and exchange would have been anathema to most Liberals.

There was, however, a distinct group within late-nineteenth-century Welsh radicalism that was developing what might be termed an indigenous proto-socialism. The Congregationalist minister and principal of Bala Theological College, Michael D. Jones, combined agrarian, decentralist mutualism with a commitment to nationalism, and a belief in the labour theory of value.[220] Similar claims for a nascent, indigenous Welsh socialist-internationalist philosophy may be made in relation to the anti-materialistic convictions of Emrys ap Iwan of Abergele.[221] A more convincing example is John Owen Jones (Ap Ffarmwr) of Anglesey. A farmer's son who studied at Aberystwyth and Manchester, in the late 1880s he began an agitation to unionise the agricultural labourers of Anglesey, initially by writing a series of powerful articles in the local press.[222] A professional newspaper editor, Ap Ffarmwr worked for the Liberal *Genedl Gymreig*, and his involvement in the Anglesey labour movement was truncated when he moved to Merthyr at the end of 1894 to become editor of the *Merthyr Times*. He subsequently moved to Nottingham, to take a post with the *Nottingham Express*, but died there in 1899 at the age of 39.[223] A founder member of the *Cymdeithas Lenyddol Moriah* at Caernarfon,[224] his

[218] Hughes, *Cymru Fydd*, p. 16.
[219] Wrigley, *Lloyd George and the British Labour Movement*, p. 5.
[220] Evan Pan Jones, *Oes a Gwaith y Prif Athraw Parch. Michael Daniel Jones, Bala* (Bala, 1903), pp. 215–76; E. Wyn James and Bill Jones (eds), *Michael D. Jones a'i Wladfa Gymreig* (Llanrwst, 2009); D. Gwenallt Jones, 'Michael D. Jones', in Gwynedd Pierce (ed.), *Triwr Penllyn* (Cardiff, n.d.), pp. 1–27; Michael D. Jones, 'Cyfiawnder i'r Gweithiwr', *Geninen* (1897), pp. 205–6.
[221] D. Myrddin Lloyd, *Emrys ap Iwan* (Cardiff, 1979); Thomas Gwynn Jones, *Emrys ap Iwan, Dysgadwr, Llenor, Cenedlgarwr: Cofiant* (Caernarfon, 1912).
[222] *Werin*, 23 November–28 December 1889.
[223] David A. Pretty, *The Rural Revolt That Failed: Farm Workers' Trade Unions in Wales* (Cardiff, 1989), pp. 20–44; R. Maldwyn Thomas and Cyril Parry, 'John Owen Jones, "Ap Ffarmwr", 1861–1899', *Transactions of the Anglesey Antiquarian Society & Field Club* (1967), 72–107; Parry, *The Radical Tradition in Welsh Politics*, pp. 12–14.
[224] *Genedl Gymreig*, 8 October and 12 November 1890.

political outlook was strongly influenced by the culture of mutual improvement. Steeped in Welsh literature, he was active in the organisation and adjudication of local *eisteddfodau*,[225] and his social activism had a strong cultural dimension. Among measures to raise the intellectual and moral condition of farmworkers, he advocated the organisation of exclusive farm servants' *eisteddfodau*.[226] He viewed these educational and cultural activities within a specifically Welsh national context, and argued for an education system that would foster Welsh culture and patriotism.[227]

Ap Ffarmwr's Welsh particularism was only one aspect of his personality. In addition to his knowledge of Welsh literature, he was well read in the canon of British radicalism, particularly the work of Ruskin and Carlyle,[228] and his interest in the land question was stimulated by Henry George, the Fabian Tracts and, most likely, Dr Rhys Jones's letters in the north Wales press. Alongside his cultural activism, he developed a methodical and clinical case for land nationalisation, arguing that the land (both rural and urban) needed to be owned and managed in the interests of the nation as a whole. He envisaged the implementation of this at a British level, but also insisted that the land issue had explicitly Welsh dimensions that were created by the disrespect of English landlords towards Wales and its customs.[229] His arguments went beyond both individualistic reformism and Welsh particularism, to embrace full public ownership of land. What was needed, he argued, was '*chwyldroad trwyadl yn ein cyfundfren dir, sef diddymu meddiant personol o dir, a gwneyd y Wladwriaeth yn berchenog, yn osodydd, ac yn rheolydd holl dir y deyrnas*'.[230] Although Ap Ffarmwr's move to Merthyr in 1894 ended his

[225] *Genedl Gymreig*, 7 January 1891, 21 December 1892, 21 November 1893 and 3 May 1894.
[226] *Genedl Gymreig*, 9 September 1891, 19 December 1893, 13 March and 8 May 1894.
[227] John Owen Jones (Ap Ffarmwr), 'Anhawsderau Gwladgarwch Cymreig', *Geninen* (1891), pp. 226–30.
[228] *Genedl Gymreig*, 7 March 1899.
[229] John Owen Jones, 'Y Tir a'r Genedl', *Geninen* (1892), pp. 111–16.
[230] John Owen Jones, 'Y Tir a'r Genedl (II)', *Geninen* (1893), pp. 33–5, p. 33 ('A thorough revolution in our land regime, namely the dissolution of personal land ownership, and the appointment of the state as owner, landlord and manager of all the kingdom's land.')

direct involvement in north Wales agrarianism, it did bring him into contact with the south Wales labour movement. He continued to combine social activism with advocacy of Welsh cultural causes, adjudicating at local *eisteddfodau* and joining the Merthyr Cymmrodorion Society. He also dabbled with Merthyr's nascent socialist movement. In December 1895 he presided over the foundation meeting of the Merthyr ILP, and in the following year he attended at least one socialist meeting in the town.[231] Ap Ffarmwr never joined the ILP, and he remained politically loyal to the Liberal Party, yet his political philosophy contained substantial elements of socialist thought. His synthesis of Welsh educationalism and collectivist politics was a significant point of connection between the worlds of Welsh radical Liberalism and the universalist ideas of socialism.

An even clearer expression of indigenous Welsh proto-socialism was provided by Evan Pan Jones of Mostyn, Flintshire. Born into poverty in southern Cardiganshire in 1834, Pan Jones spent his early years breaking stones, plaiting rush stools and stocking knitting, before completing a tailor's apprenticeship. In the 1850s he moved to industrial Glamorgan, where he worked as a tailor at Pentyrch and Blaina, and became an Independent preacher. He attended Bala Independent College, and during the 1860s studied at Carmarthen Presbyterian College and Marburg University in Germany, before settling in Mostyn in 1870. Apart from a brief spell in America in the 1880s, he remained as minister of Mostyn church until his death in 1922, writing profusely, editing newspapers (*Y Celt* and *Cwrs y Byd*) and orchestrating an energetic and impressive social campaign.[232] As with Ap Ffarmwr, Pan Jones's social philosophy was built upon the land question, which he began addressing in earnest in *Y Celt* in early 1883.[233] In August 1883 he launched *Cymdeithas*

---

[231] David Pretty, 'John Owen Jones (Ap Ffarmwr) and the Labour Movement in Merthyr Tydfil, 1894–6', *Morgannwg*, 38 (1994), 101–14.

[232] Evan Pan Jones, *Oes Gofion: Fraslun o Hanes fy Mywyd* (Bala, 1911); Tom Davies, 'Pan Jones', *Y Llenor*, 13 (1934), 144–57; Peris Jones-Evans, 'Evan Pan Jones – Land Reformer', *Welsh History Review*, 4/2 (1968), 143–59; Revd. Richard Griffith Owen, 'Evan Pan Jones', *Dictionary of Welsh Biography*.

[233] Peris Jones-Evans, 'Evan Pan Jones', pp. 149–50.

Y Ddaear i'r Bobl (Society of the Land for the People),[234] and in 1886 he was involved in organising Michael Davitt's visit to Wales.[235] In the early 1890s he commissioned and accompanied the first of a series of touring vans, of which there were eventually seven, to take the land reform message on a 'crusade' through Wales.[236]

Whether or not Pan Jones may be considered a socialist is open to debate (and this applies equally to the other individuals considered here). He considered the land question fundamental to all else: '*yr unig gwestiwn gwerth i ymdrin ag ef*.[237] It might be argued that this places him outside the socialist movement. Land reform may be seen as a radical, rather than explicitly socialist, cause. It could certainly be pursued within an individualist (rather than a socialist or collectivist) agenda, and while most late-nineteenth-century British socialists counted the land issue among their formative influences, most also argued that addressing land monopoly was only a partial solution to the social problem, and that socialism demanded the abolition of industrial monopoly and the end of the appropriation of surplus value. If this argument is seen as a definition of socialism, then neither Pan Jones, nor any of the other individuals considered here, may be considered socialist. Some elements of Pan Jones's thought would support this conclusion: his calls for families to be provided with three acres and a cow,[238] and for a general return from the towns to the countryside,[239] hark back to the radicalism of the mid-nineteenth century more than they chime with the analysis of his contemporary 'scientific' socialists. This emphasis in Pan Jones's thought

---

[234] 'Y Tir a'i Berchenogion', *Celt*, 23 February 1883.

[235] Jones, 'Michael Davitt, David Lloyd George and T.E. Ellis: The Welsh Experience'.

[236] *Tarian y Gweithiwr*, 15 January, 18 June, 27 August and 10 September 1891; *Celt*, 13 February and 22 May 1891; *Llais Llafur*, 25 June 1898; *Cwrs y Byd*, September 1891.

[237] *Llais Llafur*, 25 June 1898 ('The land question was the only question worth dealing with').

[238] *Llais Llafur*, 22 January 1898; Evan Pan Jones, 'Y Ddaear i'r Bobl', *Geninen* (1908), pp. 132-6.

[239] *Celt*, 16 December 1892.

has led Cyril Parry to conclude that he 'showed no interest in socialism or the problems of industrial workers'.[240]

In other respects Pan Jones's ideology did engage with contemporary analyses that went beyond the core issue of the land. In *Llais Llafur* in 1899 he listed what he saw as the five great (temporal) issues of the future as '*rent, enillion, llogau, cyflogau, swindle*' ('rent, profit, interest, wages and swindle').[241] He also advocated class-conscious, independent, working-class political organisation, in a way that aligned him more with the ILP than any of the other individuals considered here. He even anticipated the ILP's political philosophy before its foundation in 1892: '*Mae yn llawn bryd i'r gweithwyr gael eu lle yn y ddrama fawr wleidyddol, i gael actio eu rhan, ac nid cario coed a dwfr i ereill.*'[242] This alienated Pan Jones from Liberalism to a greater extent than other Welsh radicals, including Ap Ffarmwr (whose last act of political affirmation was to write a hagiographic biography of William Gladstone).[243] Pan Jones was harshly critical of the Liberal Party, and he took care to differentiate its leaders from *y werin*. He argued that the party's Newcastle Programme did not sufficiently address working-class concerns,[244] and launched his own ten-point workers' programme. This included standard radical objectives, such as payment of MPs, regulation of the drink trade and educational reform, alongside a number of Welsh particularist causes, such as home rule and the legal recognition of the Welsh language. It also, however, reached towards socialism in its demand for the nationalisation of royalties. Its accompanying statement '*at weithwyr Cymru*' ('to the workers of Wales') was, moreover, an unmistakable call for militant class consciousness that would have comfortably adorned the most advanced socialist programme:

---

[240] Parry, *The Radical Tradition in Welsh Politics*, p. 22.
[241] *Llais Llafur*, 16 December 1899.
[242] *Tarian y Gweithiwr*, 9 June 1892 ('It is high time that the workers had their place in the great political drama, and acted their part, rather than carrying wood and water for others').
[243] John O. Jones, *William Gladstone* (Caernarfon, 1898).
[244] *Tarian y Gweithiwr*, 19 February and 16 April 1891, 9 June 1892; *Celt*, 3 and 24 June 1892.

Yn eich llaw chwi mae y cwbl; yr ydych yn y rhan fwyaf o'r etholaethau yn y mwyafrif, ac yn yr oll yr ydych yn ddigon lluosog i droi y clorian fel y mynoch ond i chwi fod yn unol, heb uno ni fyddwch amgen teganau chwareu y cyfoethogion a phobl hunangeisiol.[245]

Pan Jones also associated with explicitly socialist individuals. Helen Taylor, with whom he organised land reform meetings in 1883, was a member of the SDF.[246] Pan Jones also greatly admired the Welsh Mancunian socialist, R.J. Derfel. He wrote to Derfel in the early 1890s, in support of his socialist pamphlet *Aildrefniad Cymdeithas*, stating '*mae eich syniadau gwleidyddol yn cydforfio yn dda ar eiddof fi*'.[247] He gave Derfel space to publish his letters on socialism in *Cwrs y Byd*, which also brought him into partnership with Ebeneezer Rees of Ystalyfera. Indeed, it is likely that Derfel's writings in *Cwrs y Byd* helped to clarify and develop the ideas of both Pan Jones and Rees, nurturing a network within which an indigenous Welsh socialism began to flourish. He also had close links with the Cardiff Fabians, and intended to celebrate May Day 1892 with them.[248] In addition to his relationship with David Rhys Jones,[249] he was close to Benjamin Evans, the Fabian secretary of the Cardiff ILP: Pan Jones sponsored Evans's membership of the Fabian Society,[250] and Evans took part in Pan Jones's van campaigns.[251]

Whether or not Pan Jones was a socialist cannot be decided on either ideological or associational grounds alone, both of which depend upon a fixed definition of an inherently fluid ideology. He was certainly viewed as a socialist by some. North Walian Conservatives saw him as a 'socialist or

---

[245] *Celt*, 25 December 1891 ('Everything is in your hand; you form the majority in the majority of constituencies, and in all of them you are numerous enough to turn the balance as you insist, but only if you are united, without unity you will be nothing but another toy to be played with by the rich and the self-seeking').

[246] Peris Jones-Evans, 'Evan Pan Jones', p. 150.

[247] National Library of Wales, Aberystwyth, NLW MS 23440D, Evan Pan Jones to R.J. Derfel, 12 December 1890 ('your political ideas converge well with those of mine'); Evan Pan Jones to R.J. Derfel, 28 May 1891, explicitly supports *Aildrefniad Cymdeithas*.

[248] *Celt*, 29 April 1892.

[249] See above pp 55–6.

[250] National Library of Wales, Aberystwyth, NLW MS 23440D, Ben Evans to R.J. Derfel, undated.

[251] *Celt*, 31 July and 11 December 1891.

semi-socialist',[252] while some among his supporters pointed out '*Ef, ac ef yn unig sydd yn ymladd ar y maes cyhoeddus dros iawnderau y gweithiwr yn gyffredinol*', and argued that this took him beyond Liberalism.[253] Ultimately, the argument must be decided by Pan Jones himself. The only reliable factor in defining any individual's relationship to the fluid and ideologically variegated late-nineteenth-century socialist movement is that individual's own self-identification. For this, Pan Jones provided conflicting evidence. Sometimes he seemed to distance himself not just from socialism, but from all other social movements, declaring his own philosophy unique.[254] On other occasions he explicitly identified himself as a socialist, by adopting the English word to describe his ideology: '*Byddaf yn cychwyn ar daith i bregethu Socialism o'r Van*', he informed R.J. Derfel in May 1891.[255] If Pan Jones may be described as a socialist, did he represent a genuinely indigenous Welsh form of socialism? He certainly combined his social doctrine with Welsh particularism: he was a fierce defender of the Welsh language, and criticised the North Wales Liberal Federation equally for its failure to use Welsh as for its attitude towards the working class.[256] He saw the land revolution as a national revolution, which would allow Wales to be itself: '*Rhaid tynu danedd y landlords cyn byth y ceir gweled Cymru yn ei lliw ei hun*', he explained in 1898.[257] He intertwined revolutionary and nationalist sentiment in his voluminous verse compositions,[258] and it would be difficult to imagine a more comprehensively Welsh character. Pan Jones nevertheless produced an uneven confection of ideas from numerous sources: Henry George's America, Michael Davitt's Ireland, the England of the Land Nationalisation Society, the Germany of Bismarck, rural Llandysul, industrial Glamorgan

---

[252] *North Wales Chronicle*, 23 April 1887.

[253] *Celt*, 12 April 1889 ('It is he, and he alone that fights in the public sphere for the rights of the worker in general').

[254] Evan Pan Jones, 'Y Ddaear i'r Bobl', *Geninen* (1910), pp. 30–1.

[255] National Library of Wales, Aberystwyth, NLW MS 23440D, Evan Pan Jones to R.J. Derfel, 28 May 1891 ('I am starting on a trip to preach Socialism from the Van').

[256] *Tarian y Gweithiwr*, 16 April 1891.

[257] *Llais Llafur*, 25 June 1898 ('There is a need to pull the teeth of the landlords before ever Wales can be seen in her own colour').

[258] E.G. Millward, 'Dicter Poeth y Dr. Pan', *Cof Cenedl*, 9 (1994), 163–90.

and theological Bala among them. That the finished product was synthesised and expressed in Wales arguably makes it Welsh, regardless of the provenance of its separate elements. At least this would be arguable if it were not contradicted by the most thorough of the synthesists to make a connection between Welsh particularism and socialism in the pre-1906 period: R.J. Derfel.

(IV) ROBERT JONES DERFEL: 'SOCIALIST CYMREIG'

Robert Jones (1824–1905) was the son of a farmer and cattle dealer from Llandderfel, Meirionnydd.[259] Having experienced child labour on a farm and in a woollen mill, he left home at the age of 11 to live with an uncle near Rhiwabon, under whose influence he became a Baptist, learnt handloom weaving and began to write poetry. He worked as a handloom weaver for ten years until, demoralised by frequent periods of unemployment and poverty, he moved to England. After several poverty-stricken years spent between Liverpool, Manchester and London, he settled in Manchester, where he became a travelling silk salesman. In this role he travelled extensively through the English Midlands, Yorkshire and Wales, while also writing a prolific amount of poetry, prose and drama. By the 1860s he had achieved considerable literary fame for work that combined a romantic celebration of nature, religion and folk life with strong nationalist and patriotic themes.[260] His literary output in the years before

[259] Jones only adopted the name Derfel (believing that there were too few Welsh surnames) in the 1850s. The main sources for Derfel's life, upon which this discussion is based, is R.J. Derfel, 'A Brief Account of My Life', *Llais Llafur*, August-December 1905 (also collected in NLW MS 23449 B); NLW MS 12525 B, Ionarwyn Williams, 'Llyfr Nodiadau o Hanesion Cymry Manceinion' also provides useful information about his context in Manchester. Secondary sources include Islwyn ap Nicholas, *Derfel: Welsh Rebel, Poet and Preacher* (London, 1945); D. Gwenallt Jones (ed.), *Detholiad o Ryddiaeth Gymraeg R.J. Derfel* (2 volumes, Llandysul, 1945); S.E. Williams, 'Astudiaeth o Fywyd a Phrydyddiaeth R.J. Derfel' (unpublished MA thesis, University of Wales, 1975); Eddie Cass, 'Robert Jones Derfel: A Welsh Poet in the Cotton Factory Times', *Llafur*, 7/1 (1996), 53–67; W.G. Evans, 'R.J. Derfel and Huwco Meirion', *Journal of the Merioneth Historical and Record Society*, 10 (1985), 48–56; Prys Morgan, 'R.J. Derfel a'r Ddrama Brad Y Llyfrau Gleision', in Prys Morgan (ed.), *Brad Y Llyfrau Gleision: Ysgrifau ar Hanes Cymru* (Cardiff, 1991), pp. 1–21; A.M. Roberts, 'R.J. Derfel, 1824–1905', *Y Traethodydd*, 165/688 (2009), 34–54.

[260] *Rhosyn Meirion* (1853), *Caneuon Min y Ffordd* (1861), *Munudau Segur* (1863),

1865 led one sympathetic contemporary to describe him as '*un o'r cenedlgarwyr puraf a welodd ein cenedl ni erioed*'.[261] Derfel's move from north Wales to Manchester positioned him between two worlds. The world of his childhood was the deeply rural, largely monoglot, Welsh cultural heartland of Meirionnydd: the world that had produced Michael D. Jones and Tom Ellis, and which provided an agrarian counterpoint to the industrial radicalism of Merthyr. From this world, Derfel made the transition to cosmopolitan Manchester, premier theatre of British class struggle: in the imagination of Engels, 'that classic soil on which English manufacture has achieved its masterwork and from which all labour movements emanate'.[262] This involved him in a profound personal journey. He went to Manchester a monoglot Welshman but quickly mastered English, and by the time he began travelling the roads selling silk, he was a fully integrated cosmopolitan. Importantly, though, part of Derfel's cosmopolitanism was a retention of Welshness. He married twice, both times to Welsh-speaking women, and his work demanded constant travelling back and forth to Wales, where he continued to preach and lecture.[263] He also sustained a correspondence, much of it in Welsh, with numerous fellow countrymen in Wales.[264]

Manchester, which had a substantial Welsh population,[265] provided a microcosm in which the cultural worlds of England and Wales coexisted, and by the 1860s Derfel inhabited both of them. He was a member of the Welsh Baptist

Caneuon Gwladgarol Cymru (1864), *Songs for Welshmen* (1865), *Brad y Llyfrau Glesion* (1854), *Traethodau ac Ariethiau* (1864).

[261] *Celt*, 24 February 1888 ('one of the purest national patriots our nation has ever seen').

[262] Frederick [Friedrich] Engels, *The Condition of the Working Class in England* (London, 1969, first published in Britain, 1882), p. 75.

[263] Bangor University Archive, Bangor MS 5019 (13), Dr Owen Davies to Myrddin Fardd, 22 September 1864, refers to Derfel's preaching at Ffestiniog. For accounts of Derfel preaching, lecturing and adjudicating at *eisteddfodau* in Bangor, Llandderfel, Bala, Holyhead and Dolgellau, see *Baner ac Amserau Cymru*, 16 December 1863, 10, 17 and 24 February 1864, 1 and 22 February 1865, 10 March 1866.

[264] National Library of Wales, Aberystwyth, NLW MS 23440D contains correspondence to Derfel from all parts of Wales.

[265] At the end of the century this was estimated at 8–10,000, NLW MS 15467 C, 'Llyfr Cofnodion Cymeithas Genedlaethol Cymry Manceinion, 1900–1911'.

Church in Granby Row.[266] He served on the committee of *Cymdeithas Lenyddol Cymry Manchester*, where he associated with other notable Mancunian Welsh poets, including William Williams (Creuddynfab) and John Jones (Idris Fychan),[267] and he frequently lectured to Welsh audiences across north-west England.[268] He acted, moreover, as a link between the two worlds. When he became involved in Manchester radicalism in the 1860s, serving on the executive of the Reform League alongside the former Chartist leader Ernest Jones,[269] he acted as a spokesman to Welsh audiences. In May 1867 he spoke in Welsh on 'Votes for Women' to the Cambrian Literary Society, in 1868 he addressed the Manchester *Cymreigyddion* on *Rhyddid Ymadrodd* (Freedom of Speech),[270] and in the election of 1868 he worked to mobilise the Welsh vote.[271]

Derfel later described his political views in this period as 'very advanced radical, in fact ... Chartist',[272] and, as a former handloom weaver, he was classic Chartist material. In this sense his politics accord with Deian Hopkin's assessment of him as a product of the early period of the industrial revolution.[273] In the mid-1860s, however, his ideological make-up was in the process of radical change. Partly as the result of a failed business venture, he seems to have experienced some sort of breakdown.[274] He ceased writing for the best part of

[266] *Baner ac Amserau Cymru*, 1 January and 16 July 1862.
[267] National Library of Wales, Aberystwyth, NLW MS 12525B, 'Llyfr Nodiadau o Hanesion Cymry Manceinion'; *North Wales Chronicle*, 19 October 1867.
[268] *North Wales Chronicle*, 9 March 1867; *Baner ac Amserau Cymru*, 7 April, 20 and 27 June 1866, 11 December 1867.
[269] *Manchester Times*, 1 June and 16 November 1867, 3 October 1868.
[270] *Baner ac Amserau Cymru*, 8 May 1867 and 12 February 1868.
[271] *Manchester Times*, 14 November 1868; For Ernest Jones and the 1868 election, see A. Taylor, '"The Best Way to Get What He Wanted": Ernest Jones and the Boundaries of Liberalism in the Manchester Election of 1868', *Parliamentary History*, 16/2 (1997), 185–204.
[272] Derfel, 'A Brief Account of My Life' (X).
[273] Deian Hopkin, 'Y Werin a'i Theyrnas: Ymateb Sosialaeth i Genedlaetholdeb, 1880–1920', *Cof Cenedl*, 6 (1991), 162–92, 167.
[274] It is not exactly clear what happened to Derfel in this period. He claimed to have experienced a business failure due to the reluctance of the Welsh community to support him when attempting to set up a Welsh bookshop, and this became a frequently repeated element of his autobiography (for example, *Llais Llafur*, 27 August 1898). There are, however, confusing aspects to his account. See Paul

twenty years, and when he began again it was as an enthusiastic and thoroughgoing socialist. He later recounted the process of conversion, which occurred when he was at his lowest ebb:

> fortunately for me, I came accidentally across some of the works of Robert Owen, and the ideas contained within them captured my convictions almost instantly, and I became a Socialist. The new ideas gave me a new life. I was, so to speak, born again. The world and all in it seemed new, and I began again to take an interest in life and its duties.[275]

This is a classic account of a conversion to the 'religion of socialism', which Derfel subsequently embraced enthusiastically. He attended a Labour Church,[276] and described socialism as 'a religion of humanity'.[277] Intriguingly, though, at least according to his own account, Derfel's conversion took place the best part of two decades before the period normally associated with such phenomena,[278] and although he did not write about it until the 1880s, his socialism had its roots in an earlier tradition of utopianism. Robert Owen's influence, explicitly acknowledged in Derfel's autobiography, was manifest in much of his political writing. He asserted the transformative possibilities of cooperation, arguing that 'by organising themselves, not to talk and fight, but to produce wealth for themselves, instead of for others, [the workers] would do more in a lifetime to bring about the desired social revolution, than can be done by political agitation in centuries'.[279] His advocacy of garden cities explicitly made reference to Owen's 'villages of unity',[280] and his

---

Ward and Martin Wright, 'Mirrors of Wales – Life Story as National Metaphor: Case Studies of R.J. Derfel and Huw T. Edwards', *History*, 95/317 (2010), 45–63.

[275] Derfel, 'A Brief Account of My Life' (III).

[276] National Library of Wales, Aberystwyth, NLW MS 23440D, J.E. Broadbent (Oldham) to R.J. Derfel, 26 October 1891.

[277] R.J. Derfel, *On the Importance of Right Methods in Teaching Socialism* (Manchester, 1891), p. 12.

[278] Stephen Yeo, 'A New Life: The Religion of Socialism in Britain', *History Workshop Journal, 1883–1896*, 4/1 (1977), 5–56.

[279] National Library of Wales, Aberystwyth, NLW MS 23446B, R.J. Derfel, *A New Departure in Socialist Propaganda*.

[280] National Library of Wales, Aberystwyth, NLW MS 23446B, R.J. Derfel, 'Garden Cities Etc.', *Manchester Evening News*, 8 September 1902.

central belief in environmental determinism – 'surround man with good moral, social, and physical conditions, and the bad will be made good, the good will be made better, and the best will be preserved in their goodness'[281] – was drawn directly from Owen's *New Moral World*.

Derfel's late-nineteenth-century assertion of Owenism might be seen as a link between socialism, utopian and scientific. His socialism was also the product of a complex geographical and cultural interplay. Owen was a Welshman, whose socialism was a product of his own journey from Wales into the wider world, and who, in the late nineteenth century, was being reclaimed by some of his own countrymen. Derfel discovered Owen in Manchester (it is even possible that he saw Owen speak in either Manchester or Liverpool),[282] and it is likely that he was introduced to Owen's work by members of the Manchester Welsh community. (He worked alongside one of Owen's biographers, another Mancunian Welshman, Lloyd Jones, during the 1868 election.[283]) Derfel, though, was also an agent in the reintroduction of Owen's ideas to both the Manchester Welsh community and within Wales. In 1898 he read a paper on Owen to the Manchester Welsh National Society, which was subsequently serialised in *Llais Llafur*.[284] It began by stressing Owen's attachment to Wales, which was contrasted with his status as a world citizen. Derfel had travelled a similar journey to that of his hero.

Whatever Derfel's ideological provenance, by the end of the 1880s he was fully located within mainstream British socialism. He joined the SDF, but, critical of the Federation's 'strong language and bitter tone', soon moved on to the Fabian Society.[285] As a Fabian he engaged in the debates, and exhibited the apparent contradictions, that were typical of late-Victorian British socialism. He rejected the concept

---

[281] National Library of Wales, Aberystwyth, NLW MS 23446B, R.J. Derfel, *Free Will or No Free Will*.

[282] National Library of Wales, Aberystwyth, NLW MS 23617E, O. Llew Owain, 'Bywyd a Gwaith R.J. Derfel', p. 13.

[283] *Manchester Times*, 14 November 1868; Lloyd Jones, *The Life, Times, and Labours of Robert Owen* (edited by William Cairns Jones) (London, 1890).

[284] *Llais Llafur*, 3, 10 and 17 December 1898; also see 'Robert Owen y Socialist', *Cymro*, 24 May 1894.

[285] Derfel, 'A Brief Account of My Life' (X).

of violent revolution in favour of 'reason, argument, and persuasion',[286] and argued that evolution was the primary agent of social change. 'Evolution works slowly but surely', he explained, 'It is a growth. It brings about greater changes than any revolution, however successful, could accomplish',[287] and although he accepted the concept of a class war, he saw it not as part of a necessary dialectical process of change, but as a negative and injurious diversion: '*rhyfel dosbarth yn fwy dinystriol i'r genedl fawr, sef y werin, na holl frwydrau gwaedlyd y byd*'.[288] He argued that society would be perfected through material improvement, education and the consequent development of superior institutions and forms of social behaviour. In keeping with one of the apparent paradoxes of late-Victorian socialist thinking, though, the shadow of revolution was never far behind the soft tones of Derfel's propaganda. 'In the sense of evolution,' he asserted, 'all socialists are revolutionary.'[289]

In this latent revolutionism Derfel followed William Morris. Morris had lectured in Manchester in the 1880s,[290] and his Marxist ideas were promoted there by a strong SDF presence,[291] so his influence upon Derfel's environment was direct. Derfel identified Morris, along with Robert Owen, as one of the few socialist leaders he would trust,[292] and his definition of socialism as 'a complete change in the basis of society'[293] was derived from Morris's own definition of revolution.[294] Indeed, Derfel was ideologically closer to the

[286] Derfel, *On the Importance of Right Methods In Teaching Socialism*, p. 3.
[287] Derfel, *An Unauthorised Programme Showing How To Abolish Poverty, Without Doing An Injustice To Anyone, or Leaving A Feeling Of Wrong Behind. A Complete Revolution Without Bloodshed, Confiscation, Or Physical Force*, p. 12.
[288] National Library of Wales, Aberystwyth, NLW MS 23446B ('class war is more destructive to the great nation, namely the common people, than all the bloody conflicts of the world').
[289] Derfel, *On the Importance of Right Methods in Teaching Socialism*, p. 2.
[290] *Justice*, 27 September 1884 and 30 October 1885.
[291] *Justice*, 22 and 29 March, 19 and 26 July and 2 August 1884, 3, 24 and 31 January and 16 May 1885, 13 March 1886, 10 September 1887, 4 August 1888; Jeffrey Hill, 'Social Democracy and the Labour Movement: The Social Democratic Federation in Lancashire', *Bulletin of the North West Labour History Society*, 8 (1982), 44–55.
[292] *Llais Llafur*, 24 June 1899.
[293] National Library of Wales, Aberystwyth, NLW MS 23446B, Derfel, 'The Most Important Thing First'.
[294] 'We use the word revolution in its etymological sense, and mean by it a change

revolutionary Morris than he was either to his fellow Fabians or to the political labour movement of the 1890s and early 1900s. His belief that palliative reform would 'do nothing more than benefit a few at the expense of the many, and at the same time will make the slavery of the masses more secure, and their emancipation more difficult to accomplish' closely echoed Morris's own uncompromising position, as did his rejection of any alliance between socialists and trade unionists and his hostility to parliamentary politics.[295] He dismissed the idea of 'practical socialism',[296] in favour of communism:

> The Socialism I believe in and advocate is Communism. To me Socialism and Communism are convertible terms – Communism is Socialism, Socialism is Communism ... Others may ... talk of social democracy, collectivism, labourism, and so forth, but I am satisfied with the word Socialism. If the other isms mean anything less than Socialism, they mean no full social salvation for man.[297]

In many respects Derfel was a typical example of the interaction between Marxism and native British thought that characterised late-nineteenth-century British socialism.[298] In his case, this ideological fusion was complicated by his national identity. One outcome of his conversion to socialism was a modification of his nationalism. He explained in 1905, 'I was an enthusiastic Welsh nationalist ... [but a] great change ... has come over myself in politics ... I am a nationalist of a sort still, but the sort is different to the old one. My patriotism is less tribal and more cosmopolitan than it used to be ... I do not place so much importance on the language as I used to.'[299] The implications of this were potentially dramatic for the Welsh language: 'a multiplicity of languages

---

in the basis of society', William Morris, 'How We Live and How We Might Live', in G.D.H. Cole (ed.), *William Morris: Prose, Verse, Lectures and Essays* (New York, 1974), pp. 565–87, p. 565.

[295] National Library of Wales, Aberystwyth, NLW MS 23446B, Derfel, 'The Most Important Thing First'.

[296] National Library of Wales, Aberystwyth, NLW MS 23446B, Derfel, 'The Housing Problem'.

[297] R.J. Derfel, *Socialism: What It Is, And What It Teaches* (Manchester, 1892), p. 3.

[298] Pierson, *Marxism and the Origins of British Socialism*.

[299] R.J. Derfel, 'A Brief Account of My Life' (IX).

is an inconvenience, a hindrance to communication, fellowship, and progress', he argued. 'Different speeches' were used by the wealthy classes 'to keep the toilers in subjection', and the adoption of an international language, which he explicitly stated would be English, was of primary importance to radicals, freethinkers and socialists, in order to 'do something real to bring about a time when all nations will be one people, and in effect of one speech'.[300] Derfel's vision of internationalism, which he viewed as concomitant with socialism, extended not just to linguistic standardisation, but to the gradual elimination of national cultures. He even suggested that the British Empire could hasten the process of national homogenisation, which he described in 1905:

> At first every man was for himself, individually. Gradually, the individual merged in a clan or tribe. Later, the tribes were absorbed in a state. It seems to me as likely that ultimately the Welsh, Scots, Manx, Irish and English will evolve into one British nation; and in the course of time I see no [im]possibility for all the nations of Europe to become one European nation, using one common tongue.[301]

The apparently straightforward displacement of Derfel's nationalism by socialism was, however, by no means as complete as he appeared to claim in 1905. Despite his ideological commitment to internationalism, and his Mancunian socialist context, Derfel did not abandon either his Welsh identity or his enthusiasm for Welsh culture. He continued his involvement with the Manchester Welsh community until the end of his life, serving as vice-president of the *Cymdeithas Genedlaethol Cymry Manceinion*, and frequently speaking at its meetings.[302] His contributions continued to address traditional Welsh cultural topics such as *Rhai Pethau Eisiau eu Gwneud yn Gymru Sydd Tuag at Ddyrchafu Cymru Fydd* (which included the nurturing of the Welsh language alongside an

---

[300] National Library of Wales, Aberystwyth, NLW MS 23447 B, R.J. Derfel, 'Language'.
[301] R.J. Derfel, 'A Brief Account of My Life' (IX).
[302] *Cymro*, 14 April and 10 November 1892; National Library of Wales, Aberystwyth, NLW MS 15467 C, Llyfr Cofnodion Cymeithas Genedlaethol Cymry Manceinion, 1900–1911.

adopted international language).[303] He also attempted to relate his socialism to Wales by using the Welsh language as a medium of propaganda. His first contribution to the debate on socialism was an article, in Welsh, published in *Cymru Fydd* in 1888, in which he advanced the argument for socialism within a nationalist framework. He argued that '*yr elfen gyntaf a'r bwysicaf mewn dyngarwch ydyw cenedlgarwch*', but then went on to demonstrate, using concepts borrowed from Marx, that the existing *Cymru Fydd* manifesto was insufficient. He introduced his own programme for national regeneration which comprised a full-scale scheme of nationalisation, beginning with the land, and the dissolution of the ruling class (*meistrolaeth*). It was, moreover, explicit that the nationalisation (*cenedleiddio*) envisaged by Derfel would take place at a Welsh, and not a British, level: '*Mae ddaear Cymru a'i holl drysorau – glo, mwnau, aur, chwareli, ac felly yn y blaen, yn perthyn i'r Cymry sydd yn byw yn y wlad.*'[304] Derfel continued to write on socialism, in both Welsh and English, until his death seventeen years later, but he never contradicted the position he set out in 1888. Rather he made a determined effort to propagandise within specifically Welsh contexts. Later in 1888, he repeated the arguments of his *Cymru Fydd* article in a speech to the Manchester Welsh National Society which he published in 1889 as *Aildrefniad Cymdeithas* – the first Welsh language tract of the Socialist Revival.[305] In 1894 he explained to the Manchester branch of *Cymru Fydd*, '*Paham yr Ydwyf yn Socialist*' (Why I Am a Socialist).[306]

Derfel's most significant work was arguably the series of letters on *Cymdeithasiaeth* that he wrote under the pseudonym *Socialist Cymreig*, for *Y Cymro* in 1892, and which were reprinted and expanded in *Llais Llafur*, *Y Cymro* and *Cwrs y Byd* during

---

[303] *Genedl Gymreig*, 16 November 1892 ('Some Things That Need Doing That Tend Towards the Elevation of the Future Wales').

[304] R.J. Derfel, 'Ein Rhagolygon a'n Gwaith', *Cymru Fydd* (May 1888), pp. 270–1 ('the first and most important element in the love of mankind is the love of nation'; 'The land of Wales and all its treasures – coal, ore, gold, quarries, and so on and so forth, belong to the Welsh that live in the country').

[305] R.J. Derfel, *Aildrefniad Cymdeithas* (Manchester, 1889); also see *Baner ac Amserau Cymru*, 5 December 1888 and 13 February 1889.

[306] *Genedl Gymreig*, 4 December 1894.

the 1890s and early 1900s.[307] Amounting to a full exposition of socialism over a total of fifty-seven different articles, they exemplify the connection between mainstream British socialism and the culture of Wales. Derfel's pseudonym – an amalgam of Welsh and English, not *Cymdeithaswr Cymreig* (or even *Cymraeg*), but *Socialist Cymreig* – hints at a sense of cultural dislocation and reconnection, and his chosen form is a direct imitation of Blatchford's *Merrie England* letters. Many of the letters are based upon the arguments of contemporary English-language propagandists, arranged around Derfel's central synthesis of *cyd-feddiant, cyd-lafur and cyd-fwynhad* (co-ownership, co-labour and co-enjoyment). They rehearse common socialist themes, encapsulated in titles such as *Aneffeithioldeb Pob Moddion ond Cymdeithasiaeth i Ddifodi Tlodi a'i Ganlyniadau* (The Ineffectiveness of all Means except Socialism to Eradicate Poverty and its Results), *Ydyw Cymdeithasiaeth yn bosibl?* (Is Socialism Possible?) and *Ysglyfaeth Y Drefn Presenol* (The Plunder of the Present System). The arguments are conducted in general terms, and their supporting statistics are drawn almost exclusively from urban England, as presented in the Fabian Tract *Facts for Socialists*. This has led some to conclude that there was 'nothing exclusively Welsh in Derfel's socialism', that it was 'manifestly alien' to the Welsh radical tradition.[308] Aspects of it were, but as a general conclusion this is insufficient. One significant way in which Derfel attempted to relate socialism to his national identity was by exploring its relationship with religious nonconformity. Derfel's attitude to religion was complex,[309] but twelve of his fifty-seven letters directly explore the relationship between socialism and Christianity. They represent a sublimation of the relationship between Welshness and socialism that foreshadowed socialism's

---

[307] *Cymro*, 17 March–6 October 1892 and 31 July–25 June 1903; *Llais Llafur*, 15 April 1899–2 June 1900 and 30 August–7 November 1902; *Cwrs y Byd*, November 1892–May 1895.

[308] Parry, *The Radical Tradition in Welsh Politics*, p. 25.

[309] He rejected Christianity and became a freethinker sometime after the 1860s, although it is not clear exactly when. He was capable of expressing virulent anti-Christian views and railed against 'priestcraft' in all its forms. See *Freethinker*, 26 July 1903–24 December 1905. Despite this, he retained many elements of his Baptist beliefs.

intense encounter with the chapels in the early twentieth century. Other aspects of Derfel's socialist writings also focus upon prominent Welsh issues, including land reform and education. More than this, several of Derfel's letters engage explicitly with Welsh national identity.

In *Gwladgarwch dan Gymdeithasiaeth* (Patriotism under Socialism) he criticised what he saw as the hollow nationalism of St. David's day, and argued that real nationalism must embrace and elevate the whole of the nation, as represented by *y werin*. He argued that the unity implied in patriotism was innate and indestructible – as testified by the unlikely survival of the Welsh nation. Arguing for the creation of a new form of non-aggressive nationalism consonant with internationalism, he went on to discuss the prospects for Welshness under socialism:

> Mae gwladgarwch o ryw fath, yr wyf yn meddwl, yn rhwym o barhau o dan Gymdeithasiaeth. Yr wyf yn methu â gweled bod dim Cymdeithasiaeth yn gofyn i mi am beidio â bod yn Gymro. Dyletswydd pob gwlad ydyw trefnu eu thŷ ei hun yn gyntaf, a chynorthwyo eraill wedi hynny, os gall. Pe byddai'n bosibl cymysgu pob cenedl â'i gilydd i wneud un genedl o'r cwbl, nid wyf yn meddwl yr enillid dim trwy hynny. Ond y mae hynny yn amhosibl. Yr hyn sydd eisiau ydyw unoliaeth mewn amrywiaeth.[310]

This new sense of nationalism, he argued, would demand a reconstruction of the Welsh nation. His programme to this end included the re-creation of the *Eisteddfod* as a non-competitive forum for the nurturing of science and culture, the secularisation of the chapels to pursue an agenda of social improvement, the creation of a secular education system to replace the influence of 'priestcraft' with rational scientific education, the maintenance of the nation's native language and a thorough redistribution of property. The outcome of this programme, Derfel argued, would create an environment that would encourage the development of a

[310] *Llais Llafur*, 3 March 1900 ('Patriotism of some type, I think, is bound to continue under socialism. I fail to see that any type of socialism asks me not to be a Welshman. The duty of every country is to organise its own house first, and after that help others, if it can. If it were possible to mix up all the nations together to make one nation out of the lot, I don't think anything would be gained. But that is impossible. What is needed is unity in diversity').

people fit for the arrival of socialism, and the whole project would be symbolised by the elevation of Robert Owen to be patron saint of Wales.[311] As a start, Derfel advocated an all-Welsh conference to consider the social condition of the Welsh nation.[312]

Derfel's call was not heeded, and historians agree that his immediate influence upon Wales was slight.[313] As the *eisteddfod* essayist O. Llew Owain put it in 1941, '*fel eos oedd Derfel i weithwyr – yn canu yn y nos*'.[314] His letters in *Y Cymro* received only a limited initial response,[315] and it is difficult to evaluate their longer-term impact. The editors of *Llais Llafur* claimed that they reprinted the letters in 1898 in response to popular demand, but although the paper subsequently received further correspondence praising Derfel's work, it was never deemed viable to meet requests to publish *cymdeithasiaeth* in pamphlet form.[316] This does not, however, detract from Derfel's significance. His contributions to the socialist press were part of the process of education and human capital building within the nascent Welsh socialist movement. Their role in the adaptation of socialist ideology to the environment of Wales was enhanced by their context. In the *Llais,* for example, his pieces on the housing issue, which advanced abstract socialist arguments on housing reform, were published alongside the writing of 'Oliver Twist', which dealt with the specifics of the housing crisis in Ystalyfera. Readers were thus invited to make the connection between the local and the universal.[317]

Derfel's influence may have been limited, but he was not unknown. *Baner ac Amserau Cymru* could refer to him in 1896

[311] *Llais Llafur*, 4 April 1903.
[312] National Library of Wales, Aberystwyth, NLW MS 23448B, R.J. Derfel, 'Cymdeithasiaeth' (LVII).
[313] John Davies, *A History of Wales* (London, 1993), pp. 417, 477; Jones, *The North Wales Quarrymen, 1874–1922*, p. 69; Richard Lewis, 'Political Culture and Ideology', in Tanner, Williams and Hopkin, *The Labour Party in Wales*, pp. 86–111, p. 94; Pope, *Building Jerusalem*, p. 23.
[314] National Library of Wales, Aberystwyth, NLW MS 23617 E, O. Llew Owain, 'Bywyd a Gwaith R.J. Derfel' ('Derfel was like a nightingale to [the] workers – singing in the night').
[315] *Cymro*, 4, 11 and 25 August, 1 September 1892.
[316] *Llais Llafur*, 29 January 1898, 13 and 20 May 1899.
[317] *Llais Llafur*, 9, 23 and 30 May 1903.

as '*y Sosialydd Cymreig adnabyddus o Fanceinion*'.[318] His primary significance, though, was not in his immediate influence. British socialism was one of the 'invented traditions' of the British nation.[319] Derfel was trying to invent an alternative, within which the national consciousness and cultural traditions of Wales had a place. He was trying to create a synthesis of the universal and the particular. This was problematic, and he was only partially successful. There were points of dislocation within his work. The possibility of a distinctly Welsh socialist ideology that he implicitly proposed was inhibited by a wide range of influences. Territorially, socialism had spread unevenly across Wales, and its penetration of Welsh culture was marginal. Derfel's Manchester was a world away from Keir Hardie's Merthyr, which was equally distant from the Caernarfonshire of Ap Ffarmwr. The elements of a genuinely rooted Welsh socialism existed, but they were disconnected. From his position as an exile, Derfel made important connections, which he passed on to the next generation. This is his primary significance. '*Y ffaith yw, y mae Derfel wedi bod yn byw yn mhell o flaen ei oes*', *Baner ac Amserau Cymru* observed in 1896.[320] If this was the case, he was not alone. Neither was he that far ahead: his death at the end of 1905, just over a month before the founding of the Labour Party, represents a watershed in Welsh socialist history. Thereafter the spread of socialism in Wales quickened dramatically, and within only a couple of years members of another generation of socialists were obliged to confront the core challenge of relating their socialism to their national consciousness and immediate environment.

---

[318] *Baner ac Amserau Cymru*, 15 January 1896 ('the well-known Welsh socialist from Manchester').

[319] Ward, *Red Flag and Union Jack*, p. 203.

[320] *Baner ac Amserau Cymru*, 15 January 1896 ('The fact is that Derfel has been living far ahead of his time').

5
PROGRESS AND PLURALISM, 1906–1912

The development of the socialist and labour movement in Britain entered a new phase around 1906, in which several different processes may be discerned. The most important of these was the emergence of the Labour Party as the primary vehicle for labour and socialist politics, and this ultimately resulted in the accommodation of socialism within the British political system. Although the Labour Party was not an explicitly socialist party, it provided a political home for the majority of British socialists. Its creation also stimulated greatly increased interest in socialist ideas across British society: the membership of socialist bodies increased, as did the circulation of socialist newspapers. Alongside this increased interest, socialists also entered another period of intense debate about the nature and strategy of their movement. The most controversial field of debate within the socialist movement centred on the calls for 'socialist unity', which, particularly after Victor Grayson's spectacular victory as an independent socialist in the Colne Valley by-election of 1907, threatened to undermine the newly formed Labour Party. This was not, however, the only live debate within the socialist movement in this period. An equally important, but historically neglected, element of the fluidity of pre-Great War socialism concerned the way in which socialists related to the pluralism of national aspirations and identities in the British Isles, and this debate was pursued with particular intensity in Wales. The final chapter of this book provides a survey of the growth of socialism in Wales in the period immediately after 1906; it then examines the emergence of a group of Welsh socialists who defined their socialism by relating it specifically to Wales and articulating it through the medium of the Welsh language.

(i) The socialist movement in Wales after 1906

Labour Representation Committees were established in parts of south Wales from the early 1900s onwards – a process that was encouraged by both the 1901 Taff Vale decision and Labour's breakthrough in the 1906 General Election – and although their formation was ad hoc and even chaotic, the Labour Party ultimately became an established part of south Wales politics.[1] The decisive factor in this was the affiliation of the SWMF to the party in 1908, which marked a major shift in the balance of power in south Wales.[2] Even the arch Lib-Lab Mabon was forced to acknowledge that the ground was moving beneath him. In 1906 he described the LRC as 'a party roaming in the wilderness without a place to put down its tent',[3] but by 1908 he was arguing that affiliation would 'make Trade Unionists better Socialists, and Socialists better Trade Unionists'.[4] When T. Mardy Jones, an organiser for the new Labour Party, claimed in 1909 that 'the divorce from Liberalism is definite and permanent'[5] he was being slightly premature: Labour did not become properly established in south Wales until the Great War. His words were prophetic, however. As Peter Stead has observed, 'deep currents were always taking things Labour's way',[6] and Labour's ultimate ascendancy was to tie Wales into a pan-British unionist political project for the remainder of the twentieth century.

In some respects this process represented less a break with Liberalism, and the Welsh particularism that it represented, than a seamless progression, and many of the old Lib-Labs – although they were now officially pure and simple Labour representatives – remained distinctly Liberal at heart. John

---

[1] Peter Stead, 'Establishing a Heartland: The Labour Party in Wales', in K.D. Brown (ed.), *The First Labour Party, 1906–1914* (London, 1985); Eddie May, 'The Mosaic of Labour Politics, 1900–1918', in Tanner, Williams and Hopkin (eds), *The Labour Party in Wales*, pp. 61–85.

[2] K.O. Fox, 'The Emergence of the Political Labour Movement in the Eastern Section of the South Wales Coalfield, 1894–1910' (unpublished MA thesis, Aberystwyth, 1965), pp. 106, 123.

[3] *South Wales Daily News*, 23 July 1906.

[4] *Rhondda Leader*, 23 May 1908.

[5] *Labour Leader*, 26 March 1909.

[6] Stead, 'Establishing a Heartland', p. 86.

Williams, the Western District Miners' Association agent and MP for Gower from 1906, was described by his supporters as 'simply a Labour candidate with Radical sympathies'.[7] He never truly abandoned his Liberal beliefs, but nevertheless remained the Labour MP for Gower through the two elections of 1910, having quietly joined the ILP.[8] His tenure there was directly due to his ability to reflect 'a network of values in which Welshness, nonconformism and, above all, community values played a part',[9] and, like Mabon, he was prepared to absorb elements of socialist ideology, so long as it was what he called 'socialism of the right sort'.[10] Indeed, in the period before the Great War, it was the more strident socialists who continued to be the political outsiders. Ben Tillett contested the Swansea Town seat in the general election of January 1910 on a straight socialist ticket, directly challenging the official Labour Party and its secret electoral pact with the Liberals. Without support from the national Labour leadership he went down to crushing defeat.[11] Even the south Wales born and bred ILP-er Vernon Hartshorn discovered that his socialism was an electoral liability. When he contested mid-Glamorgan in 1910 he found himself painted as an atheist, revolutionist and advocate of free love, and was consequently defeated.[12] At a community level it remained the case that 'those who were in sympathy with this new doctrine were considered to be very queer people'.[13] The socialists' day was yet to come, but it was not far off.

One indication of this was what Mabon described as 'the severe struggle between the old and sane trade unionism and the new socialistic unions'[14] that was raging in south Wales by

[7] Quoted in David Cleaver, 'Labour and Liberals in the Gower Constituency, 1885–1910', *Welsh History Review*, 12/3 (1985), 388–410 (403).
[8] *Llais Llafur*, 20 June 1908.
[9] Cleaver, 'Labour and Liberals in the Gower Constituency', p. 409.
[10] *Llais Llafur*, 20 February 1909.
[11] David Cleaver, 'The General Election Contest in the Swansea Town Constituency, January 1910 – The Socialist Challenge', *Llafur*, 5/3 (1990), 28–33; Schneer, *Ben Tillett*, pp. 138–46; McCarry, 'Labour and Society in Swansea', pp. 399–414.
[12] *Labour Leader*, 8 April 1910; Chris Howard, 'Reactionary Radicalism: the Mid-Glamorgan By-Election, March 1910', *Glamorgan Historian*, 9 (1973), 29–42.
[13] Cliff Prothero, *Recount* (Ormskirk, 1982), p. 1.
[14] Quoted in E.W. Evans, *Mabon (William Abraham, 1842–1922): A Study in Trade*

the end of the decade, and which ultimately resulted in the displacement of Mabon himself from the top of the SWMF. There were indications of a new militant undercurrent in parts of the coalfield even before the middle of the decade. One sign of this was a resurgence of the SDF, which had been in decline since the turn of the century. In July 1904, a reader of *Justice* reported the intention of some old SDF members in the Rhondda 'to buckle on their armour again' and begin agitation.[15] By September branch activity was reported at Abercynon, Treharris and Blaenclydach,[16] and by the end of the year an SDF club had been established at Senghenydd and another branch formed at Mountain Ash.[17] During 1905 SDF branches were established in the Rhymney Valley, at Bargoed and New Tredegar,[18] and, after a tour of south Wales in the summer of 1905, the SDF's full-time propagandist, J. Jones, was satisfied that south Wales hosted 'as enthusiastic and eager a body of comrades as could be found anywhere in the Kingdom'.[19] The SDF and its successor, the British Socialist Party, maintained a presence in the coalfield, offering a harder-edged, more obviously Marxist, variety of socialism to that of the ILP. This was boosted by visits from the party's national figures, including a return to Wales of R. Rosetti in 1905,[20] and a visit from H.M. Hyndman in 1908.[21] Like the other socialist groups, it supported its political activities with a lively social calendar of smoking concerts and recreational events,[22] and after 1905 Marxian socialists exerted intellectual and cultural influence through the Blaenclydach Marxian Club, which aimed 'to provide for working men the means of social intercourse, mutual helpfulness, mental and moral improvement, and rational recreation' through the provision of rooms for 'reading,

Union Leadership (Cardiff, 1959), p. 88.
[15] *Justice*, 30 July 1904.
[16] *Justice*, 27 August and 17 September 1904; *Rhondda Leader*, 10 September 1904.
[17] *Justice*, 24 and 31 December 1904.
[18] *Justice*, 22 April and 29 July 1905.
[19] *Justice*, 19 August 1905.
[20] *Justice*, 13 May 1905.
[21] *Rhondda Leader*, 28 November 1908.
[22] *Justice*, 25 March, 1 July and 5 August 1905.

recreation, gymnastics, lectures and concerts'.[23] The SDF and the Blaenclydach Marxians added a critical, advanced edge to the socialist and labour movement, organising lectures on themes such as 'Why the Labour Party is Ineffective',[24] and pulling it in a leftwards ideological direction.

By the end of the decade the process of radicalisation was hastened by the industrial convulsions of the great 'Labour Unrest' which were played out with intensity in south Wales through events such as the Cambrian Combine Strike in the Rhondda and the unrest in the neighbouring Aberdare Valley in 1910 and the Cardiff General Strike and the unrest at Llanelli in 1911.[25] This added a new dimension to the south Wales labour movement which was inspired by the activism of a new generation of militant leaders, such as Noah Ablett and A.J. Cook,[26] and expressed through the Unofficial Reform Committee of 1911 and *The Miners' Next Step* of 1912.[27] Many of the activists of this new working-class movement were educated at the SWMF-funded Central Labour College.[28] The CLC's ideology was profoundly universalist and classist. Its students experienced a 'scientific' Marxist education, which aimed to equip them 'to assist as effectively as possible

[23] Swansea University Archive, SWCC: MNA/PP/66/1, *Rules of the Marxian Club and Institute, Blaenclydach*.
[24] *Rhondda Leader*, 12 December 1908.
[25] Campbell Balfour, 'Captain Tupper and the Seaman's Strike, 1911', *Morgannwg*, 14 (1970), 62–80; Martin Barclay, 'The Slaves of the Lamp: The Aberdare Miners' Strike, 1910', *Llafur*, 2/3 (1978), 24–42; John Edwards, *Remembrance of a Riot: The Story of the Llanelli Railway Strike Riots of 1911* (Llanelli, 1988); Neil Evans, '"A Tidal Wave of Impatience": The Cardiff General Strike of 1911', in Geraint Jenkins and J. Beverley Smith (eds), *Politics and Society in Wales, 1840–1922* (Cardiff, 1988), pp. 135–59; Robert Griffiths, *Killing No Murder* (Croydon, 2009); Deian Hopkin, 'The Llanelli Riots, 1911', *Welsh History Review*, 11/4 (1983), 488–515; Deian Hopkin, 'The Great Unrest in Wales, 1910–1913: Questions of Evidence', in Deian R. Hopkin and Gregory S. Kealey (eds), *Class, Community and the Labour Movement: Wales and Canada, 1850–1930* (Aberystwyth, 1989), pp. 249–75; David Smith, 'Tonypandy 1910: Definitions of Community', *Past and Present*, 87/1 (1980), 158–84; L.J. Williams, 'The Road to Tonypandy', *Llafur*, 1/2, 1973, 3–14.
[26] David Egan, 'Noah Ablett, 1883–1935', *Llafur*, 4/3 (1986), 19–30; Paul Davies, *A.J. Cook* (Manchester, 1987).
[27] D. Egan, 'The Unofficial Reform Committee and the Miners' Next Step', *Llafur*, 2/3 (1978), 64–80.
[28] W.W. Craik, *The Central Labour College, 1909–1929* (London, 1964); R. Lewis, 'The South Wales Miners and the Ruskin College Strike of 1909', *Llafur*, 2/1 (1976), 57–72.

in the emancipation of [their] class'. The college's syllabus included classes on 'The History of Socialism in England', and courses in 'Foreign Languages' ('to facilitate a mutual understanding among the workers of different countries as a means to greater international unity of aim and action').[29] Within this new movement there was no place for Welsh, or any other non-class-based particularism.

The internationalist, pan-British spirit of the growing south Wales socialist movement was expressed by William Phippen, who contested a seat on the Rhondda Urban District Council in 1908. Implicitly objecting to Welsh particularism, he asked voters to support him, 'Because he is not narrow-minded, as he believes in the Universal Brotherhood of mankind ... The Printers & Compositors of the Rhondda are the brothers of the Printers & Compositors of Birmingham, and the real Foreigner and Arch-enemy of Labour is Capitalism.'[30] Rather than a URC militant, Phippen was a member of the ILP, whose propaganda was, claimed Mardy Jones, 'the dominant factor in the political life of the coalfield'.[31] To some extent the ILP overlapped with the militant miners' movement (A.J. Cook, for example, was a member of both the ILP and the URC), and many of its members espoused the same anti-particularist internationalism. It was essentially different, however. It continued to take its inspiration more from ethical socialism and (as Hardie never tired of repeating) the Sermon on the Mount in preference to the *Communist Manifesto*, and its members tended to favour the less rigidly scientific and classist education of the Workers' Educational Association to that of the CLC.[32] ILP socialism allowed a greater range of ideological possibilities than the stricter Marxism of the militants, including the accommodation of national identity. Thus Edgar Chappell, of the Swansea Valley ILP, could combine a belief that socialism was essentially consistent with both

---

[29] National Library of Wales, James Griffiths Papers, A1/15, 'The Labour College: Bound Volume of Printed Documents', The Plebs League, *What is Independent Working Class Education?* and Syllabuses of the Central Labour College.

[30] Swansea University Archive, SWCC: MNA/PP/12/2/1, William Phippen, *Electoral Address for 1908 Rhondda Urban District Council Election* (Ward 4).

[31] *Labour Leader*, 26 June 1909.

[32] Richard Lewis, *Leaders and Teachers: Adult Education and the Challenge of Labour in South Wales, 1906–1940* (Cardiff, 1993), pp. 1–47.

the culture of the chapel and Welsh national consciousness, while still declaring that 'the Socialist comes with a new message, a message of hope for humanity. Not greater privilege for a favoured race, but justice for all.'[33]

The growth of the ILP was dramatic after 1906. In January 1908 a Welsh contributor to the *Labour Leader* announced the 'awakening of Wales',[34] and by that year's annual conference at Huddersfield south Wales boasted 84 branches.[35] The 34 Welsh delegates made their presence felt by singing *Hen Wlad Fy Nhadau* from the platform, with Keir Hardie giving a solo rendition of the first verse.[36] They could also report considerable electoral progress. By 1908 the party had four county councillors, 27 urban district councillors, 18 town councillors, three rural district councillors, 18 parish councillors and 29 poor law guardians in south Wales. There were also five full-time organisers employed in the region.[37] By November, when the south Wales ILP held its own annual conference, the number of branches had risen to 95, and it was estimated that the South Wales and West of England ILP Federation had organised 2,000 meetings in the first nine months of the year.[38] The Scots ILP-er Willie Stewart toured what he called 'the huge maze' of the south Wales valleys in 1908 and 1909,[39] and he recorded his impressions of the ILP's growth.

> The facts are that the ILP is all over South Wales: that it is systematically establishing itself in every valley, and in every town and village in every valley ... Here it may be weak, there it may be strong, *but it is there*. It has taken its grip and it will not let go. These branches are not isolated from each other. They are interdependent. They all hang together. For in every district there is to be found one man or more with a genius for organisation ... And thus, bit by bit, Socialism gets a

---

[33] *Llais Llafur*, 30 May 1908.
[34] *Labour Leader*, 24 January 1908.
[35] Independent Labour Party, *Report of 16th Annual Conference* (London, 1908).
[36] *Labour Leader*, 24 April 1908.
[37] Independent Labour Party, *Report of 16th Annual Conference*; Peter Stead, 'Establishing a Heartland', p. 17.
[38] *Labour Leader*, 20 November 1908.
[39] *Clarion*, 26 June 1908.

hold, not only of the minds of the people, but of the local government machinery. South Wales will shortly be administered by the ILP.[40] This was not the first time that socialists had celebrated the 'awakening' of Wales, and the boom of 1908 ultimately showed similar cyclical features to earlier periods of ILP growth. By 1910 the party was again contracting, with only 36 branches paying fees to the South Wales Divisional Council.[41] There was, however, a qualitative change in the dynamic of ILP growth after 1906. Even during the period of contraction after 1908, there remained strongholds in south Wales where the ILP was a permanent and vibrant presence. Briton Ferry, for example, hosted a particularly active ILP branch, which bucked the cyclical trend, and by 1912 was being held up in the *Labour Leader* as a national model of success.[42] Even more significant was the territorial expansion of the ILP beyond the seedbed of the coalfield. Some of this was generated from within south Wales itself. Horatio Bibbings, one of the full-time organisers, arranged a series of meetings at Brecon in 1908 which led to an intense 'free speech struggle' with the local authority.[43] In rural west Wales D.D. Walters led the way, although not without opposition. At a meeting in Brynsion chapel at Abercych, Pembrokeshire, in October 1908, for example, 'fists were clenched and sticks were brandished', and Walters only managed to avoid injury by the strength of his personality.[44]

More promising was the emergence of an ILP movement in the quarrying and mining districts of north Wales. Activity picked up in the north Wales coalfield in 1906, with the establishment of branches at Wrexham and Rhosllannerchrugog, and by 1908 the movement was putting down roots in Caernarfonshire and Meirionnydd. An ILP branch was established at Blaenau Ffestiniog in 1908 with the declared aim of '*addysgu'r werin yn egwyddorion Sosialaeth*'.[45] A North

[40] *Clarion*, 4 June 1909.
[41] *Labour Leader*, 22 July 1910.
[42] *Labour Leader*, 16 December 1912.
[43] *Labour Leader*, 17 July and 18 September 1908; *Clarion*, 17 July 1908; *Llais Llafur*, 18 and 25 July and 19 September 1908.
[44] *Llais Llafur*, 24 October 1908.
[45] *Glorian*, 18 April 1908 ('educating the common people in the principles of

Wales and Chester ILP Federation was active by May 1908,[46] and during the year further socialist meetings were held in Bangor and Blaenau Ffestiniog.[47] Local leaders such as David Thomas and Robert Silyn Roberts began to take over the work of organising, and by the end of the decade there were ILP branches at Caernarfon, Llanrwst, Llandudno, Blaenau Ffestiniog, Llan Ffestiniog, Penrhyndeudraeth, Bangor, Llanllyfni, Portdinorwic, Llanberis, Penygroes, Talysarn and Harlech.[48] Newspapers such as *Y Glorian* and *Yr Herald Cymraeg* carried extensive discussions on socialism. When the Reverend Stanley Jones preached a sermon on socialism at Capel Pendref, Caernarfon, in January 1908, and came to the conclusion that socialists were misguided, he sparked a reaction in the press that continued for the rest of the year.[49] That this was a reflection of what was happening at a community level is suggested by a cartoon published in *Yr Herald Cymraeg* in March which shows a group of men sitting around a shoemaker, with the heading '*Senedd y Pentra – Dadl Sosialaeth yn ngweithdy'r crydd*' ('The Village Parliament – a debate on socialism in the cobbler's workshop').[50] The harvest predicted by *Llais Llafur* in 1903 was being reaped.

The growth of socialist activity in Wales in the period after 1906 was part of a national phenomenon encouraged by the electoral breakthrough of the Labour Party in the 1906 general election. Extra momentum was added by the spectacular victory of Victor Grayson, standing as an out-and-out socialist, in the Colne Valley by-election of 1907,[51] which similarly had an impact upon Wales. The socialism being preached in Wales by revivalist-style orators such as the Revd. J. Stitt Wilson and his brother Ben, on their 'Great Social Crusades' of 1908 and 1909,[52] had much in common with the socialism

socialism'). Also see *Glorian*, 16 May 1908.
[46] *Labour Leader*, 15 May 1908.
[47] *Clarion*, 12 June 1908.
[48] Cyril Parry, 'The Independent Labour Party and Gwynedd Politics, 1900–1920', *Welsh History Review*, 4/6 (1968), 47–66, 52–3.
[49] *Herald Cymraeg*, 14 January–22 September 1908.
[50] *Herald Cymraeg*, 24 March 1908. See the frontispiece.
[51] David Clarke, *Labour's Lost Leader: Victor Grayson* (London, 1985).
[52] *Labour Leader*, 17 July, 21 August and 27 November 1908, 1 January, 9 and 23 July and 17 September 1909; *Llais Llafur*, 2 January, 7 and 6 February 1909. The

of the Colne Valley. Influenced by the 'new theology' of R.J. Campbell,[53] it was built on the same nonconformist Christian foundations, and appealed to the same emotionalism that had been evident during the Welsh religious revival of 1904–5.[54] There were, moreover, direct links between the socialism of the valleys of Colne and south Wales. Grayson visited Wales on several occasions,[55] as did some of his close supporters. T. Russell Williams, who had contested Huddersfield (which was immediately to the north of the Colne Valley) in the 1906 General Election, was a frequent speaker in south Wales.[56] So too were some of the nonconformist ministers whose support had been so important to Grayson's victory. These included the Revd. W.B. Graham of Holmfirth who, when he visited the Swansea Valley in 1908, urged his audiences to create a 'socialist earthquake' there.[57]

'crusades' of the brothers Wilson often attracted hundreds to their meetings, which were accompanied by parades, teas and dancing. They were highly popular and generally supported by the ILP, although not without their critics, who accused Stitt Wilson of egotism and drawing energy away from the political side of the movement; see John Blunt in *Llais Llafur*, 13 February 1909.

[53] Revd. R.J. Campbell, *The New Theology* (London, 1907). Campbell's new theology was what he called a form of 'spiritual socialism', part of a 'great social movement which is now taking place ... towards universal peace and brotherhood, and a better and fairer distribution of wealth', and he considered it to be 'the religious articulation of the social movement' (*New Theology*, p. 14). Campbell, who was a friend of Keir Hardie, toured south Wales in 1907–8, see Christopher B. Turner, 'Conflicts of Faith? Religion and Labour in Wales 1890–1914', in Hopkin and Kealey (eds), *Class Community and the Labour Movement*, pp. 67–85, pp. 73–4. Among the many who were impressed by Campbell's ideas and the feelings that overlapped with the Religious Revival of 1904–5 was James Griffiths, see James Griffiths, *Pages From Memory* (London, 1969), pp. 11–12. Tickets for Campbell's meetings were often sold out on the day of issue, see *Llais Llafur*, 2 May 1908.

[54] D. Densil Morgan, 'Diwygiad Crefyddol, 1904–5', *Cof Cenedl*, 20 (2005), 167–200.

[55] *Rhondda Leader*, 7 December 1907, 28 November 1908; James Griffiths, *Pages From Memory*, p. 16, recounts Grayson's visit to Brynaman in 1908. True to his contradictory personality, Grayson shocked the local (teetotal) ILP-ers by asking to be taken to a bar after his address so that he could get a drink of whisky. It took a visit from the Wilson brothers to restore Griffiths's faith in socialist 'stars'.

[56] *Llais Llafur*, 28 March 1908, 2 January 1909; *Labour Leader*, 26 May 1911; *Pioneer*, 18 March 1911. For Russell Williams's views on south Wales and the ILP there, see *Swansea and District Workers Journal*, February 1912.

[57] *Llais Llafur*, 6 June 1908; *Llais Llafur*, 30 January 1909. For Graham, the most prominent of the clergymen who helped Grayson to victory, see Clarke, *Victor Grayson*, p. 36.

Other speakers from the national movement also continued to visit Wales, including John and Katharine Bruce Glasier, Margaret MacMillan, Margaret Bondfield, Mrs Despard, Philip Snowden and Ramsay MacDonald.[58] At any single, active branch there could be an almost constant throughflow of speakers from the wider socialist movement. During 1908, for example, the Penygraig ILP branch in the Rhondda hosted visits from Alderman Hartley of Bradford, Dora Montefiore, Katharine Bruce Glasier, Alderman Sanders of London County Council and the Revd. W.B. Graham of the Colne Valley.[59] Although the south continued to be the main destination for socialist speakers coming to Wales, the number of visits to north Wales began to increase too. James Parker, the Labour MP for Halifax, spoke to a large meeting at Blaenau Ffestiniog in 1908.[60] Philip Snowden spoke at Wrexham, and at the quarrymen's *Gwyl Llafur* at Caernarfon, in 1909,[61] and the Fabian Society organised a series of lectures by Clifford Sharp in north Wales towns.[62] Thus, the interplay between Wales and the wider movement intensified and broadened. Keir Hardie continued to be the most important influence, part-property of south Wales and part-property of the national movement, the 'G.O.M. of Labour'[63] stood as a living symbol of the connection between the Welsh socialist movement and the wider world. He frequently toured south Wales, but also began to play an increasing role in the north. In March 1907 he spoke at Wrexham,[64] and in 1913 he spoke

[58] *Llais Llafur*, 15 January 1908 (John Bruce Glasier at Cardiff), *Llais Llafur*, 23 May 1908 (Margaret Bondfield and Mrs. Despard in south Wales), *Llais Llafur*, 25 July 1908 (Katharine Bruce Glasier at Ferndale), *Llais Llafur*, 13 February 1909 (Margaret MacMillan and Katharine Bruce Glasier in the Swansea Valley), *Labour Leader*, 15 February 1909 (Philip Snowden at Cardiff), *Labour Leader*, 19 February 1909 (John Bruce Glasier at Briton Ferry), *Labour Leader*, 12 November 1909 (John Bruce Glasier at Cardiff), *Labour Leader* 17 October 1911 (Katharine Bruce Glasier at Briton Ferry and Philip Snowden at Cardiff), *Labour Leader*, 22 December 1911 (Ramsay MacDonald at Swansea).
[59] *Llais Llafur*, 30 January 1909.
[60] *Herald Cymraeg*, 29 September 1909; *Glorian*, 26 September 1908.
[61] *Labour Leader*, 15 January 1909; *Herald Cymraeg*, 11 May 1909; *Glorian*, 8 May 1909.
[62] *Herald Cymraeg*, 23 February 1909.
[63] *Labour Leader*, 28 January 1910 ('Grand Old Man' – appropriating the sobriquet of William Gladstone).
[64] *Herald Cymraeg*, 26 March 1907.

at Bethesda.⁶⁵ In 1911 he delivered a speech to the Literary and Debating Society at Bangor University College. The 'tremendous ovation' he received, and the way in which he 'won the respect, and, so to speak, gained the friendship of his hearers' – who considered themselves to be 'the leaders of the future' – confirmed his status as the primary representative of socialism in Wales.⁶⁶

Another expression of socialist advance in Wales was the launch of a number of new, local, socialist newspapers. Some of the Welsh Liberal newspapers, particularly *Y Genedl Gymreig*, *Yr Herald Cymraeg* and *Y Glorian*, had shown sympathy to moderate socialist ideas during the course of the decade, but until 1911 there were few explicitly socialist newspapers in Wales. The Swansea Trades Council's *Swansea and District Workers' Journal* supported socialist politics, and *Llais Llafur* provided socialism with a bilingual voice, despite the death of its founder, Ebenezer Rees, in 1908.⁶⁷ The coverage of Welsh affairs in national socialist papers, particularly the *Labour Leader*, also increased significantly from the early 1900s. After 1910, however, the range of local Welsh socialist papers expanded considerably. In March 1911, the launch of the *Pioneer* at Merthyr realised the long-standing ambitions of the labour activists there to have a paper of their own.⁶⁸ It was welcomed by local socialists as 'a paper that will keep us in touch with the doings of the Labour Party, both local and national',⁶⁹ and like *Llais Llafur* it mixed labour and socialist politics with local news, even including a football column. It also provided Keir Hardie with an efficient means of reporting his national activities to his local constituency, and so another channel was added to the ongoing interplay between Wales and the British socialist movement.

1911 also saw the launch of the monthly *Rhondda Socialist*. Produced and distributed entirely by voluntary effort, the 'Bomb', as it was affectionately known, aimed to provide 'a

[65] Bangor University Archive, Bangor MS 19301, 'Scrapbook of meetings in which David Thomas played a part'.
[66] *Magazine of the University College of North Wales*, 20/3 (1911), 44–6.
[67] *Llais Llafur*, 10 October 1908.
[68] Deian Hopkin, 'The Merthyr Pioneer, 1911–22', *Llafur*, 2/4 (1979), 54–64.
[69] *Pioneer*, 18 March 1911.

real educative medium' for the workers of the Rhondda,[70] and by March 1912 it claimed a circulation of 6,000. It survived only until 1913, when it was incorporated into the *South Wales Worker,* but during this brief period it mixed news of the ILP with articles on literature and economics, and provided a forum for the debate on the relative merits of syndicalism and political action. Both the *Pioneer* and the *Rhondda Socialist* published sections in Welsh which dealt with issues deemed to be of interest to Welsh-speaking readers. Of a different character entirely was the *Dinesydd Cymreig,* launched in 1912 at Caernarfon. The paper was founded by striking printers,[71] and by July it had been adopted as the official organ of the North Wales Quarrymen's Union.[72] Given the explicitly socialist nature of much of its content, this was an indication of how far to the left opinion among the quarrymen had moved since the Penrhyn dispute. The *Dinesydd* was not bilingual, it was an entirely Welsh medium newspaper, and by September 1912 it was declaring its Welsh national aspirations as '*Arweinydd Gwerin Cymru*' (The Leader of the Welsh Common People).[73] Like the *Pioneer, Y Dinesydd* was not formally allied to any individual political group or party; unlike the *Pioneer* it was respectful of radical Liberalism, and sought to build upon Welsh radical traditions. The contrasting tones of these newspapers represented different shades of socialism that were developing from differing local conditions. They were nevertheless unmistakably part of the same movement.

The upsurge in socialism was met by an intense reaction. By the end of the decade the Anti-Socialist Union was coordinating what it called 'a great national movement on purely Anti-Socialist lines' across the UK,[74] and it tailored this campaign to Wales by having at least one of its tracts,

[70] *Rhondda Socialist,* September 1911.
[71] Picton Davies, *Atgofion Dyn Papur Newydd* (Liverpool, 1962), pp. 129–33; Jones, *Press, Politics and Society,* pp. 140–1.
[72] *Dinesydd Cymreig,* 3 July 1912.
[73] *Dinesydd Cymreig,* 11 September 1912.
[74] National Library of Wales, David Thomas Papers, Box 1, Anti-Socialist Union of Great Britain, *Statement of Objects, Policy and Work* (1910); also see Glamorgan Record Office, Cardiff, DXEV/6, material relating to the Anti-Socialist Union in the Merthyr election of January 1910.

Socialism and the Family, published in Welsh as *Sosialaeth â'r Teulu*.[75] More effective in Wales than the largely Conservative ASU was the hostility of some chapels. Welsh nonconformity was by no means universally anti-socialist, but its membership did provide a significant deterrent to socialist activity in some places.[76] At the community level moral censure could be a highly effective means of retarding socialism. When William Phippen contested a Rhondda council seat in 1908 the pavements were chalked with 'Don't vote for William Phippen because he believes in free love'. Seventy years later, his daughter recalled that the local chapel (Bodringallt) expelled its members if they joined the ILP.[77] Nor was this an isolated incident. Socialists were frequently denied the use of chapel premises, even when they were hosting Christian ministers. Briton Ferry ILP was refused the use of the local chapels when it hosted R.J. Campbell in 1908,[78] as was another 'new theologian', T. Rhondda Williams (a Welsh Congregationalist minister at Bradford), when he visited south Wales in the same year.[79] For ministers who were sympathetic to socialism the consequences could be serious. When it was alleged that the Revd. R.W. Hughes of Moeltryfan in Caernarfonshire had chaired a meeting at which an 'anti-Christian' socialist had spoken, he was ostracised by the deacons of Capel Pendref, Caernarfon, and prevented from preaching there.[80] The Revd. George Neighbour of Nazareth Baptist Chapel at Mountain Ash was forced out of his ministry altogether in 1907, after refusing to sign an agreement with the deacons that he would not preach socialism. In response he established his own 'Brotherhood Church'.[81]

[75] Ernest E. Williams, *Sosialaeth â'r Teulu* (London, 1910).
[76] For the debate on socialism within nonconformity, see Pope, *Building Jerusalem*; Robert Pope, '"Pilgrims Through a Barren Land": Nonconformists and Socialists in Wales, 1906–1914', *Transactions of the Honourable Society of Cymmrodorion* (New Series), 7 (2001), 149–63; Robert Pope, 'Facing the Dawn: Socialists, Nonconformists and *Llais Llafur*, 1906–1914', *Llafur*, 7/3–4 (1998–9), 77–87; Turner, 'Conflicts of Faith?'; R. Tudur Jones, *Ffydd ac Argyfwng Cenedl: Hanes Crefydd yng Nghymru, 1890–1914* (Swansea, 1982), pp. 265–71.
[77] South Wales Miners Library, AUD394, Tape No. 181, Mr and Mrs D.J. Davies, Ystrad, Rhondda, interviewed by Hywel Francis, 14 October 1974.
[78] *Llais Llafur*, 18 April 1908.
[79] Turner, 'Conflicts of Faith?', p. 74.
[80] *Dinesydd Cymreig*, 18 February 1914.
[81] Christopher B. Turner, 'Conflicts of Faith?', p. 75.

The clash between nonconformity and socialism that was taking place in communities across Wales was reflected by an intense debate at Welsh national level. Some ministers published their thoughts on the matter as pamphlets, so that they could gain a wider audience,[82] but it was in the pages of nationalist journals such as *Y Geninen*, and in the denominational press that the debate was most fully rehearsed.[83] A huge amount of intellectual energy was expended before the Great War on a detailed consideration of such topics as the putative socialism of Jesus Christ, the relative merits of individual and social salvation, the relative roles of environment and spirituality in the making of human character and a host of other theological topics. Much of this debate, which represented one of the primary interfaces between Welsh intellectual culture and socialism, was conducted in a thoughtful and reasoned manner, and many ministers of religion were deeply concerned by their estrangement from the socialistically inclined among their congregations.

Less reasonable in tone was the work of the anti-socialist cheerleader of Welsh nonconformity, W.F. Phillips. Originally from Penmaenmawr, Caernarfonshire, Phillips was a Methodist minister and Oxford academic, who had allegedly once been a member of the ILP himself.[84] He poured scorn – both in print and in person – on socialism and socialists, whom he considered to be both anti-Christian and anti-Welsh. His personality, its considerable instability notwithstanding, provided a link between the national debate and the localities, as he toured Wales debating his views with all-comers.[85] The appearances of 'Willie', as he was derisively called by the socialists, were fiercely contested

---

[82] For two examples that give different sides of the argument, see Parch. W. Price (Caergybi), *"Sosialaeth": A Ddylid ei Chefnogi?* (Holyhead, 1908), which started life as a paper given to the Hebron Literary Society, Holyhead, and argues that the churches have no need to embrace socialism because they offer a superior teaching, and J. Morgan Jones MA, *Religion and Socialism* (Merthyr, 1910), which was a series of addresses given at Hope Church, Merthyr, arguing for a reconciliation between socialism and Christianity.

[83] Pope, *Building Jerusalem*, pp. 31–71.

[84] Pope, *Building Jerusalem*, pp. 62–5.

[85] For example, see *Is Socialism Anti-Christian in its Tendency?: Debate Between Mr. W.F. Phillips and Professor W.T. Mills at the Workmen's Hall, Nantymoel, Verbatim Report from the Shorthand Notes of George Thomas* (no place of publication, no date (c. 1910)).

by them, both in print and in person. T.E. Nicholas of Glais in the Swansea Valley responded to his articles in the press,[86] while his meetings frequently met with a hostile reaction. One of his appearances, at Abercynon in 1911, for example, was swamped by socialists, who repeatedly heckled him, forcing him to wander from his subject, until he eventually responded with insults, and 'The meeting, which had been a farce from the beginning, terminated in uproar'.[87] On the whole, however, socialists attempted to maintain a more neutral attitude towards the chapels. As Horatio Bibbings put it at a meeting in Trecynon in 1908, they 'had no quarrel with the churches except that they were impatient of the slowness of the coming of the Kingdom and the apathy of so many church members in helping it forward'.[88] To many socialists there was no apparent clash between the message of the chapels and the cause of socialism. Cliff Prothero, who came to socialism as a young man in the years immediately before the Great War, later reflected: 'I have no regret that I had to attend chapel so often because it gave me a firm foundation and an outlook on life which I have been able to link up with the kind of Socialism which I have attempted to follow and accept as a way of life.'[89] The dichotomy between the views of W.F. Phillips and the more materialistic socialists was, therefore, not wholly representative of the entire spectrum of opinion.

At the centre of the spectrum was the figure of Keir Hardie. Hardie realised well the importance of the chapels in Welsh politics, and he sought to demonstrate that he was on good terms with them very early in his career at Merthyr Boroughs. 'He had', the *Labour Leader* emphasised in 1901, 'during the short time he had represented the Merthyr Boroughs received more appeals for help from churches and chapels than during the three and a half years he represented West

---

A series of Phillips's articles on socialism from *Y Geninen* were reprinted as W.F. Phillips, *Y Ddraig Goch ynte'r Faner Goch? Ac Erthyglau Eraill* (Cardiff, 1913).

[86] T.E. Nicholas, 'Y Ddraig Goch a'r Faner Goch: Cenedlaetholdeb a Sosialaeth', *Geninen* (1912), pp. 10–16.

[87] *Pioneer*, 3 June 1911.

[88] *Llais Llafur*, 25 January 1908.

[89] Prothero, *Recount*, p. 6.

Ham.'[90] Hardie's socialism, like that of other 'ethical socialists', subverted rather than directly denied the principles of organised Christianity. 'The direct outcome of the teachings of Jesus upon those who lived nearest to His time, and who became His followers, was to make them Communists', he argued, and socialism was merely 'the application to industry of the teachings contained in the Sermon on the Mount'.[91] This approach attracted attention in Wales, and Hardie's *Can a Man Be a Christian on a Pound a Week?* was the best-selling pamphlet on the Merthyr ILP market stall (which was the stall with the best sales figures in Britain).[92] It also led him into conflict with local nonconformist leaders. He was refused the use of some Merthyr chapels,[93] and in 1911, as the debate between the socialists and the chapels intensified, Hardie set out his position in the pages of the *Pioneer*. His 'Open Letter to the Ministers of the Gospel in Merthyr Boroughs' challenged the local (and, by implication, national) nonconformist ministers to embrace socialism or face extinction.[94] At the same time, however, Hardie claimed that 'it was Christianity which led me into Socialism, and now Socialism enables me to understand Christianity. To me they are the complements of one complete whole.'[95] All this was too much for W.F. Phillips, who wrote his own 'Open Letter' to Keir Hardie, pointedly in Welsh, so that Hardie could not read it.[96]

The debate over socialism and religion was not unique to Wales. In Wales, however, it was tied up with the issues of Welsh identity and Welsh nationalism, which became increasingly pressing concerns within the socialist movement in the years after 1906. One sign of this was the way in which the political culture of socialism in south Wales increasingly took account of Welsh culture, through, for example, the innovation of socialist *eisteddfodau*. Socialists had been known to

[90] *Labour Leader*, 9 March 1901.
[91] James Keir Hardie, *Can A Man Be A Christian on a Pound a Week?* (London and Glasgow, 1901), pp. 9, 11.
[92] Edwards, *From the Valley I Came*, p. 123.
[93] *Merthyr Express*, 20 January 1906.
[94] *Pioneer*, 13 and 27 May, 10 and 17 June 1911.
[95] *Pioneer*, 13 May 1911.
[96] *Tarian y Gweithiwr*, 17 August–7 September 1911.

harbour mixed feelings about this aspect of Welsh culture. The competitive element of *eisteddfodau* was a problem to some (R.J. Derfel included), and others alleged that the institution was corrupt. *Llais Llafur* argued in 1899 that Wales would be better off without the national *Eisteddfod*.[97] After 1906, however, ILP branches began to hold their own local *eisteddfodau*. Pontardawe ILP held what was advertised as its second Annual *Eisteddfod* in September 1908. Mixed choirs competed for a first prize of £3 and an enlarged photograph of their successful conductor, by singing the *Marseillaise* in either English or Welsh.[98] Another annual ILP *eisteddfod* was launched at Mountain Ash in March 1909.[99] Prizes were awarded for English and Welsh essays, and a prize winning *arwrgerdd*, written by a coal trimmer from Barry Dock and subsequently published in both Welsh and English, celebrated the life of Keir Hardie in over 200 lines of epic verse.[100] The extent to which these events marked the ILP's establishment as a bastion of Welsh culture is nevertheless questionable. The advertising material and press notices of both events were in English only, and the cultural content also seems to have been overwhelmingly English in nature. At Mountain Ash only one of the ten musical test pieces was Welsh: '*Chwi Fawrion y Ddaear*' sat incongruously among 'Autumn Memories', 'Lusitania', 'A Chartists' Chorus' and 'Revolution'.[101]

If the adoption of the *eisteddfod* as a cultural form did not mark the wholesale conversion of the socialist movement to the cause of Welsh particularism, it was an expression of cultural pluralism that had political dimensions. In the same

[97] *Llais Llafur*, 18 February 1899.
[98] *Llais Llafur*, 8 August and 19 September 1908.
[99] Swansea University Archive, SWCC SC653, *Programme of First Annual ILP Eisteddfod, Workmen's Institute, Mountain Ash, Friday 22 March 1909*.
[100] ILP Archive, ILP Organisational and Regional Records, 1856–1955, Keir Hardie Papers, 'Abou Ben Adhem', *J. Keir Hardie AS, Arwrgerdd Fuddugol, Eisteddfod Gadeiriol, P.A.Ll., Aberpennar (1909)* (Mountain Ash, 1909); Daniel Owen (Ap Rhydderch), *Keir Hardie MP: The Prize Epic at the Mountain Ash ILP Eisteddfod, March 22 1909* (Mountain Ash, 1909); *Labour Leader*, 26 March 1909.
[101] For an examination of the Labour movement's engagement with Welsh culture in the early twentieth century, see Deian Hopkin, 'Llafur a'r Diwylliant Cymreig, 1900–1940', *Transactions of the Honourable Society of Cymmrodorion* (New Series), 7 (2001), 128–48.

way that socialists sought to subvert the power of the chapels, they sought to appropriate the politics of Welsh nationalism. This demanded a rationalisation of the relationship between national sentiment and socialism that was frequently achieved by drawing a distinction between 'spurious nationalism' and 'true nationalism'. Socialism was the 'only antidote to spurious Nationalism' (as represented by Welsh Liberalism), argued the *Pioneer*'s local reporter in 1911, 'The Brotherhood of Man is international'.[102] On the other hand, 'true nationalism' (which was less sharply defined) could be consonant with socialism: 'It is my contention', asserted another *Pioneer* contributor (from north Wales), 'that the present awakening among the nations of the earth is the first step in the direction of International Socialism.'[103] In debating this topic socialists were attempting to resolve an overarching tension between the universal, the national and the local that was inherent in the adoption of their doctrine. One contributor to the *Pioneer* demonstrated an acute awareness of this:

> Labour and Socialist societies are in the nature of things cosmopolitan in tendencies and sympathies, but the cosmopolitan aspect is only the obverse side of human society, and unless a corrective is supplied the cosmopolitan spirit tends to become diffuse and ineffective. The needful correction is supplied by national sentiment (and this national aspect is the reverse side of human society), which merely guarantees that charity shall begin at home, although, of course, it need not necessarily end there.[104]

Socialists used various vehicles to achieve this 'needful correction'. Hardie used the investiture of the prince of Wales in 1911 to make distinctly nationalist political capital,[105] and declared that he wished to see 'the red dragon of Wales ... emblazoned on the red flag of socialism'.[106] Socialism, he insisted at the May Day celebrations in Merthyr in 1911, 'was in the very blood of the Welsh people. It was in their

---

[102] *Pioneer*, 15 April 1911.
[103] *Pioneer*, 6 May 1911.
[104] *Pioneer*, 1 April 1911.
[105] John S. Ellis, *Investiture: Royal Ceremony and National Identity in Wales, 1911–1969* (Cardiff, 2008), pp. 115–24.
[106] *Pioneer*, 14 October 1911.

sentiment, in their history, in their language'.[107] He mobilised pan-Celticism, which he attempted to conflate with class consciousness. In 1910 he told audiences at Merthyr Boroughs that 'I too, like yourselves, am a Celt, with all the love of the homeland, its language and its literature which every true Celt feels. I love the common people to whom I belong. I am one of yourselves. *Yr wyf yn un o honoch chwi.*'[108]

On a collective level, the South Wales Divisional Council of the ILP passed several resolutions declaring that socialism was not antagonistic to Welsh nationalism.[109] The reality behind such apparent expressions of cultural and political pluralism was tense, however. Like the relationship between socialism and radical Liberalism, or socialism and the chapels, the relationship between socialism and Welsh nationalism embraced a wide spectrum. Attempts, like Hardie's, to unite the red flag of socialism with the red dragon of Welsh nationalism represented its mid-point. At one end, rooted in the beliefs of the CLC, the URC and the Marxian elements of the south Wales socialist movement, was an aggressively anti-particularist party. Its advocates dismissed any form of nationalism, maintaining that in the future 'The proletarians of all the countries will join together so that on that day there will be but one country – the earth.'[110] Their views were expressed in one 'Open Letter to a Welsh Nationalist', published in *The Pioneer*:

> Tush, man, your Nationalism is not Nationalism if it does not make for the uplifting of the masses, the betterment of people's lives, rather than the embitterment of them ... You, my Welsh comrade, have no grievance which is not shared by your comrades on the other side of Offa's Dyke, and by your Scotch and Irish comrades, too ... The national question of Germany, of Russia, of France, of Spain; and, indeed, of England and even of Wales, has been discovered to be an international one after all.[111]

---

[107] *Pioneer*, 6 May 1911.
[108] ILP Organisational and Regional Records, 1856–1955 (Reel 23), Keir Hardie, Handwritten Notes for Speech, 1910 ('I am one of you').
[109] *Labour Leader*, 17 June 1910 and 10 March 1911.
[110] *Pioneer*, 6 May 1911.
[111] *Pioneer*, 13 May 1911.

Those at this end of the spectrum represented majority socialist opinion. Among other positions of influence, they held the editorship of the *Pioneer* and dominated local ILP groups across the south Wales coalfield. At the other end of the spectrum, though, was a group of socialists whose emergence at the end of the first decade of the twentieth century marked the culmination of the relationship between socialism and Welsh national identity that has been at the heart of this book. They emerged along with the development of socialism beyond the south Wales coalfield, but were by no means absent in south Wales. The views of the two camps were irreconcilable, and it was inevitable that the two groups would clash as the latter struggled to develop a distinctly Welsh socialist tradition.

(ii) The struggle for a Welsh socialist consciousness

> I am a congregationalist minister, and am 31 years of age, have won 18 bardic chairs, and have published a book of poems on Socialism, called *Salmau'r Werin* ... So you will understand why I am a great admirer of your late father [R.J. Derfel] ... I would love to have his photo to put on my desk, to keep company to a few Labour Poets which I already have there ... I have made up my mind that the memory of so strong a man shall be kept green for a long time, and will do my best to bring the life-story and life-work of the great Pioneer before the young Comrades of Wales.[112]
>
> In a way I have taken up a part of his great work. He died in Dec. 1905. And I wrote my first Labour Poem in January 1906. Since then I have written hundreds ... He sang in the night, I sing to day in the light of the Day he made possible.[113]

So wrote Thomas Evan Nicholas ('Niclas y Glais'), minister of Capel Sion at Glais in the Swansea Valley, to two of R.J. Derfel's children in 1911. Nicholas exemplified a distinct group of socialists that emerged in early-twentieth-century Wales who, by seeking to build upon Derfel's legacy and create a distinctively Welsh socialist tradition, dissented

[112] National Library of Wales, NLW MS 23452 D, T.J. Roberts Papers, T.E. Nicholas to Edward M. Derfel, 5 May 1911.
[113] National Library of Wales, NLW MS 23452 D, T.J. Roberts Papers. T.E. Nicholas to Jane Derfel, 24 May 1911.

from the view that national consciousness was not relevant to socialist politics. In the words of Deian Hopkin, '*Cymru, ac nid y byd, oedd canolbwynt eu sosialaeth*'.[114] Prominent among them were David Thomas of Talysarn, Caernarfonshire, and Robert Silyn Roberts of Tanygrisiau, Blaenau Ffestiniog, who between them played a critical role in establishing the ILP in north Wales. Some, like D.D. Walters at Newcastle Emlyn, had been active within the socialist movement before 1906, but most were members of a new generation, born in the late-nineteenth century, who had embraced socialism in the early 1900s. They shared a common aim to achieve, in the words of David Thomas, 'the presentation of Socialism in a Welsh dress', meaning 'not only teaching Socialism to speak the Welsh language, but also saturating it with the history and traditions of the Welsh democracy'.[115]

Most of the members of this group had working-class roots: Silyn Roberts worked as a quarryman in Caernarfonshire for five years after leaving school at 14,[116] David Thomas was the son of a stone mason,[117] and T.E. Nicholas was brought up on a small upland tenant farm in Pembrokeshire.[118] In almost every case they had risen socially to occupy professional positions. David Thomas was a schoolteacher, as was Edgar Chappell of the Swansea Socialist Society, the son of a shoemaker whose contributions to the socialist press became increasingly concerned with the national issue in the early

[114] Deian Hopkin, 'Y Werin a'i Theyrnas', 165 ('Wales, and not the world, was the focus of their socialism').
[115] National Library of Wales, David Thomas Papers, Box 3, Typescript of David Thomas, 'Wales and the Politics of the Future'. Also see *Labour Leader*, 12 September 1912.
[116] David Thomas, *Silyn (Robert Silyn Roberts), 1871–1930* (Liverpool, 1956), pp. 6–11.
[117] David Thomas, *Diolch Am Gael Byw, Rhai o F'Atgofion* (Liverpool, 1968), p. 1. For David Thomas's full biography, see Angharad Tomos, 'Bywyd a Gwaith David Thomas, 1880–1967' (unpublished MPhil. thesis, Aberystwyth, 2000), published as *Hiraeth am y Fory: David Thomas a Mudiad Llafur Gogledd Cymru* (Llandysul, 2002).
[118] Bangor University Archive, Bangor MS 23359, T.E. Nicholas, Typescript of Reminiscences. For biographies of Nicholas, see Siân Howys Williams, 'Bywyd a Gwaith T.E. Nicholas, 1879–1971' (unpublished MA thesis, Bangor, 1985); David W. Howell, *Nicholas of Glais, The People's Champion* (Clydach, 1991); J. Roose Williams (ed.), *T.E. Nicholas: Proffwyd Sosialaeth a Bardd Gwrthryfel: Teyrnged Gwerin Cymru*, (Cardiff, 1971); Islwyn Pritchard, 'Thomas Evan Nicholas', in D. Ben Rees (ed.), *Herio'r Byd* (Liverpool, 1980), pp. 16–22.

1900s.[119] Thomas Jones, who had accompanied the *Clarion* vans in the late 1890s, and went on to advocate the creation of a Welsh Labour Party in 1909, was a university professor.[120] Members of the Welsh literati were also prominent. John Jenkins ('Gwili'), who had delighted the audiences at Bangor University debates in the 1890s, went on to teach, and ultimately head Gwynfryn Academy at Ammanford, where he continued to advocate socialism and *Iawnderau Dyn* (The Rights of Man).[121] Another advocate was Thomas Gwynn Jones, winner of the 1902 Bangor *Eisteddfod* chair. Most numerous among this group, however, were the nonconformist ministers. Among the most prominent, T.E. Nicholas and D.D. Walters were Congregationalists, and Silyn Roberts was the Methodist minister of several chapels in the Blaenau Ffestiniog district.[122] To this core group a multitude of names may be added, including John Puleston Jones, Calvinistic Methodist minister at Dinorwig, George Neighbour of Mountain Ash, David Gwynfryn Jones of Flint and R.W. Hughes of Moeltryfan, Caernarfonshire.[123] Together they represented an alternative face of Welsh nonconformity to the hostile one exemplified by W.F. Phillips. Socialists may have believed that the chapels were overwhelmingly hostile to their movement, and on balance they might have been right, yet without the input of these nonconformist ministers the indigenous Welsh socialist leadership would have been seriously denuded of both talent and credibility.

As exemplary representatives of *y werin*, the members of this group of socialist leaders were steeped in Welsh culture and the Welsh language. David Thomas, Silyn Roberts, T.E. Nicholas and T. Gwynn Jones were all either regular

[119] *Llais Llafur*, 30 May 1908; *Labour Leader*, 20 May and 26 August 1910.

[120] Thomas Jones, 'Y Mudiad Llafur yng Nghymru', *Cerrig Milltir* (Llandybie, 1942), pp. 7–21. For Jones's biography, see Ellis, *T.J.: A Life of Dr. Thomas Jones C.H.*

[121] E. Cefni Jones, *Gwili: Cofiant a Phregethu* (Llandysul, 1937); see esp. pp. 151–5 for his relationship to the labour movement; John Gwili Jenkins, 'Iawnderau Dyn', *Geninen*, 1912–1914; J. Beverley Smith, 'John Gwili Jenkins, 1872–1936', *Transactions of the Honourable Society of Cymmrodorion* (1974–5), 191–214.

[122] Thomas, *Silyn*, pp. 53–65.

[123] E. Morgan Humphries, *Gwyr Enwog Gynt* (Aberystwyth, 1953), pp. 40–8 (for Puleston Jones); Ivor Thomas Rees, 'David Gwynfryn Jones: Methodist, Socialist, Welshman', *Llafur*, 10/2 (2009), 101–16.

eisteddfod winners or adjudicators. Their cultural world was created by the influences of the *aelwyd werinol Gymreig*, the chapel, the literary and debating society and institutions like Watcyn Wyn's Gwynfryn Academy. This is what made them distinctive among socialists, and what led them to pursue the creation of a distinctively Welsh socialism. There is, however, a paradox here. The primary medium of their culture may have been different to that of the mainstream British socialists, but its content had significant similarities in that it shared a similar romantic heritage. All of these individuals were bilingual, and well-read in the radical-romantic canon of the English language,[124] but there was also a unity in the content of their culture that crossed the linguistic divide. The Welsh Arthurian romanticism of Silyn Roberts and T. Gwynn Jones,[125] for instance, had a great deal in common with the English romanticism of William Morris. Likewise, the pastoralism of R.J. Derfel's pre-socialist poetry was as close to the sensibilities of the young John Bruce Glasier as it was popular with Derfel's audiences of *eisteddfodwyr*.[126] The anti-capitalist revolt of the Welsh cultural socialists was driven by the same romantic impulse as that of other socialists, and in this sense there was much in their world view that located them within the mainstream of British socialist thought. This was reflected in their poeticism, which shared many elements with the period's English-language socialist poetry. The themes and imagery in the work of Derfel and Nicholas – the breaking dawns, coming days and transient working-class suffering – are more or less identical, for example, to those in the work of William Morris or J.L. Joynes.[127]

As with most socialists, the individuals in this group were converted to socialism by a multiplicity of factors. The role

[124] For example, see the notebooks kept by the young David Thomas, which reveal a wide range of English influences, including Wordsworth, Dickens, H.G. Wells, George Eliot, Conrad and many others, Bangor MS 18958 & 18961.

[125] Robert Silyn Roberts, *Trystan ac Esyllt a Chaniadau Eraill* (Bangor, 1904); T. Gwynn Jones, *Ymadawiad Arthur a Chaniadau Ereill* (Caernarfon, 1910).

[126] For a discussion of Glasier's poeticism, see Pierson, *Marxism and the Origins of British Socialism*, pp. 141–9. What Pierson calls 'the poetic impulse in British socialism' clearly did not stop at linguistic boundaries.

[127] T.E. Nicholas, *Cerddi Gwerin* (Caernarfon, 1912); T.E. Nicholas, *Salmau'r Werin a Chaneuon Ereill* (Wrexham, 1913); J.L. Joynes, *Socialist Rhymes* (London, 1885).

of socialist literature was crucial. In Derfel's case it was the work of Robert Owen, but for the following generation it was most often Robert Blatchford who was the decisive influence on the path to socialism. T. Gwynn Jones, for example, discovered Blatchford while working as a columnist for *Y Faner* in Liverpool in the 1890s,[128] and David Thomas was set on the road to socialism when he was given a copy of *Merrie England* at a *Cymru Fydd* meeting in 1895.[129] The atmosphere of the literary and debating society was also a key influence. David Thomas, for example, was a member of the Myllin Literary and Debating Society at Llanfyllin.[130] A common factor, however, in the personal evolution of many of the socialists under discussion here – and this is surely crucial to an understanding of not just their socialism, but of their need to combine it with a strong sense of national identity – was an experience of geographical dislocation. T.E. Nicholas moved from the tightly knit rural community of north Pembrokeshire, via Treherbert in the Rhondda and Dodgeville in America, before returning to Glais, in the Swansea Valley, where, in Gwenallt's memorable description, industrialism had changed even the pattern of the seasons.[131] The juxtaposition of rampant industrial capitalism upon elements already developed in Nicholas's personality by his upbringing and his time at the Gwynfryn Academy quickly turned him towards socialism, but it also confirmed the strength of his Welsh identity.[132] Early adulthood took David Thomas from Llanfyllin, via Bridgend, to the nail and chain-making region of the Black Country, before he returned to north Wales.[133] He recorded his impressions of the Black Country, the heart of Blatchford's *Dismal England*, where, he pined, 'the sky is never blue, the brooks are never clear … The sensibilities of the people are blunted for lack of sunshine, [and] their lungs are choked with the impure

---

[128] David Jenkins, *Thomas Gwynn Jones* (Denbigh, 1973), p. 92.
[129] Tomos, 'Bywyd a Gwaith David Thomas', p. 36.
[130] Tomos, 'Bywyd a Gwaith David Thomas', p. 12.
[131] Gwenallt, *Ffwrneisiau: Cronicl Blynyddoedd Mebyd* (Llandysul, 1982).
[132] Williams, 'T.E. Nicholas', pp. 4–8.
[133] Tomos, 'Bywyd a Gwaith David Thomas', pp. 11–20.

atmosphere.'[134] His experience encouraged him to read his copy of *Merrie England* more closely, and developed his socialistic inclinations. It also sharpened his national identity, as a contribution that he made to the Cradley Heath Mutual Improvement Society during his time there makes clear. In a discussion on 'The Study of Our National Mission' he argued that 'we should [not] lose our love of home and native land and change it for a vague and mystical love of humanity. We can do both – love the great and the small at the same time.'[135] This is exactly the approach that he applied to his socialist thought as it developed a little later in the decade.

These are classic cases, but the same geographical interplay may be observed in the lives of other Welsh cultural socialists, such as Tom Jones and Silyn Roberts. It was a central feature of R.J. Derfel's life, and it was a theme in the lives of many of the other socialists discussed in this book, Sam Mainwaring and David Rhys Jones being among the most obvious examples. The juxtaposition of the local and the universal, the rural and the industrial, the Welsh and the 'other' – and the tension created – was a key factor in the development of both a strong commitment to socialism and the confirmation of Welsh identity. Those who experienced it were, by the very nature of their experience, set apart from their communities. They were, however, put in a position where they could relate to those communities simultaneously as members and outsiders. From this vantage point they were in a special position to articulate the universalist teachings of socialism through both local and Welsh national levels of consciousness, and their attempt to do so as a group represents a struggle to achieve a distinctively Welsh socialist consciousness and to create a Welsh socialist tradition. In practical terms this comprised three main fields of activity: the first was to stimulate and organise the growth of the ILP, not just in the south Wales valleys but across the whole territory of Wales; the second was an attempt to create an overarching Welsh structure for the party; and the third was to provide

---

[134] Robert Blatchford, *Dismal England* (London, 1899), pp. 101–10; Bangor University Archive, Bangor MS 18959, David Thomas, Notebook.
[135] Quoted in Tomos, 'Bywyd a Gwaith David Thomas', p. 19.

socialism with a distinctive Welsh voice, by writing about it in the Welsh language.

In terms of stimulating ILP activity, the primary role played by members of this group was to supply the need for Welsh speakers at ILP meetings, which added an extra dimension to ILP propaganda. James Griffiths recalled that John James from Cwmgors in the Amman Valley was 'all the more influential because he could talk to the miners in the Welsh language';[136] when he spoke in Welsh in the Rhondda in 1908 it was reported that he 'touched strata that our ordinary propagandists have failed to reach'.[137] Figures like T.E. Nicholas, D.D. Walters and Silyn Roberts used the skills that they had developed in the pulpit to enthuse socialist meetings. Walters, for example, delivered speeches on themes, including *'Hawliau'r Werin'* ('The Rights of the Common People') and *'Iesu yn Gymdeithaswr'* ('Jesus as a Socialist'). His masterpiece was *'O Gaethiwed i Ryddid'* ('From Slavery to Freedom'), the title of which echoed Hardie's *From Serfdom to Socialism*. From the early 1900s up until the Great War Walters gave numerous versions of this speech, which varied according to the immediate circumstances of its delivery. Its epic content embraced the whole of world history, from the Garden of Eden to the Russian Revolution, and ran to 85 typed pages of foolscap. Walters delivered his socialist oratory to the coracle fishermen at Cenarth as well as to the miners and heavy industrial workers of the Swansea Valley and the Rhondda, and he prepared the way for his visits by contacting local nonconformist ministers beforehand in an attempt to overcome their prejudice.[138]

That the platform oratory of Walters and others amounted to a Welsh national, rather than simply a local, effort is indicated by its geographical coverage. Welsh-speaking socialists facilitated and promoted visits from their counterparts in different parts of Wales. Silyn Roberts brought his own earnest brand of socialist educationalism to south Wales on several occasions, including a tour of the Swansea Valley

[136] Griffiths, *Pages From Memory*, p. 14.
[137] *Llais Llafur*, 18 July 1908. For James's views on socialism and Welshness, see *Labour Leader*, 4 August 1911.
[138] National Library of Wales, D.D. Walters Papers.

in 1909 and an appearance alongside Keir Hardie at the Merthyr May Day demonstration in 1911.[139] David Thomas also spoke throughout Wales. He visited south Wales in 1911, addressing meetings at Seven Sisters, Gwauncaegurwen, Ystradgynlais and Swansea,[140] and in 1912 he undertook a speaking tour of the north Wales coalfield, holding meetings in English and Welsh at Rhosllannerchrugog, Wrexham, Brymbo, Coedpoeth, Caergwrle and Rhostyllen.[141] T.E. Nicholas, on the other hand, reached out from the Swansea Valley to the slate quarrying districts of the north when he toured there in 1913. Mixing socialism and Welsh culture, he spoke, often in chapels, to large and enthusiastic audiences on '*Paham Mae'r Werin yn Dlawd*' ('Why the Common People are Poor') and '*Telynau'r Werin*' ('Folk Lyrics'), as well as adjudicating at local *eisteddfodau*.[142] Wales had developed its own distinctive, indigenous group of socialist personalities to match what had become a professional class of socialist speakers from across the border.

In terms of organisational effort, the outstanding figure was David Thomas. More than any other individual, he was responsible for the growth of the ILP outside south Wales in the period before the Great War. He applied a meticulous and diligent personality to the tasks of arranging meetings, collecting fees, distributing literature, translating propaganda material, singling out useful or influential individuals to help the party and answering random queries. He kept up a barrage of letters to the press, and publicly debated socialism with all-comers, including local objectors to socialism as well as major figures such as W.F. Phillips or Professor Henry Jones of Glasgow University. As secretary of Caernarfonshire Labour Council, and later the North Wales Congress of Labour, he was also responsible for coordinating the relationship between the ILP and the trades unions in north Wales. This is not to mention his work as president of his local branch of the NUT, or his work on the district and

---

[139] *Llais Llafur*, 13 February 1909; *Pioneer*, 6 May 1911.
[140] *Llais Llafur*, 8 July 1911.
[141] Bangor University Archive, Bangor MS 19291.
[142] *Dinesydd Cymreig*, 29 January, 19 February, 12, 19 and 26 March, 2 and 9 April 1913.

county councils.[143] Thomas's work at a regional level may be compared with that of Henry Davies of Cwmavon (who also showed a developing interest in reconciling socialism with the national question),[144] or perhaps John Watt of Cardiff,[145] although in terms of volume, scope and quality it was unparalleled within the Welsh socialist movement.

Thomas had ambitions that went beyond regional organisation, and embraced the concept of creating an ILP structure at a Welsh national level. The question of organisational structure had arisen early in the development of the Welsh socialist movement, and by the early 1900s it had been resolved by the creation of a number of divisional groupings that separated the south from the north. Thomas led an attempt to challenge this implicit rejection of Welsh nationhood by seeking to create what he termed a 'Welsh ILP'. He set out the case in the socialist press in 1911, arguing that 'Those of us who are Welshmen in blood and language feel strongly that the Socialist movement cannot hope to succeed in Wales (outside certain districts), unless it is established upon a distinctly National basis; the twin movements of nationalism and [socialism] must grow up together

---

[143] Some insight into the diligence and thoroughness with which Thomas undertook his organisational work on behalf of the socialist movement in north Wales may be gained from an examination of the various notebooks and papers that are preserved in Bangor University Archive. In particular, for the pre-war period, see Bangor MS 19159 (Various lists of potential members); Bangor MS 19161 (More lists of members, branches etc.); Bangor MS 19162 and 19163 (More lists and accounts); Bangor MS 19182 and 19184 (Correspondence); Bangor MS 19289 (Talysarn ILP branch minutes); Bangor MS 19301 (Scrapbook of reports of meetings in which David Thomas played a role). That this represents only a small part of Thomas's activities is astounding. Another three boxes of material at the National Library of Wales also provide evidence of Thomas's work.

[144] There is no single collection of material to illuminate the life of Henry Davies, who was one of the most important ILP and Labour Party organisers in pre-war south Wales. There are scattered letters in collections such as the David Thomas papers at the National Library of Wales, and also his contributions to the press, most notably as 'Carrusk' in *Llais Llafur*. Davies's career in the labour movement was blighted in 1918, when he was convicted at the Glamorgan Assizes for the embezzlement of public funds (Report of Glamorgan Assizes, 6 March 1918). I am indebted to Aled Eurig for this piece of information. For Davies's thoughts on the issue of socialism and Welshness, see *Labour Leader*, 22 August 1912.

[145] Evidence of John Watt's work is provided in the collected material on the ILP in south Wales in the David Thomas papers at Bangor University Archive, esp. Bangor MS 19181 and 19291.

as one'. He asserted that all the ILP districts in Wales and Monmouthshire should be united in one division, that an agricultural programme and rural propaganda should be devised in order to extend the movement beyond the industrial districts of Wales, and that the study of Welsh political history should be promoted 'with a view to establishing the historical continuity of the present Labour movement in Wales with the democratic movement of the last century'.[146]

Thomas did not, however, receive the backing that he had hoped for. *Llais Llafur* was vaguely sympathetic to the idea,[147] but elsewhere Thomas ran against a bedrock of anti-particularism. The editorial response of the *Pioneer* was outright hostile. It cited the geography of Wales as a reason against creating a Welsh ILP. 'The Black mountains form a dividing line between North and South Wales, and their influence can be seen in all directions', it argued; factors such as the predominantly east to west alignment of the communications infrastructure made the organisation of two separate regions easier, and there were simply too many differences between the rural north and the industrial south to make unity feasible. Having established the case this far, the *Pioneer* then attacked Thomas's letter, with the core anti-particularist argument of the British socialists.

> Running through the letter there seems to be a hankering after what is called Welsh 'Nationalism', but what is more accurately described as Welsh 'Exclusiveness'. There is a movement in Wales today ... which parades under the name of 'Nationalism'. But it is not Nationalism. It is a spurious sentiment ... if anything distinctively Welsh is worth preserving, it will not require an Exclusive movement to preserve it ... The closer the bonds of understanding between the workers of Wales and the workers of England and the workers of other parts of the world, the greater will be their power to secure the opportunity for a full and free existence. And that is what is wanted.[148]

---

[146] *Pioneer*, 15 July 1911. Also see Bangor University Archive, Bangor MS 18964; *Labour Leader*, 7 July 1911; *Llais Llafur*, 22 July 1911. For further arguments in favour of a Welsh ILP, see the letter from John James, Cwmgors, *Labour Leader*, 4 August 1911.
[147] *Llais Llafur*, 15 July 1911.
[148] *Pioneer*, 15 July 1911.

Thomas and his supporters got as far as organising a meeting to discuss the proposal which was held, under the chairmanship of Edgar Chappell, during the National *Eisteddfod* at Carmarthen in August 1911. As well as from the more obvious Welsh cultural socialists, support came from some perhaps surprising quarters, including Vernon Hartshorn and William Harris, both SWMF activists from relatively anglicised parts of south Wales, and Mark Harcombe, one of the leaders of the striking Cambrian Combine workers.[149] The meeting concluded that 'the only party that can truly represent the democracy of Wales is the Labour Party, and that the spirit of Welsh Nationalism can only find full scope for its political and industrial activities in the policy of nationalisation of the land and industries of the country'. To this end, it urged the formation of a Welsh ILP.[150] In reality, however, the cause was lost from the outset. Even the ostensibly sympathetic Hardie argued, albeit with more tact than the *Pioneer's* editor, that branches should not act on Thomas's advice, and that the way forward was to organise separately in the north and the south.[151]

Thomas continued to argue the case. In his view, by failing to take account of the particularities of Welsh nationality, the ILP in Wales threatened to make the same mistake as the SDF had in England, and would appear to be a foreign influence.[152] His arguments, however, began to take on an almost desperate and self-defeating tone, which, if anything, merely revealed the extent of the divisions within Welsh socialism. 'Some of our comrades who have built up the ILP movement in the English speaking districts of Glamorganshire and Monmouthshire may find it difficult to appreciate this point of view', he pleaded, 'but they must try to realise that [these] districts do not constitute the whole of Wales.'[153] In one article he inadvertently admitted both the marginality

---

[149] For a full account of the meeting and related events, see Tomos, 'David Thomas', pp. 65–73; Dylan Morris, 'Sosialaeth i'r Cymry – Trafodaeth yr ILP', *Llafur*, 4/2 (1985), 51–63; Hopkin, 'Y Werin a'i Theyrnas'.
[150] *Labour Leader*, 18 August 1911; *Llais Llafur*, 19 August 1911.
[151] *Labour Leader*, 26 August 1911.
[152] Bangor University Archive, Bangor MS 18964.
[153] Bangor University Archive, Bangor MS 18964.

of the socialist movement outside the south Wales coalfield, and the defining influence of physical geography upon Welsh political life.

> In the slate quarrying districts of Caernarfonshire there are eight or nine branches, and two or three in the colliery districts around Wrexham, and between them stretches a wilderness of mountains and agricultural land sixty or eighty miles wide. What bond of union is strong enough to bind together two small movements so widely separated? The bonds of a common nationality, however, or the consciousness of having a mission to deliver to their fellow countrymen, would be sufficient to bind them to the strong labour movement in South Wales.[154]

The south Wales majority, however, was not going to be dictated to by a few scattered ILP branches in what some considered to be more or less a different country; 'there is no such thing as a Welsh nation today, there are at least two Welsh nations. One hails from North Wales and the other originates in South Wales. The two people never mix', stated the *Pioneer* in August.[155] Thomas and others continued to air their arguments in the socialist press,[156] but the overwhelming weight of the south Wales labour movement – both culturally and statistically – was stacked against them.

In other respects the Welsh cultural socialists were more successful. A third resolution passed at the Carmarthen meeting in 1911 called for the publication of more socialist literature in Welsh.[157] Its advocates believed, in the words of Henry Davies, that 'it is only in the Welsh language that the Welsh people can be made to realise that the traditions and ideals of the Welsh are not opposed to the Socialist idea',[158] and they consequently strove to create a body of Welsh socialist literature. At the pinnacle of their achievement was Thomas's much celebrated *Y Werin a'i Theyrnas*, published in 1910, which remains the most significant original work on socialism published in the Welsh language. The primacy of

---

[154] *Labour Leader*, 8 September 1911; Bangor University Archive, Bangor MS 18964.
[155] *Pioneer*, 5 August 1911.
[156] *Labour Leader*, 22 August and 12 September 1912.
[157] *Labour Leader*, 18 August 1911.
[158] *Labour Leader*, 22 August 1912.

this text should not, however, draw attention from the fact that it is representative of a wider body of work, including one other full-length text, D. Tudwal Evans's *Sosialaeth*,[159] as well as a number of pamphlets and Fabian Tracts.[160] As was the case with socialist literature generally, by far the greatest volume of Welsh socialist propaganda was the ephemeral material that appeared in the press. Like Blatchford's *Merrie England*, *Y Werin a'i Theyrnas* originated as a series of letters to the press, and was just a fraction of its author's journalistic output,[161] and although Thomas was the most prolific of the Welsh-language socialist journalists, he was not alone. The work of Silyn Roberts in *Y Glorian* was also significant, as was the contribution of T.E. Nicholas, most notably as Welsh editor of the *Pioneer*, while *Llais Llafur* carried the work of Iwan Glyn and D.D. Walters, among others. A full analysis of this body of work would require another volume, but one key question does need to be considered: to what extent does it represent an original Welsh contribution to socialist thought?

If content is taken as the decisive measure of Welshness, the question is almost impossible to answer. There were certainly Welsh influences in it. The influence of R.J. Derfel was particularly clear upon the work of T.E. Nicholas, who explicitly sought to ensure that Derfel's legacy was passed on.[162] The stamp of Welsh nonconformity is also clear upon the work of authors like Silyn Roberts and D.D. Walters.[163] Issues such as the land question, which might be considered to have a specifically Welsh – or at least Celtic – dimension, also had a strong presence. As Nicholas put it, '*Cwestiwn mawr Cymru yw Cwestiwn Gwaith, a Chyflog, a Thylodi. Ac o dan yr holl bethau hyn*

---

[159] D. Tudwal Evans, *Sosialaeth* (Barmouth, 1911). For Tudwal Evans, see Robert Pope, *Building Jerusalem*, pp. 52–4.

[160] R. Silyn Roberts, *Y Blaid Lafur Anibynnol, Ei Hanes a'i Hamcan* (Blaenau Ffestiniog, 1908); T.E. Nicholas, *Cyflog Byw* (Pontardawe, 1913); David Thomas, *Y Blaid Lafur a Dinasyddiaeth y Gweithwyr* (Manchester, 1911); *Paham Mae y Lluaws yn Dlawd* (London, 1891); Revd. John Clifford, *Sosialaeth a Dysgeidiaeth Crist* (London, 1899 and 1908); Revd. John Clifford, *Sosialaeth a'r Eglwysi* (London, 1909); J.R. Jones, *Sosialaeth yng Ngoleuni'r Beibl* (London, 1909).

[161] *Herald Cymraeg*, 11 February 1908–11 August 1908.

[162] *Pioneer*, 7, 14, 21 October, 9 and 16 December 1911; *Geninen Gwyl Dewi* (1912), pp. 23–4.

[163] For example, see 'Y Ddaear Newydd', *Glorian* 11 July 1908–26 September 1908.

gorwedd pwng y Tir.'[164] Certain elements of the Welsh socialist press made even more explicit attempts to include and appropriate the Welsh radical tradition. *Y Dinesydd Cymreig* contained features on such classic themes of Welsh radicalism as '*Arwyr 68*' and '*I Godi'r Hen Wlad yn ei Hol*',[165] while the work of authors like J.T. Pritchard of Aberdaron, who held explicitly socialist views but remained politically Liberal, indicated that there was a continuum between the Welsh radical tradition and socialism.[166] The socialists' appropriation of the radical tradition was symbolised by their use of the term '*gwerin*', which was usually associated with a particular, Liberal, nonconformist, mythical entity: a people rooted in their *milltir sgwar*.[167] Welsh socialists, however, began to use the term in a broader sense. T.E. Nicholas, who later stated, '*O werin Cymru codais i, ac ni bu ynof awydd erioed i berthyn i ddosbarth arall*',[168] wrote his *Salmau* and *Cerddi* to the *werin* and, in the opening piece of the *Salmau* projected himself as '*Bardd y Werin*'.[169] The word was also taken from its Welsh context and used in relation to the British, and even the international, working class.[170] In this sense, Thomas's choice, *Y Werin a'i*

---

[164] *Pioneer*, 6 May 1911 ('The great Welsh question is the question of work, wages and poverty. And beneath all of these things lies the issue of the land.') Also see R. Silyn Roberts, 'Hafod a Hendre i Bawb', *Glorian*, 29 February 1908–4 July 1908; Thomas, *Y Werin a'i Theyrnas*, pp. 234–46; Demos, 'Y Tir a Gollant', *Dinesydd Cymreig*, 22 May 1912; David Thomas, 'Y Blaid Lafur a'r Tir', *Dinesydd Cymreig*, 14 August 1912; *Dinesydd Cymreig* 17 July 1912 and 29 October 1913 (editorials); David Gwynfryn Jones, 'Pwnc Y Tir Yng Nghymru', *Herald Cymraeg*, 23 February–6 March 1909.

[165] '*Arwyr '68*' (The heroes of 1868) recorded the names of all those who had voted against their landlords in the 'Great Election of 1868', *Dinesydd Cymreig*, 3 July 1912–22 January 1913. The series '*I Godi'r Hen Wlad yn ei Hol*' included articles on staple Welsh radical concerns such as '*Dic Sion Dafyddiaeth*', '*Ysgrifennu a Darllen Gymraeg*', and '*Rhaglen yr Eisteddfod*', *Dinesydd Cymreig*, 17 July, 7 August, 25 September, 16 October, 27 November and 18 December 1912.

[166] For Pritchard's views, see *Dinesydd*, 11 September 1912.

[167] Price Jones, 'Gwerin Cymru', in *Radicaliaeth a'r Werin Gymreig yn y Bedwaredd Ganrif ar Bymtheg*, pp. 196–206; Prys Morgan, 'The *Gwerin* of Wales – Myth and Reality', in Ian Hume and W.T.R. Pryce (eds), *The Welsh and Their Country* (Llandysul, 1986), pp. 134–52.

[168] Bangor University Archive, Bangor MS 23359.

[169] Nicholas, *Salmau'r Werin*, pp. 5–8.

[170] See the article 'Braster Prydain' by Demos, *Dinesydd Cymreig*, 25 September 1912, and Henry O. Jones's poem, '*Deffroad y Werin*', *Dinesydd*, 23 October 1912 for its use in a British context. David Thomas uses the word in relation to the American working class, *Dinesydd*, 16 October 1912.

Theyrnas, for the title of his main work was a deliberate appropriation of Welsh radical vocabulary.

If it is possible to argue that the work of the Welsh socialists was ideologically distinct, it is equally possible to argue the opposite. Significant elements within this body of literature were direct or near-direct translations of English socialist literature.[171] This had important ramifications. It meant that there was no such thing as a socialist intellectual world free of English influence. Even in the case of original works, the extent of the influence of English texts was considerable. In the case of *Y Werin a'i Theyrnas*, while there are clearly some specific Welsh influences (the ideas of R.J. Derfel and Evan Pan Jones may be seen in the chapters on '*Dinasoedd fel Gerddi*' and '*Y Tir i'r Bobl*' respectively),[172] it is the extent of the foreign influences that is striking. These are clearly acknowledged,[173] and include Prince Kropotkin, Henry George, Carlyle and Ruskin, Blatchford, William Morris and Philip Snowden. The absence of influences from what Thomas called the 'Welsh democracy' is noticeable; it is remarkable that the major work of a socialist who sought to 'saturate' socialism in Welsh traditions and influences made reference to so few of them.

Ultimately, however, these arguments become circular. They could be applied to any aspect of Welsh thought, and would lead to the same insecure conclusion. Surely the critical point about the socialism of individuals like Thomas, Silyn and Niclas y Glais is that it was articulated through the medium of the Welsh language. If ever there was a case of the medium representing the message this was it. To write about socialism in Welsh, rather than using English, was a conscious decision. It has been suggested that this was simply a pragmatic device, adopted in order to assist in the spread of the socialist message in Welsh-speaking areas, that it was a mere

[171] Examples include Blatchford's *Altruism* (*Llais Llafur*, 5 September 1908), Keir Hardie's *The Red Dragon and the Red Flag* (*Dinesydd Cymreig*, 3 July 1912), Keir Hardie on 'The Land Question' (*Dinesydd Cymreig*, 30 October 1912), Hardie's *Liberalism and Labour in Wales* (*Dinesydd*, 16 July 1913) and Philip Snowden's *The Christ That Is To Be* (*Dinesyd Cymreig*, 6–27 August 1913).

[172] ('Cities like Gardens' and 'The Land for the People'), *Y Werin a'i Theyrnas*, pp. 198–208 and 234–46.

[173] Thomas, *Y Werin a'i Theyrnas*, pp. 344–6.

response to the challenge presented by nationalism.[174] It was rather the other way around. Using Welsh to express socialist ideas was the natural choice of culturally and linguistically Welsh socialists. If the adoption of English as the language of socialism was, as Ieuan Gwnyedd Jones suggested, a valuational statement, so equally was the assertion of socialist discourse in Welsh. This linguistic decision created a space within Welsh culture in which socialism could be discussed. The influence of *Y Werin a'i Theyrnas* was felt across Wales, as numerous letters in the David Thomas Papers testify.[175] It found its way into reading rooms and libraries,[176] and its influence permeated the labour movement, particularly in the north, where the quarrymen's union set an examination on the text.[177] The influence of *Y Werin a'i Theyrnas* also transcended the Great War. The Trawsfynydd branch of the Labour Party, for example, ran a weekly winter study class in the 1920s, in which the book was studied,[178] and the influential trade unionist Huw T. Edwards recalled that as a young man '*Fe'm trwythais fy hun yn Y Werin a'i Theyrnas a phan ddeuthum yn swyddog Undeb, hwn oedd y Beibl y dyfynnwn ohono ddydd ar ol dydd.*'[179]

One of the key achievements of Thomas and the Welsh socialists discussed in this section was to influence individuals like Huw T. Edwards, who played an important role in the development of the socialist and labour movement in Wales during the twentieth century. Edwards considered

[174] R. Merfyn Jones and Ioan Rhys Jones, 'Labour and the Nation', in Tanner, Williams and Hopkin (eds), *The Labour Party in Wales*, pp. 241–63, p. 244.

[175] For example, National Library of Wales, David Thomas Papers, Box 1, [?] Evans, Ferndale to David Thomas, 11 June 1912.

[176] National Library of Wales, David Thomas Papers, Box 1, R.W. Roberts, Bethesda to David Thomas, Christmas 1911.

[177] National Library of Wales, David Thomas Papers, Box 1, Thos G. Hughes, Cwm y Glo, to David Thomas, 11 January 1911. The questions may be found in Bangor University Archive, Bangor MS 18964.

[178] National Library of Wales, David Thomas Papers, Box 3, Morris Davies, Trawsfynnydd, to David Thomas, 13 October 1921.

[179] Huw T. Edwards, 'Dafydd Tomos', in Ben Bowen Thomas (ed.), *Lleufer y Werin: Cyfrol Deyrnged i David Thomas M.A.* (Abercynon, 1965), pp. 51–7, p. 56 ('I saturated myself in *Y Werin a'i Theyrnas*, and when I became a union official this was the Bible I would quote from day after day.') Also see Huw T. Edwards, *It Was My Privilege* (Denbigh, 1957), p. 20 – *Y Werin a'i Theyrnas* was 'a book which greatly influenced political thought in Wales for many years'.

himself a '*Sosialwr Cymreig a Chymraeg*',[180] and this self-definition would have been shared by socialists from his and succeeding generations, many of whom cited the influence of Thomas and Nicholas upon their own development.[181] In this sense, the struggle for a Welsh socialist consciousness was successful. In other senses the Welsh socialist tradition that was the product of three decades of intensive interaction between universal ideals and particular circumstances was less secure. As Britain drifted towards the Great War – a crisis that would both strengthen the forces of British nationalism and transform the nature of British socialism – the relationship between socialism and Welsh national identity remained essentially unresolved, an integral part of the ideological and cultural fluidity of a movement that would play a central role in shaping the rest of the twentieth century.

---

[180] ('A Welsh and Welsh speaking socialist'). The term is used by Edwards in notes for a speech (undated and untitled) in Huw T. Edwards Papers, C7, National Library of Wales.

[181] For example, Goronwy Roberts and Elystan Morgan, see Andrew Edwards, 'Answering the Challenge of Nationalism: Goronwy Roberts and the Appeal of The Labour Party in North-West Wales During the 1950s', *Welsh History Review*, 22/1 (June 2004), 126–52; J. Graham Jones, 'Elystan Morgan and Cardiganshire Politics', *Welsh History Review*, 22/4 (December 2004), 730–61; Andrew Edwards and Mari Elin William, 'The "Red Dragon/Red Flag Debate Revisited": The Labour Party, Culture and Language in Wales, 1945-c.1970', *Welsh History Review*, 26/1 (2012), 105–27.

CONCLUSION

The rise of socialism was one of the defining features of late-Victorian and Edwardian Wales. Although active socialists were never more than a small minority at any point before the Great War, they were nevertheless an important one. Their critique of society was penetrating and in step with the times, and their very presence changed the political dynamic of their host societies. By the end of the period discussed in this book there was a sense in which William Harcourt's oft-quoted statement, 'we are all socialists now', was applicable to Wales. To speak of the 'rise of socialism', however, is to simplify and unify artificially a number of differing, even disparate, contemporaneous processes. Socialism was an ideology with multiple manifestations. From the early 1880s onwards it spread unevenly across the territory of Wales and permeated Welsh thought and culture erratically. Its diffusion through Welsh society was governed by the complex spatial and ideological interplay of a variety of influences. The overwhelming direction of these influences may have been inwards. In other words, as its opponents insisted, socialism was an ideology that was imported into Wales.

If this is true, it is only partially so. While the 'scientific socialism' of the 1880s was undoubtedly of foreign origin, Wales was not its passive recipient. Some of the supposedly 'foreign' agitators bringing socialist ideas into Wales were themselves Welsh. Due notice should also be taken of the dynamic of socialist growth that quickly developed within Wales itself. Initially, this resulted in the spread of socialism from the coastal towns of the south into the coalfield. Coalfield socialism then rapidly developed its own internal dynamic. Critical mass was achieved during the 1898 coal strike, and although the subsequent socialist ascendancy was not immediately secure, from 1898 onwards the presence of socialism as a political force within the region was an irreversible fact. Events during the coal strike also determined the type of socialism that was adopted in Wales. Although Marxism was to play an important role in south Wales politics in subsequent decades, Britain's Marxist party, the SDF, took very clear second place in socialist politics to the ILP. During the first decade of the new century the ILP developed to political maturity in south Wales, with its own political culture and a growing political base, which was increasingly integrated into the wider British socialist and labour movement.

The growth of socialism in Wales prior to 1906 was an overwhelmingly regional phenomenon. In structural terms it was confined to south Wales, and the spread of socialist ideas beyond the heads of the valleys was a much slower process. Socialists did begin to interact with north Wales during the protracted Penrhyn dispute of 1900–3, but the spread of their ideas was retarded, not least by the barrier presented to them by the dominance of the Welsh language in the region. Consequently, the socialist movement of the south had a significant head start on that of the north. South Walian socialists had broadly adopted English as their medium of communication, and their movement had only a tenuous relationship with Welsh national consciousness. Its dominant ideology and political culture was internationalist in outlook, and tended to be sharply dismissive of Welsh particularism. There was however another socialistic tradition in Wales which fused nationalist and radical social ideology and sought to create a distinctively Welsh form of socialism. In both geographical and political terms, this tradition was diffuse. It did not have the same regional critical mass as the British-internationalist socialism of the south, and although it had advocates in the south, its adherents were scattered across and beyond Wales, and were not politically organised. They were consequently marginalised.

After 1906 socialism began to spread more evenly across Wales. This resulted in the emergence of a group of socialists within the ILP who sought to persuade the party to become more responsive to the traditions and culture of Wales. Although their calls for the creation of a political structure that recognised the territorial integrity of Wales met with a negative response, they did succeed in one important respect. They succeeded in articulating socialist ideology at a Welsh national level, through the medium of the Welsh language. Their efforts in this respect might be seen as a struggle to create a Welsh socialist consciousness. In doing this they were consciously building on the work of a small minority of socialists from the previous generation, into which they sought to integrate the traditions of Welsh radicalism. In this sense, they were seeking to establish a Welsh socialist tradition.

The defining feature of their work was less ideological than linguistic. Their use of Welsh was an act of affirmation and rejection, just as the adoption of English made the same statement for mainstream British-Welsh socialists. The linguistic and cultural tide was, however, flowing against the Welsh dissidents. The consequent dominance of a linguistically English and culturally British socialism in Wales had profound long-term implications for both Wales and Britain, many of them undoubtedly beneficial. It provided an essential component of the bedrock upon which the unionist-socialist project of the twentieth-century welfare state was built. The voice of the dissident Welsh socialists, however, was never truly silenced. It may be discerned in the debates on socialism and nationalism that took place in the pages of the *Dinesydd Cymreig* in the 1920s, or in the *Gwerin* movement of the 1930s. It was clear in the Parliament for Wales Campaign and the dramatic resignation of Huw T. Edwards from the Council for Wales in the 1950s. There are hints of it in the work of Harri Webb and in Miles's and Griffiths's *Sosialaeth i'r Cymry* of the 1970s.

The tectonic plates of history have moved considerably in recent decades and the unionist-socialist project of the twentieth century is being dismantled. It is therefore apposite to consider the process of interplay from which that project originated, and, perhaps, speculate on some of its alternative potential outcomes. After all, Derfel's *unoliaeth mewn amrywiaeth* – 'unity in diversity' – once again has a modern ring.

SELECT BIBLIOGRAPHY

1 Primary Sources

(i) Unpublished Sources
Aberdare: Aberdare Public Library
PY4/4	Aberaman Socialist Party Treasurer's Book, 1900–1903
PY4/5	Aberdare Socialist Party Minute Book, 1900–1906
PY4/10	Circular Letter to Aberdare Valley ILP, 7 November 1907
PY4/14	Aberdare Valley ILP Cash Book

Aberystwyth: National Library of Wales
NLW MS 3601E	Evidence to the Welsh Land Commission (1896)
NLW MSS 12525b	Cymry Manceinion (Collected by Ionawryn Williams, Manchester and Bethesda, 1837–1907)
NLW MSS 12698A	Pregethau gan R. J. Derfel
NLW MS 15467 C	Llyfr Cofnodion Cymeithas Genedlaethol Cymry Manceinion (1900–1911)
NLW MSS 23440–62	Robert Jones Derfel Papers (including T.J. Roberts Papers)
NLW MS 23617 E	O. Llew Owain, 'Bywyd a Gwaith R.J. Derfel'
NLW ex 2312	Papers donated by Frank G. White of Bristol in 2004 relating to the establishment of the ILP in the Swansea area
	Huw T. Edwards Papers
	James Griffiths Papers
	Thomas Jones C.H. Papers
	T.E. Nicholas Manuscripts
	A.W.L. Seaman Papers
	Robert Silyn Roberts Papers
	D.A. Thomas Papers
	David Thomas Papers
	D.D. Walters Papers
	ILP Archive (Harvester Microfilm)

Bangor: Bangor University Archive
Bangor MS 5019(13)	Letter from Owen Davies to Myrddin Fardd

SELECT BIBLIOGRAPHY 243

Bangor MS 479   Miscellaneous letters
Bangor MS 4548–4562   Thomas Jones Papers
Bangor MS 23356 & 23359   T.E. Nicholas Papers
Bangor MS 17196, 17202, 17217, 1722–3 and 19256
    Robert Silyn Roberts Papers
Bangor MS 18957–79, 19155, 19158–63, 19165, 19181–2, 19184, 19187–9, 19200, 19289, 19291 and 19301–5
    David Thomas Papers
Bangor MS 1781   Williamson Manuscripts

Cardiff: Cardiff Central Library
Cochfarf Papers
Cardiff Liberal Association, *Cardiff Free Trade Bazaar Souvenir, 8–10 October 1912*

Cardiff: Cardiff University Library Special Collections
Labour Party Archive (Harvester Microfilm)

Cardiff: Glamorgan Record Office
DXHJ2   Aberdare Valley ILP/Aberdare Socialist Society Papers
D/XIK 30/15–38   Letters and Cards from J. Keir Hardie, c.1910–1915
D/D AW H14/4   Griff Jones: Script of Swansea Socialist Party and Labour Party
DX 868 /2   Reminiscences of Hughes of Abercynon
DX EV/6   January 1910 Merthyr Election & Anti-Socialist Union Tracts
DVAU /24/1–16   1910 Election Ephemera

London: British Library of Political and Economic Science
Fabian Society Archive
Social Democratic Federation Papers

Swansea: South Wales Miners Library
Transcriptions of Interviews (South Wales Coalfield Collection):
AUD 213   Edgar Evans
AUD 335   Tom Watkins
AUD 337   Robin Page Arnot
AUD 394   Mr & Mrs D.J. Davies

Swansea: Swansea University Archive (Coalfield Collection)
SWCC: MNA/POL/5/1   Bedlinog ILP Accounts Book and Press Cuttings
SWCC: MNA/PP/69/1   Dowlais ILP Minute Book
SCWW: SC653   Mountain Ash ILP Eisteddfod Programme (1909)
SWCC D1–7   John Thomas Papers

SWCC: MNA/PP/129/1–5 ILP printed material
SWCC/MNC/PP/20/1 Sam Mainwaring Collection
SWCC: MNA/PP/131/3 Aberdare Socialist Society Banquet, 1 March 1901
SWCC: MNA/PP/66/1 Rules of the Marxian Club and Institute, Blaenclydach
SWCC: MNA/PP/12/2/1   1908 Rhondda UDC Election Papers

Online Manuscript Sources
Census Enumerators' Books and other material at Ancestry.com

(ii) Published Sources: Reports & Annuals
Fabian Society, *Conference Reports*
Independent Labour Party, *Conference Reports*
Labour Annual
Social Democratic Federation, *Conference Reports*
Socialist League, *Conference Reports*
South Wales Labour Annual

(iii) Newspapers and Journals
Aberdare Leader
Baner ac Amserau Cymru
Barry Herald
British Medical Journal
Cambria Daily Leader
Cardiff Argus
Cardiff Times & South Wales Weekly News
Cardigan & Tivyside Advertiser
Celt
Clarion
Commonweal
Cwrs y Byd
Cymro
Cymru
Cymru Fydd
Daily News
Dinesydd Cymreig
Fabian News
Freedom
Genedl Gymreig
Geninen
Glamorgan Free Press
Glorian
Goleuad

Herald Cymraeg
ILP News
Justice
Labour Leader
Labour Pioneer (Cardiff)
Labour Prophet
Liberty
Llais Llafur – Labour Voice
Lleufer
Lloyds Weekly Newspaper
Magazine of the University College of North Wales
Manchester Guardian
Manchester Times
The Merthyr Express
Morning Post
North Wales Chronicle
Nottinghamshire Guardian
Pall Mall Gazette
Pioneer (Merthyr)
Reynold's Newspaper
Rhondda Leader
Rhondda Socialist
Seren Gomer
Socialist Review
South Wales Daily News
South Wales Labour Times
South Wales Press
Swansea & District Workers Journal
Tarian Y Gweithiwr
Times
To-day
Traethodydd
Transactions of the Liverpool Welsh National Society
University College of Wales Magazine (Aberystwyth)
Wales
Welsh Outlook
Werin
Western Mail
Workman's Times
Wrexham Weekly Advertiser
Yorkshire Factory Times
Young Wales

SELECT BIBLIOGRAPHY

(iv) Contemporary Memoirs and Other Writings

Anon., *From Coal Pit to Parliament: Complete Life of James Keir Hardie MP – Stories of Success No. 10* (London, 1907).

Andrews, Elizabeth, *A Woman's Work is Never Done* (Dinas Powys, 2006).

Awbery, Stan, *Labour's Early Struggles in Swansea* (Swansea, 1949).

Atkinson, Blanche, *Ruskin's Social Experiment at Barmouth* (London, 1900).

Bailey, Revd. William, *The Higher Socialism: A Paper Read at the Cardiff Free Methodist Improvement Class, April 1889* (Cardiff, 1889).

Belfort Bax, Ernest and Bradlaugh, Charles, *Will Socialism Benefit the English People? A Written Debate Between E. Belfort Bax and Charles Bradlaugh* (London, 1887).

Blatchford, Robert, *Merrie England* (London, 1892).

Blatchford, Robert, *Dismal England* (London, 1899).

Blatchford, Robert, *Britain for the British* (London, 1901).

Blatchford, Robert, *My Eighty Years* (London, 1931).

Bruce Glasier, John, *On Strikes* (Glasgow and Manchester, 1894).

Bruce Glasier, John, *Keir Hardie: A Memorial* (Manchester and London, 1915).

Bruce Glasier, John, *Keir Hardie: The Man and his Message* (London, 1919).

Boos, Florence (ed.), *William Morris's Socialist Diary* (London and New York, 1982).

Campbell, R.J., *The New Theology* (London, 1907).

Champion, H.H., 'The Great Dock Strike', *Universal Review* 5/18 (1890), 157–78.

Clifford, Revd. John, *Sosialaeth a Dysgeidiaeth Crist* (London, 1899).

Clifford, Revd. John, *Sosialaeth a'r Eglwysi* (London, 1909).

Cole, G.D.H. (ed.), *William Morris: Prose, Verse, Lectures and Essays* (New York, 1974 ed.).

Derfel, R.J., *Brad Y Llyfrau Gleision* (Ruthun, 1854).

Derfel, R.J., *Caneuon Min y Ffordd* (Holyhead, 1861).

Derfel, R.J., *Caneuon Gwladgarol Cymru* (Wrexham, 1864).

Derfel, R.J., *Traethodau ac Areithiau* (Bangor, 1864).

Derfel, R.J., *Songs for Welshmen* (Bangor, 1865).

Derfel, R.J., 'Ein Rhagolygon a'n Gwaith', *Cymru Fydd* 1 (May 1888), 270–8.

Derfel, R.J., *Aildrefniad Cymdeithas: Papyr a Darllenwyd i Gymdeithas Genedlaethol Cymry Manchester, Nos Wener, Rhagfyr 16eg, 1888* (Manchester, 1888).

Derfel, R.J. (Munullog), *Social Songs* (Manchester, 1889).

Derfel, R.J., *Caneuon* (Manchester, 1891).

Derfel, R.J., *On the Importance of Right Methods in Teaching Socialism* (Manchester, 1891).

Derfel, R.J., *Socialism* (Manchester, 1892).

Derfel, R.J., *Socialism and the Pope's Encyclical* (Manchester, 1892).

SELECT BIBLIOGRAPHY

Derfel, R.J., *Musings for the Masses* (Manchester, 1897).
Derfel, R.J., *Hymns and Songs for the Church of Man* (Manchester, 1899).
Derfel, R.J., *An Unauthorised Programme Showing How to Abolish Poverty, Without Doing Injustice to Anyone or Leaving a Feeling of Wrong Behind* (Manchester, 1900).
Derfel, R.J., *Poverty: The Problem of Problems and the Quickest Way to Solve It* (Manchester, 1904).
Derfel, R.J., *Munudau Segur* (Caernarfon, n.d.).
Edwards, W.J., *From the Valley I Came* (London and Sydney, 1956).
Ellis, Annie J. (ed.), *Speeches and Addresses by the late T.E. Ellis* (Wrexham, 1912).
Ellis, T.I., *Thomas Edward Ellis: Cofiant* (Liverpool, 2 vols, 1944 and 1948).
Engels, Frederick [Friedrich], *The Condition of the Working Class in England* (London, 1882).
Fabian Society, *Paham Mae y Lluaws yn Dlawd* (London, 1891).
Farley, Anthony [S.G. Hobson], *Letters to My Nephew* (London, 1917).
Griffiths, James, *Pages From Memory* (London, 1969).
Gronlund, Laurence, *The Co-operative Commonwealth in its Outlines: An Exposition of Modern Socialism* (Boston, 1884).
Hardie, James Keir, *Mines Nationalisation Bill* (Glasgow, 1893).
Hardie, James Keir *A Word With Our Collier Laddies* (Glasgow, 1895).
Hardie, James Keir, *Can A Man Be A Christian on a Pound a Week?* (London and Glasgow, n.d. [1901]).
Hardie, James Keir, *From Serfdom to Socialism* (London, 1907).
Hardie, James Keir, *Llafur a Rhyddfrydiaeth Yng Nghymru* (Manchester, 1910).
Hardie, James Keir, *Killing No Murder: The Government and the Railway Strike* (Manchester, 1911).
Hardie, James Keir, *Young Men in a Hurry* (London, n.d.).
Hobson, S.G., *Possibilities of the Labour Church: An Address to the Cardiff Labour Church on February 19th 1893* (Cardiff, 1893).
Hobson, S.G., *Irish Home Rule* (London, 1912).
Hobson, S.G., *Pilgrim to the Left: Memoirs of a Modern Revolutionist* (London, 1938).
Hodge, John, *Workman's Cottage to Windsor Castle* (London, 1931).
Hodges, Frank, *My Adventures as a Labour Leader* (London, 1925).
Horner, Arthur, *Incorrigible Rebel* (London, 1960).
Hughes, Emrys (ed.), *Keir Hardie's Speeches and Writings* (Glasgow, 1915).
Hyndman, H.M., *England for All* (London, 1881).
Hyndman, H.M., *Further Reminiscences* (London, 1912).
Hyndman, H.M. and Bradlaugh, Charles, *Will Socialism Benefit the English People? Verbatim Report of a Debate Between H.M. Hyndman and Charles Bradlaugh Held at St. James' Hall, April 17th 1884* (London, 1884).

SELECT BIBLIOGRAPHY

Independent Labour Party, *Souvenir of the Twentieth Annual Conference, Merthyr Tydfil, Easter 1912* (Merthyr, 1912).
Independent Labour Party, *Keir Hardie and Harry Morris Memorial Meeting, 19 September 1926, Programme* (Merthyr, 1926).
Independent Labour Party (Briton Ferry Branch), *Socialist and Labour Hymns* (Neath, n.d.).
Jenkins, W.C. (ed.), *Trades Union Congress, Swansea 1901, Souvenir* (Swansea, 1901).
Johnson, Francis, *Keir Hardie's Socialism* (London, 1922).
Kelvin, Norman (ed.), *The Collected Letters of William Morris, vol. 1, 1848–1880* (Princeton, 1984)
Jones, J.O. ('Ap Ffarmwr'), *William Gladstone* (Caernarfon, 1898).
Jones, J.R., *Sosialaeth yng Ngoleuni'r Beibl* (London, 1909).
Jones, Jack, *Unfinished Journey* (London, 1938).
Jones, Lloyd, *The Life, Times and Labours of Robert Owen* (London, 1890).
Jones, Rowland, *Yr Eglwys a Sosialaeth* (Barmouth, 1910).
Jones, Thomas, *Rhymney Memories* (Newtown, 1938).
Jones, Thomas, *Cerrig Milltir* (Llandybie, 1942).
Joynes, J.L., *The Adventures of a Tourist in Ireland* (London, 1882).
Joynes, J.L., *Socialist Rhymes* (London, 1885).
Littlejohns, John, *Black Glamorgan* (Swansea, 1901).
MacDonald, J. Ramsay, *Socialism and Society* (London, 1905).
Mann, Tom, *Memoirs* (London, 1923).
Mardy Jones, T.I., *Mining Royalties and All About Them* (London, 1908).
Masson, Ursula (ed.), *Women's Rights and 'Womanly Duties': The Aberdare Women's Liberal Association, 1891–1910* (Cardiff, 2005).
Mór O'Brien, A. (ed.), *The Autobiography of Edmund Stonelake* (Bridgend, 1981).
Morgan Jones, J., *Religion and Socialism* (Merthyr Tydfil, 1910).
Morris, William, *News From Nowhere* (London, 1897).
Nicholas, T.E., *Salmau'r Werin a Chaneuon Eraill* (Ystalyfera, 1909).
Nicholas, T.E., *Cerddi Gwerin* (Caernarfon, 1912).
Nicholas, T.E., *Cerddi Rhyddid* (Swansea, 1912).
Nicholas, T.E., *Cyflog Byw* (Pontardawe, 1913).
Ogilvy, A.J., *Land Nationalisation* (Manchester, 1890).
Owen, Daniel ('Ap Rhydderch'), *Keir Hardie: The Prize Epic at the Mountain Ash ILP Eisteddfod, March 22, 1909* (Mountain Ash, 1909).
Owen, Robert, *Talfyriad o'r Gyfundrefn Resymol, seiliedig ar ffeithiau diwrthebbrawb yn amlygu cyfansoddiad a deddfau y natur ddynol, sef, yr unig foddion effeithiol i symud y drygau sydd yn poeni ac yn dyrysu poblogaeth y byd* (Bangor, n.d. [1841]).
Pan Jones, Evan, *Oes a Gwaith Y Prif Athraw Michael Daniel Jones, Bala* (Bala, 1903).
Pan Jones, Evan, *Oes Gofion: Fraslun o Hanes fy Mywyd* (Bala, 1911).

SELECT BIBLIOGRAPHY

Parry, W.J., *The Penrhyn Lock-out, 1900–1901: Statement and Appeal* (London, 1901).
Parry, W.J., *The Cry of the People* (Caernarfon, 1906).
Penrhyn Relief Fund, *Statement of Accounts and Balance Sheet & Report of Auditors* (Caernarfon, 1904).
Phillips, Thomas, *Sosialaeth yn Ngoleini y Bibl* (Liverpool, 1912).
Phillips, W.F., *Open Letter to Keir Hardie* (Ystalyfera, 1911).
Phillips, W.F., *Y Draig Goch ynte'r Faner Goch? Ac Erthyglau Eraill* (Cardiff, 1913).
Phillips, W.F. and Mills, W.T., *Is Socialism Anti-Christian in its Tendency?: Debate Between Mr. W.F. Phillips and Professor W.T. Mills at the Workmen's Hall, Nantymoel, Verbatim Report from the Shorthand Notes of George Thomas* (c.1911).
Price, W., *Sosialaeth: A Ddylid Ei Chefnogi?* (Holyhead, 1908).
Prothero, C., *Recount* (Ormskirk, 1982).
Pugh, Thomas, *Nodiadau Hanesyddol a Beirniadol ar Fywyd a Gwaith Robert Owen o'r Drenewydd* (Manchester, 1907).
Reid, Andrew (ed.), *The New Party* (London, 1895).
Roberts, Richard, *Robert Owen* (Caernarfon, 2 vols, 1907 and 1910).
Russel Wallace, Alfred, *Land Nationalisation: Its Necessity and Its Aims* (London, 1882).
Russel Wallace, Alfred, *The 'Why' and the 'How' of Land Nationalisation* (London, 1883).
Severn, Moses, *The Miners' Evangel: A Text Book For All Manual Workers* (Pontypridd, 1895).
Shaw, George Bernard (ed.), *Fabian Essays in Socialism* (London, 1889).
Silyn Roberts, Robert, *Trystan ac Esyllt a Chaniadau Eraill* (Bangor, 1904).
Silyn Roberts, Robert, *Y Blaid Lafur Anibynnol: Ei Hanes a'i Hamcan* (Blaenau Ffestiniog, 1908).
Stephens, T. (ed.), *Wales To-day and To-morrow* (Cardiff, 1907).
Taylor, A.J.P. (ed.), Karl Marx and Friedrich Engels, *The Communist Manifesto* (London, 1968).
Taylor, Helen, *Nationalisation of the Land* (London, 1888).
Thomas, B.B. (ed.), *Lleufer Y Werin: Cyfrol Deyrnged i David Thomas M.A.* (Abercynon, 1965).
Thomas, David, *Y Werin a'i Theyrnas* (Caernarfon, 1910).
Thomas, David, *Y Blaid Lafur a Dinasyddiaeth y Gweithwyr* (Manchester, 1911).
Thomas, David, *Silyn* (Liverpool, 1956).
Thomas, David, *Diolch Am Gael Byw: Rhai o F'atgofion* (Liverpool, 1968).
Thomas, J.H., *My Story* (London, 1937).
Thompson, A.M., *Here I Lie: The Memorial of an Old Journalist* (London, 1937).
Thorne, Will, *My Life's Battles* (London, 1925).

Webb, Sidney, *Practicable Land Nationalisation* (London, 1890).
Wedgwood, Josiah C., *Henry George for Socialists* (London, 1908).
Woollerton, Arthur, *The Labour Movement in Manchester and Salford* (Manchester, 1907).
Williams, Ernest E., *Sosialaeth â'r Teulu* (London, 1910).

2 SECONDARY SOURCES

(i) Reference Works
Dictionary of Labour Biography.
Dictionary of Welsh Biography.
Jones, Beti (ed.), *Etholiadau'r Ganrif / Welsh Elections, 1885–1997* (Talybont, 1999).
Oxford Dictionary of National Biography.
Who's Who in Wales (London, 1937).

(ii) Books and Articles
Ainsworth, A.J., 'Aspects of Socialism at Branch Level, 1890–1900: Some Notes Towards Analysis', *Bulletin of the North West Labour History Society*, 4 (1977), 6–35.
Armytage, W.H.G., 'Pant Glas: a Communitarian Experiment in Merionethshire', *Journal of the Merioneth Historical and Record Society*, 2 (1955), 232–4.
Bealey, Frank and Pelling, Henry, *Labour and Politics, 1900–1906: A History of the Labour Representation Committee* (Oxford, 1958).
Belchem, John and Kirk, Neville (eds), *Languages of Labour* (Aldershot, 1997).
Benn, Caroline, *Keir Hardie* (London, 1992).
Berger, Stefan, 'The Decline of Liberalism and the Rise of Labour – The Regional Approach', *Parliamentary History*, 12/1 (1993), 84–92.
Bevir, Mark, 'Fabianism and the Theory of Rent', *History of Political Thought*, 10/2 (1989), 313–27.
Bevir, Mark, 'H.M. Hyndman: A Re-reading and a Re-assessment', *History of Political Thought*, 13/1 (1991), 125–45.
Bevir, Mark, 'The British Social Democratic Federation, 1880–1885: From O'Brienism to Marxism', *International Review of Social History* 37/2 (1992), 207–29.
Bevir, Mark, 'The Marxism of George Bernard Shaw, 1883–1889', *History of Political Thought*, 13/2 (1992), 299–318.
Bevir, Mark, 'The Labour Church Movement, 1891–1902', *Journal of British Studies*, 38/2 (1999), 217–45.
Biagini, E.F. (ed.), *Citizenship and Community: Liberals, Radicals and Collective Identities in the British Isles, 1865–1931* (Cambridge, 1996).

SELECT BIBLIOGRAPHY

Biagini, E.F. and Reid, A.J. (eds), *Currents of Radicalism: Popular Radicalism, Organised Labour and Party Politics in Britain, 1850–1914* (Cambridge, 1991).

Bowen Rees, Ioan, *The Welsh Political Tradition* (Cardiff, 1961).

Brennan, T., 'The White House', *Cambridge Journal* (1954), 243–8.

Briggs, Asa and Saville, John (eds), *Essays in Labour History: In Memory of G.D.H. Cole* (London, 1967).

Brown, K.D. (ed.), *The First Labour Party, 1906–1914* (London, 1985).

Bryher, Samson, *An Account of the Labour and Socialist Movement in Bristol* (Bristol, 2 vols, 1929).

Campbell, A., Fishman, N. and Howell, D. (eds), *Miners, Unions and Politics, 1910–47* (Aldershot, 1996).

Cannadine, David, 'British History as a "New Subject": Politics, Perspectives and Prospects', *Welsh History Review*, 17/3 (1995), 313–31.

Casey, Michael and Ackers, Peter, 'The Enigma of the Young Arthur Horner: From Churches of Christ Preacher to Communist Militant (1894–1920)', *Labour History Review*, 66/1 (2001), 3–23.

Cass, Eddie, 'Robert Jones Derfel: A Welsh Poet in the Cotton Factory Times', *Llafur*, 7/1 (1996), 53–67.

Chase, Malcolm, *Chartism: A New History* (Manchester and New York, 2007).

Clarke, David, *Labour's Lost Leader: Victor Grayson* (London, 1985).

Clayton, Joseph, *The Rise and Decline of Socialism in Great Britain, 1884–1924* (London, 1926).

Cleaver, David, 'Swansea and District's Labour Press, 1888–1914', *Llafur*, 4/1 (1984), 35–42.

Cleaver, David, 'Labour and Liberals in the Gower Constituency, 1885–1910', *Welsh History Review*, 12/3 (1985), 388–410.

Cleaver, David, 'The General Election Contest in the Swansea Town Constituency, January 1910 – The Socialist Challenge', *Llafur*, 5/3 (1990), 28–33.

Clements, Harry, *Alfred Russel Wallace: Biologist and Social Reformer* (London, 1983).

Cole, G.D.H., *A History of Socialist Thought* (London, 7 vols, 1953–7).

Cole, G.D.H., *James Keir Hardie* (London, 1941).

Constantine, Mary-Ann and Johnston, Dafydd (eds), *'Footsteps of Liberty & Revolt': Essays on Wales and the French Revolution* (Cardiff, 2013).

Corfield, Penelope J., 'Rhetoric, Radical Politics and Rainfall: John Thelwall in Breconshire, 1797–1800', *Brycheiniog*, 40 (2008), 17–39.

Cragoe, Matthew, 'Welsh Electioneering and the Purpose of Parliament: "From Radicalism to Nationalism" Reconsidered', *Parliamentary History: Parliament and Locality, 1660–1939* (1998), 113–30.

Craik, W.W., *The Central Labour College* (London, 1964).

Crick, Martin, *The History of the Social Democratic Federation* (Ryburn, 1994).
Croll, Andy, *Civilising the Urban: Popular Culture and Public Space in Merthyr, c. 1870–1914* (Cardiff, 2000).
Croll, Andy, '"People's Remembrancers in a Post-Modern Age": Contemplating the Non-Crisis of Welsh Labour History', *Llafur*, 8/1 (2000), 3–17.
Croll, Andy, 'Mabon's Day: The Rise and Fall of a Lib-Lab Holiday in the South Wales Coalfield, 1888–1898', *Labour History Review*, 72/1 (2007), 49–68.
Daunton, M.J., *Coal Metropolis: Cardiff, 1870–1914* (Leicester, 1977).
Daunton, Martin, 'Inter-Union Rivalries on the Waterfront: Cardiff, 1888–1914', *International Review of Social History*, 22/3 (1977), 350–78.
Daunton, Martin, 'The Cardiff Coal Trimmers Union, 1888–1914', *Llafur*, 2/3 (1978), 10–23.
Daunton, Martin, 'Coal to Capital: Cardiff Since 1839', in Prys Morgan (ed.), *Glamorgan County History*, vol. 6: *Glamorgan Society 1780–1980* (Cardiff, 1988), pp. 203–24.
Davies, David, *The Influence of the French Revolution on Welsh Life and Literature* (Carmarthen, 1926).
Davies, John, *A History of Wales* (London, 1993).
Davies, Paul, 'The Making of A.J. Cook', *Llafur*, 2/3 (1978), 43–63.
Davies, Paul, *A.J. Cook* (Manchester, 1987).
Davies, Picton, *Atgofion Dyn Papur Newydd* (Liverpool, 1962).
Davies, Tom, 'Pan Jones', *Y Llenor*, 13 (1934), 144–57.
Donnachie, Ian, 'Robert Owen's Welsh Childhood: Kin, Culture and Environment, 1771–1781', *Montgomeryshire Collections*, 86 (1998), 81–96.
Douglas Pennant, Edmund, 'Landlordism: The Second Lord Penrhyn and the Royal Commission on Land in Wales and Monmouthshire', *Transactions of the Caernarvonshire Historical Society*, 57 (1996), 101–24.
Douglas Pennant, Edmund, 'The Second Lord Penrhyn and Local Government, 1861–1902', *Transactions of the Caernarvonshire Historical Society*, 61 (2000), 77–88.
Douglas Pennant, Edmund, 'Penrhynism: The Second Lord Penrhyn and Trade Unionism', *Transactions of the Caernarvonshire Historical Society*, 66 (2005), 126–36.
Dowse, R. E., *Left in the Centre: The Independent Labour Party, 1893–1940* (London, 1966).
Edwards, Ness, *History of the South Wales Miners' Federation* (London, 1938).
Egan, David, 'The Unofficial Reform Committee and the Miners' Next Step', *Llafur*, 2/3 (1978), 64–80.
Egan, David, 'Noah Ablett, 1883–1935', *Llafur*, 4/3 (1986), 19–30.
Ellis, E.L., *T.J.: A Life of Thomas Jones C.H.* (Cardiff, 1992).
Ellis, John S., *Investiture: Royal Ceremony and National Identity in Wales, 1911–1969* (Cardiff, 2008).

SELECT BIBLIOGRAPHY

Ellis, T.I., *Thomas Edwards Ellis, Cofiant* (Liverpool, 2 vols, 1948).
England, Joe, 'Notes on a Neglected Topic: General Unionism in Wales', *Llafur*, 9/1 (2004), 45–58.
England, Joe, 'Keir Hardie and the Dowlais Strike of 1911', *Merthyr Historian*, 19 (2008), 44–54.
England, Joe (ed.), *Changing Lives: Workers' Education in Wales, 1907–2007* (Swansea, 2007).
Evans, Daniel, *The Life and Work of William Williams* (Llandysul, n.d.).
Evans, E.W., *Mabon (William Abraham, 1842–1922): A Study in Trade Union Leadership* (Cardiff, 1959).
Evans, E.W., *The Miners of South Wales* (Cardiff, 1961).
Evans, G., *Seiri Cenedl y Cymry* (Llandysul, 1986).
Evans, Neil, 'Urbanisation, Elite Attitudes and Philanthropy: Cardiff, 1850–1914', *International Review of Social History*, 27/3 (1982), 290–323.
Evans, Neil, 'The Welsh Victorian City: The Middle Class and Civic and National Consciousness in Cardiff, 1850–1914', *Welsh History Review*, 12/3 (1984–5), 350–87.
Evans, Neil, 'Cardiff's Labour Traditions', *Llafur*, 4/2 (1985), 77–90.
Evans, Neil (ed.), *National Identity in the British Isles* (Harlech, 1989).
Evans, Neil and Sullivan, Kate, '"Yn Llawn o Dân Cymreig" (Full of Welsh Fire): The Language of Politics in Wales, 1880–1914', in Geraint H. Jenkins (ed.), *The Welsh Language and its Social Domains in the Nineteenth Century, 1801–1911* (Cardiff, 2000), pp. 561–85.
Evans, R. Meurig, *One Saturday Afternoon: The Albion Colliery, Cilfynydd Explosion of 1894* (Cardiff, 1984).
Evans, W.G., 'R.J. Derfel and Huwco Meirion', *Journal of the Merioneth Historical and Record Society*, 10 (1985), 48–56.
Fagge, Roger, *Power, Culture and Conflict in the Coalfields: West Virginia and South Wales, 1900–1922* (Manchester and New York, 1996).
Foot, Michael, *Aneurin Bevan, 1897–1945* (London, 1962).
Fox, K.O., 'Labour and Merthyr's Khaki Election of 1900', *Welsh History Review*, 2/4 (1965), 351–66.
Francis, Hywel and Smith, David, *The Fed: A History of the South Wales Miners in the Twentieth Century* (London, 1980).
George, William, *Cymru Fydd: Hanes y Mudiad Cenedlaethol Cyntaf* (Liverpool, 1945).
Griffiths, Gwyn, *Henry Richard: Apostle of Peace and Welsh Patriot* (London, 2012).
Griffiths, Robert, *Turning to London, Labour's Attitude to Wales, 1898–1956* (Cardiff, 1980).
Griffiths, Robert, 'Llwynog o'r Graig', *Llafur*, 3/3 (1982), 86–92.
Griffiths, Robert, *Marx and Engels on Wales and the Welsh* (Cardiff, 2006).
Gwyther, C.E., 'Sidelights on Religion and Politics in the Rhondda Valley, 1906–26', *Llafur*, 3/1 (1980), 30–43.

Haig Mackworth, Margaret (ed.), *D.A. Thomas: Viscount Rhondda by his Daughter and Others* (London, 1921).

Hannam, June and Hunt, Karen, *Socialist Women: Britain, 1880s–1920s* (London and New York, 2002).

Harrison, Stanley, *Poor Men's Guardians* (London, 1974)

Hauben, Ronda, 'A Pioneer in Workers' Education: Mark Starr and Workers' Education in Great Britain', *Llafur*, 4/2 (1985), 96–102.

Hechter, Michael, *Internal Colonialism: The Celtic Fringe in British National Development, 1536–1966* (London, 1975).

Hill, Jeffrey, 'Manchester and Salford Politics and the Early Development of the Independent Labour Party', *International Review of Social History*, 26/2 (1981), 171–201.

Hill, Jeffrey, 'Social Democracy and the Labour Movement: The Social Democratic Federation in Lancashire', *Bulletin of the North West Labour History Society*, 8 (1982), 44–55.

Hilton, Kenneth, 'John Spargo, The Social Democratic Federation and the 1898 South Wales Coal Strike', *Welsh History Review*, 16/4 (1993), 542–50.

Hobsbawm, Eric, *Labouring Men: Studies in the History of Labour* (London, 1964).

Hobsbawm, Eric and Ranger, Terence (eds), *The Invention of Tradition* (Cambridge, 1983).

Hoffman, P.C., *They Also Serve: The Story of the Shop Worker* (London, 1949).

Hopkin, Deian, 'The Membership of the ILP, 1904–10: A Spatial and Occupational Analysis', *International Review of Social History*, 20/2 (1975), 175–97.

Hopkin, Deian, 'The Merthyr Pioneer, 1911–1922', *Llafur* 2/4 (1979), 54–64.

Hopkin, Deian, 'A.J. Cook in 1916–18', *Llafur*, 2/3 (1978), 81–8.

Hopkin, Deian, 'Y Werin a'i Theyrnas: Ymateb Sosialaeth i Genedlaetholdeb, 1880–1920', *Cof Cenedl*, 6 (1991), 162–92.

Hopkin, Deian, 'The Rise of Labour in Wales, 1890–1914', *Llafur*, 6, 3 (1994), 120–41.

Hopkin, Deian, 'Llafur a'r Diwylliant Cymreig 1900–1940', *Trafodion Anrhydeddus Cymdeithas Y Cymmrodorion*, (New Series) 7 (2001), 128–48.

Hopkin, Deian and Kealey, Gregory S. (eds), *Class, Community and the Labour Movement: Wales and Canada, 1850–1930* (Aberystwyth, 1989).

Hopkin, Deian, and Williams, John, 'New Light on the New Unionism in Wales', 1889–1912', *Llafur*, 4/3 (1986), 67–79.

Howard, Chris, 'Reactionary Radicalism: the Mid-Glamorgan By-Election, March 1910', *Glamorgan Historian*, 9 (1973), 29–42.

Howell, David, *British Workers and the Independent Labour Party, 1888–1906* (Manchester, 1983).

Howell, David, *A Lost Left: Three Studies in Nationalism and Socialism* (Manchester, 1986).
Howell, David, 'When Was the Forward March of Labour?', *Llafur*, 5/3 (1990), 57–78.
Howell, David W., 'Labour Organisation Among Agricultural Workers in Wales, 1872–1921', *Welsh History Review*, 16/1 (1992), 63–92.
Howell, David W., *Niclas Y Glais, The People's Champion* (Clydach, 1991).
Hughes, Dewi Rowland, 'Y Goch a'r Gwyrdd: Cymru Fydd a'r Mudiad Llafur Cymreig (1886–1896)', *Llafur*, 6/4 (1995), 60–79.
Hughes, Dewi Rowland, *Cymru Fydd* (Cardiff, 2006).
Hughes, Emrys, *Keir Hardie* (London, 1956).
Hughes, G.A. (ed.), *Men of No Property: Historical Studies of Welsh Trade Unions* (Caerwys, 1971).
Hume, Ian and Pryce, W.T.R. (eds), *The Welsh and Their Country* (Llandysul, 1986).
Inglis, Kenneth, 'The Labour Church Movement', *International Review of Social History*, 3/3 (1958), 445–60.
James, David, Jowitt, Tony and Laybourn, Keith (eds), *The Centennial History of the Independent Labour Party* (Halifax, 1992).
James, E. Wyn and Jones, William (eds), *Michael D. Jones a'i Wladfa Gymreig* (Llanrwst, 2009).
Jenkins, David, *Thomas Gwynn Jones* (Denbigh, 1973).
Jenkins, Geraint H. (ed.), *Language and Community in the Nineteenth Century* (Cardiff, 1998).
Jenkins, Geraint H. (ed.), *The Welsh Language and its Social Domains, 1801–1911* (Cardiff, 2000).
Jenkins, Geraint H. and Smith, J. Beverly (eds), *Politics and Society in Wales, 1840–1922: Essays in Honour of Ieuan Gwynedd Jones* (Cardiff, 1988).
Jenkins, Gwyn, 'The *Welsh Outlook*, 1914–33', *National Library of Wales Journal*, 34 (1986), 463–92.
John, Ken, 'Sam Mainwaring and the Autonomist Tradition', *Llafur*, 4/3 (1986), 55–66.
Johnson, Graham, 'Social Democracy and Labour Politics in Britain, 1892–1911', *History*, 85/277 (2002), 67–87.
Johnston, W. Ross, 'The Welsh Diaspora: Emigrating Around the World in the Late Nineteenth Century', *Llafur*, 6/2 (1993), 50–74.
Jones, Aled, *Press, Politics and Society: A History of Journalism in Wales* (Cardiff, 1993).
Jones, David J.V., *The Last Rising: The Newport Insurrection of 1839* (Oxford, 1985).
Jones, D. Gwenallt (ed.), *Detholiad o Ryddiaeth Gymraeg R.J. Derfel* (Denbigh, 2 vols, 1945).
Jones, D. Gwenallt, *Ffwrneisiau: Cronicl Blynyddoedd Mebyd* (Llandysul, 1982).

Jones, Emrys (ed.), *The Welsh in London, 1500–2000* (Cardiff, 2001).
Jones, E. Cefni, *Gwili: Cofiant a Phregethu* (Llandysul, 1937).
Jones, Ieuan Gwynedd, *Explorations & Explanations: Essays in the Social History of Victorian Wales* (Llandysul, 1981)
Jones, Ieuan Gwynedd, *The Observers and the Observed: Mid-Victorian Wales* (Cardiff, 1992).
Jones, John Graham, 'Y Blaid Lafur, Datganoli a Chymru, 1900–1979', *Cof Cenedl*, VII (1992), 167–200.
Jones, John Graham, 'Michael Davitt, David Lloyd George and T.E. Ellis: The Welsh Experience 1886', *Welsh History Review*, 18/3 (1977), 450–82.
Jones, John Gwynfor, 'Edward Thomas (Cochfarf): Dinesydd, Dyngarwr a Gwladgarwr', *Trafodion Cymdeithas Hanes Bedyddwyr Cymru* (1987), 26–45.
Jones, John Gwynfor, 'Y Ddelwedd Gymreig Ddinesig yng Nghaerdydd, c. 1885–1939', in Hywel Teifi Edwards (ed.), *Merthyr a Thaf* (Llandysul, 2001), pp. 325–63.
Jones, Philip N., 'Some Aspects of Immigration into the Glamorgan Coalfield Between 1881 and 1911', *Transactions of the Honourable Society of Cymmrodorion* (1969), 82–98.
Jones, R. Merfyn, *The North Wales Quarrymen, 1874–1922* (Cardiff, 1982; 2nd edn 2015).
Jones, R. Merfyn, 'Beyond Identity? The Reconstruction of the Welsh', *Journal of British Studies*, 31/4 (1992), 330–57.
Jones, R. Merfyn, 'Labour Implantation: Is There a Welsh Dimension?', *Tijdschrift Voor Sociale Geschiedenis*, 18/2–3 (1992), 231–47.
Jones, R. Merfyn and Rees, D. Ben, *Cymry Lerpwl a'u Crefydd: Dwy Ganrif o Fethodistiaeth Galfinaidd Gymreug/The Liverpool Welsh and their Religion: Two Centuries of Welsh Calvinistic Methodism* (Liverpool, 1984).
Jones, R. Tudur, *Ffydd ac Argyfwng Cenedl: Hanes Crefydd yng Nghymru 1890–1914* (Swansea, 1982).
Jones, Thomas Gwynn, *Emrys ap Iwan, Dysgadwr, Llenor, Cenedlgarwr: Cofiant* (Caernarfon, 1912).
Jones, William D., *Wales in America: Scranton and the Welsh, 1860–1920* (Cardiff, 1993).
Jones, Wyn, *Thomas Edward Ellis, 1859–1899* (Cardiff, 1986).
Jones Evans, P., 'Evan Pan Jones – Land Reformer', *Welsh History Review*, 4/2 (1968), 143–59.
Jowitt, J.A. and Taylor, R.K.S. (eds), *Bradford, 1890–1914: The Cradle of the Independent Labour Party* (Leeds, 1980).
Kellas, James G., 'The Mid Lanark By Election, 1888 and the Scottish Labour Party, 1888–1894', *Parliamentary Affairs* 18/3 (1965), 318–29.
Kidd, A.J., 'The Social Democratic Federation and Popular Agitation Amongst the Unemployed in Edwardian Manchester', *International Review of Social History*, 29/3 (1984), 336–56.

SELECT BIBLIOGRAPHY

Kirk, Neville, '"A State of War in the Valley of Glencoe": The Ballachulish Quarries Disputes, 1902–1905', *Scottish Labour History*, 38 (2003), 14–36.

Kirk, Neville, *Custom and Conflict in the Land of the Gael: Ballachulish, 1900–1910* (Monmouth, 2007).

Lawn, Martin, 'Mark Starr, Socialist Educator', *Llafur*, 4/2 (1985), 91–6.

Lawrence, Jon, 'Popular Radicalism and the Socialist Revival in Britain', *Journal of British Studies*, 31/2 (1992), 163–86.

Lawrence, Jon, *Speaking for the People: Party, Language and Popular Politics in England, 1867–1914* (Cambridge, 1998).

Laybourn, Keith, 'The Failure of Socialist Unity in Britain, c. 1893–1914', *Transactions of the Royal Historical Society*, 6th Series, 4 (1994), 153–75.

Laybourn, Keith and James, David, *The Rising Sun of Socialism: The Independent Labour Party in the Textile District of the West Riding of Yorkshire between 1890 and 1914* (Wakefield, 1991).

Leng, Philip J., *The Welsh Dockers* (Ormskirk, 1981).

Lewis, Richard, 'The South Wales Miners and the Ruskin College Strike of 1909', *Llafur*, 2/1 (1976), 57–72.

Lewis, Richard, 'Protagonist of Labour; Mark Starr, 1894–1985', *Llafur*, 4/3 (1986), 5–18.

Lewis, Richard, *Leaders and Teachers: Adult Education and the Challenge of Labour in South Wales, 1906–1940* (Cardiff, 1993).

Lieven, Michael, *Senghennydd: The Universal Pit Village, 1890–1930* (Llandysul, 1994).

Lloyd, D. Myrddin, *Emrys ap Iwan* (Cardiff, 1979).

Mackenzie, Norman and Jeanne, *The First Fabians* (London, 1977).

Manning, H. Paul, 'The Streets of Bethesda: The Slate Quarrier and the Welsh Language in the Liberal Imagination', *Language in Society*, 33 (2004), 517–48.

Marsh, Jan, *Back to the Land: The Pastoral Impulse in Victorian England from 1880 to 1914* (London, 1982).

Martin, David and Rubinstein, David, *Ideology and the Labour Movement: Essays Presented to John Saville* (London, 1979).

Masson, Ursula, *'For Women, for Wales and for Liberalism': Women in Liberal Politics in Wales, 1880–1914* (Cardiff, 2010).

Masterman, Neville, *The Forerunner: The Dilemmas of Tom Ellis, 1859–1899* (Llandybie, 1972).

Matthews, Ioan, 'The World of the Anthracite Miner', *Llafur*, 6/1 (1992), 96–104.

Matthews, Ioan, 'Maes y Glo Carreg ac Undeb y Glöwyr, 1872–1925', *Cof Cenedl*, 8 (1993), 133–64.

May, Eddie, 'Charles Stanton and the Limits to 'Patriotic' Labour', *Welsh History Review*, 18/3 (1997), 483–508.

McBriar, A.M., *Fabian Socialism and English Politics* (Cambridge, 1962).

McKenna, Vicki, 'A Miner on a Mission', *Your Family Tree* (September 2010), 34–6.
McKibbin, Ross, 'Why Was There No Marxism in Great Britain?', in *The Ideologies Of Class* (Oxford, 1990), pp. 1–41.
McKinlay, Alan and Morris, R.J., *The ILP on Clydeside, 1893–1932: From Foundation to Disintegration* (Manchester, 1991).
McPhillips, Kevin, *Joseph Burgess (1853–1934) and the Founding of the Independent Labour Party* (Lewiston, 2005).
Mendilow, Jonathan, *The Romantic Tradition in British Political Thought* (London and Sydney, 1986).
Millward, E.G., 'Dicter Poeth y Dr Pan', *Cof Cenedl*, 9 (1994), 163–90.
Moore, James Robert, 'Progressive Pioneers: Manchester Liberalism, The Independent Labour Party and Local Politics in the 1890s', *Historical Journal*, 44/4 (2001), 989–1013.
Moore, Jane, '"Parallelograms and Circles": Robert Owen and the Satirists', in Damian Walford Davies and Lynda Pratt (eds), *Wales and the Romantic Imagination* (Cardiff, 2007), pp. 243–67.
Mòr-O'Brien, A., 'Keir Hardie, C.B. Stanton and the First World War', *Llafur*, 4/3 (1986), 31–42.
Morgan, D. Densil, 'Diwygiad Crefyddol, 1904–5', *Cof Cenedl*, XX (2005), 167–200.
Morgan, J. Vyrnwy, *Kilsby Jones* (Wrexham, n.d.).
Morgan, Kenneth O., 'The "Khaki Election" in Gower', *Gower*, 13 (1960), 20–5.
Morgan, Kenneth O., *Wales in British Politics, 1868–1922* (Cardiff, 1963).
Morgan, Kenneth O., *Keir Hardie* (Oxford, 1967).
Morgan, Kenneth O., 'The New Liberalism and the Challenge of Labour: The Welsh Experience, 1885–1929', *Welsh History Review*, 6/3 (1973), 288–312.
Morgan, Kenneth O., *Keir Hardie: Radical and Socialist* (London, 1975).
Morgan, Kenneth O., *Rebirth of a Nation: Wales, 1880–1980* (Oxford and Cardiff, 1980).
Morgan, Kenneth O., 'Peace Movements in Wales, 1899–1945', *Welsh History Review*, 10/3 (1981), 398–430.
Morgan, Kenneth O., *The Red Dragon and the Red Flag: The Cases of James Griffiths and Aneurin Bevan (Welsh Political Archive Lecture 1988)* (Aberystwyth, 1989).
Morgan, Kenneth O., 'Leaders and Led in the Labour Movement: The Welsh Experience', *Llafur*, 6/3 (1994), 109–19.
Morgan, Prys, 'R.J. Derfel a'r Ddrama 'Brad Y Llyfrau Gleision'', in Prys Morgan (ed.), *Brad Y Llyfrau Gleision: Ysgrifau ar Hanes Cymru* (Llandysul, 1991), pp. 1–21.

SELECT BIBLIOGRAPHY

Morgan Humphries, E., 'Profiadau Golygydd', *Caernarvonshire Historical Society Transactions*, 2 (1950), 81–92.
Morgan Humphries, E., *Gwyr Enwog Gynt* (Aberystwyth, 1953).
Morris, Dylan, 'Sosialaith i'r Cymry – Trafodaeth yr I.L.P.', *Llafur*, 4/2 (1985), 51–63.
Nicholas, Islwyn ap, *Derfel: Welsh Rebel, Poet, and Preacher* (London, 1945).
Nicholas, James, *Pan Oeddwn Grwt Diniwed yn y Wlad* (Llandysul, 1979).
Olivier, Hermia, *The International Anarchist Movement in Late Victorian London* (London, 1983).
Owen, James, 'Dissident Missionaries? Re-Narrating the Political Strategy of the Social Democratic Federation, 1884–1887', *Labour History Review*, 73/2 (2008), 187–207.
Page Arnot, Robin, *South Wales Miners: A History of the South Wales Miners Federation, 1898–1914* (London, 1967).
Parry, Cyril, 'Fabianism and Gwynedd Politics, 1890–1918', *Transactions of Caernarvonshire Historical Society*, 29 (1968), 121–36.
Parry, Cyril, 'The Independent Labour Party and Gwynedd Politics, 1900–1920', *Welsh History Review*, 4/1 (1968), 47–66.
Parry, Cyril, *The Radical Tradition in Welsh Politics: A Study of Liberal and Labour Politics in Gwynedd, 1900–1920* (Hull, 1970).
Parry, Cyril, 'Gwynedd Politics, 1900–1920: The Rise of a Labour Party', *Welsh History Review*, 6/3 (1973), 313–28.
Parry, Jon, 'Trade Unionists and Early Socialism in South Wales, 1890–1908', *Llafur*, 4/3 (1986), 43–54.
Parry, Jon, 'Labour Leaders and Local Politics, 1888–1902: The Example of Aberdare', *Welsh History Review*, 14/3 (1989), 399–416.
Pease, Edward, *History of the Fabian Society* (New York, 1916).
Pelling, Henry, *Origins of the Labour Party* (London, 1954).
Pierce, Gwynedd, 'The Welsh Connection', in Gwyn Jones and Michael Quinn (eds), *Fountains of Praise: University College, Cardiff, 1883–1983* (Cardiff, 1983), pp. 25–40.
Pierce, Gwynedd (ed.), *Triwr Penllyn* (Cardiff, n.d.).
Pierson, Stanley, 'John Trevor and the Labour Church Movment in England, 1891–1900', *Church History*, 29 (1960), 463–78.
Pierson, Stanley, *Marxism and the Origins of British Socialism: The Struggle for a New Consciousness* (Ithaca and London, 1973).
Pierson, Stanley, *British Socialists: The Journey from Fantasy to Politics* (Cambridge, MA and London, 1979).
Pope, Robert, 'Lladmerydd Y Deyrnas: Herbert Morgan, 1875–1946', *Trafodion Cymdeithas Hanes Y Bedyddwyr* (1994), pp. 47–65.
Pope, Robert, 'Facing the Dawn: Socialists, Nonconformists and *Llais Llafur*, 1906–1914', *Llafur*, 7/3–4 (1998–9), 77–88.
Pope, Robert, *Building Jerusalem: Nonconformity, Labour and the Social Question in Wales, 1906–1939* (Cardiff, 1998).

Pope, Robert, '"Pilgrims Through a Barren Land": Nonconformists and Socialists in Wales, 1906–1914', *Transactions of the Honourable Society of Cymmrodorion* (New Series) 7 (2001), 149–63.

Powell, Geoffrey, '"They shall no longer see as through a glass darkly": Robert Owen and the Welsh Enlightenment', *Montgomeryshire Collections*, 91 (2003), 53–69.

Pretty, David, *The Rural Revolt That Failed: Farm Workers' Trade Unions in Wales, 1889–1950* (Cardiff, 1989).

Pretty, David, 'Caethion y Tir: Gwrthryfel y Gweithwyr Fferm yng Nghymru', *Cof Cenedl*, 7 (1992), 133–66.

Pretty, David, 'John Owen Jones (Ap Ffarmwr) and the Labour Movement in Merthyr Tydfil, 1894–6', *Morgannwg*, 38 (1994), 101–14.

Price, Emyr, *David Lloyd George* (Cardiff, 2006).

Price Jones, Frank, *Radicaliaeth a'r Werin Gymreig yn y Bedwaredd Canrif ar Bymtheg* (Caerdydd, 1975).

Prynn, D., 'The Clarion Clubs, Rambling and the Holiday Associations in Britain Since the 1890s', *Journal of Contemporary History*, 11/2–3 (1976), 65–77.

Pye, Dennis, 'Fellowship is Life: Bolton Clarion Cycling Club and the Clarion Movement, 1894–1914', *North West Labour History Society Bulletin*, 10 (1984), 20–30.

Rees, D. Ben (ed.), *Herio'r Byd* (Liverpool, 1980).

Rees, D. Ben, 'Sosialaith Farcsaidd Cymreig T.E. Nicholas', *Trafodion Anrhydeddus Gymdeithas Y Cymmrodorion*, New Series, 3 (1996), 164–73.

Rees, D. Ben, *The Welsh of Merseyside* (Liverpool, 2 vols, 1997 and 2001).

Rees, Ivor Thomas, 'David Gwynfryn Jones: Methodist, Socialist, Welshman', *Llafur*, 10/2 (2009), 101–16.

Rees, Ivor Thomas, 'Thomas Evan Nicholas, 1879–1971', *National Library of Wales Journal*, 35/1 (2010).

Rees, Ivor Thomas, 'Charles Butt Stanton, 1873–1946, M.P. for Merthyr Tydfil, 1915–1918', *Merthyr Historian* 25 (2013), 161–78.

Reynolds, Jack and Laybourn, Keith, 'The Emergence of the Independent Labour Party in Bradford', *International Review of Social History*, 20/3 (1975), 313–46.

Roberts, A.M., 'R.J. Derfel, 1824–1905', *Y Traethodydd*, 165/688 (2009), 34–54.

Roberts, Dafydd, *Y Chwarelwyr a'r Sowth* (Bethesda, 1982).

Roose Williams, J. (ed.), *T.E. Nicholas, Proffwyd Sosialaeth a Bardd Gwrthryfel* (Cardiff, 1971).

Roose Williams, J., 'T.E. Nicholas, Bardd Gwrthryfel', *Cyffro*, 1/2 (1970), 45–51.

Roose Williams, J., *Quarryman's Champion: The Life and Activities of William John Parry of Coetmor* (Denbigh, 1978).

Samuel, Raphael (ed.), *Patriotism: The Making and Unmaking of British National Identity*, vol. II: *Minorities and Outsiders* (London, 1989).
Samuel, Raphael, 'British Dimensions: "Four Nations History"', *History Workshop Journal*, 40/1 (1995), iii–xxii.
Savage, Mike, 'Understanding Political Alignments in Contemporary Britain: Do Localities Matter?', *Political Geography Quarterly*, 6/1 (1987), 53–76.
Schneer, Jonathan, *Ben Tillett: Portrait of a Labour Leader* (London and Canberra, 1982).
Schwarzmantel, John, *Socialism and the Idea of the Nation* (Hemel Hempstead, 1991).
Smith, David, *Aneurin Bevan and the World of South Wales* (Cardiff, 1993).
Smith, David (ed.), *A People and a Proletariat: Essays in the History of Wales, 1780–1980* (London, 1980).
Smith, David, *Wales! Wales?* (London & Sydney, 1984).
Smith, Joan, 'Labour Tradition in Liverpool and Glasgow', *History Workshop Journal*, 17/1 (1984), 32–56.
Smith, J. Beverley, 'John Gwili Jenkins, 1872–1936', *Transactions of the Honourable Society of Cymmrodorion* (1974–5), 191–214.
Smith, J. Beverley Smith (ed.), *James Griffiths and His Times* (Ferndale, 1978).
Smith, Robert, *'In the Direct and Homely Speech of the Workers'*: Llais Llafur, *1898–1915* (Aberystwyth, 2000).
Stead, Peter, 'Vernon Hartshorn: Miners' Agent and Cabinet Minister', *Glamorgan Historian*, 6 (1969), 83–94.
Stead, Peter, 'Working-Class Leadership in South Wales, 1900–1920', *Welsh History Review*, 6/3 (1973), 330–53.
Stead, Peter, 'Establishing a Heartland: The Labour Party in Wales', in K.D. Brown (ed.), *The First Labour Party, 1906–1910* (London, 1985), pp. 64–88.
Stedman Jones, Gareth, *Languages of Class: Studies in English Working Class History, 1832–1982* (Cambridge, 1983).
Stewart, William, *Keir Hardie* (London, 1921).
Tanner, Duncan, *Political Change and the Labour Party, 1900–1918* (Cambridge, 1990).
Tanner, Duncan, 'The Development of British Socialism, 1900–1918', *Parliamentary History*, 16 (1997), 48–66.
Tanner, Duncan, Williams, Chris and Hopkin, Deian (eds), *The Labour Party in Wales, 1900–2000* (Cardiff, 2000).
Taylor, A., '"The Best Way to Get What He Wanted": Ernest Jones and the Boundaries of Liberalism in the Manchester Election of 1868', *Parliamentary History*, 16 (1997), 185–204.
Thomas, Ben Bowen, 'Mabon', *Y Traethodydd*, 17 (1948), 167–73.

Thomas, Brinley, 'Robert Owen of Newtown', *The Transactions of the Honorouble Society of Cymmrodorion* (1960), 18–35.

Thomas, David, *Silyn: Robert Silyn Roberts, 1871–1930* (Liverpool, 1956).

Thomas, R. Maldwyn and Parry, Cyril, 'John Owen Jones: "Ap Ffarmwr", 1861–1899', *Transactions of the Anglesey Antiquarian Society and Field Club* (1967), 72–108.

Thompson, E.P., *William Morris: Romantic to Revolutionary* (London, 1955).

Thompson, E.P., *The Making of the English Working Class* (London, 1963).

Thompson, E.P., 'The Peculiarities of the English', in Ralph Miliband and John Saville (eds), *The Socialist Register*, 2 (1965), 311–65.

Thompson, E.P., 'Homage to Tom Maguire', in Asa Briggs and John Saville (eds), *Essays in Labour History: In Memory of G.D.H. Cole* (London, 1967), pp. 276–316.

Thompson, E.P., 'Hunting the Jacobin Fox', *Past and Present*, 142 (1994), 94–140.

Thompson, Laurence, *Robert Blatchford, Portrait of an Englishman* (London, 1955).

Thompson, Noel and Williams, Chris (eds), *Robert Owen and His Legacy* (Cardiff, 2011).

Tomos, Angharad, *Hiraeth Am Yfory: David Thomas a Mudiad Llafur Gogledd Cymru* (Llandysul, 2002).

Tsuzuki, Chushichi, *H.M. Hyndman and British Socialism* (Oxford, 1961).

Vaughan, Herbert M., *The South Wales Squires: A Welsh Picture of Social Life* (London, 1926).

Wallace, Ryland, *Organise! Organise! Organise! A Study of Reform Agitations in Wales, 1840–1886* (Cardiff, 1991).

Ward, Paul, *Red Flag and Union Jack: Englishness, Patriotism and the British Left, 1881–1924* (Woodbridge, 1998).

Ward, Paul, *Britishness Since 1870* (London and New York, 2004).

Ward, Paul and Wright, Martin, 'Mirrors of Wales – Life Story as National Metaphor: Case Studies of R.J. Derfel & Huw T. Edwards', *History*, 95, 317 (2010), 45–63.

Waters, Chris, *British Socialists and the Politics of Popular Culture, 1884–1914* (Manchester, 1990).

Watmough, P.A., 'The Membership of the Social Democratic Federation, 1885–1902', *Bulletin of the Society for the Study of Labour History*, 34 (1977), 35–40.

Watson, Katherine, 'Some Letters Concerning the Fabian Summer Schools in Merioneth, 1907–10', *Journal of the Merioneth Historical and Record Society*, 13/4 (2001), 392–400.

Wilkes, Ivor, *South Wales and the Rising of 1839: Class Struggle as Armed Struggle* (London and Sydney, 1984).

Williams, Chris, 'The South Wales Miners' Federation', *Llafur*, 5/3 (1990), 45–56.

Williams, Chris, *Democratic Rhondda: Politics and Society, 1885–1951* (Cardiff, 1996).
Williams, Chris, *Capitalism, Community and Conflict: The South Wales Coalfield, 1898–1947* (Cardiff, 1998).
Williams, David, 'Chartism in Wales', in Asa Briggs (ed.), *Chartist Studies* (London, 1959), pp. 220–48.
Williams, Glanmor (ed.), *Merthyr Politics: The Making of a Working Class Tradition* (Cardiff, 1966).
Williams, Gwyn A., *The Merthyr Rising* (London, 1978).
Williams, L.J., 'The First Welsh "Labour" MP: The Rhondda Election of 1885', *Morgannwg*, 6 (1962), 78–94.
Williams, L.J., 'The New Unionism in South Wales, 1889–92', *Welsh History Review*, 1/4 (1963), 413–30.
Williams, L.J., 'The Strike of 1898', *Morgannwg*, 9 (1965), 61–79.
Williams, T.L., 'Thomas Jones and the *Welsh Outlook*', *Anglo-Welsh Review*, 64 (1979), 38–46.
Williams, Vivian P., 'Cipolwg ar Lyfr Confnodion (1902–04) "'Caban Sink y Mynydd", Chwarel Llechwedd, Blaenau Ffestiniog', *Journal of the Merioneth Historical and Record Society*, 14/3 (2004), 240–55.
Wrigley, Chris, *David Lloyd George and the British Labour Movement* (Brighton, 1976).
Yeo, Stephen, 'A New Life, The Religion of Socialism in Britain, 1883–1896', *History Workshop Journal* 4/1 (1977), 5–56.
Young, J.D., 'A Very English Socialism and the Celtic Fringe, 1880–1991', *History Workshop Journal*, 35/1 (1993), 136–52.

(iii) Unpublished Theses and Dissertations

Baggs, Christopher, 'The Miners' Libraries of South Wales from the 1860s to 1939' (PhD, University of Wales, Aberystwyth, 1995).
Barrow, Logie, 'The Socialism of Robert Blatchford and the *Clarion* Newspaper, 1889–1918' (PhD, University of London, 1975).
Davies, Ioan Rhys, 'Popeth yn Gymraeg? Yr Iaith Gymraeg a Delwedd Ddinesig Caerdydd, c. 1885–1912' (MA, Cardiff University, 2007).
Daunton, M.J., 'Aspects of the Social and Economic Structure of Cardiff, 1870–1914' (PhD, University of Kent, 1974).
Demont, S.E., 'Tredegar and Aneurin Bevan: A Society and its Political Articulation, 1890–1929' (PhD, University of Wales, Cardiff, 1990).
Fincher, Judith, 'The Clarion Movement: A Study of a Socialist Attempt to Implement the Co-operative Commonwealth in England, 1891–1914' (MA, University of Manchester, 1971).
Fox, K.O., 'The Emergence of the Political Labour Movement in the Eastern Section of the South Wales Coalfield, 1894–1910' (MA, University of Wales, Aberystwyth, 1965).

Hopkin, Deian, 'The Newspapers of the Independent Labour Party, 1893–1906' (PhD, University of Wales, Aberystwyth, 1981).

Howys Williams, Sian, 'Bywyd a Gwaith Thomas Evan Nicholas, 1879–1971' (MA, University of Wales, 1986).

Humphries, E. Margaret, 'Edgar Leyshon Chappell (1878–1949): A Biography' (Diploma in Continuing Education (Local History), Cardiff University, 1993).

John, Kenneth, 'Anti-Parliamentary Passage: South Wales and the Internationalism of Sam Mainwaring (1841–1907)' (PhD, University of Greenwich, 2001).

Matthews, Ioan, 'The World of the Anthracite Miner' (PhD, University of Wales, Cardiff, 1995).

McCarry, T.J., 'Labour and Society in Swansea, 1887–1918' (PhD, University of Wales, Swansea, 1986).

Parry, Cyril, 'Socialism in Gwynedd, 1900–1920' (PhD, University of Wales, 1967).

Tomos, Angharad, 'Bywyd a Gwaith David Thomas, 1880–1967' (M Phil, University of Wales, Aberystwyth, 2000).

Treharne, S.E., 'Astudiaeth o Fywyd a Phrydyddiaeth R.J. Derfel' (MA, University of Wales, Cardiff, 1974).

Index

Aberbeeg 98
Abercanaid 118
Abercych 209
Abercynon 77, 98, 205, 217
Aberdare 24, 25, 26, 27, 29, 73, 74, 78, 88(n), 91, 98, 101, 103, 112, 116, 119, 120, 124, 125, 126, 129, 130, 132, 133, 134, 136, 138, 141, 169, 206
Aberdare ILP 78, 124, 126, 129, 132, 133, 136, 138
Aberdare Liberal Association 29
Aberdare Nationalist Society 29
Aberdare Socialist Society 73, 125, 130, 141
Aberdyfi 157
Abergavenny 99
Aberystwyth 100, 145, 148, 151, 152, 153, 157, 158, 159, 182
Aberystwyth University College 145, 148
Abraham, William (Mabon) 17, 38, 48, 76, 90, 121, 180, 181, 203, 204, 205
Ablett, Noah 178, 206
Aildrefniad Cymdeithas (R.J. Derfel) 147(n), 187, 197
Alexander, H. 61, 65
Alpass, Bert 100, 117
Ammanford 61, 169, 224
America 16, 17, 26, 27, 44, 49, 69, 184, 188, 226, 235
'American Wales' (Zimmern) 89, 96, 144
anarchism 25(n), 26, 27, 43, 67, 97, 146
anarcho-syndicalism 26
Andrews, Elizabeth 127
Anglesey 148, 182

Anti-Socialist Union 121, 214
ap Iwan, Emrys 182
Arnold, A. (Swansea) 65
Arnold, Matthew 49
atheism 14, 62, 79, 96, 176, 204
Auld Langsyne 47(n)
Australia 16, 53, 55
Aveling, Edward 178

Bailey, William (Revd) (Penarth) 40
Bala 158, 159, 182, 184, 189
Ballachulish Quarry dispute 172
Baner ac Amserau Cymru 96, 146, 200, 201
Bangor 145, 151, 153, 161, 177, 180, 210, 213, 224
Bangor Fabian Society 153–4
Bangor University College 213, 224
Baptists 36, 51, 62, 168, 189, 190, 198(n), 215
Bargoed 205
Barmouth 10, 31–3, 157, 161
Barnes, George 166
Barry 3, 58, 69–80, 127
Barry Dock 34, 219
Bedlinog 88(n), 91, 99, 116, 117, 118, 128, 132, 144
Beddgelert 157
Belfort Bax, Ernest 29, 30, 76(n), 79
Belt, George 99
Bellamy, Edward 40–1, 48, 105
Bethesda 144, 161, 163–72, 213
Bettws y Coed 158, 161
Bevan, Aneurin 1, 96, 129(n)
Bevan, W. (Swansea) 59, 60
Bibbings, Horatio 209, 217
Birmingham 121, 141, 157, 207

INDEX

Black Glamorgan (J. Littlejohns) 137
Blackburn 71
Blaenau Ffestiniog 17, 18, 162, 163, 164, 209, 210, 212, 223, 224
Blaenclydach 205, 206
Blaenclydach Marxian Club 205–6
Black Country (English) 226
Blaina 98, 184
Bland, Hubert 43–4, 152
Blatchford, Robert 3, 84, 95, 96, 101, 102, 131, 133, 135, 136, 138, 149, 153, 159, 163, 165, 166, 198, 226, 234, 236
Bloxwich (Staffs) 31
Bondfield, Margaret 212
Bolton 46(n), 84(n), 168
Brace, William 46, 76
Bradlaugh, Charles 49, 76(n)
Bristol 35, 45, 46, 90, 92, 99, 128
Bristol Channel 38, 92
Britain for the British 131, 133
British Socialist Party 205
Briton Ferry 138, 140, 209, 212(n), 215
Broadhurst, Henry 59
Brocklehurst, Fred 46, 87, 90, 152
Broughton 156, 157
Bruce Glasier, John 84, 107(n), 119, 120(n), 121, 122, 126, 158, 159, 212, 225
Bruce Glasier, Katharine (née Conway) 45, 57(n), 132, 212
Brymbo 229
Brynamman 169
Brynmawr 20
Builth Wells 155, 156
Burgess, Joseph 34
Burne-Jones, Edward 179
Burns, John 38, 159, 163
Butler, Jesse 90

Caergwrle 229
Caerphilly 52, 92, 93, 94, 134
Cadoxton 34, 71
Caernarfonshire 34, 159, 201, 209, 215, 216, 223, 224, 229, 233
Caernarfonshire Labour Council 229

Cambrian Combine Dispute 7, 181, 206, 232
Campbell, R.J. (Revd) 211, 215
Can a Man be a Christian on a Pound a Week? (Keir Hardie) 218
Cardiff 3, 16, 21, 24, 27, 34–58, 69, 72, 73, 77, 78, 80, 85, 86, 87, 88, 90, 91, 92, 93, 95, 97, 115, 121, 122, 123, 124, 125, 126, 133, 134, 135, 136, 141, 152, 154, 176, 187, 206, 212(n), 230
Cardiff *Clarion* clubs 136, 134
Cardiff Cymrodorion 36
Cardiff Fabian Socialist Society 42–58, 187
Cardiff Free Methodist Improvement Club 40
Cardiff General Strike (1911) 206
Cardiff ILP 85, 86, 87, 91, 123, 187
Cardiff Labour Church 45–7, 126
Cardiff Junior Liberal Association 41
Cardiff Progressive Labour League 45, 48
Cardiff SDF 77–8
Cardiff Society for the Impartial Discussion of Political and Other Questions 42
Cardiff Trades Council 37
Cardiff Socialist Party 78
Cardiganshire 53–5, 102, 154–5, 184
Caernarfon 157, 162, 182, 210, 212, 214, 215
Carlyle, Thomas 49, 183, 236
Carmarthen 53, 104, 147, 184, 232–3
Carmarthenshire 9, 175
Cenarth 228
Central Labour College (CLC) 206–7, 221

Cerrigydrudion 157
Chamberlain, Joseph 180
Champion, Henry Hyde 16(n), 39(n), 60

INDEX

chapels 33, 36, 61, 62, 63, 66, 97, 102, 145, 147, 168, 171, 172, 199, 208, 209, 215–18, 220, 221, 224, 225, 229
Chappell, Edgar 139, 140, 207, 223, 232
Chartism 9–10
Chatterton, Joseph 70, 71, 73, 74, 77, 79, 87, 107, 108(n), 111
Cheetham's Phrenological and Cinematic Entertainment 157
Chester 156, 157, 170, 210
choirs 51, 99, 109, 113, 126, 136, 163, 166, 168, 169, 219
Christian Socialism 12, 32, 148, 151, 157, 178, 180, 211, 218
Cilfynydd 91
  Albion Colliery Explosion (1894) 50, 88
Clarion (movement) 3, 84, 133–5, 136, 158, 160, 161, 166, 168
Clarion (newspaper) 95–6, 105, 132, 133, 138, 156, 157, 163, 165, 174
Clarion support for Penrhyn quarrymen 165–6, 173
Clarion vans 97–101, 114, 117(n), 126, 132–3, 158
Clarke, E.J. (Swansea) 92
Clayton, Joseph 107, 114(n)
Cleeves, Edmund A. 61, 62, 64, 67–8
Cliffe Leslie, T.E. 75
Clifford, J. 167, 234(n)
Coal Strike (1898) 3, 76, 85, 91, 105–21, 124, 137, 141, 173, 239–40
Coedpoeth 148, 229
Colne Valley 211, 212
  by-election (1907) 202, 210
Colton, James 77, 78
Commonweal 24, 25, 27, 29, 30, 31(n)
Comte, Auguste 27
Communism 26, 27, 39, 41, 145, 149, 195, 207, 218
Congregationalism 33, 182, 184, 215, 222, 224

Connah's Quay 150
Conwy 158, 161
Connell, Jim 99, 140
Conservatives 120, 145, 152, 187, 215
Cook, A.J. 206, 207
Cooper, Mrs (Nelson) 125
Co-operative Commonwealth (Gronlund) 44
Co-operative Society 176, 177
Co-operative Holidays Association 160–1
Cornwall 69
Corwen 157, 158
cosmopolitanism 10, 11, 37, 42, 43, 47, 48, 52, 56, 57, 58, 72, 73, 77, 80, 195, 220
Crooks, Will 48
Curran, Pete 94, 95, 107, 165, 166
Cwmavon 90, 92, 104, 128, 138, 170, 230
Cwmllynfell 123, 169
Cwrs y Byd 101, 146–7, 184, 187, 197
cycling 84, 99, 134–5, 157, 158, 160, 161
Cymdeithas Ffabianaid Dyffryn Orllwyn 154–5
Cymdeithas Genedlaethol Cymry Manceinion 196
Cymdeithas Lenyddol Cymry Manchester 191
Cymdeithas y Ddaear i'r Bobl 55
Cymdeithas y Ddraig Goch 139
Cymro 101, 197, 200
Cymru Fydd (movement) 63, 72, 73, 100, 178, 180, 197, 226
Cymru Fydd (journal) 12, 29, 197

Daniel, D.R. 166, 170, 180
Daniel, John (Iwan Glyn) 119, 139(n), 234
Darby, W.H. 152
Dave, Victor 26
Davies, Ben (Liverpool) 147
Davies, Dai (Merthyr) 110
Davies, Henry 92, 104, 119, 128, 138, 170, 230, 233
Davies, Rose 127

268   INDEX

Davies, T.E. (Trimsaran) 123
Davitt, Michael 15(n), 17–18, 28, 162, 180, 185, 188
Debating and mutual improvement societies 22, 40, 42, 101, 147, 148, 153, 154(n), 156, 191, 213, 216(n), 225, 226, 227
De Mattos, W.S. 45, 57(n)
Derfel, Robert Jones 29, 71(n), 101, 102, 104, 147, 149, 177, 187, 188, 189–201, 219, 222, 225, 226, 227, 234, 236, 241
Despard, Charlotte 125, 212
Dinesydd Cymreig 214, 235, 241
Dinorwig 148, 224
Diwygiwr 27
dockers 39, 49, 59, 67, 70, 90, 117
Dolgellau 157, 190(n)
Dowlais 30, 91, 95, 98, 112, 114, 121, 123, 130, 131, 137, 139(n)
Dunn, W.J. (Swansea) 138
Dyfi Valley 159

Eames, William 153
Ebbw Vale 91, 98
Education Act (1902) 123
Edwards, Huw T. 237–8, 241
Edwards, O.M. 176, 178
Edwards, Thomas (Twm o'r Nant) 175
Edwards, W.J. 138
eight hours day 131, 147, 181
Eisteddfod (national) 24, 100. 176, 199, 200, 219, 224, 232, 235(n)
eisteddfodau (local) 104, 149(n), 164, 183, 184, 190(n), 218, 219, 225, 229
Ellis, Thomas Edward 9, 17, 177–9, 180, 190
Emerson, Ralph Waldo 49
England for All (Hyndman) 14
Engels, Friedrich 12, 13, 190
England Arise (Edward Carpenter) 72, 140
Erith 168

Evans, Ben 86, 87, 90(n), 97, 147, 187

Fabian Essays in Socialism 43, 49, 51, 52
Fabian Tracts 43, 55, 153(n), 166, 179, 183, 198, 234
Fabian Society 3, 13, 35, 42–58, 72, 77, 80, 82(n), 86, 92, 94, 100, 131, 144, 151–3, 153–4, 154–5, 160, 179, 187, 195, 212
    Aberystwyth 100, 144, 151–3
    Bangor 153–4
    book boxes 131
    Cardiff 42–58, 187
    Llandysul 154–5
    Newport 92
    summer schools (Llanbedr) 160
Felinfoel 61, 62
fellowship 133, 135, 160, 161
feudalism 171
Ffestiniog 158, 190(n)
Fielding, John 21–4, 40, 41
Flint 17, 224
Flintshire 146, 179, 184
Fochriw 117
Fors Clavigera (Ruskin) 10
Foulkes, Edwards (Llanberis) 34, 80
Francis, Llew (Penydarren) 110, 111, 116, 128, 131, 131(n)
free love 79, 127, 204, 215
French Revolution 8

Gee, Thomas 17(n), 119
Genedl Gymreig 57, 149, 153, 162, 182, 213
General Election
    1868 178, 191, 193
    1900 119, 120–1
    1906 121, 139, 203, 210, 211
    1910 (January) 121, 204
    1910 (December) 121
    2015 1
Y Geninen 34, 216
George, Henry 16, 18, 41, 180, 183, 188, 236
Giles, Matt 128

INDEX

Gladstone, William 119, 162, 186, 212(n)
Glais 217, 222, 226
Glamorgan 34, 97, 134, 184, 187, 204, 232
Glanamman 169
Gore, Hugh Holmes 45, 90
Gorseinon 61, 62, 169
Gower 59, 63, 120, 139, 180, 204
Grady, Joe 94
Graham, W.B. (Revd) 211, 212
Grangetown 37, 58
Grayson, Victor 202, 210, 211
Gregory, R. (Treforest) 30
Griffiths, James 1, 105, 211(n), 228
Gronlund, Laurence 44
Guild of St George 10
Gwaencaegurwen 116
Gwalia, Lewis J. (Ynysybwl) 29
Gwynfryn Academy 224, 225, 226
Gwynedd 5, 6

Halliday Sparling, Henry 46, 57(n)
Hamilton, J.S. 88
Harcombe, Mark 232
Harcourt, William 162, 181, 239
Hardie, James Keir 7, 45, 46, 50, 52, 57(n), 59, 84, 85, 87, 88, 90, 103, 107, 108, 110, 111, 112, 116, 119, 120–2, 123, 126, 127, 128, 136, 137, 138, 139, 141, 146, 155, 156(n), 159, 160, 163, 164, 165, 166, 180, 181, 201, 207, 208, 212, 213, 217, 218, 219, 220, 221, 228, 229, 232, 236(n)
Hark the Battle Cry is Ringing 39, 47(n), 72
Harlech 210
Harris, William 232
Harrison, Amy 100
Harrison, Frederic 49
Hartshorn, Vernon 128, 204, 232
Hen Wlad fy Nhadau 18, 47, 141, 208
Hobart, Harry 61–3, 64, 65, 67
Hobson, Sam 49–51, 52, 56, 57, 58, 85, 86, 87, 92, 94, 138
Hodge, John 120

Hollett, George (Swansea) 67
Home Rule 15, 16, 50(n), 140, 178, 186
House of Commons/Parliament 7, 44, 50, 59, 88, 110, 120, 124, 165, 167, 179, 181, 195
Huddersfield 208, 211
Hughes, R.W. (Moeltryfan) 224
Hyder, Joseph 70
Hyndman, Henry 13, 19–20, 21, 34, 76(n), 162, 181, 205

Independent Labour Representation 5, 6–7, 35, 90, 103, 171
Independent Labour Party (ILP) 3, 7, 46(n), 49, 58, 64(n), 70, 74(n), 77, 78, 80, 82–8, 90–5, 106–18, 122–42, 155, 156, 157, 163, 164, 170, 171, 172, 173, 174, 184, 186, 187, 204, 205, 207, 208, 209, 210, 212, 214, 215, 216, 218, 219, 221, 222, 223, 227, 228, 229, 230, 231, 232, 233, 240.
ILP Annual Conferences 85, 107, 121–2, 163, 208
ILP National Administrative Council (NAC) 94, 114, 132
ILP Regional Structure 92–4, 114, 128, 138, 141, 208, 209–10, 230
Isaac, T. Daronwy 76(n), 100
Ireland 14, 15, 16, 17(n), 18, 28, 50, 145, 188

James, John (Cwmgors) 228, 231(n)
Jenkins, John (Cardiff) 37
Jenkins, John (Gwili) 153, 224
Jenkins, Oliver 97, 129
Jevons, Stanley 43, 52
Jones, David (Penrhiwllan) 154
Jones, David Gwynfryn 224
Jones, David Rhys 53–8, 73, 86, 87, 94, 103, 154, 183
Jones, Ernest 191

INDEX

Jones, Evan Pan 28, 55, 56, 57, 100, 101, 104, 146, 54–5, 174, 184–9, 236
Jones, Griff 66, 96
Jones, Henry (Professor) 229
Jones, John (Blaentir) 154
Jones, John (Idris Fychan) 191
Jones, John (Jac Glan y Gors) 175
Jones, John Owen (Ap Ffarmwr) 182–4, 186, 201
Jones, Kilsby 11
Jones, Lloyd (Manchester) 193
Jones, Michael D. 119, 174, 182, 190
Jones, Stanley (Revd) 210
Jones, Thomas 50, 86, 100, 153, 158, 177
Jones, Thomas Gwynn 224, 225, 226
Jones, Professor Viriamu 40
Jones, W. Lewis (Bangor) 151
Jones, W.W. 166
Joynes, James Leigh 15(n), 18–19, 21, 225
Justice 14, 16, 19, 21, 60, 61, 64, 65, 67, 69, 71, 74, 77, 107, 108, 173, 205

Kenney, Annie 124
Kidwelly 61
Kingsley, Charles 12
Kitz, Frank 24–30, 34, 35

Labour Elector 60
Labour Leader 52, 85, 105, 108, 110, 113, 135, 137, 172, 208, 209, 217
Labour Church movement 45–7, 49, 53, 125, 126, 168, 192
Labour Representation Committee 203
Labour Party 1, 2, 92, 201, 202, 203, 204, 206, 210, 213, 230(n), 232, 237
Labour Unrest (1910–12) 206
Lambeth Trades Council 165
land agitation 16–18, 28, 29, 41, 42(n), 54, 55, 170–1, 174, 182, 183, 184, 185, 186, 187, 188, 199
land nationalization 29, 40, 55, 61, 70, 179, 197, 232
Land Nationalisation Society 55, 188
Landore 21, 64, 65, 133
Lassalle, Ferdinand 75
Liberalism 6, 22, 42, 48, 60, 64, 119, 121, 138, 150, 151, 162, 171, 177, 178, 181, 184, 186, 188, 203, 214, 220, 221
Lib-Labs 108, 180, 203
Liberty 67
Littlejohns, John 129, 137, 140
Liverpool 19, 90, 141, 147, 156, 157, 189, 193, 226
London 9, 10, 21, 24, 25, 26, 27, 30, 35, 38, 39, 41, 42, 43, 45, 46, 49, 53, 56, 61, 65, 66, 68(n), 69, 70, 94, 100, 109, 113, 117, 126, 163, 166, 168, 176, 178, 179, 189, 212
London County Council 45, 212
London Dock Strike (1889) 39, 49, 117
London Trades Council 70, 109
Looking Backward (Edward Bellamy) 40, 48, 105
Lowe, David 110
Llais Llafur – Labour Voice 103–5, 115, 119, 123, 130, 139, 140, 142, 169, 170, 173–4, 186, 193, 197, 200, 210, 213, 219, 231, 234
Llanbedr 160
Llanberis 19, 34, 157, 162, 210
Llanbradach 91
Llandrillo 158
Llandudno 17, 18, 19, 147, 148, 157, 158, 210
Llandysul 55(n), 57, 154, 188
Llanelli 6, 58, 59(n), 61, 63, 64, 65, 88, 125, 206
Llanfairfechan 145
Llanfyllin 226
Llangollen 157, 158
Llanhilleth 98

INDEX

Llanidloes 10
Llanllyfni 210
Llanrwst 158, 210
Llantrisant 35, 112
Llan Ffestiniog 210
Llechryd 155
Lloyd, Hugh (Maerdy) 110, 116, 128
Lloyd, W.W. 166, 167
Lloyd George, David 17, 166, 180, 182
Llyswen 9

MacDonald, James 70, 72, 77, 78
MacDonald, James Ramsay 45, 84, 95, 152, 212
MacMillan, Margaret 212
MacPherson, Mary and Fenton 99
McCarthy, Tom 90
Machynlleth 145
Maerdy 88(n), 90, 91, 95, 98, 110, 114, 116, 118, 128
Maesycymmer 91, 95
Mainwaring, Sam 24–9, 30, 31, 34, 35, 55, 64, 65, 66, 67, 68, 87(n), 92, 94, 227
Manchester 45, 46, 71, 90, 101, 118, 124, 144, 175, 177, 182, 189, 190, 191, 193, 194, 196, 197, 201
Mann, Tom 16(n), 27(n), 38, 59, 87, 88, 103, 126, 138, 156
Manning, Revd J.E. 22
Mardy Jones, T. 203, 207
Marseillaise 47, 136, 141, 219
Marx, Karl 12, 27, 52, 75, 107

Marxism 2, 13, 14, 16, 26, 31, 33, 43, 69, 75, 79, 104, 111, 178, 194, 195, 205, 207, 221, 240
Maurice, F.D. 12
Mazzini, Giuseppe 49, 75
McCorde, Sam 69
Meirionnydd 9, 160, 175, 176, 189, 190, 209
Men of England (Shelley) 47
Men of Harlech 39, 72

Merrie England 84, 87, 95, 96, 97, 99, 101, 102, 131, 133, 148, 149, 153, 164, 198, 226, 227, 234
Merthyr 24, 30, 51, 76(n), 88(n), 89, 91, 92, 95, 98, 99, 109, 110, 112, 112, 114, 117–23, 126, 127, 128, 129, 131, 132, 138, 139, 164, 165, 181, 182, 183, 184, 190, 201, 213, 214(n), 217, 218, 220,221, 229
Merthyr Boroughs 7, 119, 132, 217, 218, 221
Merthyr Vale 91, 98, 112, 114, 117, 118
Miall Edwards, D. 153
Mill, John Stuart 43
miners 7, 17, 26, 28, 29, 38, 46, 48, 52, 59, 75, 76, 88, 89, 100, 101, 104, 106, 107, 108, 109, 110, 111, 112, 113, 114, 115, 117, 119, 127, 130, 146, 156(n), 165, 168, 169, 171, 172, 204, 206, 207, 228
Miners' Evangel 75–6
Miners' Federation of Great Britain 75, 104, 108, 109
Miners' Next Step 206
Most, Johan 26
Montefiore, Dora 212
Montgomeryshire 10, 145
Morgan, David (Dai o'r Nant) 38
Morgan, Pritchard 120, 121
Morganwg, Iolo 9
Morris, William 14, 26, 60, 68, 72, 140, 159, 178, 179, 194, 195, 225, 236
Morris, William (Swansea) 67
Morriston 64, 65, 38(n), 90
Mostyn 146, 184
Mountain Ash 77, 91, 103, 112, 114, 117, 205, 215, 219, 224
music/singing 18, 39, 47, 51, 52, 71–2, 112, 125, 132, 135–6, 139, 141, 145, 163, 166, 169, 205, 206, 208, 219
mutual improvement 130, 136, 137, 147, 183, 205, 227

Myddleton-Worral, Mrs (Julia Dawson) 166, 173

Nant y Glo 98
Nantlle 162
National Health Service 1
National Union of Teachers (NUT) 229
Nationalism 1, 4, 13, 20, 28, 50, 177, 178, 182, 195, 199, 218, 220, 221, 230, 231, 232, 237, 238, 241
navvies 70
Neath 26, 55(n), 64, 68(n), 38(n), 88, 90, 92, 158
Nelson 88(n), 91
Nelson (Lancashire) 125
Neighbour, George 215, 224
New Theology 211
New Tredegar 205
Newcastle Emlyn 53, 223
Newport 9, 34, 71, 86, 87, 88(n), 90, 91, 92, 93, 95, 98, 99, 100, 114, 115, 133, 134, 135
Newport Rising 9
News from Nowhere (Morris) 14
Newtown 9, 10, 175, 176
Nicholas, T.E. 33, 217, 222, 223, 224, 225, 226, 228, 229, 234, 235, 238
Nonconformity 11, 18, 60, 138, 198, 215, 216, 224, 234
North Wales and Chester ILP Federation 210
North Wales Congress of Labour 229
North Wales Property Defence Association 174
North Wales Quarrymen's Union 170, 214, 237

O Gaethiwed i Ryddid (D.D. Walters) 228
Osborne, Dan (Treharris) 116
Oswestry 155
Owen, Hugh 11
Owen, Jenkyn 100

Owen, Robert 9, 12, 175–8, 181, 192, 193, 194, 200, 226
Owenism 9, 175, 176, 193

Paethsyllydd 23
Pan-Celticism 36, 221
Pankhurst, Emmeline 124
Parker, James 212
Parker, Tom (Porth) 117
Parr, Charles Arthur Edward 21, 40, 41–2, 43, 46, 48, 51, 53, 54, 57
Particularism 2, 4, 47, 56, 139, 183, 188, 189, 203, 207, 219, 240
Mary Parry (Mary Silyn Roberts) 152
Parry, W.J. 165
Paterson, John (Colne) 60
Paton, A.J. (The Flying Scotsman) 134
Pearson, W.G. 70
Pease, Edward 155
Penclawdd 61
Penderyn, Dic 120
Penny, John 132
Penrhyndeudraeth 210
Penrhyn Quarry disputes 4, 144, 163–74, 214, 240
'Penrhynism' 170
Penry, John 175
Penygraig ILP 212
Penygroes 210
Perkins, C.H. 21, 22
Phillips, Tom 62
Phillips, W.F. 216–17, 218, 224, 229
Phippen, William 207, 215
Pioneer (Merthyr) 213, 214, 218, 220, 221, 222, 231, 232, 233, 234
Ponkey 148
Pontardawe 102, 219
Pontarddulais 62
Pontlottyn 98
Pontmorlais 98
Pontypridd 7(n), 24, 25, 26, 74, 76, 79, 90, 91, 98, 99, 112, 114, 118
Portdinorwic 210

INDEX 273

Porth 77, 111, 114, 117, 118, 124, 148
Porthmadog 148
Powell, John (Abertillery) 46
Powell, Thomas 9–10
Preston 120
Price, John (Waun Avon) 20
Price, W.W. 133
Primrose League 145, 157
Pritchard, J.T. (Aberdaron) 235
Proctor, Tom 109
Prothero, Cliff 217
Proudhon, Pierre Joseph 12
Puleston Jones, John (Revd) 148, 224
Pwllheli 147, 148

quarrymen 18, 146, 161–74, 212, 214, 237

Radcliffe, Henry 121
railwaymen 69, 70, 90, 129
Randell, David 59, 60, 63, 64, 180
Rechabites 67
Rees, David (Y Cynhyrfwr) 27, 175
Rees, David (Ystalyfera) 117
Rees, Ebenezer 103–4, 115, 117, 128, 146, 187, 213
Rees, John (Dowlais) 30
Rees, Seth 116
Rees, W. (Llechryd) 155
Rees, W.J. (Neath) 64, 92, 94, 138
Religious Revival (1904–5) 211
Rhondda 6, 24, 29, 30, 63, 66, 87, 109, 112, 114, 115, 116, 117, 134, 180, 205, 206, 207, 212, 214, 215, 226, 228
Rhondda Miners Association 29
Rhondda Socialist 213, 214

Rhosllannerchrugog 209, 229
Rhostyllen 229
Rhyl 155, 157(n)
Rhys, Morgan John 175
Rhymney 98, 100, 101, 112, 115, 117, 205
Ricardo, David 43, 52
Richard, Henry 11, 28, 120

Richards, David (Landore) 133
Richards, George (Aberaman) 129
Roberts, John H. 87
Roberts, Richard (Revd) 100, 163, 176–7
Robinson, E.T. 46, 87
Rocking Stone (Pontypridd) 7, 24
Rosetti, R. 70, 71, 205
Royal Commission on Land (1894) 54
Ruskin, John 10, 49, 67, 75, 161, 179, 180, 183, 236
Ruthin 150

Saint Simon, Henri de 12, 75
Salford 93
Salvation Army 99
Samuel, G.A.H. (Marxian) 135, 141
Sanders, Haydn 31–3,
Salt, Harry 39, 47, 72
scientific socialism 12, 56, 58, 185, 193, 206, 239
Scotland 1, 5, 14, 17, 83, 84, 99, 168, 172
Senghenydd 89, 205
Seven Sisters 229
Severn, Moses 74–6
Sexton, James 90
Shallard, S.D. 127, 128
Shaw, George Bernard 152
Sheffield 168
Sheppard, Matthew 69, 70, 73
Shrewsbury 10, 158
Silyn Roberts, Robert 210, 223, 224, 225, 227, 228, 234
Smart, Russell 94, 95
Snell, Harry 94
Snowden, Philip 84, 132, 212, 236
Social Democratic Federation 13–16, 18, 19, 20, 21, 26, 35, 40, 41, 43, 58, 60–81, 86, 87, 93, 94, 107, 109, 110, 111, 163, 173, 174, 178, 179, 187, 193, 194, 205–6, 232, 240
Socialist League 13, 24–6, 28, 29, 30, 31, 43, 178
Socialist Revival (1880s) 5, 8, 197
'Socialist unity' 82, 93, 94, 202

Sorley, Professor 40
South Wales Divisional Council (ILP) 209, 221
South Wales ILP Federation 64(n), 92, 93, 94, 114, 128, 138, 141, 208
South Wales Labour Annual 138, 140
South Wales Miners Federation 7, 106, 108, 169, 203, 205, 206, 232
Spargo, John 69, 70, 71, 73, 74, 76, 78, 107, 108, 109, 111
Sparkes, Joseph (Bedlinog) 116, 128
Splott 86
Stacy, Enid 46, 70, 88, 94, 124, 152
Stanton, Charles B. 128
Stalybridge 168
Stepniak, Sergius 42
Steward, Ira 27
Stewart, Willie 208
Stitt Wilson, Ben 210, 211(n)
Stitt Wilson, Revd J. 210, 211(n)
Stonelake, Edmund 128
Swansea 3, 6, 17, 21, 22, 23, 58, 59, 60, 64, 65, 66, 67, 68, 78, 80, 87(n), 88, 90, 92, 96, 115, 117, 120, 125, 128, 129, 133, 134, 135, 137, 138, 139, 169, 204, 208, 211, 213, 217, 222, 223 229
Swansea and District Workers Journal 128, 135, 213
Swansea ILP 138
Swansea Liberal Club 22
Swansea Literary and Debating Society 22
Swansea Socialist Society 66, 78, 96, 117, 125, 128, 129, 133, 137, 139, 223
Swansea SDF 64–8
Swansea Trades Council 213
Swansea Valley 59, 80, 115, 134, 211, 217, 222, 226, 228, 229
Swansea Valley ILP 208

Taff Vale Dispute 203
Talysarn 210, 223

Tarian y Gweithiwr 96, 101, 102, 103, 112, 126
Tawney, R.H. 12, 150
Taylor, Helen 55(n), 187
Taylor, Tom 70, 88
temperance 36, 64, 67, 99, 178
Thelwall, John 9
Thomas, David 210, 223, 224, 225(n), 226, 229, 230, 232, 234, 235, 237
Thomas, D.A. 89, 120
Thomas, Edward (Cochfarf) 36–7, 47, 48, 50, 95
Thomas, R.E. 51–3
Thompson, A.M. 165, 172
Tillett, Ben 38, 39, 46, 59, 120, 156, 163, 165, 204
tinplate workers 52, 59, 60, 62
Tiplady, Isabel 100
Today 30
Tonyrefail 77
Tonypandy 74, 114
Toynbee, Arnold 179
Trawsfynydd 237
trades councils 37, 48, 59, 64, 67, 68(n), 70, 109, 128, 165, 168, 213
Trades Union Congress 59, 60
Treharris 88(n), 90, 91, 92, 93, 95, 97, 98, 99, 112, 114, 116, 118, 124, 130, 135, 205
Troedyrhiw 91, 98, 112, 114
Tuckwell, Revd W. (Stockwell) 40
Tylorstown 24, 117

Undy (Monmouthshire) 69, 73
Unofficial Reform Committee 206, 207, 221
University College of South Wales 40, 125
Utopian socialism 12, 175, 192, 193

Vincent, Henry 9

Wallace, Alfred Russel 55(n), Walsall 31
Walters, D.D. 102, 103, 209, 223, 224, 228, 234